SSF

a moveable thirst

Tales and Tastes from
a Season in Napa Wine Country

Rick Kushman and Hank Beal

BICENTENNIAL
1807
WILEY
2007
BICENTENNIAL

JOHN WILEY & SONS, INC.

Published by John Wiley & Sons, Inc., Hoboken, New Jersey
Published simultaneously in Canada

For general information about our other products and services, please contact our
Customer Care Department within the United States at (800) 762-2974, outside the
United States at (317) 572-3993 or fax (317) 572-4002.

Wiley also publishes its books in a variety of electronic formats. Some content that
appears in print may not be available in electronic books. For more information
about Wiley products, visit our web site at www.wiley.com.

LIBRARY OF CONGRESS CATALOGING-IN-PUBLICATION DATA:

Kushman, Rick.
 A moveable thirst : tales and tastes from a season in Napa wine country / Rick
Kushman and Hank Beal.
  p. cm.
 Includes bibliographical references and index.
 ISBN: 978-0-471-79386-1
 1. Wine tasting—California—Napa Valley—Anecdotes. 2. Napa Valley (Calif.)—
Description and travel. I. Beal, Hank. II. Title.
 TP548.5.A5K87 2007
 641.2'20979419—dc22

                    2006005471

Book design by Richard Oriolo
Wiley Bicentennial Logo: Richard J. Pacifico

Printed in the United States of America

10 9 8 7 6 5 4 3 2 1

contents

a season
in napa valley

the tasting rooms
of napa valley

acknowledgments

WE FIRST NEED to thank our wives—Deborah Meltvedt and Tina Beal—for their love, infinite patience, logistical support, and for putting up with this Quest and all our harebrained ideas. In our defense, most involve wine.

Speaking of patience, thank you to our agent, Bob Mecoy, whose advocacy, energy, and out-and-out smarts helped propel this book. A similar thank you to our editor, Justin Schwartz, whose enthusiasm for the book and serenity in the face of what had to be mind-numbingly minute questions made him a joy to work with.

Many of our friends and many of our colleagues at the *Sacramento Bee* and Nugget Market provided encouragement and showed stamina listening to a season's worth of stories from two hyped-up authors. Thanks to all. But we owe special thanks to *Bee* food editor Mike Dunne, for tirelessly answering pesky questions, to Tom Sellers for a thorough and smart read through, to Becky Boyd for determined research help, and to Rita Blomster, Jack Vaughn, and Julie Owens for game and witty help trying to name this book.

At Nugget, we need to give special thanks to the Stille family for their unflinching and whole-hearted support, and to Hank's wine steward team for their constant encouragement and for listening with interest time after time, and not just because they had to.

In Napa, a special thank you to Stu Smith and Julie Ann Kodmur of Smith-Madrone Vineyards and Winery, whose help, instant friendship, and spirited company were a huge bonus prize of this project, and to Lee Hodo at Bouchaine Vineyards for her quick and vigorous support of our book.

There were also many people who gave us more time and answers—and sometimes wine—than we seemed entitled to, including Bob Trinchero of Trinchero Family Estates; Michael Honig, president of Honig Vineyard & Winery; Vince Bonotto, the director of vineyard operations for Diageo Wines; Richard Camera, the director of vineyard operations for the Hess Collection Winery; Mike Smith, owner of Sunshine Foods; Nile Zacherle, winemaker at Barnett Vineyards; Ron Vuylsteke, winemaker at Tudal Family Winery; Cliff Little, who runs the tasting room at Milat Vineyards; Bonnie Zimmerman, general manager at Pope Valley Vineyards; Katarena Arger, winery manager and tasting room boss at Arger-Martucci Vineyards; Toni Nichelini-Irwin of Nichelini Winery; Brent Trojan from the Napa Valley Wine Train; and Hildegard Heymann, a University of California, Davis, professor of Viticulture and Enology who runs the school's sensory research efforts.

We also need to thank two friends, Mark Kreidler and Marley Klaus, who never knew it but supplied cheerful and badly needed pick-me-ups during a few dark moments in the writing process.

And finally, a thank you and a toast to the hundreds of people working in tasting rooms throughout Napa Valley who made every day of our Quest a joyful adventure and who make the region a happy place for visitors.

Introduction

WE'RE STANDING IN the sunny tasting room of Luna Vineyards at the south end of Napa Valley. I can't resist.

"I have a dumb question," I say.

My best friend, Hank, is standing next to me. He doesn't know what I'm about to ask, but he's heard this sort of start before. He begins to distance himself from me. There's no real motion. It's almost a metaphysical move. It just becomes clear he is no part of what's coming.

"We hear everything," says the woman pouring the wine for visitors. Her name is Joyce and she is friendly. I take that as encouragement.

"I read somewhere," I say, "that you're supposed to swirl wine counterclockwise. "Because we're in the Northern Hemisphere. That's the way water goes down a drain. Counterclockwise."

Joyce looks at me. That's all, just looks at me for a bit.

"You know, I've never heard that," she finally says. "I don't know."

There is no one else in the tasting room. Joyce says maybe she could ask their winemaker, because, you never know. She picks up a phone behind the little tasting bar and gets him after a couple tries.

"I have someone here with a question," she says, and tells him what I asked.

"Yes, uh-huh, yeah," she says into the phone. "Really? Me, too. Hey, thanks."

Joyce hangs up and turns toward me.

"He says that's the stupidest thing he's ever heard," she says.

That, right there, was pretty much our story for most of a wine season. Hank and I were on our trip—our Quest, really—to visit every tasting room in every winery in Napa through one cycle of the valley, spring to fall, from bud break to crush. Despite the sporadic flare-up of a stupid question, the Quest gave us a nine-month, cheerful adventure and a running tutorial in the ways of Napa Valley and of wine.

It let us watch a season on the vine, it let us see the whole of Napa—its personality, its people, and its enchantment—and it let us glimpse the enormous, lively soul of American wine. That's the trip we're about to take you on, but first, you need to know two things.

It started, as so many rash ideas do, with a bottle of wine. That's often explanation enough.

The other point fills in the rest, and it should be obvious: Hank and I are wine guys. Very different sorts, but, still, wine guys. I like to think we both get something from the friendship, but, honestly, most of the time I'm mooching from him.

Hank is a pro. I—so very clearly—am not. He's the executive wine buyer for Nugget Market, a Northern California supermarket chain, and, for everyone who asks, he's an agreeable, patient wine coach. I'm his frequent test of patience. My most advanced wine credentials are I can name the five Bordeaux grapes. (They are Cabernet Sauvignon, Merlot, Cab Franc, Malbec, and, I think, Dopey.)

We both love talking wine, learning about it, and, surely, drinking it. We're just at very different levels and my level is the ground floor. Like most people.

For me, wine is a glass of happy. It's good food, laughing friends, and cheery settings. It's the smell of barrels, the sizzle of a grill, the rolling lines of vineyards, the comfort of a sunny deck. And it's that first sip from that first glass, always a surprise that the taste is so, so . . . happy. For details, I go to Hank.

And he's there for me. Hank gets energized when he tastes something good. He loves wine that's interesting. He reads fruits and flavors in a way that makes sense, even to me. Usually. "There's cigar box," he'll say. "Can't you taste the cigar box?" Hank's been through sommelier classes, he samples 1,000-plus wines a year, and sells more than one million bottles annually. (A couple dozen go to me. I try to help out.) The University of California, Davis, the school that is, in essence, the academic arm and training center of the American wine industry, takes students to see the wine departments Hank's created in his Davis stores.

And, professional or not, wine is a happy thing for him, too. It's those parties and people and the magic of vineyards, just like it is for me. That's why, as vastly different wine guys, we share a fixation on Napa Valley. And that's why our rash idea, our obsessive little notion to visit every tasting room in Napa—every room that lets average people visit without requiring reservations months in advance or the sacrifice of a toe—worked itself into our Quest.

Don't mock. Napa has more than 300 top-notch wineries, and almost half have public tasting rooms. We could find no record that anyone had done this before, spent serious time in every tasting room. And the question, we think, is, why not? Napa Valley is the heart—and the essence—of American wine country. For wine guys, and pretty much anyone who doesn't live for theme parks, Napa is the real magic kingdom.

It's thirty miles of paradise and moveable feast. It's cafes and grocers, picnics and world-class restaurants, luxury spas, tiny getaways, and inns crammed with charm. Napa is also gentle weather, soft hills, and vineyards. Oceans and oceans of vineyards.

Napa was the core for the big bang of the American wine boom, and its quality and romance still power the industry. The names of the Napa wineries have a near-mythic ring: Robert Mondavi, Beauleau Vineyards, Beringer, Chateau Montelena, Stag's Leap Wine Cellars. That's the early royalty of American wine. And there are wineries that say big quality, big California reds, and, frankly, big bucks, like Opus One, Silver Oak, or Caymus. Or there was that bottle of Screaming Eagle—the ultimate prestige wine—that brought $500,000 in a Napa Valley Wine Auction. It was a big bottle, but, still.

Napa is also the engine of American wine. If Napa accounts for just four percent of California wine, its style, panache, and quality dictate American wine tastes—and by extension, drive world wine trends. The U.S. is one of the world's top four countries in wine imports, exports, production, and consumption, and when winemakers across the globe put their wines into barrels, American dollars are on their minds. That makes Napa a major player in world markets. Only Bordeaux—maybe—is a region with as much influence on the world of wine as Napa.

But its biggest lure isn't commerce, it's fantasy. Napa Valley feels like a blend of European style, country ease, congenial elegance, and pastoral casualness—all wrapped in postcard-ready scenery. If the valley's image is as carefully nurtured as any vineyard, so what? We're happy to buy into Napa's engaging sense of place. Makes tasting wine there more fun.

But it's more than fantasy. Wine gets in your blood there. You feel great wine in the air and on the vines. You feel it oozing from the dirt. From the terroir, as wine folk say. Napa Valley is everything you taste in a glass of wine. Everything I taste, anyway; Hank gets a bit more.

Wine is the culture in Napa; it's like the home team. People talk wine, make it, sell it, and drink it. We ran into wine people in stores, at gas stations, in the market in St. Helena looking for a Sauvignon Blanc to go with their take-out chicken. We couldn't meet people there without feeling their enthusiasm for wine, and without getting their advice on where we should go to drink it.

When you're looking to drink wine in Napa Valley, it starts with the tasting rooms. They're the gateway, the first link between all those wineries and people like us rambling around the kingdom. To that end, we've also compiled the most complete and detailed guide to Napa Valley tasting rooms that exists. Not to the wineries, the tasting rooms. So many travel guides say, "Beringer opened in 1876 and has a lovely Rhine House." But they don't say if you get to taste in there or if it's any fun. (Answer: yes, you do, and yes, it is.)

Tasting rooms have a spell about them, almost in the way of a glass of wine. It's hard to enter a tasting room without getting jolts of anticipation and optimism. In Napa, they run the scale—luxurious, sleek, rustic, boisterous, hushed—but almost every one has something about it, something a little bit wonderful.

And so, we had a Quest. For me, it also became a rolling education: about tasting wine, about vineyards and barrels, about finer points like whether the glass matters or, you know, how they make wine. For Hank, it was a different voyage of discovery. He was looking for that next wine gem, and, frankly, he was hoping he could make his friend a little less of an idiot. And for both of us, it was a chance to drink some very good wine.

ONE

Downtown Napa

LEARNED SOMETHING ALREADY. Spitting wine isn't easy.

You'd think you would, you know, just spit. But it turns out, like so much else involving wine, it's a bit complicated. Spit buckets aren't especially large, and they sit on counters in nice public places full of nice adults. You do not just haul off and spit.

I'm grasping this inside the Wineries of Napa Valley tasting room, a friendly wine shop on an outdoor mall. It's one of ten tasting rooms in downtown Napa, and if Hank and I are going to survive the day standing, we need to spit.

Hank is smooth. He leans over. *Voosh.* Wine is gone. Me, I lean over and try not to splash. I just open my mouth carefully. Wine dribbles into the bucket. It also dribbles down my chin and onto my shirt. I look to Hank for support.

"Nice," he says.

The woman pouring for us is sympathetic. "I haven't really gotten the hang of spitting either," she says. "I usually just avoid it."

First helpful hint for a wine tasting tour: Don't wear white clothes. Dark colors are just a consistently good idea with everything wine.

That's what we are up to, a search for everything wine. My best friend and wine mentor, Hank, and I are on Day One of our Quest to sample in every one of the tasting rooms in Napa Valley. We are optimistic, without knowing exactly why, but that's how we operate, that our expedition to discover and absorb Napa—the heart and essence of American wine country—will also lead us through the whole vast, vibrant world of wine.

Hank already knows a lot of it. He lives in it. He's the executive wine buyer for Nugget Market. Whatever I know, I learned from Hank. I'm hoping to expand my horizons on this Quest, maybe get to feel like I'm connected to Napa and that wine world, too. But right now, I'm working on fundamentals: basic tasting and spitting technique.

I turn to Hank. I'm counting on him to carry me through the rough patches over the next few months, which, at this rate, look like they'll be considerable.

"You have to put something into it," he says when the wine lady walks down to the other end of the little bar. "Not a lot, but something. And aim for the side of the bucket; you don't want splashback."

I'm holding the 2001 Goosecross Napa Zinfandel. I think it's pretty good, but I'm focusing on other things. I'm also not convinced I can tell if it's good because I'm not convinced you taste the wine the same when you spit. Hank has already explained why I'm wrong, but that discussion is beyond me at the moment.

So, Hank's doing what he can. "Work on getting it all over your tongue," he says. "Leave it there a few seconds. Then put some effort into the spit."

I sip, swish it around a little, and try not to sound like I'm gargling. I lean over. *Voosh*. Dribble. Still, it's better. I solve my problem by putting on my black sweater. Dark colors. I'm telling you.

At the other end of the wine bar, there's now a middle-aged couple from Ohio. They walked over from the Napa Valley Visitor's Center next door. This tasting room is a common first stop for newcomers to Napa, and to wine tasting. The people working the tasting bar have both the attitude and apparent endurance for it. The wine lady who ignored my spitting woes now good-naturedly explains to the couple how to look for flavors in their Sauvignon Blanc. She says think about how it smells and what the fruits might be. "You'll taste all kinds of things like melon and apricot in the wine," she says, and to her credit, without sounding like a grade-school teacher.

"You mean they put apricot in the wine?" the very nice Ohio woman asks.

"Why do they call it a finish?" the very nice Ohio man asks.

I feel suddenly expert again. It seems like a good time to move along.

IT'S MARCH AND WE'RE STARTING OUR trip in Downtown Napa at the bottom of the Napa Valley. It's a town that just began latching onto the wine boom after forty years of merrily steering millions of tourists out to Highway 29 on its western edge, and keeping its Victorian mansions, blue-collar core, and anonymity to itself. Then, in the mid-1990s, Napans—they seriously call themselves Napans—had a communal epiphany. "All those cars heading up the valley," they more or less said, "are full of money."

The city bounced back with a rush of redevelopment, a push for high-end restaurants, boutique hotels, and a shiny new walking mall. Now, Napa has two dozen Zagat-rated restaurants and a charming little California-style downtown, its wood and brick facades and refurbished historic buildings coexisting with the mall's modern earth tones and vaguely grape themes.

Downtown Napa is also happily, for our purposes, lousy with wine tasting rooms. Many of them are like Wineries of Napa Valley, shared storefronts for wineries too small to have rooms of their own. A $20 card gets you 10¢ pours in all of them, and, in case you give up on walking the four or five blocks to the outer edges, there's a regular shuttle. The shuttle also goes to the Napa outlet stores, but they warn you first.

We view all this as a perfect launch spot for our Quest, partly because of the tasting room wealth, partly because it seems a safe place to work on my tasting proficiency, and partly because Copia is here.

Copia, a $55-million, 80,000-square-foot temple to all things epicurean, is named after the Roman goddess of abundance. Its official title is the American Center for Food, Wine and the Arts. We have a long road ahead of us through this valley that is its own thirty-mile-long shrine to food and wine, and we figure some early cultural grounding can only help.

Copia, it turns out, seems to be about a lot of things, maybe too many things, but not particularly Napa Valley. It was funded in big part by Robert Mondavi, and his approach to food and wine as joyful art is apparent in the exhibits and general esteem for the subject. There are rotating art shows about food or wine, there are classes and films, and there's a large, playful science-fair section.

But it's lacking, ironically, what has always been Robert Mondavi's greatest charm: a sense of excitement and charisma, a sense that there is something larger in these connections than just the idea that food and wine and art go together. Mondavi always made it feel like they belong together, and that together they make a special magic. Copia could use a dose of magic.

It could also use a bit more Napa. Despite the tributes to the miracle of winemaking, there isn't much feel of vineyards or wineries or the lush valley. Outside, the building looks like a modernist factory, despite the fountains, long rows of trees, and the three and a half impressive acres of what they call "organic, edible gardens." Inside, it's tall and sleek, with pale colors and lots of metal, glass, and open space for events and festivals.

What Copia feels like, really, is a high-end mall for grown-ups. You can see teenagers dropping off parents with a firm, "We expect you to call right when your food-and-wine pairing gets out." Instead of a food court, there's a wine bar, a Julia's Kitchen, an American Market cafe with designer sandwiches, and a Wine Spectator Tasting Table. That is our target.

The Tasting Table is a curved bar out in the ground floor mall section. Today they're pouring New Zealand whites. We walk up and the genial guy behind the bar, without a word, slides a couple crystal glasses across to us with something in them, then moves away to talk up other tasters. Hank guesses Pinot Grigio. I would have said Chardonnay, but I nod because, what do I know. I go look for something to tell us what we're drinking.

I walk down the bar and cock my head sideways to read the bottle the genial guy is pouring for two women. Kumeu River Pinot Grigio. That Hank, he's good. Meanwhile, genial guy, a burly, sixtyish man wearing a green Copia apron and a permanent happy look, is telling the women, "C'mon, what am I gonna do with the rest of the wine? Have some more." They relent under his assault of hospitality, and he nearly fills their glasses. He looks around for another mark.

A young couple walks up and he dishes them each a healthy pour with the air of a barkeep serving ale. They try to ask about the wine, but genial guy moves on with a happy "Enjoy." He picks up a new bottle and comes to us with a Stoneleigh Marlborough Sauvignon Blanc. Hank starts to say this should be good, but genial guy is having too much fun. "You look like men who like wine," he says. "Help me finish the bottle."

We're guessing genial guy is a Copia volunteer, just a nice man donating his time, and that when the winemakers pour their own stuff on weekends, it doesn't go quite like this. Still, you have to love the irony. Copia calls itself a "monument to the elegance of food and wine," and we're sitting through possibly the least elegant wine tasting in Napa.

ONE BLOCK EAST OF THE TWELVE acres of Copia, and across the Napa River as it bends away from downtown, is JV Wine & Spirits. There may be nothing in Napa Valley that is more of a polar opposite in mood to Copia.

The Napa River separates the new Napa downtown from what it was. JV looks like a warehouse store and sits in an industrial district. Across the street is Furniture 4 Less. Where contemporary Copia is about modernity and form, JV Wines & Spirits is nothing but function. Its rows and rows of wine are stacked alphabetically and mostly in their boxes. If Copia is designed for tourists, JV is a place for locals. A very good place for locals. It's got a mammoth wine selection, including 800 labels from wineries that produce no more than 600 cases a year. Because they, like almost everyone, are out of Rombauer Chardonnay, the valley's current "it" Chardonnay, JV has a display with twenty suggested replacements, similar in style and price. They promise more Rombauer the day it's released in the fall. You wonder if maybe Robert Mondavi, after an appearance at Copia, sometimes pops into JV to see what they've got.

JV's tasting bar is a major contrast, too. It's in a side pocket of the store, inside a little room for pricey wines, and it's just a simple L-shaped counter looking at a cinder block wall painted grape purple. It's quiet and lighted well-enough, but here, it's about the wine. They are pouring twelve good wines this afternoon. Even I recognize a few.

One is Sedna, from a small winery on the valley floor just a few miles north, and I know I've liked their Cabernet. Hank can't resist his wine-retailer impulses and he's wandering around the store when Brad, a clean-cut young guy in JV's purple shirt, comes to pour for us. We chat. I say I like that Sedna Napa Valley Cab. He pours me a bit. I still like it. Hank walks up and gives the look I've seen many, many times.

"What I have told you," he says with overacted exasperation, "about starting with a Cab?"

I know this. There are rules. You go white to red, light to heavy. Taste buds get worn out or overwhelmed or whatever it exactly is. The question, I ask, is can I go back? No problem. A couple crackers, a swallow of water, I'm golden. I'm also hoping Brad will forget I've already tasted the Cab when we get back to it.

The thing about tasting, actually, is there really are no exact rules. Everything's a guideline because everyone does it differently. And because everyone is different. There are, however, key points.

It starts with your nose. You get thousands of scents in your nose and your olfactory system. You taste, however, only a few basic flavors: sweet, salty, sour, and bitter, plus your tongue picks up what's called "umami," a Japanese word for "savory" or "meaty" or, I dunno, "not fish."

"Your nose is everything," Hank says. That's why you swirl your wine. The smells come from the alcohol evaporating, and swirling helps it along, spreads the wine around the glass and creates more surface area for evaporation. I'm now sure it does not matter which direction you swirl—thank you, Luna Vineyards—but there are some guidelines for this, too.

We would meet a winemaker named John at Signorello Vineyards a few days later who would give us some of them.

"Why do you swirl the glass?" he would ask.

"Open up the wine?" I say tentatively. I know the phrase.

"How do you know it worked?" John says. "Smell first, then swirl. Smell it, swirl, smell again. If the nose doesn't change, you know it's a simple wine. You can keep swirling as much as you'd like. When you smell, stick your nose right in there. In wine country, I promise no one will laugh at you.

"And put the glass on the bar or the table before you swirl it. If you try to be too cool and swirl it mid-air, you'll end up with half the bars' cleaning bills."

Been there. At JV Wine & Spirits, I swirl carefully, if multi-directionally. I'm also dribbling less during the spitting action, so Hank figures it's time to move my lessons along.

The actual tasting has its techniques, too. Hank lets me sip the 2002 Sedna Napa Valley Chardonnay. I get all that crème brûlée/toasted marshmallow big Chardonnay flavor. Now, Hank says, try it again.

"Take a healthy sip," he says. "Leave it in your mouth a few seconds and move it around. Try to coat your tongue."

The taste buds, as limited as they already are, have regional issues, too. They're bunched, rather than spread evenly, which is why you try to cover your whole tongue with a little wine. Then, you pucker your lips and suck in a little air, kind of like a reverse whistle. You look like a fish and the gurgle isn't pretty, but it gets a huge flavor spike. I mean huge.

"It's aerating the wine," Hank says, "just like when you swirl. Then spit."

This time I taste a lot more fruit. Hank says it's green apple and pear and I'm buying it. I'm also starting to buy the idea spitting doesn't kill the taste, but I think that's because you still swallow a little. Or maybe that's me.

WE LEAVE JV AND HEAD BACK across the river to the little center of town. It's hard to stand at First and Main Streets in this newly polished downtown and not be happy about the proximity of so many tasting rooms. Also such wildly different styles of tasting rooms.

Through the day, we go to places like Vintner's Collective in one of the oldest buildings in Napa, the Pfeiffer building constructed in 1875, and once the home of, among other things, a saloon and brothel. From the outside, the old bricks and stone show some history. Inside, there are no signs of the Pfeiffer's shady past. The room is proudly upscale, with polished blond wood and a jet-black tasting bar. There's bright, progressive art everywhere. It would feel like an ultra-trendy restaurant, the kind of place Hank and I usually can't get into, if the guys behind the bar weren't so amiable.

Vintner's Collective is one of the shared shops. They serve wines from eighteen small-but-premium wineries, and they have the winemakers come in and pour regularly. The wine is very good—my favorite is a huge 2000 Richard Perry Napa Syrah—and so are the crackers, which, instead of the usual full basket, are laid out flat, four to a plate.

But, all you really need to know about Vintner's Collective is their website quotes the sommelier from The French Laundry, certainly Napa's, and one of America's, most respected restaurants, as the wine shop he'd visit if he could only visit one.

Down the block, there's Napa Valley Traditions, which is, barely, the tasting room for Bayview Cellars, a family winery just north of Napa in the Oak Knoll District. Napa Valley Traditions is really a country store and gift shop. They sell stuffed animals, jams, ceramics, and, of course, checkered country linens. And they have a very nice espresso bar. The "tasting room," on the other hand, is a table in the back, around two corners, tucked in a section that can't decide if it's retail space or storage area.

The wine is OK, about what you'd expect, but everyone in the store is so adorably friendly, and so happy to see us, we buy a couple bottles of Wine Away stain remover just to buy something.

We eat an early dinner in the Napa General Store, which, like so much in this enjoyably inconsistent little downtown, is also not what it sounds like. It's mostly a restaurant in a high-ceilinged room in a refurbished building on the river. It's got an open kitchen, huge windows leading out to a deck, and a warmly lit wine bar.

We get our 10¢ taste at the bar, courtesy of the Downtown Napa

Tasting Card, then move to a table in the dining area. I have a 2003 Cakebread Napa Valley Sauvignon Blanc and Hank's gets an '03 Praxis Pinot Noir from Monterey to go with our Asian fusion meals, and, no, I do not spit. There is such thing as taking your lessons too far. The room is a spacious, inviting place, and it would be good to just sit here a while, but we have tasting rooms to get to. Work. Work. Work.

BACK ROOM WINES, JUST A BLOCK down from the walking mall, has the feel of a place for locals. And for wine folk. It's a modest-sized, nothing-fancy wine shop with an expansive world view. Since most of its customers have plenty of access to Napa wineries, there's a good stock from other regions and other countries.

Owner Dan Dawson is pouring for his weekly Friday night tasting, and the theme tonight is Cabernets Under $30. The range of regions includes the Columbia Valley, Lake County, and Alexander Valley. I spot my Sedna on the list, too, but I'm holding back. It got me in trouble once already. Now I'm doing what Hank does.

The shop has about ten people in it, most of them young and with that yippee-it's-Friday-night brightness. They look like people who'd hit TGIF spots if this weren't Napa. Instead, they're in a small, quirky wine shop talking about finishes and balance and oak. The sense isn't a bar's flirty wariness; instead it's almost collegial, like, maybe, we can learn a little about wine from each other. Not from me. I'm just saying. The three women next to us, in their twenties, locals, and attractive, ask us what we're tasting, what we think of it, and why. This is not standard bar talk.

For the record, Hank and I are both married. Any incidental chatting up of attractive Napa locals is purely for research purposes. We learn that two of the women, Michelle and Jen, are servers in a St. Helena restaurant and are here to taste wines they don't carry. Their friend, Terri, works in a tasting room at a winery just north of Napa.

That gets us asking about tasting room behavior, and, more specifically, what isn't cool. I can't be briefed too much on this subject.

Some of it is obvious: Tasting rooms aren't for happy hour. It's not all-you-can-drink, and it's not part of a pub crawl. (That's why you buy a bottle and find your own spot.) Just be moderate and don't hang around the same room all day.

Also, there really are no stupid questions—except for my counterclockwise swirl theory—but you can look stupid trying to look smart. That's a big point with Hank.

"You guys taste your wines every day," he tells them. "You're always going to know more about them than we will." And this from a guy who knows a lot.

Terri says she gets men—it's always men—who lecture her about her wines, which would be boorish enough even if they weren't often wrong.

"Just be nice," she said, "we'll end up pouring you more. I like beginners, and I like people who ask questions. It's never a problem talking about our winery and our wine. But, you know, what we hate is snobs."

That gets us to what Terri, Michelle, and Jen—and we would learn, half of Napa Valley—consider a scourge of wine country: limousine tasters. A lot of wineries restrict limos to certain hours. It isn't everyone in a limo, particularly not the small groups looking for a different tour of Napa, but there are two annoying classes of limousine tasters. One group is the partyers, who are a general pain for obvious reasons, but at least they aren't driving themselves around. The other bunch is what Michelle calls the elitists.

The elitists, she says, only buy the most expensive wines. Not the best, the priciest. Michelle sees them at her restaurant. Wine isn't a passion for them, it's a way to keep score, to show their elevated social status and general grandness. "Those people," Michelle says, "are such wanna-bes. When those guys show up, it's a buzz kill for the whole room."

Lower on the annoyance scale for locals, actually more lame than irritating, are the people who've seen the movie *Sideways* too many times. Great movie. A classic for wine lovers. But if you don't have the inner warning light about tired and overused jokes, here's what you should know: Don't recite lines from the movie, don't brag about your love for Pinot Noir, and do not, seriously, do not say you're not drinking fucking Merlot. It's already been done too often.

Another repercussion from *Sideways*, apparently, is more guys now hit on the women working tasting rooms. "Honestly," Terri says, "I don't know why people see something in a movie and think they should do it. It's not like we suddenly need bouncers or anything, but some guys are such morons."

And then there is this move, and I am so entirely with them: Holding your wine glass by the base. That's just stupid.

"God, I hate that," Terri says. "I'm not even sure why. But when people come in and do that, I want to pour wine on their lap."

I decide, after all this conversation, I won't brag that I've almost learned to spit.

OUR LAST STOP, EVEN WITH A strong endorsement from our three friends, is an energetic, hospitable surprise. It's a place called Bounty Hunter. It's a wine bar/pub/bistro on First Street down at the river that is everything a wine bar, pub, and bistro should be. There's lots of wood and light, and the room is somehow both crowded and airy. There's one brick wall with shelves of wine, tall community tables seating eight, scattered smaller tables, and an unfussy feel at the bar. One bar stool is a saddle.

If you closed your eyes and wished for an end-of-the-day wine and social spot, it would be Bounty Hunter. They're also serious about their wine. The stemware is high-end crystal, they offer rotating wine tasting flights—what they call Taste Drives—forty wines by the glass and more than 400 labels. The menu lists a wine's retail price, its Bounty Hunter's price—with a minimal markup—and a standard restaurant price, which in here looks like gouging.

Bounty Hunter opened in 2003, more than a decade after its owner, Mark Pope, started his rare wine catalog and his service tracking down tough-to-find wines for customers—which explains the bounty hunter name and gear displayed around the room, like the snowshoes and western-style topcoat. Nothing exactly explains the polo mallet.

Hank and I eventually land spots at the bar and order glasses of wine. On Hank's suggestion, I have a 2002 Herbert Brochard Sancerre, a French white from the Loire Valley. Hank has a 2001 Talisman Thorn Vineyard Pinot Noir from the Sonoma Coast. Both are terrific. As we sit there, a cooked chicken, standing on its tail end, goes by on a platter. It's Beer-Can Chicken, the bartender says—a chicken, cooked with a half empty can of beer stuffed inside and its top plugged by a lime. The whole thing steams on the grill. Hank and I swear that chicken is our next Napa meal.

As we sit at the bar and watch this humming crowd, so many of them drinking good wine, we see a guy we met earlier today, Andy, who was pouring at Vintner's Collective. We keep meeting people like Andy, who just moved to Napa. They're here to be at the epicenter of wine.

Andy is in his twenties and came from Boston after working in a wine shop for two years. His reason for moving was both vague and very specific. He wants to live in the wine world. We also met Karen, pouring at Napa Wine Merchants, who was a TV promotions exec in Sacramento—our home—and who sold her house to move to Napa.

She loves the industry and if you're going to learn about wine, she says, you need to be in Napa.

That's the thing about this valley. Its fantasy mixes with a clear truth: There is no wine region in America so wholly and resolutely engaged in the notion of wine. People come here to visit that, and they come here to live it, to learn about wine, to make wine, to just be around it all.

There is nothing like wine in the world, no other foodstuff or agricultural crop that has such a quixotic grip on us. Nothing that will make people pick up and move just to be around a product. Wine has a mythology, a free-standing significance, an almost primal lure that can seem utterly irrational if you think too hard about it.

It makes food and social connections better, and, yeah, sometimes that's just the alcohol. But mostly it's more. It's the complexity of winemaking, the seemingly endless variations on something so simple as juice from grapes. It's the way good wine evokes a sense of place, a sense of the region and the countryside it comes from. Sometimes, it's just the taste.

Sitting here in Bounty Hunter, watching the people and just sipping good wine, stirs something in both of us. Wine is at its best, we decide, at the human level. That's what Copia missed. You don't worship wine, you drink it. If wine is art, as Copia says, then it's best when it's experienced, not revered.

That's why, maybe, the elitists in the limos rub so many people the wrong way in this valley. They turn something that should be a joy into a prize, and they miss what wine should be: a pleasure everyone can get a piece of.

And that's why, at least for us, Bounty Hunter strikes such a chord and seems such a fit for Napa Valley. This is a place connected to some very good, and sometimes very expensive, wine. But the connection is at the street level, or maybe it's the people level. This bouncy, obliging place has a joyfulness to it, and if it, and everyone here, has bought a little into the romance of wine, that just adds to the basic fun of finding a new wine, or of uncorking an old, reliable one, and of drinking it.

After all that, after sitting there and deconstructing our connections to this world of wine, it dawns on us both: We haven't even left town. It's time, we decide, to get out into the vineyards.

Oak Knoll District

SPRING CAN BE a scary time in Napa Valley. The vines are waking up and the defenseless baby grapes are about to pop out. So much can go wrong, Hank is telling me.

We're driving up Silverado Trail, the two-lane highway on the east side of the valley that's the quieter of the two main roads running the length of Napa. It's an early day in April and everything around us is intensely, thoroughly green. There are some wildflowers trying to make a statement, but the overwhelming sense of the hillsides, the vineyards, the trees, and the mountains up to Atlas peak, is a soft, pervasive Mediterranean green.

It's hard for me to focus on Hank's warning on this sunny, optimistic day. The vines are getting leaves, the air is warm, you can smell freshness in the dirt. I'm thinking, "God, I love spring."

But Hank is talking pestilence and ruin. The guy can be such a downer.

"Even when everything goes right, you're always guessing with vineyards. Little things like the amount of sun or rain can change the flavor of the grapes. It's kind of like playing poker with God," Hank says.

Vineyard managers up and down the valley scramble at this time of year to keep ahead of the weather. Sometimes they have to make moves—prune leaves, cut off shoots, change the canopies of the vines, even remove some of the tiny grapes—based on what they think is coming. And sometimes they just have to react. Their enemies are frost, rain, sudden heat, rot, and bugs. Some can nearly kill a crop; more likely, if not handled right, they'll mess with the flavors and substance of the wine.

This early on, frost is the first likely killer. Despite the brilliant sunshine today, recent nights have been near or below freezing. "I'll bet there are a lot of tired people around here who have been spending their nights in the fields," Hank says. "You kinda forget this all starts with farming."

That's exactly what they tell us at Van Der Heyden Vineyards, a couple miles up Silverado Trail from downtown Napa. Van Der Heyden is the dictionary definition of a family winery. You drive up what looks like a long, private driveway to a couple houses, and park among the family cars and some farming vehicles. The tasting room is inside a tiny, proudly cluttered, converted carport. Outside the small windows, a few workers are in the vineyards, and so are two kids and a Border collie carrying his own leash in his mouth.

In the tasting room, a big, animated guy with the ruddy look of a man who's bounced around vineyards for many of his sixty-plus years is exuberantly talking wine and quizzing us. Do we know Merlot can be a deep, powerful wine? What do we think forty-three months in French oak does to their 2000 Napa Valley Cabernet? I guess it makes the Cab seem like it's been aging much longer. "Right," he nearly shouts. I thought we might high-five.

"Taste it," he says. I tell him I get chocolate in it, but I get chocolate in almost everything. I like chocolate.

"Nothing wrong with chocolate," he says.

Then I ask if the frost has been bad. Our host is not Mr. Cheery anymore.

"Every vineyard manager has been up at 2 a.m. with the smudge pots or something for a week," he says. Dead serious now. "We've got it under control but those guys are wearing out."

Bad year? I ask.

"Nah," he says. Mr. Cheery is back. "That's just the wine business."

One of the many reasons Napa Valley is such a choice wine-growing region is that, even with the spring weather mood swings, the range of those swings is relatively mild. In parts of France, our host says, a bad spring could mean ice storms or freezing temperatures deep into June. A bad European spring can be harsher than a normal Napa winter, and that's why vintages there matter so much more.

Some years are just brutal. In Napa, the differences are mostly matters of degree. What a bad spring can do here, is change the yield or the quality of grapes, but generally not destroy them.

Frost is the exception. Frost can kill the young buds and vines. But there are tools to fight the cold. The smudge pots Mr. Cheery was talking about are one of the oldest tricks, though they're becoming a rarer sight. They're large, oil-burning cauldrons, maybe two feet wide, with a large exhaust pipe extending up four feet or so. In part, they're vineyard heaters that keep a flame lit through a cold night. They also create a layer of smoke over the flat vineyards that acts like a blanket to hold in some of the daytime warmth. For obvious reasons, an increasingly crowded Napa Valley is less and less enthusiastic about blankets of smoke.

More common, particularly in the flat vineyards where the cold air dives to the valley floor and seals out warmer air above it, are the huge wind machines, giant fans set in towers sometimes four stories high. They suck cold air up and out of the rows and let warm air drop into the vineyards.

Vineyards that have access to enough water also use a logic-defying system of spraying the vines with a thin layer of mist. The water freezes and the ice actually insulates the vines, holding them at a temperature just above freezing that is safe for vulnerable young grapes and vines.

"Those guys out there work pretty hard," Mr. Cheery says.

Walking out, I'm thinking maybe this idyllic life does take some effort. As we get to our car, the Border collie runs up to play, still holding his rope leash. We hear someone calling from one house, "Andre. Hey Andre." So I walk the dog over and say he's right here.

The woman is sympathetic and tries not to make fun. "No, that's the dog," she says. "Andre is our winemaker. He was in the tasting room all morning."

Right. Andre Van Der Heyden. Founder of the place. So, that's who that was. I wonder what the dog's name is. I'd call him SmudgePot.

WE MOVE A BIT UP SILVERADO Trail. In spring, everything, I mean, everything, looks like a winery. Maybe it's the all-encompassing green and the general tone of the valley; certainly it's that vines are growing on every small patch of land. We look at our map and turn down a driveway in front of a wide, two-story Victorian. Then we see the sign. Silverado Trail Tractor Rental. OK. At least we know where that is now.

Up the road is Darioush, and there's no confusing this with a trac-tor yard. The 22,000-square-foot, gold-tinged winery, fronted by a long, tree-lined driveway, sets of low fountains, and sixteen free-stand-ing stone columns, looks like a Persian palace.

It's built that way partly as a nod to its Persian wine roots. Owners Darioush and Shahpar Khaledi, who left Iran for California in the 1970s during the Islamic Revolution, grew up in one of the world's first wine regions—in an Iranian town called Shiraz—and they didn't want to forget where they came from. That's not likely. Besides their buzz-worthy premium wines, their startling building is something of a shock sitting among vineyards and against low, vine-covered hills, and now and then you'll hear someone complain it doesn't fit in.

But this is Napa, where people build wineries suggesting Germany, Greece, Italy, every region of France, and, here and there, Disneyland. What's one more acknowledgment of wine's interna-tional pedigree? And as shiny and flamboyant as it may be, Darioush is also welcoming, with big walkways and doors, and with tons of light pouring into the tasting room.

We sit at the glass-topped bar in the center of the huge room, under a skylight and among more stone columns. It feels like a sleek nightclub bar rather than a tasting table. We watch a twenty-foot-high indoor waterfall. It's more of a water wall, actually, smooth and firm looking. I'm just as dazzled by the big, firm 2002 Signature Cabernet Sauvignon, which might explain what happens next.

A young couple sitting at the bar beside us asks our server for a dinner recommendation. Don Giovanni, she says. That's Bistro Don Giovanni, an Italian-style hot spot that's been one of Napa's top—and coolest—restaurants for more than a decade. It's almost directly across the valley floor from Darioush on Highway 29.

For some reason, they all look over at me. It's possible I snorted. I give them that hand waggle—palm flat and straight down, fingers wobbling—that means only so-so. It's also possible I sneer a little when I do that.

"Really?" the woman tourist says innocently enough.

"I dunno," I say, "it's got such a big rep and everyone recommends it. I think it's overrated."

"Really." That's the server, and it's a statement of disagreement and, maybe a little, hurt feelings. "I love that place," she says.

It's dawning on me I should have shut up.

"I'm just saying the last time (only time) I was there, I wasn't impressed." Which is true, and I'm usually impressed easily. Still, why won't I stop talking?

"I recommend it all the time," the server says.

"It just seemed sort of ordinary," I say. I'm trying to backtrack and doing it badly. "But lots of people like it and it's been popular forever and it gets great reviews and . . ."

"I have friends who work there," the server says as she starts to move off to pour for another group. She says something I can't hear to the couple. They nod.

"Go to Don Giovanni," I say to them. "You'll have a great time. Don't listen to me." That may be the best advice they'll get their whole trip.

They leave with a mumbled something that could have been "thanks," but I doubt it. Hank has wisely remained silent. "I'm not huge on Don Giovanni, either," he says in a bit. Now I get backup.

The server comes back and is enormously nice to Hank. She is not impolite to me. I notice, however, my pour is smaller than his. The life of a critic is hard.

THIS PART OF THE VALLEY IS officially called the Oak Knoll District of Napa Valley, and it gets fewer tourists than northern Napa. So many of the tourist targets are Up Valley, as they say here, from Yountville on north, and especially in the Oakville and Rutherford areas, where the big-name wineries line Highway 29. But that's too bad, considering how viscerally you experience the look and texture of the vineyards right here. This is the widest flat spot in Napa, at points nearly five miles wide. The roads that cut through it—Big Ranch Road running north-south or Oak Knoll Avenue going east-west—take you into a wonderland of vineyards, their ruler-sharp lines running elegantly off across the valley floor and disappearing toward the mountains.

It's early afternoon and we're standing outside the Monticello Vineyards buildings, in the middle of the valley, breathing in the rows and rows of vines, feeling engulfed, almost overwhelmed by them. Monticello, a well-regarded winery with some monumental Cabernets, was built by a former Virginian who modeled the place after the home of Thomas Jefferson, one of America's founding wine guys. The buildings are about one-third the size of the originals, and as graceful as they may be, what is so much more affecting here is this sense of being deep in the vineyards. It might be the straight lines, or the way the rows accent slight changes in the landscape, but something here makes us feel serenely connected to the spot and to the valley.

"It's ironic," Hank says, "that a winery with one of the great views in the valley is right in the middle of the floor. And that a lot people never find it."

We both just stand for a while. Neither of us wants to get back in the car.

WE'VE BEEN BOUNCING AROUND THIS STRETCH of lower valley and it's nearing the end of the day. We're at Koves-Newlan Vineyards, on a side road that runs alongside and just a few yards west of Highway 29. It's another of the off-the-beaten-path wineries in this district that are right on the path. The tasting room is down a short flight of stairs and, essentially, jury-rigged in an enormous barrel-storage warehouse with concrete floors and racks of barrels stacked three stories high. It's a comfortable mix of feeling casual and professional, and the short, dark woman pouring for one couple and for us is chatty and matter-of-fact. We're all insiders, she's implying, or we wouldn't be here. We're tasting in a warehouse. That's where wine people taste.

Then she stops, her brown eyes get large just for a moment—Is that terror?—and she takes a deep breath.

"Uh-oh," she says to no one. "A limo. They're supposed to make reservations."

The scourge of the valley is upon us. We hear them approach. Large shadows loom at the door above the room. We all look up. There are four of them, two big, dark-haired guys in loud Hawaiian shirts and two dark-haired women in dresses who, frankly, look a little embarrassed for their guys. The guys operate on the same volume setting as their shirts as they try to say hello and handle the steps.

The couple next to us says a quick thanks and leaves. Hank and I want to see this, so we just move away from the bar. Besides, I have a nice pour of their spicy 2001 Napa Valley Pinot Noir and I'm not giving it up.

The four of them try mightily. They know a little about wine, it sounds like, and try to taste gracefully, despite the occasional slurred word. They ask the kinds of questions people ask when they're trying not to sound like they've been drinking all day. "Where do these Pinots come from?" "Is this all from Napa Valley?" "Where are those vineyards?" They are all, basically, the same question.

"We close at 5," the server says. It's quarter to. There's no hope they'll get the hint.

This horde is not really doing anything wrong, except, I suppose, being drunk. That happens. Their real transgression, though, is something larger and more ethereal: They stomped on the mood. They stomped on the fantasies of wine tasting that we so happily buy into—that we're all slightly refined, slightly erudite and cultured, yet down-to-earth and simpatico with the hard work and dirty hands good winemaking requires. Wine tasting is the oh-so-mature—or so we say—joy of mixing a little intellect with a lot of pleasure. And these guys, these limousine tourists, make enough noise to wake everyone from that fantasy. They're just out here crashing around having fun. It's so uncivilized.

Whatever else they may be, however, they are extremely loud.

"Is there a Macaroni Grill or something around here?" one guy asks.

"What's that?" the server asks back.

"Good Italian restaurant," he says.

"Good chain Italian," says one of the women.

"No chains like that," the server says. "But there's Don Giovanni."

Hank gets that smile he gets, and he looks at me, like, well? This time I shut the hell up.

IT IS NOW LATE APRIL, A Sunday morning between two spring storms, and the day is a mix of sun and clouds. The air is more humid than Napa is used to. This spring is turning out to be wet, and that's another bucket of concerns for the wineries.

We're standing among the vines at Trefethen Vineyards, one of the oldest wineries in the valley. The elegant, dusty redwood building, built in 1886, stands in a grove of ancient oaks, and is surrounded by 600 acres—about a square mile—of its own vineyards. We have drifted out into one of them on a semi-tour and we're looking at infant grapes. An entire bunch is the size of a fingernail. This is bud break; the grapes are peaking out and, if I can say this without sounding too idiotic, they look adorable. Also helpless.

This is one of the times—and there are many—when vineyard managers earn their pay, Karen Nielsen, our tour guide, is telling us. We met Karen before at Napa Wine Merchants. She's the woman who sold her house in Sacramento to move to Napa Valley. Working the tasting room in downtown Napa is her second job. Hosting and giving tours at Trefethen is her main gig. But she's still new at this. Hank and I are, actually, her first tour, which consists mostly of Hank wandering around and Karen and me following him. He answers questions for both of us.

"I'm still learning this place," she says. Karen is thirtyish, blond, and athletic looking. She and Hank talk about how the rain is starting to affect the vineyards. I mostly nod.

Rain is a pain in a bunch of ways for the wineries. Too much water through the season can, basically, dilute the taste in grapes.

Winemakers tend to want small, concentrated grapes because those have big flavors and make the best wines. Over-hydrated grapes make thin wines, and they can have lower sugar concentration—called Brix—and it's the sugar that turns into alcohol when the wine ferments.

Heavy rain can also cause "shatter." That's when the rain washes away pollen before the grape flowers get fully pollinated, which reduces the yield and means fewer grapes per cluster. Later in spring, a hard rain—or worse, hail—can even cut the grapes or the leaves.

There is more, because this is farming and with farming there is always something else to worry about. The wet can bring mold and rot and pests. The list of pests that threaten young vines sounds like the lineup for a horror movie. It includes the orange tortrix, the grape bud mite, and the western grapeleaf skeletonizer. The most common fear—though it's not rain related—is phylloxera, a microscopic aphid that feeds on the vines' roots and destroyed most of Napa at the end of the 1800s, the valley's first, doomed, bloom. It struck again in the 1980s, though wineries were better equipped to react. The only real treatment, however, is to rip out infected vines and replant a more resistant root.

"I think they don't want us to even say the word," Karen says. Never provoke the wine gods, she says.

Trefethen and its neighbors are willing to wrestle the gods a little, however. Hank is poking around in another field looking at the system of trellises holding the vines in place. This group has the vines aimed straight up. It's called vertical shoot positioning, Hank tells us. That lets air flow through the vine—the better to dry the grapes quickly—and it means more sunlight for the grapes and the leaves. It will also let the vineyard people spray if they need to.

Karen says the vineyard workers have been doing something they call "suckering," cutting off excess shoots so all the vines will grow as ordered. Removing some vines also means the remaining ones will be more stressed and produce more concentrated fruit. But cut off too many, and those remaining vines don't have enough leaves—the solar panels of the grapevines, as Hank calls them—to keep the rest of the vine healthy.

"I'm starting to learn," Karen says as we walk back toward the main building, "this winemaking thing is a lot more complicated than I thought it was."

"Wait till harvest," Hank says.

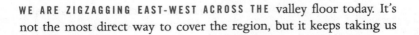

WE ARE ZIGZAGGING EAST-WEST ACROSS THE valley floor today. It's not the most direct way to cover the region, but it keeps taking us through those astounding expanses of vineyards. We stop at Andretti Winery, a bright set of buildings that looks like an Italian countryside villa complex designed by the architects of Disneyland.

It's painted a range of Tuscan yellows and mustards, has a stone courtyard, a Renaissance-looking fountain, huge rounded wooden doors, and seems so permanently cheerful you want to giggle. Inside, the tasting room is more of the same cheerful, which includes Marilyn, our server. She's a little busy, but so what.

Marilyn opens a 2003 Napa Valley Sangiovese for us, and pours herself a quick taste, to make sure the bottle is OK. "Boy, that's good," she says. Marilyn pours herself another taste—to be more sure—pours for us, then again for her. "Yes, that is good," she says. Nice to see diligent quality control.

This winery sits on fifty-three perfect acres of flat wine country, and was started in 1996 by race car driver Mario Andretti. He designed the buildings to recall Montona, the village in Northern Italy where he was raised. Andretti shows up every now and then, for a new release, for a winery dinner, sometimes just to hang out. There's a small table with some racing memorabilia in a corner of the tasting room, but this place is not about past glories. It's simply a piece of the Napa Valley dream that Andretti had the sense and the means to embrace.

Hank and I wander out to the patio behind the tasting room. It's surrounded by flowers and looks at the Tuscan mustard guest house and across the green vineyards beyond it. The view could have been designed by the architects of Disneyland, too, it's so perfect. Nice life, I'm thinking, being a race car driver.

BY MID-AFTERNOON, WE ARE AT ANOTHER Italian-style villa—a popular motif, we are learning—but this has a stone façade and a hillside flair. This is home base for Signorello Vineyards, on the east side of the valley, up a short, sudden hill. It's more of a real villa because the owner, Raymond Signorello Jr., stays there often. The back has a huge deck, a dozen patio tables, and a good-sized, vanishing-edge pool that appears to flow off into the valley below.

Signorello is one of the many wineries that is, in theory, appointment only. But, really, that's just what it says on the permit. As much as Napa County wants tourists, it's also trying to keep the tourist traffic down—something taught, I guess, in Contradictory Land Use 101 at This Will Never Work University—so most tasting room permits issued since 1990 are "Appointment Only." Except if you happen to walk in.

We walk into Signorello and a big guy behind the tasting bar waves us over before we can even ask. "C'mon in," he says. "Step right up, guys."

The tasting room is done in earth tones and tile, and has a big kitchen across from the long tasting bar and a couple of light-wood community tables. It seems as much a rec room as anything else. There's a mix of blues and rock playing in the background and the big guy is talking with a foursome that appears to be in no hurry to leave.

"The only thing you have to remember about wine," he says as they taste a red, "if you love it, you're absolutely right. If you hate it, you're absolutely right."

He is having a good time, and it feels like a house party in here. He comes to our end of the bar and introduces himself. John. He's fortyish, six-foot-four, with a barrel chest and the slightly weathered look of a man who spends some time outside. He wears a subdued, tan Hawaiian shirt that blends with the colors of the room.

John, it turns out, is a winemaker from the Dry Creek region of Sonoma County, just east and north of Napa. He's the guy who tells us to smell-swirl-smell when we're tasting. John says he's working here because he loves Signorello wines, and he likes how people here look at wine.

"Mother nature makes something different every year," he says. "There is rain, sun, heat on different days in different order. All of that matters to the fruit and you can't make wine without the grapes. Winemakers get all the glory, but the vineyard managers—we call them winegrowers—they matter just as much. That's why good winemakers are out there with them."

Signorello, despite the Italian name and villa, advertises that it makes wine in the classic French style. Like many other wineries in Napa, they figure much of a wine's flavor and character is determined by what happens in the vineyards. How they prune, what canopies and trellis systems they use, how they stress the grapes, how much or little they irrigate, all of that plays on the grapes. Signorello wants lush, concentrated fruit, so they try to grow relatively stressed grapes using relatively low amounts of water.

But what about the spring rain, we ask?

"We're OK," John says. "So far we're only 1.18 inches more than last year. If we get more, we might have to prune or thin the fruit. That makes a good wine, too."

That's part of the poker game Hank was talking about. Thinning the fruit is a lot like cutting back the shoots. If some clusters are cut out, all of the vine's energy and nutrients go into the remaining grapes. That means a lower yield—and less wine—but you get more concentrated flavors.

There are other tools for dealing with spring weather. Growers put cover crops—flowers and greenery—in between the vines that use up some of the moisture in the soil. They also house the friendly, we-love-wine insects that eat the evil, vine-destroying pests. The cover crops, after they're plowed under, also put nutrients back into the earth.

"You just have to pay attention," John says.

There's a lot to pay attention to, I say.

"That's why not everybody can make wine," he says. Then he laughs. "Though, if you look around, there sure are enough people trying."

BY THE END OF THE DAY, we're back on the west side of the Oak Knoll District, at Laird Family Estate, a new winery from an old Napa Valley family. The tasting room is the glass-enclosed top to a modern pyramid sitting high on man-made caves. Behind the pyramid is a substantial, high-tech winery used as a shared facility by a number of Napa's winemakers.

The tasting room is surrounded by glass and is high enough to feel like you're floating over the vineyards. It's nearly 5 p.m. when we get there. Hank says we need to "power taste" if we're going to check this one off our list today. But the woman behind the tasting bar is in no real hurry. She tells us the story of the place as she pours for us and washes wine glasses.

In 1970, owner Ken Laird, starting with a few acres of worn-down prune trees near Calistoga, began buying Napa farmland and orchards and turning them into vineyards. He farmed the first acres with his family and sold grapes to founding wineries like Robert Mondavi, Inglenook, and Beringer. Then in the early 1980s, he bought land in the Carneros region when most of his neighbors there raised trees or goats. By 1998, he owned 1,400 acres throughout the valley, and Laird wanted to do more than farm. So he broke ground on these caves and this community winemaking facility—called a custom crush—that's now used by a range of winemakers and vineyard owners. When it opened in 2000, Laird also started making his own wine.

It is, in a way, the story of Napa Valley. Or one of the stories. Laird was like Eugene Trefethen and Andre Van Der Heyden and the pioneers in the valley in its early resurgence in the 1960s and 1970s, people who wanted to be here, who had the vision to see its potential as a wine region, and who were smart, and, frankly, tough enough, to stick it out. What they have now looks huge and romantic and tranquil, but we can't see the sweat, the muscle, and, no doubt, the anxiety that went into building it.

The other story is Mario Andretti's and Darioush Khaledi's. They got their tickets somewhere else—Mario drove a grand prix car, Khaledi built a grocery business in Los Angeles from scratch—then came to Napa with the resources and bought into the life. In their own ways, they're part of the valley lore, too. They made good wines, created energetic wineries, showed how to grab onto the Napa Valley fantasy. Their route, honestly, is the one most of us daydream about: striking it rich and buying a winery.

But taking unproven land, planting vines, creating vineyards and a winery from the dirt, that's the enduring legend of wine country. It is the aura that surrounds us when we trundle through the vineyards. It's the notion of working the land and the grapes, of building something from scratch, of being part of the wine life. That's what adds a special layer of romance to this valley.

"Why didn't we buy land here in 1970 and turn it into vineyards?" I say to Hank as we start to drive away from Laird.

"You mean other than the fact we were in high school?" Hank says.

"Yeah, other than that."

Hank doesn't often engage in the sin of jealousy. Or maybe it's really hindsight. I can't help myself sometimes. So much of Napa's rise seems so recent and enticing, it feels like anyone could have just reached out and snatched a piece. That, of course, is not true, despite that wave of dot-com money a decade ago and, still, the occasional rich guy buying in. But one of the fables woven into Napa's atmosphere now is that this good life, this wine life, was sitting there for the taking.

The better story, however, is Ken Laird's. The idea of a foolhardy farmer turned big landowner turned winemaker gets as close to the American dream as you can imagine. And it makes you see this whole winery-owning endeavor isn't so easy. It's oddly reassuring that it took vision and guts and hard work, because if I'm honest with myself— rarely an enjoyable prospect—I can admit I never would have done it.

It's much easier, I'm thinking, just to get a bottle of wine and have a glass.

We are both quiet driving down the road. The sun is down behind the Mayacamas now and the fields have a dusky softness to their look. It's finally Hank who speaks.

"I think we need to go back to Bounty Hunter," he says.

THREE

Carneros

ARTESA IS A great club spot. It's high on a peak with a titanic view looking down on rolls and rolls of vineyards, then across the San Francisco Bay and out to the mountains that ring it. Inside, the tall, open room is all glass, sleek wood, and art deco. The crowd at the bar is young, attractive, and cool. A great club spot.

As a wine tasting room, it's more complicated. This is a semi-rainy Sunday afternoon in early May and still the place is hopping. "You should have been here yesterday," a server whose name-tag says Natalie tells us. "That was busy. This is nothing." On Natalie's nothing day, there are twenty people in front of the midsized tasting bar, chatting, laughing, occasionally trying a new wine. It feels like a place to drink wine, not just to taste it, right down to the servers with name-tags who I keep calling bartenders.

That is not a complaint. Artesa Vineyards and Winery has decided to be a destination winery of sorts. There's a small indoor reflecting pool, tables scattered around the airy room, and more tables outside on the deck with that view of the hills and the bay. It gets a San Francisco circle, and lots of people are here for the feel, the view, and the hot-spotness of it. They drive out to Napa to hang at Artesa. They buy a bottle of wine and sit on the deck. They could do worse.

For us, that's working out just fine. We decide this upscale, let's-celebrate kind of tasting room is ideal for diving into sparkling wines, though I suspect the truly cool don't use "diving in" and "sparkling wines" in the same sentence. Those are the people to whom French Champagnes, Roederer Cristal, or Artesa's Grand Reserva have become the new Sour Apple Martini or, forgive me, Long Island Ice Tea.

I, on the other hand, would be classified somewhere between novice and totally uncool in this area. All I know—I think—is that unless the wine comes from the Champagne region of France, it is not officially Champagne. It's sparkling wine in America and the better stuff has *méthode champenoise* somewhere on the label, though I'm not sure why. I will be wrong about most of that, for reasons involving global politics and World War I, but that's for later.

Right now, I'm diving into Sparkling Wine 101. We cross the room to the slightly less crowded reserve and wine club tasting bar where there's some sparkling action. A server/bartender named Dan pours us three tastes in three Champagne flutes.

They tell you to look at the bubbles. Small, fine bubbles mean a more delicate wine. Big, clunky ones are for savages. They do have a purpose, but it's in a Big Gulp. I've heard that and I'm trying to sound informed, so I proudly note that the bubbles are itty-bitty and coming straight up from the middle.

Dan is patient and, I might add, kind. The glasses are etched in the center, he says, so the bubbles will be centered. It's mostly for display, but these flutes do more than show the fizz. They're better than the old-fashioned bowl-like glasses because they keep the wine from going flat and they don't fill your nose with those bubbles.

I stick my nose in, swirl, and sniff again. Smell, swirl, smell, as I was taught. Hank tries not to laugh. He's had practice at that. "Not necessary," Hank says. "The bubbles already aerate the wine. And it's not so easy to swirl a flute." He points to the wine on my shirt.

Dan by now is feeling sorry for me. "It's just a habit," he says. "I'll be at a party and I'm standing there swirling Champagne. Then I'll look down at my glass and go 'oops.'" Bless you, Dan, for trying. I'm guessing he's just saying that. Dan's a big, slightly heavyset, fiftyish guy with an athletic bounce to his step, though that may come from pouring good wine all day. He and Hank both like the Grand Reserva, Artesa's upper-end sparkling wine. They say there are layers and complexity in the fruit. It's a little too tangy or something for me, but, only a little. I'm happier with the Codorníu Cuvée Raventos. There's an earthy, bread-like taste Hank says comes from the yeast. And my wine costs $15 a bottle, about a third of his favorite. There are advantages to an underdeveloped palate.

That's the thing about sparkling wine, Hank says. It's a fit for a lot of palates, and is way more approachable than a lot of people think. But many would-be fans are either scared away by the steep prices of the top-end stuff, or they've been driven off by the junk they drank at some under-capitalized wedding.

But there are so many good, interesting—and not-exorbitantly-priced—sparkling wines, you could argue for keeping a bottle in the fridge as an everyday wine, the way lots of people do in Europe.

"It's the perfect food wine because it's so versatile," Hank says. "In this country, we only drink it at celebrations, but it goes with so many things. It's really good with potato chips or popcorn. When people ask about some of the hard food-and-wine pairings, I say drink sparkling wine."

You would think that's because of the bubbles. Maybe they work as a scrubbing palate cleanser. Actually, it's that the grapes are picked with a relatively high level of acidity, and some acid in the wine helps food flavors pop out.

All of that makes sense—versatility, food friendly wine, high acid, over-dramatic reputation—but I'm standing there looking at that happenin' crowd thinking what sparkling wine really does is make you feel cool. Like a guy wearing a tux in a James Bond movie. Possibly it's the sharper, more refined taste. Probably it's the slick-looking flutes and those thin bubble lines. Whatever the exact reason, it's hard not to feel classy and polished with that sparkling brut in my hand. I just lean against the tasting bar for a moment being Mr. Smooth. Then I notice I'm still swirling.

"You got more wine on your shirt," Hank says.

ARTESA IS IN THE CARNEROS REGION of Napa, the southwestern toe of the valley that opens to the top of the San Pablo Bay and the entire San Francisco Bay below. It's a cooler land of Chardonnay and Pinot Noir grapes, two core ingredients of bubblies, besides being fine wine grapes in their own right. Artesa has recently become better known for its still wines—that's what we sparkling drinkers call regular ol' Cabs and Chards: still wine—but it has a sparkling history. Its owners come from the world's second oldest winemaking family—the Codorníu clan of Spain—who planted grapevines in the Spanish Penedès region in 1551. Until 1999, their Carneros winery was called Codorníu Napa and was all about making wine à la *méthode champenoise*.

As great a fit as Carneros grapes are for Artesa, the ultra-modern winery itself doesn't really match the tone of this piece of Napa. Carneros is, if anything, Napa's rural annex, and a peek at what Napa was thirty years ago—and at what neighboring Sonoma County was, too, because half of the Carneros AVA is in Sonoma. (AVA means American Viticulture Area. It signifies an official U.S. Alcohol and Tobacco Tax and Trade Bureau sanction as an appellation, or, basically, a place where the grapes are unique.)

Because Carneros is right on the bay, many wine growers ignored it for decades, figuring that the soil was too thin or had too much salinity, and that the weather was too cool to support decent wine grapes, particularly the big Cabernet Sauvignons being groomed around Napa. It really wasn't until the 1980s—when much of the main valley floor was spoken for—that wineries in big numbers began buying land and planting vineyards in Carneros.

That was also when Chardonnay exploded across our national wine palate. Chard is now America's top-selling varietal by barrels and barrels. We drink more than 400 million bottles a year—that's collectively—and it's become the definition of white wine for many people. "I can't believe how much Chardonnay we sell," Hank says. "Our Chard section is always double the size of any other varietal in our stores. If we have four feet of shelf space for Cabs, we have eight for Chardonnay. By the bottle, we sell at least twice as many Chards as we do anything else."

When the wineries looked seriously at Carneros, they found an area perfect for Chardonnay, not to mention those finicky little Pinot Noir grapes, with the cool breezes and fog off the bay keeping the temperature down in the summer and up a bit in the winter. The coolness gives the grapes a touch of the acidity that makes for great food wines, too, but unlike some of Europe's cooler regions, Carneros also gets plenty of hearty California sunshine and the good, hearty fruit that goes with it.

Many of the major wineries in Napa and in Sonoma now grow grapes in Carneros, and many more buy from vineyards there, but most of the area still looks only semi-developed. The side roads off Highway 12/121 lead to quiet fields, pastures, and orchards among the vineyards, and, as an occasional rustic embellishment, a house with a dilapidated car parked in some weeds.

More in this region's pastoral tone—though far from any rusted cars—is Mahoney Vineyards, just down the hill from Artesa. Mahoney was first known as Carneros Creek and is one of the veterans of the area, going back to 1972. Standing outside its cheerful yellow tasting room, we can see how different the Carneros region is from the rest of Napa Valley. The air smells like salt water, the light has the diffused, slightly filtered softness it gets when an ocean is nearby, vine-covered hills ripple off seemingly into open space, and, instead of the valley's snug, tucked-in feel, the sense is of unlimited expanse. Inside the spacious, two-story room with high windows and an easy country charm, there is another difference from Artesa: fewer visitors. Many fewer visitors.

"It's kind of slow today," our server tells us. She doesn't wear a name-tag. We ask how many people she's had by mid-afternoon. She says maybe twenty.

We tell her there was a steady twenty people at all times in front of the tasting bar at Artesa.

"Well, the weather is a little iffy," she says.

Even less Artesa-like is a small restaurant called Moore's Landing. It's connected to Cuttings Wharf, which is really just a parking lot with a small launch ramp and an overstatement in its name. It's at the end of Cuttings Wharf Road, south of Highway 12/121, where the Napa River brushes along the bottom of Carneros and where, a century ago, there was a commerce center and a legit working wharf.

Moore's Landing is a ramshackle diner with Formica counters, beat-up red booths, and a cement deck out back that faces some marshes and the calm Napa River. This funky spot is so opposite any lunch place in the heart of Napa, it's hard to believe we're in the same time zone, let alone the same valley.

Until the food shows up. Big plates. Big taste. And a bit of the Napa flair. Hank's grilled fish sandwich and my Cajun chicken spring off the plates. All we need is a flute of sparkling wine.

MAYBE THE PROTOTYPE CARNEROS WINERY IS Bouchaine Vineyards. This treasure of a spot is down a couple country roads south of Highway 12/121. It's not too far from Moore's Landing, but we're almost lost looking for it. Then we hit Buchli Station Road and a huge, new redwood winery looms up suddenly, sitting incongruously among farmland and some low, vine-covered hills. A couple more road signs would help, but Napa County allows wineries just two small, blue signs. So Bouchaine sticks one out about a mile east and another about a mile west and hopes for the best.

We walk into the bright little tasting room and feel like we stumbled into a neighbor's house. Neighbors with class, who like flowers and pour you their wine. Great neighbors, really. A middle-aged guy in a red golf shirt behind the bar is folding together a wine-carrying box and apologizing to his two customers.

"You need a pilot's license and an engineering degree to put these damn things together," he tells them. "Sometimes I don't get it just right and I hear 'Crash, Tinkle' outside. I just point to Barbara here."

His name is Dan Robson and, like his winery, he seems to personify the spirit of Carneros. He's casual, engaging, and completely unstuffy. When he sees us, his sudden mission in life is to make sure Hank and I have fun. His hands fly around as he tells us Bouchaine focuses on Chardonnay and Pinot Noir because the Chardonnay and Pinot are so damn good here.

Their wines seem to be classic Carneros, lots of crispness, lots of fruit, and lots of layers. I'm liking the Pinot Noir from the less expensive line, called Buchli Station, and I ask where the name comes from. Dan's colleague, Barbara, jumps in, grabs us by the arms, and drags us down a hall to look at black-and-white photos of a train station that was operating in the area in the late 1800s.

She talks like a proud mom, tells us this winery is the oldest in Carneros, going back to those late 1800s when it was owned by a man named Boon Fly. Boon Fly. Best wine guy name ever. Barbara shows us pictures of the area in the 1940s when it was Garetto Vineyards, and points to big redwood casks in some photos. "That's the wood that's the siding on the winery now," she says.

Barbara is not done. She takes us outside the tasting room, and across the deck. We're momentarily stunned by the view. It looks out at low vine-covered hills, each vineyard on a different heading, all undulating off into the distance. Then it expands across pastures to the bay. What makes the view so affecting is its simple balance. I'm thinking some artist-in-residence placed every vine, every tree, and every sheep. I immediately want to have a picnic.

The vines are a few yards past the deck. Barbara sort of pets the leaves as she talks about how she's worried because the spring is staying wet and the rain could wash the pollen away before the grapes pollinate themselves. "They're so vulnerable right now," she says, peeling back some leaves to show us the tiny buds, "and if . . . hey." She stops and looks at me. "Your glass is empty."

We hustle back inside to fix that. Another couple is there tasting Pinots now, and Dan is making dinner recommendations. "You guys have to try Moore's Landing," he tells them. "It doesn't look like much but they're nice people and the food is great." We agree as enthusiastically as we can, but we're no match for Dan.

"Or if you're looking for Italian, everyone loves Don Giovanni," Dan says. The couple looks at us for more agreement. I smile gracefully. "Who are we to argue?" I say.

When they leave, packing off bottles in another precariously assembled carrying box, Dan asks if he can make us reservations anywhere. We say we're about done for the day. "I can't let you leave without tasting this," he says and pulls out a 2000 Gee Vineyard Pinot

Noir. "We don't have any to sell, but you'll love it." The grapes come from a vineyard that's dry farmed, meaning the vines aren't irrigated and have to scrounge for water from rain or moisture in the dirt. The result is sometimes a near-useless crop, but more often it means stressed grapes with concentrated flavors and wine that is, in technical terms, really good. This one is deep and full of all those Pinot flavors from spice to cherries to mushrooms.

We're the last in the tasting room, so Dan and Barbara walk out with us and down the driveway like we're family, suggesting other wineries, asking where we've been, telling us other good seasons in Carneros—they say winter is fun with fireplaces going in tasting rooms—and generally chatting about vineyards and wine. I thought Dan was going to hug us. As we're getting in our car, another foursome drives up. Barbara looks at her watch.

"It's four," she says to Dan. "We're closed."

Dan walks over to the car as the two young couples get out. "We close at four every day. Sorry," he says.

They start to say, oh well, but Dan speaks first.

"You know what, what the hell," he says. "C'mon in. I don't have to be anywhere."

They all walk up the driveway. Dan's asking where they've been, what they've liked, how much of Carneros they've seen. I thought he was going to hug them, too.

DOMAINE CARNEROS, WITH ITS GRAND CHÂTEAU on a hill, is a landmark in Napa. It also represents the other side of the sparkling wine equation. Domaine Carneros is old school: regal, elegant, and reeking of European roots. If Artesa is energetic and youthful, Domaine Carneros is Old World and rooted. It's a place where the word Champagne means something.

The château looks like a movie-set version of a French Champagne house, which makes some sense. Domaine Carneros is owned by the Taittinger family of Reims, France, and this Louis XV–style, terra cotta–colored building is trimmed in brick and wrought iron. It's modeled after the Château de la Marquetterie, which is, according to a plaque on the stairs, a country home for the Taittingers. Makes you wonder about their big house.

Hank and I are here on a sunny, warm Friday. If there is a better spot on the planet for regular folk to toast a sunny, warm Friday than Domaine Carneros's stone and brick terrace, I can't imagine where it would be.

Tasting at Domaine Carneros is different from most Napa wineries. You sit at tables on this terrace or inside the marble-floored salon under crystal chandeliers. But as graceful as the salon is, on a day like this, if you stay inside, you're an idiot.

The ornate stone rails are low enough so you can see the Pinot Noir and Chardonnay vines that roll right to the terrace. Beyond that are gardens, a pond, and the Famous Gate, a twenty-foot-tall, eighteenth century–style black iron gate that was built to say this is the entrance to California's best wine country. In the distance are hills trimmed with vineyards and the Vaca Mountains beyond that.

The special view is looking to the side, due north of the château. There, on a small rise leading to Winery Lake, a dozen sheep dot the landscape. Wooden sheep. There's one black one, too, but he's off to a side, shunned by the flock. Even wooden sheep have class issues.

I'd worry about the loner if we weren't feeling so good just being here. We order a tasting flight of three sparkling wines, a Brut Vintage, a Brut Rosé, and the Le Rêve Blanc De Blancs. I'm thinking it's time to start defining terms. I've been reading since our trip to Artesa a week ago. Now I'm sure I have a new understanding about the words *méthode champenoise* on the label.

"I thought," I ask one of the servers who stops near our table, "that only wines made in France can say they are made *méthode champenoise* and that other sparkling wines made like those have to say *méthode traditionelle.*"

"Pardone?" she says.

Uh-oh. Strong French accent. I start to speak louder.

"I . . . thought . . . Americans . . . can't . . . use . . . *méthode champenoise,*" I say again. "I mean, can you, is this, you can't call it Champagne, right?" Oh good, that'll clear things up.

"No, no. Theese ees OK," she says, and does that move where she pretends someone is calling for her. She half smiles at me and walks away quickly around a corner.

Hank tries to help me out before I drive off more servers. I'm confusing a couple things, as is my way. He starts at the beginning.

Most Champagne-style sparkling wines come from three grapes: Chardonnay, Pinot Noir, and Pinot Meunier. Each is made into a base wine in a large tank, like any other non-bubbling wine. The sugars in the grapes, with the help of yeast, ferment into alcohol, and the by-products—heat and carbon dioxide—escape out of the tanks, like with other wines.

Next comes what they call the secondary fermentation. Wine makers blend the base wines in the proportions they prefer—sometimes they also add older, reserve wines for flavor—then mix in more yeast and more sugar.

In the traditional method, that mixture of wine, yeast, and sugar is poured into thick bottles and sealed. The always-hungry yeast eat the sugar and start another round of fermentation that creates more alcohol and more CO_2. But this time, the gas stays in the bottle and, voilà, bubbles. The yeast eventually expire—no doubt happily—and leave a sediment called lees. The now-sparkling wine will sit, sometimes for years, with the yeast in it, absorbing different levels of toast-y, bread-y, yeast-y flavor.

To start to remove the lees, the bottles are stored nose slightly down. Over months, they are turned slowly—it's called riddling—to move the sediment toward the cork but without jostling the wine inside, which would get bubbles going and damage the wine. (That's why, by the way, it's a bad idea to store sparkling wine at home on things that vibrate, like a refrigerator or stereo speaker—and, yeah, it's been done.)

When all the sediment is at the cork, the neck of the bottle is frozen, the cork is pulled and the plug pops out. They call this disgorgement. A sweetening solution called dosage usually gets added to adjust the flavor of the wine and it's resealed. The bottles that go to market are the bottles in which all this happened.

"You can see why sparkling wine is so expensive, it's so much more work," Hank says. "It's like making wine twice. And the slower they go, the better it is, but the more it's going to cost."

That, Hank says, is *méthode champenoise.* The traditional, wine-ferments-in-the-bottle process. There is a cheaper, faster, bulk alternative called the Charmat method, named after the Frenchman Eugene Charmat. To answer the first, obvious question: Yes, some Frenchmen are named Eugene. This route tosses the first wine and the second round of yeast and sugar into one big tank, then seals it. The secondary fermentation and carbonation take place in the tank, getting big bubbles and, often, inexpensive, clunky wine. Then it's bottled and sold to kids going to proms.

I still have my base question, but Candice arrives with our samples. She is almost as effervescent as the wine, but has none of that fake sweetness of a Charmat-made bubbly, and it is indeed starting to worry me that I'm describing people in wine terms.

I love, absolutely love, the 2001 Domaine Carneros Brut Vintage. It's not at all sweet or tangy—or whatever that is I don't seem to like—and there's some flavor of nuts mixed in with the fruit. Hank absolutely loves the 1998 Le Rêve Blanc De Blancs, the big-money wine on the list. That is Candice's favorite, too, and, she says, that's what most people are absolutely loving out here today.

I say I don't quite get it. I wonder if maybe it's too dry for my primitive taste buds. *Au contraire,* she says, though a bit more nicely. I am, again, mixing my terms.

"There are five main levels of dryness," she says. "The Le Rêve is a Brut, too, that's the driest. From dry to sweet, it goes Brut, Extra-Dry, Sec, Demi-Sec, and Doux. That's way sweet."

There is also Brut Natural or Brut Nature, which is sometimes called Extra Brut, that is even drier. This means Extra-Dry is actually about in the middle and a little sweet. It sounds like the same marketing approach that calls the smallest coffee at Starbucks a tall.

Candice also tells me Blanc de Blancs means the wine is from all white grapes, generally Chardonnay. Blanc de Noir is predominantly red grapes—Pinot Noir or Pinot Meunier—but in Europe, red grapes are called black, hence the "noir." Most sparklings have a mix.

We realize the more questions we ask Candice, the more she refills our supposedly one-shot-only glasses. She's in her mid-twenties, has dark hair and eyes, and her smile is quick. We've learned she is a former flight attendant but never liked traveling. Eventually it dawned on her she was in the wrong profession. Like so many other people in Napa, she loves wine and says she's happy to be working in the business at any level. We need more questions, so I get back to my original: When can you use Champagne and *méthode champenoise*?

Candice says she knows there's a twist in there somewhere, so she heads off to get Michael, the guy who seems to be in charge out here. Tragically, she takes the bottle with her. Michael, slightly heavyset with dark hair, is another effervescent person. We're starting to think there's something about working around bubbles all day.

He says the name thing all has to do with the Treaty of Versailles.

I laugh. I like that Michael.

"Really," he says. "It's in the Treaty of Versailles."

"World War I?" I say.

"Actually, before that even," Michael says. "The Treaty of Madrid, which was, like, 1891. They take their wine seriously over there. I'm told wars have started over lesser things than Champagne."

It turns out, the Treaty of Madrid dealt with nineteenth-century international trademark issues, and it included an agreement that only wines made in a region could use that region's name on the bottle. For instance, a Burgundy had to be from Burgundy. Champagne, of course, had to be born in Champagne. In 1919, when the 440-article Treaty of Versailles was signed ending World War I, that rule was restated.

But the thing is, the United States didn't officially sign the Treaty of Versailles—American representatives signed the document, but the U.S. Senate wouldn't ratify it for a variety of political reasons, none of them remotely connected to wine. America made its own peace with Germany in 1921 and it didn't involve wine, either.

In 2005, U.S. and European Union trade negotiators agreed to a few restrictions, but, basically, they only prevent new American wineries from using names like Burgundy or Champagne. U.S. wineries already calling their sparkling wines Champagne can keep doing it until they run out of bubbles.

So here's what that means: In Europe, and in much of the rest of the wine world, Champagne can only be used on French wines from the region of Champagne, and *méthode champenoise* only goes on a bottle of the legit French stuff. Everyone else in Europe has to use *méthode traditionelle,* which tells you the secondary fermentation was in the bottle, not in a tank. So Spanish sparkling wines, and there are some good ones, are called Cavas and their labels say *méthode traditionelle.* Same for Italian (Spumante) or German (Sekt) sparkling wines.

In the U.S., winemakers can use *méthode champenoise* because who's going to stop them?

"But most high-end winemakers here won't put Champagne on the bottle," Michael says. "Our owners are French, and they wouldn't do that for sure. And most people who drink the good sparkling wines know it's not really, truly Champagne when it's not. Most of the time, Champagne gets on American wine only when it's the cheap stuff. Their drinkers don't know any different. Kinda funny, huh? If you see American Champagne, you usually know it's crap."

OUR HEADS ARE A LITTLE LOOPY as we're leaving, but we think it's from the politics, not Candice's generosity. We buy a couple sandwiches from a deli at the bottom of Old Sonoma Road and head over to Acacia to see if there's a picnic spot. There is, but there isn't.

Acacia is a midsized winery with a reputation for stellar Pinot Noirs and Chardonnays. It's a modern hangar-looking building on a bluff above the hills of Carneros and the San Pablo Bay. Just outside its small tasting room is a deck with a picnic table. Looks like a perfect spot for us. The tasting room entrance sits beneath a green awning and is guarded by a small black dog with white paws named Jelly Bean—Jelly to her friends—who requires a couple good pets before she rolls out of the way.

Inside, we say we'd love to taste, but first desperately need to eat our sandwiches, so we'll be out at the picnic table, if that's OK. Actually, they say, we can't. No permit for picnics. We can't sit on the grass below the deck, either. "Unless we don't see you," the woman behind the counter says deadpan.

There it is again. A county that wants tourists but doesn't want tourists. Meanwhile, we need to eat.

"Thank you," I say loudly and clearly, because you never know if a Napa County regulator is listening. "We will leave now and eat somewhere else. Definitely somewhere where they have proper permits, but certainly not on your property. Good-bye."

"Travel well," the woman says, loudly and carefully back.

The tables on the grass below the deck are perfect, too. Jelly—and we think we can call her Jelly—wanders down to see if we're legal, but she's an easy bribe with a couple bites of sandwich.

OUR LAST STOP IN CARNEROS IS Truchard Vineyards and it's a special one for us. In a way, though, it breaks the rules we set for this tasting room Quest. But we also blame them, more or less, for starting the whole thing.

Our rules, we think, are pretty simple. We're going to every tasting room we can walk into or get into with a quick phone call. Basically, any winery someone driving around Napa might find and want to try. We decided to ignore the weeks-in-advance, reservation-only, limited-guests places, because most people can't go to them. Also, just because. It's our Quest.

There is no good reason for that, except, I suppose, that we're operating with a bit of an egalitarian, everyman complex. Or I am. Hank takes most developments in life far less personally than I do. But I figure, if a winery makes it hard for me to get in, I don't want to go there. I never said I was mature.

That doesn't include quasi-appointment-only wineries like Acacia, where you really can walk in. Most of the wineries in Acacia's class want visitors but can't get the come-one, come-all permits. So they have you sign a book, or fill out a card, or just make an appointment for the minute you walked through the door. Others truly are too small for walk-in traffic, or they're simply not interested, and we say let them be.

Truchard is a family-run winery and genuinely cannot handle drop-ins. But we're going there anyway, because it was a bottle of Truchard wine that gave birth to this particular rash idea of ours for a Quest. It was a still summer night almost a year ago. We were on Hank's back deck, which is a fine place to be when your best friend is a corporate wine buyer. The later it gets, the better the wine gets that Hank pulls from the cellar he built into his house.

There is a game we've been playing for years. Hank pours a taste, and we try to guess the wine—region, varietal, and vintage. Or anything. My wife, Deborah, is pretty good at it. Hank's wife, Tina, is even better. I'm always wrong. Always. Rarely uncertain, but I'm predictably, reliably wrong. That night, the mystery wine Hank poured was full of fruit and spice and pepper and earth and I can't even begin to describe the rest of it. It was spectacular. No one guessed because no one wanted to break the spell.

That's another thing about wine, sometimes there is just a spell. It's the setting and the people and the weather. Surely it's also the wine. Together, they create an alchemy, a sudden magic, when life in that place, at that instant, is profound and perfect. Maybe the next time, that same wine, the bottle right next to it on the shelf, won't taste quite as good. For all the science and art in each bottle, wine is a creature of the moment, of circumstance, too. That moment on Hank's deck was enduring and wonderful.

The wine, it turned out, was a 1994 Truchard Syrah. I'd never heard of Truchard. I wanted to see where it came from. I wanted more bonding with that moment, and with the wine. It works the other way, too. Seeing the winery, seeing the vineyards, the barrels, the place the wine was conceived, makes you connect. I wanted to connect with Truchard. And when we talked about it, I wanted to connect with Napa and all those other places where all those other wines come from. That's a huge reason millions of people visit Napa Valley every year. They want their own connection, their own bond and sense of belonging to the place and the people and the wine. So did Hank. Next step: Our Quest. We would bond with them all.

So we make an appointment at Truchard Vineyards, which is in the northern part of Carneros, up a small driveway off the top of Old Sonoma Road. We miss it once because, from the road, it's basically a home with a small patch of Cabernet Franc vines and a rose garden. Beyond the house, the driveway passes a wooden barn-like building and ends at an arched stone entrance to hillside caves. Above the caves, vineyards fan up the hill and off toward a ridge.

We park by the house. Jo Ann Truchard, wearing dark pants and a colorful silk blouse, is waiting in front of the barn/barrel room to lead our small tour. Across the driveway on a patch of grass are two Angora goats. (Gigi is the sheared one; Sayde still wears what look like dreadlocks.) Jo Ann's husband, Tony, keeps the goats because he doesn't already have enough to do looking after 400 acres of grapes.

Our little tour group includes the Truchards' banker in Napa and two of her friends from Hawaii, a Montana couple, and a doctor from Reno who knew Tony when he was practicing medicine there. In 1974, though they lived in Reno in the high desert east of the Sierra Nevada, Tony and Jo Ann bought twenty acres in Carneros because they fell in love with Napa and couldn't afford land anywhere else in the valley.

"Land was $4,000 to $5,000 an acre in Napa," she told us as she was pouring healthy tastes of their 2002 Roussanne. "People told us to go to Carneros because it wasn't discovered yet, which usually means no one's buying there for a reason.

"We asked a grape advisor if it was a good idea. He said, 'No. It's too cool, the soil's too shallow and there's no water.' We bought it anyway."

They paid $3,000 an acre, dug a pond, lined it with clay, and started growing grapes. Tony grew up on a Texas farm, and, doctor or not, he wanted to work some land. He drove across the Sierra, 200 miles from Reno to Carneros and 200 miles back, every chance he had, almost every weekend in those early years.

"It's just in his blood," Jo Ann tells us as we walk up a dirt road that rises past their pond and through the vineyards above the caves. We have our Roussanne with us, and it's creamy and tastes like apples and honeysuckle. As usual, I keep forgetting to pay attention when the wine is good.

Eventually, Jo Ann says, Tony quit his practice and the Truchards became full-time grape growers. In 1989, they began making wine, too. Jo Ann, tall and graceful still, stops to look back at the vineyards. Theirs all line up straight toward the bay. She says Tony planted then to run parallel with the regular Carneros wind so it wouldn't beat at the vines from the side.

"Our weather patterns are very predictable," Jo Ann says. "If you're having an outdoor lunch, the breeze comes up just about the time you try to put the tablecloth on."

There is a gentle confidence to Jo Ann Truchard. She is proud of their land and their winery, but it's more than that. It's the air of someone who remembers building what she has, who understands how it all works and is happy with her choices. Looking at their hills of vineyards and drinking their wine, I'm thinking it would be hard not to be content.

Jo Ann takes us back down the hill and into the 11,000-square-foot caves. They're cool, with rough gray walls, and are lined with pale wood barrels. The air is filled with the thick, rich smell of aging wine. We ask Jo Ann about some of the world-class rankings they've received. Their 2003 Chardonnay, for instance, was ranked number forty-six on the *Wine Spectator*'s 2005 top 100 wines in the world.

"We knew something happened that day," she says. "The fax machine started spitting out orders. That was fun."

We circle back to the barn and barrel room that doubles as a small tasting area. Jo Ann has poured us the 2001 Syrah, and if it's not the magic 1994 from that summer night, it's lush and full of strawberries and white pepper. I only get white pepper because Hank tells me it's there. But once he does, the taste is distinct. Wine, it seems, is also a creature of suggestion.

Tony joins the group, wearing jeans and a denim shirt, back from poking through his vineyards. He's tall and thin, and his slightly weather-beaten face is red from the sun. Hank and I wonder if we should tell the Truchards what they started with us, but Tony is talking to his old doctor friend, saying the late spring rains that stopped only a few days ago have him worried about the Chardonnay crop. He's afraid the rain washed some of the pollen off the grape flowers and that not all the bunches will mature.

"It's never a good thing when it rains during bloom," Tony says, sipping from a small glass of his own Syrah. "We won't know for two or three weeks (when the grapes start to grow more). By August, it could all just be little nubs."

Despite the weather difficulties, Tony's face has a perpetual half-smile. He's got that same gentle confidence as Jo Ann. It makes both of them appealing, comforting people. It's like being around sturdy, deep-rooted trees. Trees that make good wine.

Tony asks everyone what they think of the wine, genuinely interested. I gurgle something about yummy. He and Hank talk in more detail. After a few minutes, Tony gets back to chatting with his buddy. The thing is, Tony says, he's worried about the press. I shove my pens deeply into my pocket. If the press writes about the rough spring even before anyone sees the grapes or tastes the wine, this year will get a bad reputation. You can't undo that, no matter how good the wine turns out. There will be a blanket perception this was a bad year, and prices will drop.

"I hate to whine about it," Tony tells his friend. "We've done pretty well by the press. But I'm not taking any calls or talking to anyone until I get my grapes in and my wine made."

His friend is nodding. I'm nodding. Stupid press, I will write later in my reporter's notebook.

We decide we like these people, Jo Ann and Tony. We decide we're glad it was their wine that started us off, glad we came here, glad we met them. We will like their wines even more, now, because we were here, because of the beauty of the place and the solid, earnestness of the Truchards. And because we left feeling as if we understood Carneros a bit more.

We need to tell them all this, we think. They should hear how glad we were to meet them. But not just yet. We'll wait until Tony gets his wine made.

FOUR

Yountville/ Stags Leap

ED BURTON FROM Houston, Texas, looks like a guy from Houston, Texas. He's about sixty, has a bushy white mustache, is wearing jeans and a baseball cap, and he's leaning against a bar with a drink in his hand. But here's the thing: His baseball cap says "Stag's Leap Wine Cellars," the bar is in the neat, pet-filled tasting room of Elyse Winery, and his drink is a glass of Rosé.

Not just wine, pink wine. And Ed came here specifically for the 2004 California Rosé. He's excited about it, too. It's zippy and fruity and dry. A great wine for food, he says. He's thinking of pairing it with a spicy little tomato-based pasta.

I'm thinking, what would the stereotypical guys back in stereotypical Texas say? But the truth is, probably nothing. First off, the notion of matching good wine with good food is getting to be universal. And for all its beer-and-whiskey street rep, Texas is the fourth biggest wine-consuming state in the U.S. (after California, New York, and Florida). But mostly, Ed looks like he can take care of himself just fine. The guys back home, stereotypical or not, would likely shut the hell up about his Rosé.

Not that we expect to see Ed in any wine brawls. He's an amiable, engaging guy who's game to make new friends. That's one of the side joys of wine tasting, particularly in a place like Napa. It is, in a way, a rolling party, a valley-wide social event with an automatic conversation starter. Everyone visiting here, the sometimes hundreds of thousands roaming the valley on the same day, all have something in common: an interest in wine, at least at some level. And they're not just talking wine, they're drinking it. Instant festivities. Put simply, a lot of people are game to make new friends in these tasting rooms.

That's what Ed is telling us. He's been meeting folks throughout the valley and gleaning their advice for a couple days now. He's visiting Napa because his son is getting married in wine country in October, just over the Mayacamas Mountains from here in a town called Kenwood. Ed's wedding gift is the wine for the reception, and because he's a man who can make the brutal sacrifices, he's not just buying the wine, he's shouldering the job of choosing it, too. Taste by taste.

"This is hard, hard work," he tells us. "And I only get to do it for a few more days."

Elyse is a friendly little winery on a country road just outside Yountville. It's run by Ray and Nancy Coursen and, I guess, their pets. Their dogs meet you in the driveway. Their gray, one-eyed cat, Misto, sits behind tasters, waiting to get his head scratched. Right now, Misto, who, by the way, has a wine named after him, sits behind Ed. Ed periodically bends down to oblige. Elyse makes some smokin' big reds, like Zinfandel, Cabernet Sauvignon, and Petite Sirah, but Ed was sent here by a restaurant in Yountville for that Rosé.

He's been going down the list of reception dishes, matching them up with wines. For an oyster-based appetizer, he's getting a dry sparkling Brut. For the steak, he's planning a monster Syrah, though he hasn't ruled out the classic, a big Napa Valley Cab, because, as he says, "who ever rules out a great Napa Cab?" Flawless choices, I'm thinking. And he's making me hungry.

"I wanted one that was out of the box, too," he says, holding up his Rosé. "This might be it."

We ask him if he's gotten the hang of food-and-wine pairings and he almost does a spit take with his Rosé.

"Everyone's got a rule for me," he says, "and every rule just about contradicts every other rule."

No kidding. The wine should complement the food. The wine and food should contrast. Don't get a huge difference. Don't make them too similar. Match the textures. Go for opposites. Don't overpower the food. Don't be wimpy. Rich wine fits rich food. Crisp wine fits rich food. Acid works with salt. Acid works with sweet. Sweet works with sweet. Don't end a sentence with a preposition. Never run with scissors. You need a glass of wine just thinking about it.

"I get that this can be pretty complicated," Ed says. "Here's what I do, and it's been workin' for years. I get wine I like. I eat food I like. I figure that way, I'm startin' off a winner. If they go together, man, I'm having a good night.

"But you know what? Trying to figure it all out is a heck of a lot of fun." He turns to the server behind the bar, Alice, who has moved in front of him. "Since I'm here anyway," he says, "mind if I try a couple of those Cabs?"

ELYSE IS ON HOFFMAN LANE. JUST across that little road and 100 yards down is Havens Wine Cellars, a place with a reputation for making wines that go with food, partly because its owners, Michael and Kathryn Havens, publicize that they met and fell in love drinking wine and eating food. Like most people, really. But they did it in Europe, actually remembered what they were doing, and opened a winery built around the wine-belongs-on-the-table concept.

The tasting room at Havens is, technically, a well-appointed foyer. It's mostly just a pleasant little reception area with a window looking into the winery. There's no bar, just a large buffet against one wall, and a line of wine bottles sitting under lights on the buffet's white counter.

Nicole Lockett, who's been working at Havens about six months and combines professionalism with the youthful joy of having a good job, stands face-to-face with us as she pours. She has dark hair and a slightly round face, and is the kind of low-key person you instantly want to treat nicely. With no bar between us, this feels way more personal than usual, like we're in Nicole's house and it's her wine. I make a note not to do anything too stupid.

Havens makes some unusual wines for Napa, like Albariño, a white Spanish varietal that seems part Viognier and part Sauvignon Blanc with a lush feel and a crisp taste, or Bourriquot, a Bordeaux blend red with the less-than-common mix of Cab Franc and Merlot. Both wines have some substance in your mouth, but neither is what we call "huge."

Nicole says they're designed to be versatile with food. I ask what is it in a wine that does that, beyond just saying good acid? How does it work?

For just a moment, she gets a look—that "they didn't tell me this" look—and I instantly regret the question. I don't want her to feel awkward. Nicole is nice. She's pouring us her wine. I try to back off. "Don't bother," I sort of blurt. But she regroups. "That's a good question," she says. "Let me go ask Jeff."

Jeff, it turns out, is Jeff Keene, the winemaker. Nicole went to get the winemaker to answer what I thought would be a simple question. That Nicole is a trouper. Hank gives me that look of infinite patience yet again.

"A lot of it is balance," Hank says while we wait for Nicole to interrupt Jeff from whatever he was doing, which has to be more important. "You don't want it to be too high alcohol, 'cause that overwhelms your food and all you taste is the wine. But you want some tannins because that gives it some structure. You know, some feel in your mouth.

"And you definitely want a decent amount of acid. Acid kind of cleanses your palate."

Nicole comes back around the corner with Jeff. He's a medium-sized guy who looks maybe thirty and has the casual/cool accent of someone who grew up in New Zealand. I start to apologize but he'll have none of it, so I ask what makes a wine good with food.

"A lot of it is balance," he says. Seriously. He and Hank must read the same newsletter. "We want it to have a round mouth feel, but not the big, big alcohol or the big, big tannins. That dominates your food. We're trying to make the wine part of the meal and help all the flavors pop out a bit."

I give Hank my "sorry to ever have doubted you" look. He's used to it.

Mostly, Jeff is saying, wine works great with food when it refreshes the palate between bites, but also when there are complementary tastes, or even similar ones, that come more alive. Those giant wines, the trophy reds Napa is famous for, he says, tend to crush the flavors of a lot of dishes, and they're best with meat or sometimes just by themselves.

Jeff goes back to doing real work and Nicole tells us the Havens loved how Europeans mix wine and food and people. Drinking wine with a meal slows everyone down, makes people more social, makes them treat meals like they're special occasions. It's a celebrate-each-day approach to life.

As she is talking to us, a middle-aged couple comes in. They are the Browns, from Lexington, Kentucky, and they made an appointment at Havens on the say-so of their restaurant last night. They admit to not knowing a lot about wine, but, Mr. Brown says, "where we're from, everyone knows about Bourbon."

Nicole starts to explain to them about Havens, then sees one of her wine bottles is empty, so she leaves to get another. I make chitchat and ask what restaurant it was that recommended Havens.

"Bistro Don Giovanni," Mrs. Brown says.

Christ. Doesn't anyone eat anywhere else?

"How was it?" I say amiably enough.

"It was great," she says.

"Really?" I say. "You liked it?"

"They were terrific."

I nod. Of course they were.

"That's nice," I say.

"Nice to meet you," Hank says, heading out the door and all but dragging me with him. We walk down the pathway to the car. "You do know," he says, "we're going to have to go back to Don Giovanni pretty soon."

⁂

ALL THE TALK OF FOOD AND wine fits this piece of Napa. We are near the town of Yountville, which is more or less the epicenter of good eating in a valley with plenty of good eating to be done. Just as the Havens say, great wine and great food seem to find each other, and in the past decade or so, Napa has grown into a culinary wonderland where even the tiny grocers and sandwich joints do some high-level work. It also doesn't hurt that the Culinary Institute of America at Greystone, up the road in St. Helena, is pumping out good young chefs who will work anywhere beyond a McDonald's so they can stay in the valley.

National-class restaurants are all over Napa Valley—Bistro Don Giovanni is not part of this discussion for the moment, OK?—ranging from Pilar's and Cole's Chop House in Napa city, to Auberge du Soleil and The Grill at Meadowood in the valley's eastern hills, to La Toque in Rutherford, Catahoula in Calistoga, and Martini House, Tra Vigne, and Terra in St. Helena. But around Yountville they grow in clusters. And they're many of the names people know when they come to Napa: Domaine Chandon's restaurant, Piatti, Brix, Mustards Grill, Bouchon, and Bistro Jeanty, all original, interesting, roundly delicious places. But above them all is the big dog, the unchallenged boss of the Napa food pack: The French Laundry. If the only restaurant in Yountville was The French Laundry, it would still be the bull's-eye of Napa food.

The French Laundry is a very good place to eat. It makes national top-ten lists every year. So does its owner, Thomas Keller, who was named the best chef in America in 1997 by the James Beard Foundation. Hardened reviewers often stumble out mumbling things like "best meal ever." However, the Laundry, as some people call it around here, is not cheap. Guidebooks run out of dollar-sign logos trying to estimate the price. Some just offer search tips for good equity loans. The corkage fee at The French Laundry is $50. Translation: Don't even think about it. (It's also designed to keep out the tourist bottle of White Zinfandel.) Dinner for two runs $400 to $500, easily. No one seems to complain.

But what puts The French Laundry over the top, what gives it mythic stature, goes beyond the spectacular food and the spectacular price. It's the spectacular—and eccentric—exclusivity. Actually, The French Laundry welcomes everyone, but it's everyone who can make a reservation. (Cue the laughter.) You have to be as dogged and lucky as a rich gold miner to get one. There are, swear to God, websites devoted to the subject of getting a French Laundry reservation.

The restaurant has seventeen tables, just two seatings, and takes reservations two months in advance. Exactly. To the day. Only by phone or through the opentable.com website (one a day for each seating). Mostly you gotta do it by phone. Call on June 15 if you want to eat on August 15. I have no idea how you make a reservation for August 31. The French Laundry starts taking reservations each day at 10 a.m. and by some accounts gets 400 calls a day. When they're filled for two months hence—which happens in minutes—they just don't answer the phone. If you get past all the busy signals, there's no answering machine, no "Thanks for playing along," they simply let it ring while they're off making fantastic food. I'm not sure what happens if you make a reservation then cancel, but my guess is they send a guy around to beat the crap out of you.

Hank and I talk about trying to get into The French Laundry in some two-month future though the fiduciary repercussions would be serious. We even call a couple times, just for the sport of it, and to our financial relief, we don't get close. We don't even get the ringing, just the busy signal. I was thinking if we called, got an answer, then hung up, they'd star-69 us, and that big guy would come beat the crap out of us both.

On this day, we take a much safer route and eat an early meal at Cucina à la Carte, a lively place in Yountville with a huge, tree-covered deck that calls itself a Franco/Italian Marketplace. Hank has a spicy albacore tuna wrap and I have a Dungeness crab burger. It costs us about 1/20th of a French Laundry meal and is terrific. We are proud of our discretion and frugality.

"This was a good move," I say.

"Great spot," Hank says.

"Really great spot," I say.

"Glad we did it."

"Good food."

"Really good food."

When we drive past The French Laundry on our way out of town, we slow down for a minute and try to feel smug. But we both really, really want to eat there.

IT'S THE SUNDAY BEFORE MEMORIAL DAY, and we're in the valley today as much for the challenge as anything else. Napa Valley, like most great vacation spots, gets a tad busy on major holidays. But we figure if we don't taste through at least one of the summer majors, we're just wimps.

Still, courage has its limits. We're back on the quieter Silverado Trail, avoiding the parts of Highway 29 that will become near–parking lots by mid-afternoon, and, instead, are moving through the Stags Leap District on the east side of the valley around Yountville Crossroad.

Our first stop is venerable Clos Du Val, a classic winery not just because it's been operating here since 1972, but because it has the deep-rooted feel of an Old World monastery, with reddish brown, ivy-covered walls, massive arched doors, and a large, simple tasting room under a twenty-eight-foot-high ceiling.

Clos Du Val's founders, John Goelet and Bernard Portet, have definite Old World roots—Goelet, an American from a French family, joined with French winemaker Portet, whose family is rooted in Bordeaux—and it shows in everything from their style of wine to the Bordeaux tradition of planting roses at the end of vineyard rows. (The roses are more than ornamental. They're like coal-mine canaries; they'll react to vineyard pests before the grapevines show they are there.)

But there is another tradition of sorts here, too. Clos Du Val is the long-established home of hundreds and hundreds of swallows. They nest in the forty-foot-high eaves in front of the winery and return every March 19, just like their more famous cousins in San Juan Capistrano. These swallows may not get the hype, but they associate with way better wine.

In the end of May, the birds are swooping and diving, and climbing in and out of their little mud-looking nests, and they appear very Old World in their own right. They'll hang around until mid-July, and during the heavy-swallow stretch, any visitor bombed by the little birds gets a free tasting.

Hank and I sit outside in the sun for a bit watching the swallows cruise the vineyards that run up to the lawn in front. I'm secretly hoping to earn a free tasting just because I think it would be kinda cool. We talk more about this food-and-wine thing and how there's a difference in approaches between Old World and New World.

"Americans drink wine at bars and parties," Hank says. "We get a glass and sip and it's just the wine talking. We want that fruit-forward big red or the crème brûlée, oak-y Chard when we do that.

"But for Europeans, the meal is the party. They're drinking wine while they're eating and they make their wine to go with food. That gets back to the higher acid, the more balanced tannins, and a little less oak and fruit. They almost think of wine as another spice or a condiment, and you wouldn't sip ketchup without food around." Hank kinda looks at me funny when he says that. "Most people wouldn't," he says.

But how, I'm wondering, do they cope with all the contradictions? If it's supposed to match and contrast and highlight every food—all at once—how do one or two wines fit everything for a big meal and a lot of people?

The answer gets back to the "Old" in Old World. For centuries, people who made wine also grew most of their own food. They weren't doing a lot of online shopping for boutique Cabernets and shipping cases across the country. They were growing whatever their land would give them and traveling to the market in the local village. The food and wine all came from the same earth and had some naturally compatible elements and flavors. Everything just fit.

"New World wines are more fruit. Old Worlds are more earth. It's almost a too-simple explanation," Hank says, "but a lot of it was nature."

Makes sense. The elemental/terroir connection works in a lot of ways. If everything in nature is linked, why wouldn't the local grapes match the rest of the local food? There's probably even an explanation somewhere in there about the swallows and how they find their old nests when it's March 19. But I have one more question for Hank. "OK, Nature Boy," I say. "Tell me how these birds know when it's a leap year?"

WE MOVE NORTH THROUGH STAGS LEAP, a region best known for Cabernet Sauvignon, and some great Cabs at that. Many of its vineyards run up the hillsides against the eastern Vaca Mountains and over the little knolls and crags that poke up throughout the area. Those Cabernets have an international reputation, behind only the Cabs of Oakville and Rutherford in Napa—and maybe a few small mountain vineyards—though some critics argue Stags Leap fruit, with its flavors of chocolate, black currant, raspberry, and black cherry, is more elegant and restrained than some of the powerful Oakville and Rutherford wines.

At Chimney Rock, the winery just north of Clos Du Val, a server named Mike Morf tells us the story he's heard for how the region got its name.

It's all Native American legend, Mike says, and it goes back to a longtime rivalry between a great chief and an equally great stag he'd been hunting for years. One day—every legend starts its key point with "one day," Mike reminds us—the great chief had finally trapped the noble stag on a cliff high up a rocky palisade.

"Just as the chief was about to loose his arrow, the two eyed each other for one long moment," Mike says, "then the stag leaped an impossible leap off the palisade, across a chasm, and onto another cliff."

The chief declared that any stag so great it could make that leap should never be hunted again. And so it was. Later, the chief and the stag joined forces, opened a small, premium winery and started making elegant, restrained Cabernets.

It's a great story, except, probably, the winery part. The real one is even better. It starts in 1893 when Horace Chase, a San Francisco businessman, bought a 240-acre estate and created a winery in the area. He named it, along with his manor house, Stags Leap—no apostrophe; that will matter later—and is generally credited with concocting the stag-and-chief legend. The winery failed a few years later, done in by the phylloxera that swept through the region.

Leap, if you will, almost a century forward. In 1970, Warren Winiarski, a respected winemaker in the valley, left the Robert Mondavi Winery and bought some land near the old Chase manor house. He opened a winery in 1972 and called it Stag's Leap Wine Cellars. Meanwhile, in 1971, Carl Duomani, a Southern California businessman, bought the old Chase property and eventually rebuilt and restarted the winery. He called it Stag's Leap Winery.

Here's where it gets good. And grammatical. Winiarski and Duomani fought in court over the name. It was a great battle and reminded all who knew them of the stag and the chief. Yeah, not really. But they did seesaw through the courts. One day (of course), a judge finally ruled that both could use that stag with hops, but Winiarski's would be Stag's Leap Wine Cellars, single stag a-leaping, and Duomani's Stags' Leap Winery would suggest a pack cruising the palisades. When other wineries in the area wanted Stag's Leap designated an official AVA in the early 1980s, Winiarski and Duomani worked together to fight it. They lost on the big issue, but at least won the punctuation battle. The AVA is officially the Stags Leap District, no apostrophe. That'll show 'em.

For what it's worth, Stags' Leap Winery pushes the great chief-noble stag story and credits it to the Native American Wappo tribe. Stag's Leap Wine Cellars has a much bigger, and more valuable, legendary status attached to it.

This goes back to the epic 1976 Paris Tasting, the France vs. America wine contest that woke the world to California wine. The memory of the Paris Tasting is a catechism in Napa.

It seems those French had been sniffing about the quality of New World wines for decades, and even if American vintages won an occasional tasting contest, it was always on American soil with American judges, and what could Americans know about judging wine if they made such slop.

Then on May 24, 1976, Englishman Steven Spurrier, who owned a Parisian wine shop, staged a tasting at the InterContinental Hotel in Paris. He collected some American wines, all of them Californian, most from Napa, and put them head-to-head in a blind tasting with some of France's best, including Bordeaux like a 1970 Château Mouton-Rothschild and a 1970 Château Haut-Brion. It has been described as a mischievous stunt for Spurrier, but it ended up a gut punch to French wine snobs.

The nine judges were all French and they were particularly sniffy that day. They near-gagged on what they thought were American wines. At one point, a judge sighed, "Ah, back to France," as he sipped a white. Turned out to be a 1972 Freemark Abbey Napa Valley Chardonnay. Three of the top four whites were California wines, including the winner, a 1973 Chardonnay from Chateau Montelena. Even worse, the top red was from Napa, a 1973 S.L.V. Napa Valley Cabernet Sauvignon from Stag's Leap Wine Cellars (single stag).

The French press would whimper how they had been tricked and how, well, whatever. They implied everything but steroid use and blood doping. The whining didn't take. This was major league good news for American wine in general, Napa Valley in particular, and sure as hell for Winiarski's Stag's Leap. It was an enormous event that would make wine history—the *Time* magazine story and winemaker notes from Winiarski and Mike Grgich, who made the Chateau Montelena Chardonnay, are in the Smithsonian. The contest transformed the industry and gave an indelible cachet to California and Napa.

And to Stag's Leap Wine Cellars (single stag). That prestige still shows in the packed, and surprisingly understated, tasting room. It's the most crowded tasting room in this area today, because sometimes there are places people go just to bend a knee. If half the visitors are here for the FAY Cabernet or Cask 23 and don't know the Paris Tasting story—or the chief-and-stag story, for that matter—they still know this is an important visit.

I have to say I am disappointed, in my own hyper-competitive, adolescent little way. I half expected "We Rule" and "Screw French Wine" banners to be flying three decades later. But I can find nothing in the otherwise simple room except some tasting counters, a couple very large wine holding tanks, and the usual appreciation of wine and vineyards.

We only see it when we're leaving. Many visitors probably don't notice. High over the door is a list of French names: Pétrus. Latour. Cheval-Blanc. Pichon Longueville. There are more. They are the names of great French Châteaux. Most were not at the Paris tasting. There's no explanation, they're just written across the wall. It certainly is not bragging. All I can think of is that this is a simple tribute to the grand traditions of winemaking and its Old World roots. Just a tip of the hat to the greats. Yeah, OK. Classy isn't a bad approach either.

<hr />

YOU WOULDN'T KNOW IT'S MEMORIAL DAY weekend, or any weekend, in the cheery tasting room at Steltzner Vineyards. The square space is enclosed by glass doors and large windows that look out on a terracotta patio, vineyards, and some of those sharp Stags Leap knolls. There's a stone floor and a big, soft couch. It feels more like a comfy cafe with a view, except it's empty.

The quiet is not a source of joy for Nate Page, who appears to be in charge of the room. "Everyone's going up the road to Pine Ridge or Silverado," he tells us. "Or down the road to Stag's Leap. I watched a guy drive into our lot a minute ago, but he was just using it to make a U-turn."

Yeah, Nate's a little bitter. But just a little. Mostly, he's earnest. He tells us it's because he thinks Steltzner has some good wines (they do), this is a great place to taste (it is—$10 for a bunch of pours), and it's such a pretty spot (that, surely, is true).

Nate's a tall, loose-jointed, dark-haired guy. His business card just says "Wine Enthusiast." Hard not to like an enthusiast, particularly when he keeps bringing out new wines to taste, including their line of Stags Leap Cabs, and a Pinotage. Nate says it's a South African hybrid that came from cloning Pinot Noir with a grape called Cinsaut, which is a Rhone varietal but in South Africa it's also called Hermitage so you get Pinotage and just never mind the name, he says, but it's pretty good anyway.

It is, full of cherry like a Pinot and kind of earthy like those Rhone Syrahs. That's from Hank. I'm mostly thinking this wine would kick ass in a name-that-wine blind tasting because who's even heard of it.

I also like the Oak Knoll Estate Chardonnay. There's a bunch of fruit flavors in it—a lot of them are tropical, Hank says—but it's different from the big Chards. There's not much of the butter/caramel thing. That's because it was fermented completely in stainless steel, Nate brags, though it seems funny to be bragging about that when Chardonnay drinkers love their oak.

"This is a food wine," Nate says. "This is a Chard that could stand up to asparagus."

Whoa. I wait for the thunder clap and the deep voice booming, "Heresy!" Asparagus? Nothing pairs with asparagus, the nemesis of all wine, the evil, astringent little vegetable that looks so innocent on the plate and turns all wine metallic. Except maybe sweeter wines like a Muscat, but who drinks Muscat with dinner? Asparagus is the Darth Vader of the food world. It starts innocently enough, but eventually leaves ruin in its wake.

Actually, Nate says, a lot of wines go with asparagus, but the problem, often, is that food wines have the good acid that turns oh-so-bad with asparagus. What works is a balanced wine, and maybe one with more fruit, he says.

I ask again about the food-wine thing. Why does the acid work with almost everything else?

"For me it's kinda like a toothbrush," Nate says. "It makes you ready for the next bite. If you had something like a big, creamy Chard with a cream sauce, you'd just get this big glob in your mouth and all the flavors would get dull."

He says our mouths get blasé through a meal. Like any of our senses, which function by registering changes in our environment, our taste buds stop relaying food info quite so eagerly as a meal wears on. That's one reason the first bite tastes the best. Acid recharges our tasting batteries, starts us over, in a way. And it brings out flavors in a lot of foods, the way lemon brings out the flavors of fish or the way vinegar makes salads so much more alive.

Still, you can only take that so far. "You know, I'm always looking for that wine that makes a meal better," he says. "But you shouldn't think, 'I'll get this wine to go with dinner even though I don't like it.' Start with wine you like, go from there."

I have more questions, but four women walk into the room, and behind them a young couple is climbing out of a car. Nate looks so happy for the company, I don't want to spoil the moment.

THERE'S A REASON LOTS OF PEOPLE are going to Pine Ridge—great wines, cozy spot—and Silverado Vineyards—great wines, spectacular view—and the crowds at both wineries remind us that, while we may not be wimps, we aren't all that smart to be cruising the valley on a holiday afternoon. The pack is only a bit smaller at Cliff Lede, another exceptional place, with a long, intriguing wine list and a Southwestern-feeling sculpture garden set against the vineyards.

By the end of the day, we are at Robert Sinskey at the top of the Stags Leap District. We shouldn't be here. We're worn out, and we're way beyond the suggested maximum daily winery intake, which is three or four. This is a terrific winery and it's, of course, packed. We're almost grumpy about it. Really, anyone who gets grumpy wine tasting should be slapped.

We wouldn't be here right now if we weren't on this little Quest of ours. A long day of tasting wine wears out your palate and—at least on holidays—your patience. There is no sane reason to keep going when you're tired and need to be slapped. But we have our Quest. Nothing sane about it.

Robert Sinskey is another winery with Old World roots, though these come mostly in the way of attitude. Founder Bob Sinskey and his son and now-owner, Rob, are New World guys—Bob is a doctor who invented a widely used artificial human lens; Rob is a graduate of the Parson's School of Design in New York—but they both believe that American diets should be evolving toward the European model of fewer saturated fats and, among other things, meals benefiting from the ol' food-with-wine concept.

The narrow tasting room, with its thirty-five-foot-high cathedral ceilings and hanging spot lights, has the feel of a restaurant, and there's a high-grade kitchen at the far end. They use it a lot to make snacks for the wine tasters. The servers behind the bar are moving fast—definitely New World pace—but staying surprisingly cheerful. Hank says he feels bad for being a grump watching these people hustle. I huff at him.

One server, I think her name is Melissa, offers something made in the kitchen to pair with our 2004 Los Carneros Pinot Blanc. It's pesto Parmesan on shortbread. It's stunning with the wine. More pesto-y, more Parmesan-y and the wine seems loaded with honeysuckle or jasmine—honestly, I can never tell which is which—and it's good.

"We say here that wine should be good on its own and great with food," says Melissa. Or maybe she's Jasmine. Either way, I'm with her.

We hang around a bit and, frankly, chill out. Robert Sinskey makes some terrific Pinot Noirs, and we are both feeling much happier tasting them. Eating snacks helps, too. It's possible both of us were hungry. Another lesson learned about wine tasting: eat regularly.

A different server, an energetic young guy named Jesse, or, possibly, Jasmine, bounces over. I ask about the snacks and he says they're fundamental to the approach at Robert Sinskey.

He brings up that Old World concept again about regional foods matching regional wines. "In the U.S.," he says, "we tend to compare wine to other wines. That means we're usually asking for big, powerful wines, and that's not always great with food. In Europe, when they started making wine, they compared it to their food."

The theory at Robert Sinskey, and at more and more Napa wineries, is to make wines that are more or less Old World style: less aggressive, less pushy, and, actually, more patient. I don't miss the irony.

Hank and I are among the last to leave the tasting room. We resolve to try to be less aggressive, more patient tasters. Old World tasters, we say.

IT'S AN EVENING IN EARLY JUNE, one of those perfect June evenings in Napa when the light is just a little golden and the valley seems to be a carpet of supple green. The vineyards are filling out, their rows meshing together and losing their lines as the leaves blanketing the flats merge into one lush layer.

We're in Yountville proper because we decide we're going to put all this food-and-wine, Old World-New World theory to work. We're going to eat dinner somewhere really good. That we can afford.

We have reservations at Bistro Jeanty, a small restaurant on Washington Street, Yountville's main drag, that says it's styled after little neighborhood French bistros. It's run by Philippe Jeanty, the former executive chef at Domaine Chandon and one of Napa's most popular restaurateurs. Our wives are with us. A guiding principle on our Quest is, if we go anywhere special, we take Deborah and Tina along, because we are caring, decent men who understand that, no matter what, our wives are in charge.

First, we stop at the tasting room for Jessup Cellars, just a few blocks up Washington. Hank and I are always working. It's a storefront room in a California/Western style, with pale walls, high ceilings, wood trim, square windows, and a light marble bar. A hundred years ago, a horse would've been tied up out front.

Adam Jessup, a son of Jessup founder and winemaker, Mark, is pouring behind the bar. He's telling us how he's about to release a Cabernet on his own label, and how, despite growing up in a wine industry family and going to U.C. Davis, he never thought he would go into the wine business.

"You just don't expect to do what your family does," Adam says. In his mid-twenties, he's tall, and has dark hair and a confident smile. "Now, I'm glad to have the opportunities and I wonder what I was thinking."

He says he hasn't decided on the name of his Cab, and that his girlfriend would love it to be named after her. He laughs. We laugh. Everyone sees the issue. Why not just tattoo her name on your forearm, I say. We laugh again. Just in case, I say we are sure she's a wonderful woman. We all nod enthusiastically. Adam, too.

Adam asks where we're headed and we tell him about dinner and our food-wine fascination.

"Then you need to try this," he says.

He takes out small, port glasses. We get pours of a 2001 Napa Valley Zinfandel Port. He brings over some simple cookies and a bowl of Zinfandel Chocolate Port Sauce. Chocolate and Port. Good chocolate and great Port. Oh . . . dear . . . God. I try to hug the bowl of chocolate sauce, but Deborah and Hank get it away from me and give it back to Adam. I consider going over the bar to get it.

"Good, huh?" Adam says.

This is a perfect case of two great, well-paired tastes making each better. The Port softens; the chocolate gets bigger and becomes textured; they blend mid-taste and reach some third flavor. Some third dazzling flavor.

"Please, sir," I say, "may I have some more."

To her great credit, Deborah doesn't warn me that we have a big dinner ahead. Also, she knows I don't listen well around chocolate. I have more of the Port and more of the sauce, as much as Adam will give me, which is not near enough. But it's time for dinner.

***

BISTRO JEANTY IS COMFORTABLE AND CASUAL, exactly like those French neighborhood bistros, I would say, except that I've never been to one. Still, the half-curtains, simple wood tables, slightly busy decor, and just-crowded-enough room give it a fun, relaxed feel. Our waiter, Atyeh, is doing neighborhood restaurant, not stuffy, high-end polite.

We explain to him we're working on some food-wine pairings and have brought our own white wine for appetizers. He's supportive because it sounds intriguing and because it's his job to be supportive. Either way, we all like Atyeh.

The wine is called Shoo-Fly. It's Australian and blends Sauvignon Blanc, Viognier, and Verdelho. It's supposed to have fruit, body, and some acid, and sounds like a versatile food wine. We will give it a challenge.

The problem for most people trying to match food and wine becomes quickly obvious. Variety. Damn that variety. We start with four wildly different first courses. Deborah has crudités, an assortment of little vegetable salads that make for a challenge by their assorted little selves, I have smoked trout on potato salad, Tina goes with a beet-and-greens salad with feta cheese, and Hank, trooper that he is, has asparagus soup.

How does any wine deal with all this, I ask Hank.

"There never really is one solution," he says. "There's no universal wine. We've got one with a lot of things going for it, but, watch, someone's won't work out."

The wine goes surprisingly well with Hank's soup. He says because the cream in the base softens the asparagus. His wife isn't as lucky. Hank says beets are a tough pairing. If it's me, it's easy: Beets match perfectly with a garbage disposal. I am not a beet guy. Tina likes beets but her salad makes the wine bitter. She's not letting on. "Anyone want to try mine?" she asks faux-sweetly. "It's really good."

I have the smoked trout on potato thing and it is terrific by itself. I have a sip of wine and something happens midway through. Maybe it's the salt-acid mix, maybe it's just alchemy, but I get that taste you get when you know you've bull's-eyed. I can still taste the wine and the trout, but something else happens. They both get bigger and better, and different. It is a moment of indescribable, perfect deliciousness. If I weren't the classy person I am, I would do my happy dance right here on the table.

With our main courses, we make an attempt to stay a bit more similar. This is no big sacrifice because everything we've tasted has been devastatingly good. Except the stupid beets. Hank orders the special, a hanger steak, Tina has a pork chop in onion sauce, Deborah goes coq au vin (chicken in a smoky red wine stew), and I get a grilled, crusted salmon special that's also got smokiness involved. Smoky is our theme. We are proud of our teamwork.

For our wine choice, we put it to Atyeh. He is again supportive, and he seems to actually like playing our game. He suggests a Longboard Russian River Syrah. It has good tannins and its own hint of smokiness.

I like the Syrah a lot. Hank thinks it might be a bit high-alcohol and jammy. That explains why I like it, but Hank says it may not pair as well as we think. We taste all around and, it turns out, the Syrah goes well with my salmon and Deborah's chicken, only so-so with Tina's pork chop because there's something in the sauce that makes the wine a bit tart, and it absolutely rocks with Hank's hanger steak. There you go. Even the pros have trouble predicting matchups sometimes.

So what have we learned? A lot and nothing and it's pretty simple: Everyone is right. Are there pairings that go well? Yes. I stumbled onto two great ones today. Are there some that suck? Yes, and it starts with beets. Are there rules that work and contradictions to every one of them? Sort of. But there is one impeccable pairing: food and wine and people you love.

It's the heart of the Old World argument for this food-wine thing. It's not magic and it's not religion. Food and wine can be special in so many ways. The tastes, the textures, the sensory encounters, the simple wonder of it all. And the part I like the best—the part that makes me happy just thinking about it, and that most defines how I think about wine—is the idea of celebrating meals, and celebrating life, by mixing wine, food, family or friends, or, most perfectly, all of the above. Spot-on food-wine pairings can be astounding sometimes, particularly if they involve a form of chocolate. But as Ed, my new friend from Houston says, looking for them and playing with them and reveling in it all is how it's supposed to be done. And if your wine is great, even better.

FIVE

Oakville

IT'S WARM AND sunny today. The vineyards have become a late-June carpet of green. Beyond them, the mountains on both sides of the valley are starting to show some edges of brown and a few signs summer is coming.

We can see this because we're standing on the launch pad on top of Opus One—very expensive winery; looks like a spaceship—and we're gawking at the heart of Napa Valley. This is Oakville, the rich home of some of the world's great Cabernet vineyards and ground zero for Napa's—and, truthfully, America's—modern wine boom.

From this trellis-covered, pale stone deck, you can see so much of Napa. It's not the widest view of the valley, it's what's right here: the signposts of Napa's past and the keystones for much of what it's become.

There's a view of the Oakville Grocery, a food-and-social center for 125 years and currently Napa's reigning designer deli in a valley filled with new twists on old sandwiches. At Oakville Crossroad is the Napa Wine Co., holder of the oldest working winemaking permit in California and now Napa's premier custom crush facility where winemakers make small lots—a few of them as top end as top end gets—without the baggage of an actual winery.

And you can see west, over those lush, lush vineyards—including To Kalon and Martha's Vineyard, two of America's most eminent stands of grapevines—to the ridge at the bottom of the Mayacamas. Among the trees, there're hints of the huge, ornate gray stone house with green copper trim that is Far Niente, one of the nineteenth-century wineries revived with twentieth-century money.

Up Highway 29, there are more names: Nickel & Nickel, Turnbull, Cakebread. To the east, through the trees, there's a glimpse of the pink mission-style winery of Groth and the square water tower that's on the label of Silver Oak. Crowds still line up twice a year when Silver Oak lets loose a new vintage.

But it's what's straight ahead, just across the highway, that commands our attention: The long, tan, mission-style building with the unmistakable tower and arch. It is the Robert Mondavi Winery, older sister to Opus One, but more significantly, it's the cornerstone of the modern Napa wine industry.

So much of new Napa—post-phylloxera, post-Prohibition, post–jug wine, and post–European scorn—flows from this winery and from the towering spirit and communicable enthusiasm of the man who founded it.

Robert Mondavi is a legend in this valley and an icon to anyone who knows wine. It was Mondavi who sold the notion of Napa that's since grown to near myth. It was Mondavi who encouraged other Napa vintners to think grander, to be greater. It was Mondavi who shared what he knew about growing grapes and making wine, who donated tens of millions to wine and food and art centers around California, who stopped people and made them try his wine. And it was Mondavi who spread the gospel of Napa's soil and climate and wines to San Francisco, New York, and the hallowed fields of Bordeaux.

We need to spend some time at Robert Mondavi Winery, possibly the most visited winery in the valley. We need to stand there and feel the place. But not today. Sometimes you have to experience a bit more of the kingdom before going to see the king.

Besides, at Opus One, we're in one of the king's castles, and there's some high-profile wine below us in the tasting room waiting to be sampled for the everyday bargain price of $25 for one two-ounce pour. We're not complaining. Hank isn't, anyway. I'm mostly confused. This is new to me. Hank explains.

This is a one-wine house in the style of the great French châteaux. Opus One just makes Opus One wine, a Bordeaux blend based on Cabernet Sauvignon that's always co-starred Cabernet Franc in the mix. The wine's changed over the years, gotten less showy, maybe grown a little more French, Hank says, and the vintage we're about to taste, the 2001 Opus—you call it Opus if you're any kind of cool—used all five major Bordeaux grapes. By the way, now I'm pretty certain Dopey is not one of them.

Opus, like those great châteaux, actually makes a second wine, called Overture, in years when there's enough leftover grapes or juice—they don't like it when I call it run off—of fitting quality. Overture goes for $45 a bottle; Opus One is $145. Considering that some new, instant-trophy wines get nearly double the price of Opus, and that Opus may have the most prominent, and bi-continental, winemaking lineage in the valley, that it ranks right up there on the world pedigree list, $145 starts to sound like a steal. Not for us. I'm just saying.

When you talk about Opus One, you have to start with that pedigree. It's there in profile on the label, side views of Robert Mondavi and Baron Philippe de Rothschild. That would be a Rothschild from Bordeaux's top-of-the-line, Premier Cru, Château Moton-Rothschild. The men first met in Hawaii in 1970, when the Baron approached Mondavi about a joint venture.

1970. Even before the Paris Tasting, let alone Napa's growth as a world wine power. In 1970, the French considered American winemakers to be something akin to retarded children. Yet here was a Frenchman, and not just any Frenchman, but a baron from a Premier Cru—one of the five, government-sanctioned, best-of-the-best winemaking houses in Bordeaux, and by some definitions, anywhere—approaching a puny Californian, not waiting, lowering himself to speak first, to say let's do a deal. And Rothschild said let's take your grapes—*your grapes*—your Napa Valley, not–Premier Cru, Holy-Christ-not-even-French grapes, and make some wine together. In California. Oh the humanity.

They talked over a few years and the plan came together in 1978 when Mondavi traveled to Bordeaux as a guest of Rothschild. The exact details took twenty-five minutes to decide, Mondavi has said. As big a personal moment as it was for Mondavi, it was also an enormous step for all of American wine. They would blend American technology with French winemaking, progressiveness with tradition, in a way, science with art.

The first vintage was made in 1979 by Rothschild winemaker Lucien Sionneau and Timothy Mondavi, Robert's son. It was released, along with the 1980 vintage, in 1984. The winery didn't open until 1991, cost $27 million, and was then, hands down, the most expensive winery built in Napa.

Much of the money went into the technology, the cellars, the gravity-flow mechanics, the caves under the building that create a small hill on the Oakville flats. But they surely paid a lot to their architects, Johnson, Fain & Pereira—the people who designed San Francisco's Transamerica Pyramid. And here's where you might quibble. Opus One's official line is that it's "inverted like a jewel." OK. Sure. The first time I saw it coming down Oakville Crossroad, I seriously thought it was a water treatment plant. We turned the corner and I said missile launch pad. Mostly, you see stone and the flat metal top that looks like a Frisbee worn as a hat.

When we got closer, however, everything changed. The walk-up is wide open, with cream-colored limestone walls and graceful stairs leading to a courtyard. That's surrounded by colonnades and leads to a huge, polished wood door. It feels like a temple. Except for the Frisbee hat.

Inside, we signed in at a desk—they call the nice man sitting there the concierge, but he's just sitting there giving directions. Opus One didn't allow public visitors for a while, which may have added to its cachet or mystery—and certainly fed the jokes, like calling it Pompous One—but that ran counter to the Mondavi theme of being inviting and of making wine something for everyone. Plus, some of those other trophy wines were getting the headlines and a little exposure never hurts. The doors opened in 1995.

The interior is more blending of California and Europe. It's open and tall, mixes the pale tan and cream stone with redwood and stainless steel, has outdoor hallways, and lets sunlight stream through huge windows and skylights. It's sleek and modern, mostly. A sitting room mixes contemporary art, new stuffed couches, and ornate furniture that might be Eighteenth-Century Italian or Louis-the-Something French. Most of the details are lost on me, except that it's impressive.

So is the wine. We take our time getting to the actual tasting room, because it just seems so uncool to rush it. At the small tasting bar, the young, well-dressed woman treats us as if we belong. I try not to disappoint her. It dawns on me that, in my limited-but-enthusiastic wine-drinking career, this will be the most expensive wine I've ever tasted. I'm not sure what to do. I hold it up and look at it for, apparently, a long, long time.

"You eventually have to drink it," Hank says.

Yes, and there will be no spitting here. It's too rich for my saliva.

It is very, very good. Powerful and intense, and, I guess, a word would be polished. This is a Big Red, capital B, capital R. It feels silky and forceful and tastes like deep, God, I don't know, deep grapes.

I'm a little rattled by the price and the place and the wine that's so overwhelming. I have to admit, the price really has an impact. Is it worth $145 a bottle? And lots more for older vintages? Is it worth three and a half bottles of the Jessup Cab we had a week before? Hell if I know. Probably not to me, because I might actually buy the Jessup Cab. But if you have the money, why not? Or if you just believe it's worth it.

We sip and taste slowly. I notice Hank doesn't spit, either.

"What do you think?" he asks.

"We haven't been to a lot of places like this," I say.

MORE MY SPEED IS OAKVILLE GROCERY. They have large, only barely overpriced chocolate chip cookies, and I am back in my element. Oakville Grocery, actually, is pretty much everyone's element. It's a great deli, a bit of a cafe, a major league wine shop, a general store, and a good spot to sample cheese, olives, salsa, tapenades, and all kinds of stuff crammed along the narrow aisles. You spend a lot of time squeezing past strangers, here. Oakville Grocery is not for claustrophobics.

But it is nearly a tourist attraction on its own. The grocery was built in 1881, became the mercantile and post office for the nineteenth-century Napa hub that was Oakville, and the big Victorian next door is still the area's post office. There's a throwback feel here with the covered porch, the wooden benches, and the giant picture of a Coke bottle on the side of the building. And they have working public telephones. Throwback, I'm telling you.

Oakville Grocery draws a steady crowd—lunchtime, of course, gets nuts—but it looks more packed from the road than it is when we drive up because everyone's on the front porch, sitting in shade. Actually, the Grocery handles crowds well. The short stretch between order and pickup barely leaves me time to sort through my cookie options. Cherry Chocolate Chunk. Peanut Butter Chocolate Zebra. White Chocolate Macadamia Nut. When pressed, I go old school. Straight-up chocolate chip. They also handle sandwiches well. Hank's roast beef with some kind of blue cheese spread, and my hot chicken and melted Gruyère, are big-time tasty.

We find a table out back in the shade under trees looking at vineyards. Hank is talking about what a great little pause this is in our grueling and thankless Quest. Or maybe just that it's a nice spot, or that his sandwich is good. I'm not really listening because I'm still doing the math on Opus One. My sandwich and big cookie cost about $10. I could get fourteen of those for one bottle of Opus. On the other hand, I can't really see putting a chicken sandwich away for ten years.

JUST OVER ON OAKVILLE CROSSROAD IS Napa Wine Co., a place that started in 1877 as Nouveau Medoc Winery, and is, as it says across one large outside wall, "Bonded Winery No. 9." The translation: It holds the ninth permit to make wine issued in California, the oldest still operating. There are a couple older wineries, but this permit stayed in continual use (by the likes of Inglenook and Beringer at points) and the others lapsed. For instance, Charles Krug, Napa Valley's oldest remaining winery, had a dormant period and operates as Bonded Winery No. 3110.

I am thinking about that, and about how, more than a century later, star winemakers like Helen Turley, Heidi Peterson Barrett, and Randy Mason used or still use Napa Wine Co.'s facilities. I'm thinking about the Robert Mondavi Winery across the highway, about Opus One, Oakville Grocery, the big SUVs humming by on the road, and the rows of world-class vineyards around us. I'm thinking, what an extraordinary place Napa is.

It's been called a lot, good and bad: a quintessential California tale; a great modern Eden; a model showing how money changes everything; an example of American drive; a prototype for preserving open land; a case of people losing sight of what they have; a real-world Disneyland; and the closest thing to paradise not on an island. All of that is true. Napa's history and its present are complicated. So is the world. And so is the world of wine.

Napa's wine history is, if nothing else, a classic American story. It could be a Hollywood epic. It starts with hard work and big success, then there's disaster, some bleak years, and more disaster. Slowly, one resolute man by one resolute man, Napa wine climbed back, until it exploded across the planet, its panache and wine style growing into an economic force, probably *the* economic force, in the wine world. The industry here is now a complex web of opportunity, restraint, and pressures from both inside and out.

Napa's wine story started long before Bonded Winery No. 9, in 1831, when a North Carolina trapper named George C. Yount was guided into Napa Valley and ended up hunting, trapping, and working for two nearby Spanish missions. In 1836, the Mexican governor granted Yount 11,814 acres in the heart of the valley—Napa land was cheaper then—that was called Rancho Caymus, a name that still shows up around the valley. Yount's name does, too, in the form of Yountville. It is uncertain, however, if he were alive today, whether he could get into Yountville's French Laundry.

Yount planted vines in 1838, and since there were no tourists to speak of, he drank most of the wine himself. The first commercial wine enterprise was started in 1857 by John M. Patchett. He bought 100 acres on the north end of Napa town, grew and crushed grapes, and sold the wine for $2 a barrel. The record is not clear on his *Wine Spectator* points rating. Patchett built what was, more or less, Napa's first winery in 1858, a fifty-foot-by-thirty-three-foot stone building. Tours were by appointment only.

German immigrant Charles Krug started making wine in Patchett's winery, then founded his own in 1861. (Besides being the oldest surviving winery in Napa, it's notable for another reason. Krug opened the first Napa tasting room—in 1882—and for me and Hank, that makes the man a hero.) Jacob Schram started Schramsberg in 1863, H. W. Crabb planted what was to become the To Kolan vineyard in 1868, and the floodgates, by nineteenth-century standards, were open.

In 1876, the Beringer bothers, who had been working for Krug, opened their own winery and in 1877 built the seventeen-room Rhine House where visitors taste now on Beringer tours. 1877 was also when Nouveau Medoc Winery fired up.

Gustave Niebaum, a Finnish fur trader, came to Napa in 1879 and started Inglenook (which morphed in the late twentieth century to Niebaum-Coppola, then in 2006 to Rubicon Estate). Later, in a nineteenth century version of the Paris Tasting, Inglenook won an award for "excellence and purity" at the 1889 Paris Exposition. Had the French realized Niebaum made his wine in America, they likely would have thrown it out.

There were lots more. Vittori Sattui came in 1885, Christian Brothers Greystone Cellars opened in 1888, Anton Nichelini started his Chiles Valley winery in 1890. By 1890, Napa had more than 140 wineries and over 18,000 acres of grapevines planted. Then came the first disaster.

Phylloxera is a word of terror in wine country. It is actually an aphid, a microscopic louse, which feeds on the roots of grapevines and deprives them of nourishment. Phylloxera was on a worldwide tear and came to the valley in 1890, after trashing nearby Sonoma wine country a decade earlier. By 1900, only 3,000 acres of vines were left in Napa.

Most of the wineries shrank or closed. Charles Krug died a sad, beaten man. Maybe worse, his tasting room shut down. The Beringer brothers were barely holding on. Schramsberg's vineyards were destroyed. Most Napa wineries went under.

Some help came at the turn of the century. French immigrant Georges de Latour had seen phylloxera in France, and he also knew of a grapevine that was resistant to it. He imported the rootstock and sold it around the valley for ten years, and helped save the wineries that were left. He also helped finance his own winery, Beaulieu Vineyards, which he started with a four-acre parcel in 1900 and opened in 1907. BV was a major producer by 1910 and some other Napa wineries bounced back, too, though the valley was nothing like the booming wine country it was in the nineteenth century.

If you know anything about Hollywood epics, you know it's time for even more devastation. That came on October 28, 1919, at the hands of the United States Congress: Prohibition. It was America's puritanical roots rearing up again, and, in hindsight, one of the most harebrained moves in American history.

Prohibition gave a huge boost to organized crime, encouraged government corruption at every level, turned average citizens into felons, and pissed off most of the American population. Other than that, it worked out fine. It also turned the lights off for most of what remained of Napa's, and America's, wine industry. A few of the biggies, like BV, Inglenook, and Beringer, survived by making sacramental or kosher wine, which was allowed by the Volstead Act—the law enacting the details of Prohibition—and some others made the 200 gallons a year the act also allowed, theoretically, for private use.

But for the enormous majority of wineries, it was good night. They became orchards or ranches or ghosts.

Hank and I are talking about the notion of Prohibition, and how unfathomable it seems today, as we walk inside the tasting room of the Napa Wine Co. The tasting room, technically, is called Cult Wine Central for the range of wines, some very popular, some on the hard-to-find lists, produced there. It's a big, square area with two long bars, and it feels like a wine shop with its variety of bottles on shelves behind the counters.

Napa Wine Co. houses more than sixty labels, including its own, and wines that have launched or still produce there include Bryant Family, Colgin, Staglin, Pahlmeyer, Marcassin, and Volker Eisele Family Estate—a near–who's who of those high-end trophy wines.

Napa Wine Co. is also the facility for Marilyn Merlot, which has a different drawing of Marilyn on each vintage and has become more collector's item than wine. The first release, a 1985, now sells for $3,750 each, and a twelve-bottle vertical from 1985 through 1996 goes for, I swear, $7,000. See, Opus is sounding reasonable.

We meet Maureen Donegan, whose title is Fine Wine Specialist. Her story is not rare in Napa. She studied viticulture and enology, worked in a bunch of wineries, and wants to make her own wine. That's why she's here at Napa Wine Co. She can watch a range of winemakers using the custom crush to see the different styles. Her plan is to travel some, probably to Italy and Australia, to see how winemakers work there. I'm thinking her research isn't all work.

Maureen is tall, has blond hair and a quick laugh. She clearly knows her wine, which she says is another reason she likes working at Napa Wine Co. She gets a good deal on a huge list of wines.

"I like the freedom of drinking what I want to drink," she says. Take that, Prohibition.

WE MOVE EAST ON THE OAKVILLE Crossroad and turn into the vineyards looking for PlumpJack Winery. In some ways, this is a polar opposite to Opus One. Not all ways, though. The signs leading to the little tasting room are medieval-style shields with a comic-like scrawl on them. You'd think they belong to some loopy roadhouse in Cartoon Town. The winery is named after Shakespeare's Sir John Falstaff, a rogue whose nickname was Plump Jack and whose impish spirit seems to be embedded in the winery.

The relatively small tasting room is half Renaissance Faire and half of that roadhouse pub, with a round, metal-trimmed bar, lots of windows, and oddly shaped objects around the room. The walls have goofy-looking shields and swords mixed with modern wine art.

No one takes themselves too seriously here, although PlumpJack makes some seriously good, and seriously priced, wines. The 2004 Reserve Chardonnay has lots of fruit and vanilla and is a mouthful, but it still stays crisp. The 02 Estate Cab, which is their lesser Cabernet—relatively speaking—has a plum-y, chocolaty finish that lasts for, like, a week.

And both of those wines, at $44 and $62, come with screw tops if you want them. Their Oakville Reserve Cab, at $160 a bottle—and, yes, I notice, it's more than Opus One—also has the screw-top option.

Hank loves screw tops. You lose the flourish of the corkscrew moment, but screw tops truly protect the wine against being "corked," which is when a chemical called TCA—officially: 2,4,6-trichloranisole—gets in the bottle. TCA can form lots of ways, most often during cork processing, and it makes wine taste like a wet dog wrapped in soggy cardboard, never the best expression of the fruit.

Hank says he's seen different numbers quoted on how many bottles end up corked, from one to ten percent—every study seems to have either a statistical flaw or a glaring conflict-of-interest—but he tastes thousands of wines a year and figures five percent minimum, one bottle in twenty, are corked at least a little.

"If you have just a few bottles at home," Hank says, "the odds are pretty good that one of them is corked. And if you're saving one to take to dinner on a special night, you won't know till you get there."

Denise Moffit, who's pouring our tastes at PlumpJack, is totally with Hank. That's not entirely unexpected since she works for PlumpJack, but she also makes good sense. "It can be expensive and embarrassing," she said. "You bring your own wine to dinner, the waiter opens it, and it's corked. Now you feel like an idiot, you have to order off the wine list, and you probably still have to pay the corkage fee.

"If I'm buying one of our Cabs, which, you may have noticed, aren't cheap, I want to know I'm going to get to drink it."

This is not the prevailing view in the wine world. At least, not the publicly stated view. We talked to one winemaker who said it seems silly to seal your hyper-expensive Cabernet with oak bark—cork is actually a piece of tree—but even if his wine would be safer, demand would go down. Sales are sales. The debate over corks vs. screw tops or synthetic cork-like stoppers is growing some, but in the tradition-laden culture of wine, pushing some newfangled modern device is no way to get popular. Or make sales.

And let's be honest, there are big economic interests at stake, too. For instance, Portugal's Amorim Group, the biggest cork producer in the world, sells about 3.5 billion of those little guys a year. Here's a shock: They're not thrilled with screw tops.

But for some people, on a more human level, it's all about the pop. I remind Hank about the server we met earlier pouring for visitors at Napa Cellars. His name is Rich Lowitz and he's a funny, high-energy guy who is completely engaged in the subject of wine.

Rich is not your wine-is-ritual zealot. When we walked in, he was reassuring a young couple who looked to be tasting-room rookies.

"It's grape juice," he said. "Don't be intimidated. If you like it and your husband doesn't, you're both right. Just drink what you like and don't listen to anyone. Nobody started out drinking $100 Bordeaux." It didn't look like Bordeaux rang any bells with the couple, but they liked Rich anyway.

We did, too. The guy is Mr. Enthusiasm. He is also, it turned out, Mr. Cork.

"Oh, no, no, no," he said when the subject of screw tops came up. "No, no, no. I don't like it. You're out to dinner on a big night, your date is waiting to be impressed, and, what, you open your wine with a little twist? It's like opening a jar of pickles. Where's the impression? Where's the romance? You'll end up asking 'Where's my date?'"

That's the crux of the argument for corks. Not so much the losing-your-date part, but losing the ceremony, the grand gesture. That is, indeed, a very nice moment when the cork pops out. The pro-cork forces also say—and Hank disagrees—that synthetics have a subtle hint of petroleum product and that screw tops give wine a lovely metal finish. Those still aren't wet dog, but there you go.

The fight goes on. There's disagreement over whether wines with screw tops will age too slowly, or not at all, because the seal might not let in enough air, or whether more porous synthetics make it age too fast. Hank says that's hoo-hah. Only a fraction of wine drinkers hold wine for any great time.

"For most people who buy wine, probably ninety-nine percent of them," Hank says, "careful aging means buying a bottle and not crashing on the way home from the store. Then they drink it."

Hank's solution would be to keep the corks or—the way PlumpJack does it—the cork option for expensive wines. That would also mean fewer corks on the market and an overall higher quality, though Amorim Group's stock price would probably drop.

"We're talking about the masses, not collectors. Why use such a risky closure and possibly waste millions of gallons of wine?" Hank says. "It doesn't make sense when technology has come so far just to do it for tradition."

I'm on Hank's side on this, first, because I'm always on Hank's side on principle, and because I get a little nervous bringing an expensive wine to dinner, or at least my version of expensive, since I'm worrying it will be corked. Also, I may drop it, but that's off point. My favorite solution is a thing called a Zork. It's basically a screw cap with a little plunger so, when you pull it out, it makes an almost-cork-like pop. I like that for its ingenuity and for the compromise. I also like saying Zork.

GROTH'S GRACEFUL, MOORISH/MISSION-STYLE winery, with high ceilings, huge windows, pale walls, and bright paintings, is an extremely cheerful place on a sunny morning at the start of July. But Lisa, a veteran employee and something of an ironic wit, isn't feeling it.

"I was saying to my doctor I don't know what's wrong," she tells us. Lisa would be approaching the too-much-info level, except she has a conspiratorial air about her that makes us insiders. Plus, I'm nosy. "I've been so depressed," she says. "He told me, 'Everyone is. It won't stop raining.'"

That's the way it seems around Napa. May started wet then got warm, pretty much like a normal spring. But in June, odd storm after odd storm moved through Northern California. Usually by July, Napa has seen a month or two of seventy- to eighty-five-degree days. This year, it's only been the last week.

For Lisa, a midsized blond woman with a pretty oval face, the rain's been depressing because it feels like she missed spring, and because she knows the grapes have missed some spring, too.

The good news, she says, is that most of the fruit set during the warm and dry stretch in early May—meaning the grape flowers got pollinated and didn't get washed away by rain—so the yield looks to be healthy. The bad news is, the soil is so saturated by water, the vines are growing like crazy plants.

Lisa takes us through a roomy, open dining room that feels like an art gallery. The walls have the energetic modern paintings of Suzanne Groth, daughter of owners Dennis and Judy. We've never met her, but my guess is Suzanne's not afraid of color.

We go out onto a deck looking straight north, and out over some very lush vineyards. The rows point straight north, too, and the impression is of thick green lines running through the distant trees and, basically, to forever.

"We replanted them to go north-south so the wind can dry them out," Lisa says. "But there's so much moisture, we have to keep cutting back to let the light and air get through. And we're dropping a lot more fruit (cutting off some bunches to make the remaining grapes more concentrated). Normally, in a good year, we might drop thirty percent of the fruit; this year we're dropping I think twenty percent more."

It's hard to tell how that will add up at harvest time, she says, but they're hoping the summer will be steady and warm—grapes like it hot, but not too hot—and they'll probably start picking these vines in September. Most of Groth's Cabernet Sauvignon is planted in Oakville, so most of their Cab grapes ripen at the same time and things get slightly hectic around here.

"If I'm still depressed then" she says, "then I'll know it wasn't the rain. Or if it's still raining in September, then we'll be screwed, but at least I'll have a reason to be depressed."

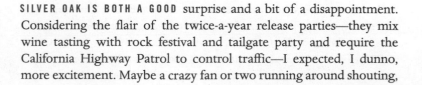

SILVER OAK IS BOTH A GOOD surprise and a bit of a disappointment. Considering the flair of the twice-a-year release parties—they mix wine tasting with rock festival and tailgate party and require the California Highway Patrol to control traffic—I expected, I dunno, more excitement. Maybe a crazy fan or two running around shouting,

"I got a bottle." Also, considering the status of Silver Oak, I expected more exclusivity. I was ready to beg our way in.

The winery is off Oakville Crossroad, just west of Groth, and driving up we see the square-topped water tower from the label. That's a fun little moment (though there's no actual oak tree near it). There's tons of parking. No guards, no gates, just wisteria-covered trellises and neat, rose-lined walkways. The big stone winery, with a rounded wooden door, a peaked roof, and a series of tall, narrow windows, looks like a great country church.

All of that fits my expectations, except the lack of gates, and maybe the absence of crazy fans. But inside, it's just a tasting room, not a particularly special one, more retail space than shrine. The light from the low ceiling is bland and the brick-colored tile floor is worn. I want more specialness. Messy piles of shirts and hats sit on a table in the middle of the room and I think about finding a winery worker and asking, "What have you people done?"

It's also pretty busy, which makes sense, but adds to the retail store feel, not the rare church thing I want. I'm liking Opus One's missile station more and more.

My disappointment aside, Silver Oak is something of a story. It's a very well-known label—probably the single wine most likely to impress your average in-laws (so long as they don't live in France), based on price, reputation, and name recognition. And it has the image of a limited-issue, impossible-to-get wine, which drives up the price and brings out the folks for release days.

But the thing is, these days you can find Silver Oak everywhere. They make close to 70,000 cases a year. A server shows us a five-page, tiny-type list of just Northern California outlets that carry their wine. Hank's Nugget Markets are on it, but we know that. About the only stores not on it are Target and Ace Hardware.

Hank explains to me a little about how this happened. When Silver Oak started in 1972, it was among the first Napa wineries to focus on one varietal, Cabernet Sauvignon. They used American oak—which means more vanilla and a bit more impression of sweetness—and held it in barrels and bottles for four to five years, to make it softer and more approachable. The result is a complex, but rich, ripe, and accessible wine—essentially a big, expensive wine you can drink when it's released. The average American palate is not looking for a tight, tannic wine that needs to sit in a cellar for ten years. The average American palate, if it's spending big bucks on wine, wants to drink the damn stuff now.

Silver Oak was probably hottest in the 1990s when new money—much of it dot-com money—was creating new prestige-wine drinkers whose bank accounts were more mature than their wine tastes. Silver Oak's approachability was perfect for them, but it was, and still is, a genuinely serious wine and scores some genuinely serious ratings.

The folks at Silver Oak did not leave it at that. They took one more—near genius—step. To be truly desirable, you need to seem like a hard-to-get treasure. There's something about wine that makes people go nuts over anything that's limited. It implies care, and quality, and something I have that you don't. Silver Oak was produced in small quantities when it started but grew reasonably large, reasonably fast. So some very smart people there limited the places you could find it. Not the amount, just the access. "I couldn't get it to sell," Hank says. "There was already one place in town that had it, and that was it."

And then there were the release parties. The Silver Oak folks played on the desirability, on the fact their wines show well right off, and on the American propensity to stand in a line that's already formed. Hence the raucous release parties. Big lines. Big publicity. More reputation for exclusivity. More raucous release parties. They reached critical mass and a cemented reputation. Silver Oak is a big winery that pretends it isn't. Hard not to admire how well they do that.

Some of that has changed recently. There are new hot, cult-like trophy wines—such as Colgin Cellars, Araujo Estate Wines, and, of course, Screaming Eagle—that are genuinely made in small amounts, maybe a couple thousand, or even a couple hundred cases. Plus, the dot-com bust, the 9/11 attacks, and some general economic downturns have cut demand for very expensive wines. That doesn't mean Silver Oak isn't selling. It is, because a) it isn't the priciest of pricey wines, b) it's everywhere, and c) it's Silver Oak. Most wine drinkers have never heard of Colgin, Araujo, or even Screaming Eagle, but everyone knows Silver Oak. And the release parties still draw festival crowds. It's just that the exclusivity, now, is myth.

As for the wine, I'm a little lost, maybe for the opposite reason I was lost at Opus One. I'm underwhelmed inside here, thrown by the contrast between image and reality, at least for the tasting room. It's not a bad place, and the outside is pretty cool, but this room just isn't the big-time, super-special, God-isn't-this-wine-great tasting room I wanted. I'm pretty sure I like the 2000 Alexander Valley Cabernet, price $60, better than the 2000 Napa Valley Cab, price $100, but I'm not sure why. And at this point, I've completely given up trying to assess value.

I do think going to a release party would be fun, though the crowds might make it tough to get into, and wouldn't that be ironic?

The one time Silver Oak still might really be exclusive is during its public open house.

WE ARE ALMOST READY. THERE'S ONE more winery first. We drive west on Oakville Crossroad over Highway 29, and head through the vineyards on a road that will turn into a winding climb up the Oakville Grade.

As the hill starts up, maybe a quarter mile and before it gets crazy steep, there is Diamond Oaks Winery, which used to be La Famiglia di Robert Mondavi and before that Vichon. Only Diamond Oaks is not owned by Mondavi.

It's a small, charming spot with a killer view. The wines are good. I love the Carneros Reserve Chardonnay because I get all that butterscotch with still some fruit and crispness. And the tasting room is mostly window. Outside is even better. The hilltop-like picnic area has a bocce ball court—like, it seems, just about everyone in Napa—and on one side it looks over a very steep hillside covered with the wavy lines of vines.

On the other side it looks across the valley, down on the flats of the Oakville vineyards, and at the tan bell tower of Robert Mondavi Winery, tiny in the distance. Hank and I look at all this, at the layer of green, at the mountains rimming Napa Valley, at the wineries surrounded by vines.

"Time to go see the king," I say.

THERE IS AN AIR OF AMUSEMENT park excitement in the parking lot of the Robert Mondavi Winery, which, to a lot of other winemaking houses, would be an insult. But not here. Mondavi wants the visitors. In 1966, Robert put the winery on Highway 29, not back up against the mountains, so people would come in and try the wine. And, he figured, spread the word.

Robert Mondavi has done much for Napa wine, and for California and American wine, from raising standards and experimenting, to cheerleading and just being a symbol of a good wine life. But maybe above it all, what he's done is spread the word, about taking chances, about wine, about Napa.

Post-Prohibition, there was not a lot of cheer in Napa. The biggest wineries—Beaulieu, Beringer, Inglenook, Christian Brothers— survived by making sacramental wines or selling grapes, and started up again in 1933, but it was during the Depression and, then, World War II.

A few names that were to become legends in Napa entered the valley. Louis Martini opened a winery in 1933. John Daniel, grand nephew of Gustave Niebaum, inherited Inglenook in 1937 and turned it toward making fine wine. In 1938, BV's Georges de Latour hired a Russian named André Tchelistcheff, who had been studying wine in Paris, and convinced him to come to Napa. Tchelistcheff would raise up Beaulieu, then many other wineries, and become the valley's Yoda of winemaking for decades. In 1947, Mario Trinchero and his family from New York bought Sutter Home Winery just outside St. Helena.

And an Italian immigrant named Cesare Mondavi, who was living in Lodi in California's Central Valley, bought first a bulk winery called Sunny St. Helena, then in 1943, at the urging of his son, Robert, the old Charles Krug Winery. But that was mostly it for Napa, lots of bulk wine, lots of wine shipped in railroad cars. Only a few wineries tried to make the great wines that, frankly, few people in America would drink, anyway. Robert Mondavi has said when he drove past BV and Inglenook in those days, he would bow his head out of respect for what they were trying to do.

In the 1960s, there were maybe two dozen wineries in Napa. But change was coming. Joseph Heitz bought a small winery off Highway 29. It had been called "The Only One Winery" because it was the only one making Grignolino, a fruity Italian varietal. Slow times call for being obvious. In 1965, Jack and Jamie Davies restarted Schramsberg and made sparkling wine in the hills above Calistoga. And in 1965, there was The Fight.

Robert and Peter Mondavi were then typical brothers, which is to say similar and different and competitive and often in total disagreement. Robert, who had visited Europe in 1962, had discovered French winemaking, how they treated each varietal differently, how small oak barrels added texture and complexity to wine, and how there could be magic when great food and great wine were put together. He wanted to do that at Charles Krug, which was making good money in the mass wine business. Peter, correctly, said there's no market in the U.S. for fine wine. Robert, it turned out, also correctly, said let's create a market.

Those tensions and a natural rivalry lingered, but The Fight—at least on the surface—was over Robert buying his first wife, Marge, a mink coat because they had been invited to a dinner at the White House. As Robert describes it in his 1998 autobiography, *Harvest of Joy*, Peter implied Robert used winery money for the coat. Robert, even at age fifty-two, acted like any brother. "Take it back," he told Peter.

Peter didn't. Robert hit him. They had to be separated. That started a real rift, long since healed, that sent Robert out of Charles Krug—the family actually suspended him, Robert later sued and won millions—and down the road to these flats of Oakville.

He bought a large chunk of the To Kolan vineyard, and in 1966 started Robert Mondavi Winery, the first new winery to be built in Napa since the end of Prohibition. Then he gave it the Robert Mondavi treatment.

Mondavi had access to some first-class Sauvignon Blanc grapes—a varietal barely used in California then—fermented the wine dry and aged it in oak to round it out. Then he invented the name Fumé Blanc, a twist on the French wine Blanc Fumé, so as not to scare people off with Sauvignon Blanc. His test group was a PTA meeting back in Lodi. The Fumé Blanc went over well with the moms. Mondavi started selling it for $1.79 a bottle, something of a high price, but, he has said, he wanted people to know it was good stuff.

Over the next few years, he found other ways to let people know Mondavi Winery—and Napa—made good stuff. Stories have him flagging down cars on Highway 29 and directing them into his winery, which Mondavi has said are an "exaggeration." For sure, he would go to restaurants and push his wine, sometimes giving a bottle to diners just so they could taste it.

He would go to East Coast restaurants, in tough markets like New York or Boston, where they had no use for California wines or, probably, California, and order the best French wine, often a Premier Cru from Bordeaux. Then he'd order a second Premier Cru, get people talking, and invite the chef, the sommelier, or the owner to try some great French wine. In the middle of the hubbub, he'd produce a Robert Mondavi Cabernet and have them compare. Usually that earned his wine respect. Always that earned him a rep as an odd guy.

A few years of that, and of more conventional cheerleading, general marketing, and of undiminished enthusiasm, helped spread Mondavi's and Napa's word in restaurant and wine circles. Then came the 1976 Paris Tasting. Both winning winemakers, Warren Winiarski and Mike Grgich, like many winemakers in Napa Valley, were Mondavi alumni who, along with Robert, had done their share of experimenting.

As Napa would grow and expand, other trends would sweep America's attention toward wine and toward Napa, including Sutter Home's invention in the late 1970s of the lightly sweet White Zinfandel, a national love affair with Chardonnay starting in the 1980s, then a 1991 *60 Minutes* report on the health benefits of red wine that had a mammoth effect on the industry.

It wasn't just Mondavi's doing to be sure, but he kept pushing Napa and wine, food and art, reaching for the magic he found in Europe on that first visit. And he brought much of Napa, and much of the American wine world, with him. Mondavi and company experimented with cold fermentation, with steel tanks, and with levels of toast on oak. They messed with trellising, yeast, storage temperatures, and growing technique. More recently, they went to big oak storage tanks. Mondavi called it a "test-tube winery." And much of what he learned in those early days, he gave away to growers and other winemakers, because Mondavi wanted wine to be great and for Napa to be a place—the place—for great wine.

Now we are standing under that famous arch, waiting for our tour guide, thinking how familiar this long, flat, mission-style winery looks, not just because it's on the label and in every Napa guidebook, but because these mission-style buildings are all over this valley and half the West Coast. Through the arch, we can see the vineyards and the green Mayacamas range maybe a mile away. Mondavi's vineyards run all that way west.

Our guide is a middle-aged, part-time teacher named Noel Lucas who just started doing tours this summer. He is, if not the most knowledgeable guy just yet, the embodiment of enthusiasm. I'm thinking Robert Mondavi would like him.

The tour wanders through the edge of the 550-acre To Kolan vineyard, which is a pretty cool thing. They've built paths and a couple "talking areas"—basically shaded benches in small circles—and it's fun to be out here. I want to pepper Lucas with questions about the place and about Mondavi, but, first, he's still pretty sketchy on details, and also, I think the rest of our tour just wants to get to tasting and would probably kill me.

Instead, I go with my standard Plan B: ask Hank. Lucas had said a valley-wide outbreak of phylloxera in the mid-1980s actually helped a lot of wineries. That isn't computing with me.

Hank says when Napa started to boom in the 1970s and 1980s, a lot of winery owners planted grapes for wines they wanted to make, not necessarily the grapes that were best for the soils and micro-climates around Napa. As they all got more sophisticated—in part, Lucas has mentioned, because of work done at Mondavi—a lot of vineyard owners realized they maybe had planted less-than-perfect varietals. But ripping out vineyards isn't cheap. The twentieth-century phylloxera, though much more controlled by twentieth-century technology and information, still eventually forced a lot of vineyard owners to replant through the late 1980s and early 1990s—with even more resistant root stock, and with grapes better suited for their locale.

For Mondavi Winery, which has 1,400 acres planted in Napa, phylloxera was good and bad. Some of the rootstock was already resistant, but many vineyards, including stretches of To Kalon, had to be replanted. The plus side was, they got better results in many places and it gave Mondavi more chances to experiment. Block H—thirty-one acres of this precious To Kolan vineyard—is dedicated to studying how different Cabernet varieties perform.

We pull a trick here—technically cheating on the rules of our Quest. Because this is Mondavi, and because what's the point of hanging with a guy like Hank if we can't take advantage now and then, we use Hank's status as an industry insider and wine buyer, and get a trade tasting after our tour. Inger Shiffler, a smart, casual woman, whose title is Wine Educator, walks us around some more, then sits us down to taste some astoundingly good wine. I like that Inger seems to enjoy them as much as we do, and I'm only saying that because she stops talking and almost goes away for a moment when she gets a mouthful of the 2001 Reserve Cabernet Sauvignon. Hank does the same thing.

I like the Reserve Cab, but I go away on the 2001 Oakville District Cabernet. My wine costs $40, theirs costs $110. I don't know what that says about my palate, but I do know it makes me the cheaper date. We all wiggle around in happiness when we taste the 2000 Sauvignon Blanc Botrytis, a sweet wine that's made by letting the grapes hang extra long, get a little of the mold Botrytis—called noble rot—which shrivels the grapes some, makes them very concentrated, and leaves some residual sugar after they're fermented. The result is sweet and fruity and wiggling around when you taste it.

I ask Inger if Robert still comes to his winery much, now that he's in his nineties and it's gone public and is controlled by Constellation Wines, a corporation considered a good winery owner but still a corporation. She says he drops in now and then, still cheers people on, and still has a bash with his wife, Margrit, at his house in the Stags Leap hills for winery staffers on Christmas. Hank and I look at each other. I know he's thinking what I'm thinking: Robert Mondavi, Mr. Wine-Food-and-Cheer, the man who forever pushed the notion that the wine life means joy and hospitality, who instilled a sense of celebration into this valley, throwing a party. That must be one hell of a party, I say. It is, Inger tells us.

SIX

Chiles Valley and Pope Valley

TONI NICHELINI-IRWIN is complaining about traffic. Who doesn't in Napa? Toni's saying there are so many more cars these days, and all those big trucks, rolling past her little winery. It's crazy. It used to be so quiet.

Here's the thing. Toni is standing in the middle of the road, arms spread wide, one foot on the dotted yellow divider of Highway 128. There are no cars in sight. Even in Napa, there's a road less traveled, though it might not feel that way to everyone.

Eventually a tan car rolls past the Western-style house and the old, dark-wood front of Nichelini Winery that's been there since 1890. Toni gives us a look, like, See? It was minutes later.

These two buildings on a wooded bend in Highway 128 look like the entrance to Western World or a movie set for California's 1800s. The house has big, white posts, a wrap-around porch, and tall, Victorian-style windows on both floors. The dark-brown, weathered winery has big barrels in front, a slanted roof, and looks like it's itching to fall down the hill.

It won't, Toni swears. They've been making wine in there more than a century. This winery and this family are not going anywhere. Even with all that damn traffic.

We are off on the back roads of Napa, in the mountains to the east of the valley floor, and we're finding little treasures of history and charm and, frankly, pretty good wine. Not much traffic, though, and it feels especially light since this is mid-July and the rest of Napa has its roads full. The wineries up here aren't big names or big producers—though some first-class wines come from these hillsides and high meadows, and many of Napa's biggest wineries grow grapes in these parts. All the wineries, though, are fountains of hospitality, and they're reminders of what all of Napa was like not so long ago.

Nichelini Winery is at the bottom of Chiles Valley, a ten-mile-long, more-or-less north-south slot in the Vaca Mountains. It runs parallel to the Silverado Trail and separates Napa Valley from Lake Berryessa, a recreational area and reservoir. If you make wine up here, 800 to 1,000 feet above Napa, you still get to put Napa Valley on your label. Or Chiles Valley. But do not call it Pope Valley, which is a few miles north and east, and though both areas are connected by the Chiles Pope Valley Road, there's some regional rivalry at work around here.

"A lot of people weren't happy when they added Pope to the name of the road," Toni tells us. We're pretty certain that includes her, though we think that covers the two subjects—traffic and dumb ol' Pope Valley—that get a rise out of her. Toni seems to laugh about everything else. She has an oval face, short brown hair, and the ubiquitous Napa-look of having lived a life in some sunshine. She's one of four family members who own the winery and is the granddaughter of Anton Nichelini, the man who built the place.

We walk down a steep hill between the winery and the house, and stand on the terrace that is the tasting area for Nichelini. There's a small wood tasting bar and we're facing a heavy stone wall that is both a foundation for the house and the entrance to the old barrel room.

Nichelini makes a range of wines, some of them unusual like a Sauvignon Vert, an "off-dry" (or slightly sweet) white, with still a bit of bite from the fruit; an old-vine Zinfandel from grapevines that were planted in 1930 and look like the withered hands of a witch; and a Chiles Valley Red, which is a blend of Zin and Petite Sirah, not something you see every day. I like the Chiles Valley Red a lot because it's lush and ripe. It's a little too ripe, maybe too jammy, for Hank. It's the kind of wine we always disagree on. What does he know?

Toni is telling us this is the oldest winery in Napa run continuously by one family. Anton Nichelini, who was part-Swiss and part-Italian, learned winemaking in Switzerland and chose this spot in the hills above a creek because the area was similar to Switzerland. Anton homesteaded 160 acres, thirty to forty of them planted with vineyards, and started building the hand-hewn stone cellar and the wood winery above it in 1890. He finished the house in 1896, where Toni's grandmother, Caterina, had the last eight of her twelve children.

Like a lot of wineries in Napa, Nichelini had some rough periods, but one family member or another kept it going through the years in some form. We ask how it was Anton survived during Prohibition.

"Very quietly," Toni says.

Not entirely, actually. Prohibition was one of America's dumbest constitutional blunders. Beyond the social repercussions, the organized crime, the citizen-vs.-citizen anger, it devastated the wine industry. For men like Anton Nichelini, whose worlds were built on making and selling wine, there were not a lot of options. He kept making and kept selling wine.

Only the second part of that was completely illegal. The law allowed heads of households to make 200 gallons a year of wine for their private use, so Nichelini could run the winery, as long as his sales stayed out of sight. And there were some sales—around Chiles Valley, in neighboring towns, as far away as San Francisco. Generally, the Nichelinis avoided trouble, though there was the occasional car chase or the hiding from federal revenuers in the night. But there was only one really bad day, and it involved Caterina.

Toni shows us a framed letter displayed inside the old barrel room like a trophy. It was written anonymously in 1920 by a buttinsky in Monticello, a tiny town then in the Berryessa Valley and now at the bottom of Lake Berryessa. He sent it to the Napa County sheriff.

The letter complains that there's a jug of wine kept hidden at the hotel in Monticello. "There is no question but what the wine comes from Nichelini," it says. "If the revenuers would get busy and put the lid on him, I am satisfied drinking would end here."

So revenuers drove over the hill from Napa and stopped at the watering trough in front of Nichelini Winery to cool their cars and themselves. Caterina, being the gracious woman she was, saw men in suits splashing in her water trough and offered them lunch. And being the gracious host she was, Caterina poured them wine with lunch, so far, all on the up-and-up. The men said they liked it so much, they'd love to buy some, as Toni tells it.

"They said, 'Oh Mrs. Nichelini, this is wonderful. Can you sell us a jug?'" Toni says. "As soon as she took the 50 cents, they arrested her."

But Caterina was the mother of twelve. No one wanted her in jail. Everyone was happy to let Anton take the rap. He got sentenced to six months as a trustee, staying at the St. Helena Hotel. Anton did odd jobs and visited friends during the day, and got back to his "cell" by sundown.

The worst of it, says Toni, was the revenuers dumped everything in the tanks and barrels, maybe 15,000 gallons of wine. And though they didn't destroy any equipment, the wine killed an ancient redwood tree down near the creek.

We've been wandering around as Toni tells us the story, and now we're back on the stone terrace by the tasting bar. We sit on a bench and I almost plop down on Boots, an orange cat who, I notice now, has been pulling that cat trick of never technically following us but always appearing, and sleeping, next to wherever we go.

Toni says he functions as a better-than-you'd-expect guard cat. "He doesn't really like other animals," she says. "He attacked a seventy-pound pit bull once. It was a really sweet dog, and Boots sent the poor thing jumping into his mom's arms."

But Boots has developed a tolerance for a new winery cat, a little fluffy brown guy with some kitten still in him. Boots is on the bench trying to ignore the brown cat, who's working hard to get his attention to play.

"He's never let another cat get that close," Toni says.

The brown cat wandered in a couple weeks back, his heavy fur covered with stickers and thistles from his cheeks to his tail. Toni figures some moron dumped him. They cleaned him up, cut out some fur, and patched him up. They named him Stickers.

We walk up the little hill and stand by our car. A big truck rumbles past.

"It never used to be like this," Toni says with a shrug.

"Horrible," I say.

"You adjust," she says.

WE BACKTRACK DOWN 128 TOWARD NAPA because, honestly, we're fairly inept at planning a trip. We're heading for Kuleto Estate, which is off the highway—above it, really—more than a mile up a narrow, winding dirt road that barely fits our not-big car. They've installed mirrors on trees along the road so you can see oncoming cars, which still doesn't stop us from nearly ramming a delivery truck.

"Which one of us is supposed to back up?" Hank asks. He's driving.

"The guy coming down," I say. "I think. That way, if he slips, he doesn't keep rolling off a cliff."

We sit there. So does the truck.

"Not sure he knows that," Hank says.

We sit some more. Then, for no reason I see, Hank and the truck both opt for forward. We try to go around each other, and that puts our two outside wheels right at the steep edge. My nose is out the passenger window and I'm looking straight down a wall of rock. The truck has wheels up the inside wall. I'm holding my breath. The truck driver and his passenger are calm and smiling.

We fit. Barely. The driver shouts a happy "thanks" and waves.

"They were nice, anyway," I say.

At the top, Kuleto Estate is dazzling. It's owned by Pat Kuleto, the big-time restaurateur who's responsible for, among others, Fog City Diner, Boulevard, and Farallon in San Francisco and Martini House in St. Helena. I've been to all, and they all rock. Each is different, but all have this way of being slightly showy or fancy but in a fun, unpretentious way. Besides knowing food, Pat Kuleto is a man with a sense of how to entertain without overdoing it.

The winery on the top of the mountain is the same way. It's huge, some kind of cross between California mountain lodge and Italian villa, with lots of natural stone, lots of heavy wood, lots of terrace, and lots of heart-stopping views. To the west, straight off a cliff, is Lake Hennessey then Napa Valley, maybe 1,000 feet below. To the south, straight ahead of us, is a mélange of vineyards running up and down and along different hillsides in every possible divergent angle and slant.

Hank and I just gape for a minute. It's almost too dazzling to absorb. There's also a fire truck up here—they'd need their own equipment in an emergency—a small lake, gardens, and some sheep, and off somewhere on this 761-acre ranch, vineyard, and fairyland, there's cattle, goats, and, probably, unicorns.

Inside the winery, there's more wood and a bigger-than-life scale to everything. The views are still everywhere. Winemaker Dave Lattin is our tasting guide, and he apologizes because, he says, he's the least interesting guy in the place. The usual guide, Gordie Larum, is apparently a legend in Napa for his wit and unstoppable energy. (We would meet his wife, Silvia, a week later. She works at Esquisse. "People ask, 'Is Gordie always like that? It must be great,'" she would tell us. "I say, you don't have to live with it.")

Dave has also sent another winery worker, who was going to help us, down the mountain because an eighteen-wheeler was at the gate down on Highway 128, the driver mistakenly thinking he could handle a few turns before tumbling into a gully. The worker will unload the truck—whatever is in it—and bring it up in his pickup.

"The best we could come up with is me," Dave says.

Dave Lattin has been making wine for twenty years, which is about how old he looks. He's got sandy brown hair, is slim and sort of loose-limbed when he walks. He wears what we've decided is the uniform of Napa wine folk, a short sleeve shirt, jeans, and work shoes. He and Kuleto make some stunning wines. We start with a Rosato di Sangiovese, a lively Rosé with strawberry and raspberry all over it, and run through a list that includes a rich, balanced Chardonnay—available only at the winery and worth the climb—a spicy Sangiovese, a powerful Zinfandel, and a lush Cab. I say they all seem so different, which, I guess, they're supposed to, being different varietals and all.

Dave says, actually, they really do try to give each wine its own style—not just make a bunch of big, mountain reds—and they can do that with their vineyards.

Of those 761 acres, ninety are planted with vines. Eventually there will be about 120 acres planted. The vines sit at altitudes between 800 feet and 1,450 feet on hillsides, in valleys, on flats, atop rolls of land. With all those angles, exposures, and elevations, they can plant a huge range of varietals. They grow Pinot Noir, for instance, in a cooler notch at a lower elevation, and grow grapes like Syrah and Cabernet Sauvignon near the top of the mountain in more sunlight.

That range lets them choose the almost precise location best for each grape. The downside is, planting the vineyards was expensive and hard, and included creating a sustainable system of farming and of recycling and storing their water. Now that these vineyards are set on hills and nooks and inside tiny valleys, there's no easy, or cheap, way to work the grapes.

Dave says they have a large, full-time vineyard team because, basically, they need it. "If we're trimming the canopy and tying to keep, like, just morning sun on the grapes, you have to keep changing the sides of the vines you cut as the hills turn," he says. "I almost need to give guys a compass out there."

All of those different conditions and angles mean they harvest slowly here, which is a good thing. Dave says it generally takes more than forty days to get all the grapes in because they're ready at such a staggered rate.

"In places like Oakville, everything's ready at once," he says. "You've got winemakers screaming 'Pick it now!' Here, I can go, 'Take in these ten rows here and those ten rows there.'"

We wander over to the house Pat Kuleto built up here, another mix of California mountain and Tuscan styling, and stand on the tree-covered stone patio. There's a pool that, like the patio, seems to drift off the edge of the mountain, down toward the lake and the town of Rutherford. The Villa Cucina, as Kuleto calls it, has more natural wood and stone and earth tones, and tons of huge windows. It looks like the home of a man who figured out how to enjoy his life.

I ask if Pat spends a lot of time here.

He does, Dave says, but he also seems to be perpetually off on his next project.

"I tell him sometimes he needs to just sit here," Dave says.

No kidding. I'm thinking, if it were me, I'd be sitting on this patio drinking my wine for days at a time. Of course, that explains, at least in part, why I don't have a patio like this and Pat Kuleto does.

Back inside the main building, a woman visiting the winery staff is about to leave.

"Tell me again," she says, a little embarrassed to be asking, "is it the car going downhill or uphill that's supposed to back up if we meet on the road?"

Uphill, they say. Less chance of losing control.

"Really?" she says.

We decide to give her a few minutes head start, just in case. And it's not a bad excuse to sit on the deck for a little longer.

UP IN THE HEART OF CHILES Valley, back again past Nichelini Winery, then up that perversely named Chiles Pope Valley Road, we hardly see another car. It's a little freaky considering this is a perfect summer Friday afternoon. We're just over one tall ridge from a busy Napa Valley proper, and a little more than an hour from major cities like San Francisco and Sacramento. But back here, with the big oaks, the rolling brown hills, and the flats of drying grass corralled by long dark-wood fences, it feels like Western farm country circa 1850.

The one giveaway is the vineyards. This is wine country, too, now, and those flats of tall drying grass and the horse pastures are separated by neat lines of green vineyards. In truth, this is what most wine country outside of Napa Valley, and neighboring Sonoma, looks like in California and throughout the U.S. There aren't a lot of places where world-class wineries are lined up, almost door-to-door, along the highway. Wine country is farm country, and it's something you can forget in Napa because often the sleek wineries, the Victorian buildings, and the charming villas hide the agriculture.

In this quiet, narrow valley, the farming is more visible. So is the ranching and, in a way, the sweat that goes into it all. Still, for a Californian reared on the charms of Napa, I can't help thinking Old West. To my unsophisticated sensibilities, Chiles Valley is a place where the Lone Ranger could've been a winemaker.

RustRidge Ranch and Winery is almost exactly that. It started as a 400-acre thoroughbred horse ranch in the 1950s. They added the winery operations in the mid-1970s and have about fifty-five acres planted with grapes. RustRidge is also a bed-and-breakfast, and a generally laid-back place where the dogs, horses, and cats are as much in charge as anybody. That's a sort of a pattern back here, too.

We drive past the ranch house, corrals, and horse paddocks, and are waiting at the converted barn that's now the winery, watching Mark Serrano, the sales and marketing manager, come bombing up the dirt road on his mountain bike, leaving a plume of dust behind him like a vapor trail. It's my kind of winery where they keep appointments via mountain bike.

Mark lets us into the winery/barrel room/tasting area and we get licks and tail wags from Charlie, a yellow Labrador mix and the third generation of Labs who figure significantly into the mood of the place—he's on the label of the Sauvignon Blanc with his mom, Tosca, in adorable cartoon form, along with a wine-tasting horse. There are no upper-crust pretensions here.

Mark is maybe thirtyish, with dark hair, and he's not broken a sweat from his ride. He's telling us the owners are Susan Meyer, who's the winemaker, and her husband, Jim Fresquez, who's the horse trainer. The tasting area is a small, neat bar among the barrels. Behind it are medals for the wines, and pictures of some of the horses. Charlie lies on my foot.

I say that the 2001 Estate Zinfandel has a spectacular nose, deep and maybe forest-y and rich. Mark says it's blackberries and huckleberries. I just inhale for a moment. I want to inhale it in, even more than I want to taste it.

"I call those feedbags wines," Mark says. "You'd love to strap them on and smell them all day."

I say that's a good theme for a winery that's also a horse ranch, but Mark suddenly looks a little pained. He's not so convinced a horse theme is the best way to sell wine—other than the Sauv Blanc label, the wines have labels with a dignified horse's profile on them.

"This is a great place," Mark says. We nod.

"I love the horse ranch," he says. We nod more.

"Susan and Jim love the horse ranch." Still nodding.

"I'm just not sure it's the best image for a pretty sophisticated wine." Again we nod. We agree about the wine.

"I just wish they'd call it something besides RustRidge Ranch and Winery."

"What would you call it?" Hank asks.

Just RustRidge Winery or maybe RustRidge Estate, he says. Gives it more heft. Or, if push comes to shove, just flip it, RustRidge Winery and Ranch. "Anything to emphasize the wine part," Mark says.

Me, I like the horses. But I'm a guy who likes tasting wine with a dog sleeping on my foot.

WE ARE STANDING BEHIND THE ENORMOUS —I mean huge—pale wood and granite tasting bar at Catacula Lake Winery, pacing off with careful steps to see how long this sucker actually is. It's me, Hank, and Rick Keith, son of the owner, Edward Keith. We're the only ones in here, but if there were fifty more people, a dozen cows, and a flock of ducks, it would still feel empty. This place is mammoth.

From the front, the winery is a large, mission-style building with a two-story arched entrance under vaulted thick-wood trellises. Inside, the rooms are mongo-sized. The front room—it's way too big to be an entranceway—is assembly-hall scale, with vaulted ceilings, heavy posts and beams, thick wood furniture, and an old wagon with hay that you hardly notice because the room's so big. Across all the walls is a 245-foot-long color mural showing the history of Chiles Valley.

That all eventually opens into the tasting area, which has that gargantuan, L-shaped tasting bar. The wall behind the bar is all windows—no real frames, just glass—so you feel like you're on the patio, which is also vast and looks out to Catacula Lake.

"My dad likes things big," says Rick. Wouldn't have guessed.

Just how big is what we're trying to figure. Rick is an easygoing guy who looks a bit like what Charlie Brown might have become had he grown up to help run a winery. He's as into it as we are. Rick paces out twenty-five feet to the corner of the L. "That can't be right," he says. "Way too small."

All three of us pace together and count out loud. We get about forty-five approximate feet to the corner and another twenty after the turn. That's sixty-five feet, more than twenty yards, of tasting bar—and I still think we've undercounted—just for us.

"We have some pretty good parties here," Rick says.

"I think you can invite the entire state," I say.

Catacula doesn't exactly fit the more rustic, back valleys of Napa. It's a little modern and it's way big. But it is fun, and they are serious about their wine. Rick is telling us that the late spring rains hit harder here than down below. They came after most of the grapes had already blossomed and set on the floor of Napa Valley, so there was little damage there. But Chiles Valley was still in the pollination period, so some clusters are thin because the pollen got washed away.

"We lost some Zinfandel," he said. "What's left seems to be really good, but we'd love to have more of it."

Chiles Valley runs a couple weeks behind the main of Napa, because the winters and springs are a few degrees colder, and because the summer nights get cooler. That means their growing season is longer and they're vulnerable to bad weather on both ends, but the cooler nights help the grapes keep that nice level of acidity they need to make complex and balanced wines.

"This is one of the first places around here where people started growing grapevines," Rick says.

As that giant mural shows, the region that is Chiles Valley was first settled by the Native American Wappo tribe, then the valley was given to Joseph B. Chiles in 1844 in a Spanish land grant that called the area Rancho Catacula. It would, like almost everything else, eventually get renamed for the white guy who got there first. The 8,000-acre grant's boundaries were drawn to include most of the farmable flatland, and one of the first things farmed there was grapes.

When Edward Keith bought the 1,025-acre ranch that surrounds Catacula Lake in the 1960s, it was then called the Bar 49 Estate, and he ran it as a nonprofit summer camp for boys and girls for two decades. The Keiths closed the ranch for a few years, then could not get the permits to reopen it as a kids' camp. They had been growing grapes since the 1970s, so it was time to try winemaking. The first vintage was 1999 and the oversized-but-cool tasting room opened in 2002.

Rick is telling us the history as we walk through a 15,000-square-foot cave system, with room for 5,000 barrels. "My dad deeded the whole Bar 49 Estate to the Napa Valley Land Trust," he says, "so most of the land is supposed to stay the way it always was."

For all of that, the Keiths are not beyond writing a little history on their own, or technically, concocting it. Back in the tasting expanse, Rick shows us a 2002 Zinfandel and a Rosé under the label Cheyanna. It's an elegant, black-and-white drawing of a long-haired maiden riding a noble-looking horse bareback. Both the horse and the maiden have their manes blowing behind them.

On the back, the label tells a bit of Cheyanna's story. She seems to be a venerable legend. "Passionate and capricious, this Zinfandel exemplifies the essence of Cheyanna," the bottle says. "Celebrate your high spirit with your own Cheyanna."

Inspiring, I say.

"Yeah," Rick says, "we made that up. Looks pretty good, doesn't it?"

WE HEAD NORTH AND CHANGE VALLEYS as the road jogs through the town of Pope Valley—total business district: four buildings. There's a post office in a small hut, a general store that's closed on weekends, a garage that doesn't sell gas, and a historic hotel that's been empty a very long time. The road dumps "Chiles Valley" from its name and becomes just Pope Valley Road. You can see Toni Nichelini-Irwin's beef.

Two miles north of "town" is the Pope Valley Winery, a tragic tale wrapped in a cheery winery. It has more of that historic back-country feel, with the century-old, barn-like winery built over a tiny creek— back in the day, they just opened a hatch and dumped stuff into the water. Up the creek a few yards is an ancient blacksmith shop, circa 1885, and beyond that, a dilapidated, barely standing shack, maybe ten-by-eight feet, that homesteader, winery-founder, and all-around hard-luck guy, Ed Haus, built and lived in for years before he constructed the farmhouse and winery.

We ring a big, old bell hanging from a much-older tree to let them know we're here. I ring it a few extra times because it's fun. How often do you get to ring a bell for a reason? It brings out Bonnie Zimmermann, general manager and do-everything-person, who doesn't mind the extra rings.

"I love that bell," she says and bangs out a round of her own.

Bonnie takes us to the sunny little tasting room that looks like someone put a roof on what was once a chicken coop. "You got it," she tells us. It was also once a tack room. "We cleaned it up."

Nicely. Now it has the feel of a friendly, closed-in porch. Besides the usual wine knickknacks, the room has lots of crafts—pottery, small paintings, knitted figures—on shelves in one corner.

"I let the old ladies in the valley display their stuff," Bonnie says. "If I sell anything, I just put the money in an envelope and mail it to them."

The wines are solid and downright economical—the 2001 Cabernet is $12, the 2000 Zinfandel is $15, both huge bargains, especially considering what we see around Napa. My favorite, as it often is, is a Napa Zinfandel Port. Love that Zinfandel Port.

They've also discounted a few slightly older wines, including a 2001 Chenin Blanc that's going for $25 a case. "I know this has been around too long," Bonnie tells us. "I'm figuring someone will buy it on sheer price. Where are the college kids when you need them?"

We instantly take to Bonnie. She has short hair, talks fast, and has a sense of playfulness about her. Sometimes she conducts blind tastings when the four or five wines she gives tasters to evaluate are all the same wine. Just to see what happens. "It doesn't always go over well," she says.

Bonnie is a former television producer who bailed on Hollywood to find a job, any job, in the wine world. "I did anything I could get my hands on," she says. "When I got here and looked at this valley, I said, 'I'm staying. I'll live a lot longer.'"

As she tells the winery's history, however, it becomes clear that ol' Ed Haus probably never shared those sentiments. Big Ed, as Bonnie sometimes calls him, came to Pope Valley from Switzerland and apprenticed as a blacksmith. He homesteaded the land, built that little shack in 1880, and started the blacksmith shop in 1885.

But Ed was pining for his girlfriend back home, Ida Leimbacher. He wrote her family, asked if they would send her to America, then went down to San Francisco to meet her ship. But the Leimbacher family—according to tradition, Bonnie thinks—had sent Ida's older sister, Bertha. Bertha was as chagrined to be in the backwoods of California with Ed as Ed was to have her here.

"It was grim," Bonnie says. "And, yet, they married anyway. They were miserable."

Their special day was in 1886. As the years passed, they grew to hate each other's guts, Bonnie says. Ed eventually started building the winery and used some huge timbers hauled over from a silver mine, but the caves for the barrels were the hard part. Ed and Bertha dug the caves together. It took them nine years. Nine bleak, aching years. This did not help them bond. Ed and Bertha were rarely seen in public together. The few pictures there are of them, always show the couple with pinched mouths and cheerless eyes.

Still, they opened the winery in 1897, which they called the Burgundy Winery and Olive Factory, and they sent for Ed's two brothers, Henry and Otto. This, too, could have turned out better for Big Ed.

"When they showed up," Bonnie says, "it was kinda hard on Ed. His brother Otto had married Ida."

Somehow, Ed and Bertha had two children, Sam and Lily, but neither ever married. No wonder, Bonnie says, considering the wretched example of married life they grew up with. The kids ran the winery until Lily, the last of them, died in 1959.

"Somebody once asked me if this winery is haunted," Bonnie says. "I told 'em there's actually a pretty good feeling to the place. But we are lucky it didn't have a murder."

Bonnie says the winery was always small but steady, though they shut down—in theory—during Prohibition. Big Ed did what a lot of winery people did back then. He sold barrels of grape juice with the words painted on the side: "Caution: Don't add yeast. Alcoholic beverage will result." It was obvious, but it was legal.

There was one Prohibition venture that may have been a bit less than legal. When son Sam was in the army in 1915, he met a kid from Chicago who knew people. Unfortunately, those people worked for Al Capone.

"Sam came up with the bright idea to sell wine to Capone," Bonnie tells us. "He was getting a good price back then, 75 cents a gallon. But there was a downside."

They shipped wine to Capone for about a year, then Sam got a tip from his friend. People supplying Capone with wine and spirits were disappearing. Capone, apparently, found it cheaper to kill his contractors than to pay them. Sam told Ed maybe they should stop the shipments to Chicago.

"That must have been a fun conversation to have with Ed," Bonnie says.

Bonnie is looking through a book on the Haus family history as she tells the story. She runs across a picture of Sam, who looks squat and sturdy. There's a bird on his shoulder.

"It's a quail," Bonnie says. "Sam had a pet quail and it sat on his shoulder."

A few minutes later, we're in the car and we've passed back through the metropolis of Pope Valley. We're winding up Howell Mountain Road, heading back to the center of Napa Valley. Hank's wondering if Sam Haus trained his quail or if it just sat there naturally. I say, considering the family history, the quail might have been the sanest creature at the place. Hank says the bird probably had commitment issues.

We're driving up the wooded road, thick trees all around, then quick breaks to a view of some vineyards, then more trees, all of it glimmering a little in the rich, dusty light of a summer late afternoon. The traffic is starting to get busier, and we've seen more cars on the drive over the mountain than we did all day on the roads in Chiles and Pope Valleys. Neither of us wants to leave. Our minds are still in those two quiet valleys.

"I like the horse on the RustRidge label," I say. "And they should use more dogs."

"So how big do you think the bar at Catacula really is?" Hank says.

"How come," I say, "we've never been back there before?"

SEVEN

Rutherford

THIS SUMMER IS turning out kinda weird. It's 11 a.m., and we're standing on a small hill above Quintessa's modern, dug-into-the-earth winery, looking out at a view of rolling vineyards, hills, a sweet little pond, ancient oaks, and half of Rutherford. Frankly, I'm freezing.

The fog is still in. Rutherford, like most of Napa Valley, usually gets evening and morning fog. It's one of the qualities of this great Cabernet Sauvignon region—the fog helps the grapes, uh, sleep, I guess it is, and helps them ripen evenly. But this is not just that cooling blanket from the Pacific that tucks the grapes snuggly away, as I read someone overwrite it. This is too cold. This is San Francisco summer cold.

Justin Talley is showing us around. He's a young guy dressed way too nice for a Sunday morning in wine country, wearing a pale gray dress shirt and slacks, and he's explaining the Quintessa magic, which I sort of get because this place is beautiful and I'd probably fully get if I weren't so damn cold.

Quintessa is another of the elite, single-wine wineries. They just make Quintessa, a Cabernet-based blend, the way Opus One just makes Opus One, in the style of a classic Bordeaux château. Quintessa is not quite a trophy wine because you can actually buy a bottle—they make about 10,000 cases—if you can pay the $110 price. No one normal can find real trophy wines, let alone afford them.

Justin allows that, yeah, it's a little cold today, and tells us how this mild August will probably stretch out the growing season another couple weeks. It also means the grapes are developing more evenly through the prime growing days, which makes a better, more balanced wine. The risk is, they'll be picking into October and could run into rain. Rain brings mold. Mold sucks for wine. Makes it taste like mold.

"Picking late is good for another reason," Justin says, mostly to Hank. I'm standing behind Hank, trying to have him block the wind. "Normally, we start at 2 a.m. and quit as soon as it starts to get hot. That way we can control the Brix. The sugar level goes up in the grapes as the day gets hot, and goes back into the vine when it's cool. If we pick a little later in the season, the days stay cool longer."

Quintessa is meticulous about its growing, picking, and winemaking. They use eco-friendly techniques, have a slick, gravity-flow winery, built massive caves, use expensive French oak, and have large crews tending the grapes and the wine. That explains, at least in part, the price tag.

And some of it, surely, is image. If you want to be a top-of-the-line winery, price matters. Too high, of course, and your market slice is tiny. But too low—as idiotic as this sounds—and there's a portion of the wine world that assumes you're making purple soda. The wine world is not always rational.

Justin takes us back to the elegant-but-sturdy tasting room—there's sleek wood, black metal posts, stone walls and floors, and a mix of light from overhead spots and from skylights—and pours us the 2001 and soon-to-be-released 2002 Quintessas. They are very different. For me, the '01 is softer, the '02 riper. I like the '02 a lot. I ask Hank why, considering the same winery, vineyards, and people, the wines come out so differently.

"So many components, so many things go into wine like the weather, the yield, the oak, the toast, the time in barrels, all of that," he says. "A lot of times there is no clear reason why a wine tastes exactly like it tastes. You can work on the balance or the ripeness or making sure there's a lot of complexity, but some of it is the fruit and some is just a mystery.

"It's individual, too. You and I probably taste different things in a wine. Sometimes it's based on what you're looking for. Like, you tend to go for the bigger, riper fruit, and you probably pick that out in wines."

True. I'm a sucker for up-front, instant-gratification wines. I am a guy looking for big reds, which are often the big-point, big-price wines. Turns out, I'm part of the problem.

IF YOU WANT TO SEE VAST variations on a similar theme, there's probably no place like Rutherford. This is not just Cabernet country, this is the land of Rutherford Dust, and of big, powerful Cabs coming from soil that gives them some earth or spice or, I guess, dust. Together, Rutherford and neighboring Oakville have always been the core of Napa Valley. They're the place wine-growing started in Napa, and together they have become one of the best regions on earth for Cabernet Sauvignon, though the French beg to differ. (So might some winemakers running near-micro wineries in the hills rimming Napa, but it's on the flats of Oakville and Rutherford where vineyards can grow world-class Cabernet grapes in any kind of affordable volume.)

Yet the range and style of wineries here is as varied as in any part of the valley. There are powerhouses like Beaulieu, St. Supéry, Franciscan, Grgich Hills, and Rubicon Estate (formerly Niebaum-Coppola); high-end names like Quintessa, Caymus, and Mumm; and places with great-but-medium-priced (for Rutherford) reds like Provenance, Sequoia Grove, Frog's Leap, and Honig. There are three wineries—all extremely different—starting with Rutherford: Grove, Ranch, and Hill. Rutherford Hill is the one with the crowds.

Since it's a Sunday, we're sticking to the Silverado Trail side of Rutherford. The sun is finally out and, once again, I'm warm and happy. And you want to talk contrasts, we're at Conn Creek Winery, just up the road from Quintessa, and here they make, and let us taste, a ton of wines.

We can tell this is a more casual place right off because there's a twenty-five-pound orange cat, named Sebastian, sitting in the doorway of the stucco, Mediterranean-style winery. He doesn't move when we step over him, mostly, I think, because he's a twenty-five-pound cat. There's also a normal-sized orange cat, Simon, running around. I liked Quintessa, but it clearly is not a place that would tolerate tasting room cats.

Conn Creek and its sister winery, Villa Mt. Eden, produce a range of good-to-terrific, and far more humanely priced, wines. Tasha, a medium-blond woman with a British accent, pours seemingly all of them for us. I lose count at twelve, then she takes out the Conn Creek Anthology, a Cab-based blend that's full of plums and cherries and some kind of spice that must be Rutherford Dust. It's their most expensive wine, at $50, which isn't cheap but it isn't $110, or, like some of the mountain-side micro Cabs, $310.

My favorite is a 2001 Villa Mt. Eden Tall Trees Vineyard Cabernet. I love it. It's big and lush, still has some tannins, and has chocolate and bunches of berries in the flavor. It costs $15. I'm sure this is partly me because, as we've established, I am no one to judge value or price, but I think this is groovy wine. Conn Creek advertises that it got eighty-eight points from *Wine Spectator* magazine. I wonder if, blind tasting or not, it would have gotten a higher rating if it had cost more. Not supposed to matter, Hank says, but maybe.

I buy a bottle as we head up the road. Immediately, I wish I had bought a couple more. I can't even judge value when I'm holding it in my hand.

OUR DAY GOES BACK AND FORTH like that. Big, small, pricey, semi-less pricey. We like Rutherford Ranch, a comfortable little tasting room right on the Silverado Trail. Their prices are low—their 2001 Napa Valley Cabernet costs $16—the wines are solid, tasting is free, and the room is empty.

"Marketing," says Bob Hayes, who's pouring for us here, "is just as magic as making wine."

We climb up past the Auberge du Soleil resort, where price is no object, to Rutherford Hill Winery. This spot is teeming with people. There are lots of good reasons for that. They have picnic tables up and down the hillside under 100-year-old olive trees, they have tours of their enormous cave system, and they have a huge, almost scary-looking winery building that's shaped like a massive, rounded house for a fifty-foot dog.

Rutherford Hill also has a range of good-to-terrific wines. The top-of-the-line is their four-star Reserve Merlot that's $92. But it's very crowded. As good as their wines are, as impressive as the building and caves might be, as lovely as the picnic area is, I don't know why everyone is here on a busy Sunday and not down the road at Rutherford Ranch, where, for crissakes, tasting is free. Maybe the wine doesn't cost enough.

WINE AND MONEY SEEM TO HAVE a primal attraction. And that combination, particularly in recent years, has been a force in Napa, just as it is in other wine-growing regions. It's maybe more democratic in America, or, maybe, more nakedly simple. Price means different things in different parts of the wine world. In Bordeaux and other places, old wineries with old reputations—sometimes decades old reputations—can command big prices just on name alone. In Napa, there's usually at least a ballpark connection to quality.

Wine is a luxury item. As much as I might argue otherwise, it is not necessary to sustain life. Or even to live a good life, people tell me. Like most luxury items, it can also be as much about cachet as anything. As the respected wine writer Dan Berger says, no one wears a Rolex because it keeps better time than a Timex. Wine has a status attached like few other food stuffs—you could argue cheese or caviar, but, seriously, how many people are you going to impress with cheese?

And if you're seeking cachet, and can afford it, good wine lets you show off and appear generous all at once. Break out that $300, limited-release Cab, or even that $92 Rutherford Hill Merlot, and you're saying, I'm successful, I'm informed, and, doggone it, I'm swell enough to serve it to friends.

That, of course, is a little unfair, too. There are plenty of genuinely swell people pouring their friends good wine, and some serious wine drinkers who put money aside to spend on great wine because they love great wine. I'm just saying that ego-streak exists. And the thing is, most wine buyers, the enormous, overwhelming majority of wine buyers, even when they're seriously looking for great wine, are often guessing. So they go with price. Location and price. If it's a Rutherford Cab, say, and it costs enough, we assume it's quality stuff.

That's what Chuck Custodio, an assistant winemaker at Piña Cellars, is telling us. He says most people outside of wine country and the wine business—which is most people—don't remember vintages or appellations, and barely remember wineries. So they use simple cues.

"It's human nature," Chuck says. "If you're looking for a good wine, you go to Safeway and look to the top shelf and grab the coolest label with a big price."

That makes pricing a skill and an art, and maybe a game, too. A Rutherford Cabernet like Piña's could command serious money, because it's a Rutherford Cabernet and Piña is a small winery. Small wineries making good Rutherford Cabs are expected to be expensive. The market almost demands it.

"That's a little too much for me," Chuck says. "We just try to make good wine."

They're apparently succeeding, if you go by the high ratings they get. Or by their wine. Piña's owned by four brothers whose family has been in the vineyard management business for generations. They finally started their own winery in 1996. It's in a simple, garage-looking building off Silverado Trail and has a couple pieces of ancient farm equipment out front for decoration. They own six acres on Howell Mountain and thirty acres here, most of it running up the steep hill behind the winery. They're slowly developing the hillside for vines, putting in some landscaping and—because what's a Napa winery without one—building a bocce ball court.

Chuck is pouring for us on a folding table in the barrel room that feels more like a basement, with its cement floor, racks of barrels, and equipment in the corners. "Usually my dog (a German shorthair named Sadie) is knocking things over," Chuck says. "People come here and go, 'We hear you guys have this killer wine and a crazy dog running around.'"

He opens a 2001 Cab for us. It's intense and balanced and, it seems to me, as good a wine as anything I've tasted. It sells for $48. Chuck pours a couple more, including a 2004 from a plastic pitcher. Everything is outstanding. He said there will be 530 cases of that '04, plus—he points to a small stack of boxes—thirty cases of his own label, Trahan. I ask why they don't charge more.

"The brothers didn't want to be the place where you have to get on a list to be on the list," he said. "They're respected in vineyard management, but this wine has their name on it. They want people to be able to drink it."

I want to talk more about this. I also want to stay because Chuck keeps pouring more wine, but we have an appointment down the road. As we leave Silverado Trail and go west on Skellenger Lane, I'm thinking, again, I should have bought a bottle of that Cab. I could still afford that one.

OUR TASTING AT CAYMUS VINEYARDS IS scheduled for 3 p.m. We pull into the small parking lot about two minutes after. The driver of a limo parked next to us under a tree is reading a newspaper as we walk past. He doesn't look up.

"Better hurry," he says. His eyes are still on his paper. "If you're late, they'll turn you away."

It's true, our host, Stan tells us as we sit down at a big wood table in what feels like an old hacienda dining room. A couple more minutes and we would've been outside with the limo driver. But Stan's demeanor is the opposite of what we expected from a big-name, big-price winery that requires you to show up bang on the hour. He is welcoming, reassuring, and confidently casual in the way of a good teacher. Hard to believe ol' Stan would've locked us out.

The punctuality thing, Stan says, is not about status, or exclusivity, or Caymus is so cool it can reject tasters offhand. It's that they want to make the tasting relaxing and to make visitors feel a bit pampered. Since Caymus tastes in small groups, someone barging in halfway through kills the mood.

We're sitting with Stan and six other people. Each of us has three glasses at our place settings. There's almost nervous giggling in the group because we know we're about to get some very good wine for very free. They don't charge here. Hospitality, Stan says. A lost art.

He's also telling us how Caymus, respected for decades as a top Cabernet producer, has decided to focus here in Napa entirely on its Napa Valley Cab and its Special Selection Cabernet Sauvignon. They're still selling a little Sauvignon Blanc and Zinfandel at the winery, which we'll be tasting, and there's a Pinot Noir called Belle Glos that's also made by the Wagner family (Caymus's owners), but it's bottled outside Napa under its own label.

So is Conundrum, a dry, complex white that blends Chardonnay, Muscat, and Sauvignon Blanc, plus a bit of Sémillon, and Viognier. Hank introduced me to Conundrum and I've found, when you order it in restaurants, the waiter or sommelier treat you a little better. Not, of course, that I care about that sort of thing. I'm just relaying research data. (By the way, it's not that Conundrum is pricey—it's $20 to $25 in stores—it's that mostly only wine people know about it. So I'm told. I don't give it a thought.)

Anyway, Stan says we won't be tasting the Conundrum or Belle Glos, since they aren't technically Caymus wines. And we won't be tasting the Special Select Cab. He doesn't say why. My guess is because it costs $136 a bottle and this is free.

The wines we do taste are not slackers. The 2002 Napa Valley Cab—at $70, if you're counting—is ripe and fruity. It's almost sweet, though I think that's really the taste of berries or vanilla, and the finish lasts a while but doesn't give me that big tannin sandblast. Stan says Caymus has changed its style some in recent years, to go a little riper and fruitier right off. That's happened a lot in Napa as both American wine palates and American wine critics have moved toward those more-accessible big reds.

Someone asks how long this Cab should be put away. Couple years, Stan says. Don't overdo it. Or just drink it now (a suggestion I'm trying to follow right here).

"A lot of people who hold onto wine, tend to hold it too long,"

Stan says. "They all start to taste the same. You're going, 'Where's the fruit?'"

That is even more true for the kinds of Cabs and big reds most popular now. They're ripe, and have that big fruit and high alcohol. Hang on too long and the ripeness goes away, the fruit softens, but the alcohol doesn't change. It ends up overpowering the wine.

Another reason lots of people hold wine too long, he says, is they're collecting. There are wine people—a small sub-group of wine shoppers—who buy and trade and hold onto cases of the highest-end wines. They treat them as precious commodities, like gold or gems, not as, well, food. Stan says some wines can age and improve for years, maybe for decades, but a lot of wines can't.

"Some of those old wines can go up in value almost as fast as they go down in quality," Stan says. "If you're asking me, I like the idea of buying wine to drink it."

THE ROUGHLY FOUR-MILE STRETCH OF HIGHWAY 29 that runs through Rutherford is as dense with name—and quality—wineries as any four miles in America. Cakebread, Beaulieu, Sequoia Grove, St. Supéry, Rubicon Estate, Grgich Hills, Provenance, Franciscan, Whitehall Lane. That's a short list. It can get pretty dense with wine tasters, too, so Hank and I have a plan. We're not entirely following it, but it's good plan nonetheless.

Part 1: Stay off Highway 29 in Rutherford on weekends, especially weekend afternoons.

Part 2: When you work this stretch, move in one direction and stay on one side of the road. Put simply, keep turning right. Left turns are just dreams during busy times.

Great advice. We don't take it. It's a Thursday in August, which is almost like a weekend in terms of visitors, but we want to start at Rubicon Estate right in the middle of things.

Rubicon Estate is one of the three or four most-visited wineries in Napa and was Niebaum-Coppola until 2006. It was also once Inglenook. The story is sort of complicated.

Inglenook was the cornerstone Napa winery started by Finnish sea captain Gustave Niebaum in 1879. It struggled after phylloxera and through Prohibition until Niebaum's grandnephew, John Daniel Jr., came in 1934 and took over in 1937. He turned it into one of the two high-class wineries—along with Beaulieu Vineyards—in Napa at the time. Inglenook's 1941 Cabernet Sauvignon is still sometimes called the best wine ever produced in Napa Valley, maybe the best wine of the twentieth century, though, seriously, how you would compare is beyond me. The point stands, though, that Daniel made some rip-roaring wine.

He sold the winery and the Inglenook name in 1964. It was sold again five years later to Heublein Inc. To make a long, tragic story short—but still tragic—Heublein turned Inglenook into jug wine in the 1970s.

Film director Francis Ford Coppola bought the old Niebaum Victorian home and 110 acres of the vineyards in 1975, then acquired the actual winery and the rest of the estate and vineyards in 1995 and called it Niebaum-Coppola. But after he bought Chateau Souverain in Sonoma and renamed it Francis Coppola Estate, he wanted to avoid confusion. So this winery got named after its signature wine, Rubicon.

Depending on your point of view, Coppola either rescued a piece of Napa history, or he turned it into a tourist attraction. Me, I like the notion he rescued it. True, Rubicon Estate now has something of a Hollywood feel. It's showier, fancier, bigger than reality, a bit like those ersatz city streets at theme parks. There are real stores and restaurants, and real people walking around buying things and eating dinner, but it's not like actual, you know, life. In a lot of ways, it's more fun than real life, and certainly more splashy, but it's not exactly authentic. Same story here.

In this case, I say, so what? Good for Coppola. As much as Hank and I love the small, surprising tasting rooms, the simple, elegant wineries, and the faithfully historic spots, there's nothing wrong with a winery owner putting on a show. Napa does not have to be one thing, have one tone. If a movie director sinks his money into restoring one of the grand wineries of Napa, he can name it what he wants and do it in the style he chooses. Coppola chose the style of a movie director. There's a certain authenticity to that.

We drive up to Rubicon Estate through a long, elegant line of trees, then walk across a park-like collection of grass, trees, lampposts, and fountains. The enormous winery building itself is stately and covered with well-tended ivy. You can imagine some old wagons, probably pulled by Clydesdales, sitting in front. The whole look is thoroughly beautiful.

Inside is where you hit the intersection of Hollywood and Wine. There's stained glass and an elegant wooden staircase—it looks Niebaum, it's built by Coppola—that goes upstairs to a collection of movie memorabilia. There's an original 1948 Tucker car, costumes from *Bram Stoker's Dracula*, a desk from *The Godfather*, a collection of movie awards including Coppola's Oscars. Real Oscars. Not something you see every day in wine country. There's also an old desk belonging to Captain Niebaum with a history of his life.

Downstairs, the two big tasting rooms are as much wine-and-food department stores as they are tasting bars, and they're lively enough. Coppola named a sparkling wine after his daughter, Sofia, and has a line of Director's Reserves, in case anyone forgets where they are. Tour guides wear vaguely seafaring-looking outfits, a nod to Niebaum's sailing days before he landed in Napa.

Whatever else happened here, Coppola did not forget the history he bought, and that's the special part. Away from the tasting departments, along a walk through the old winery, there are small, cellar-like rooms behind gates. They house collections of old Inglenook wines. One is the Daniel Cellar, with wines from vintages 1935 to 1964, when John Daniel made the wine. There are some '41s in there, including three bottles Roman Coppola, Francis's son, bought at a Los Angeles auction in 2004. He paid $24,675—per bottle—for the first two, and $27,025 for the third. That last price seems a wee high. There's also the Niebaum Collection room, vintages from Gustave, circa 1882 to 1908. Now we're talking serious aging.

WE TURN RIGHT OUT OF RUBICON Estate, but, against our own advice, make a left across Highway 29 to start—finally—our one-direction, right-turn-only swing through Rutherford.

At Sequoia Grove, we are about as far across the style-scale from Rubicon Estate as we can get, which includes Dusty, the old black dog lying in the doorway who just looks at us when we step over her. She later works up the energy to come into the airy, rustic tasting room and get petted, but her enthusiasm level would never make the grade at Rubicon.

As friendly as everyone is here, including Dusty, I'm thinking they're stretching things a bit when they call the redwood trees around the refurbished 135-year-old farmhouse a "grove." More like a bunch. Maybe a gathering. I counted seven trees. Seven is not a legitimate grove.

The wines, on the other hand, are very legit. National class, Hank tells me. He says Sequoia Grove is one of those wineries—of which Napa has a few, I'm learning—that has a sterling name and a great reputation among wine people, particularly people not looking for status or flash. I can see why. All the wines are exceptional. My favorite so far is the 2002 Napa Valley Syrah. It's dark reddish and feels almost plush. There's something in the finish I can't describe but Hank says he gets black tea.

Jesse Petrick, a mid-twenties guy working the tasting room, shows us a bottle of 2001 Reserve Cabernet Sauvignon with medals draped all over it. "Feel free to peruse," he says deadpan. We'd rather taste.

Wow. I get that right-there, huge-but-soft fruit thing I like and, I think, chocolate and spice. Or maybe it's vanilla and spice. Something and spice. It's smooth and still big, and this wine has itself a finish. Hank likes it, too.

"I'd put that up against any wine we've tasted," he says. "It doesn't have the power of Opus One, but it's big, it's balanced, and it's interesting."

And it's only $55, which isn't remotely cheap, but in relative terms, it's a two-for-one deal compared with the $110 Quintessa. I ask how they arrived at $55. Vicki Reza, who's also working the tasting room, says it's a price that covers them and they think works.

"We make 40,000 cases and it all goes pretty quickly," she said. "You don't have to be crazy big to do well in this business. Honestly, I don't know how some wines get priced like they do. Some wineries could easily get more, and some charge big prices partly to get publicity or a big name, I guess. We like our size and our reputation now."

REPUTATION IS A FUNNY THING. AN important thing in the wine world. And at Peju Province, we run into a reputation for funny. Peju makes some good wines, and is one of the most distinct-looking wineries in the valley, with a bit of a wonderland touch to the flowers, fountains, and sculpture garden out front.

The winery and tasting room mimic French Provincial style, in big part because owner Tony Peju grew up in Aix-en-Provence. His winery includes a pointed, fifty-foot tower with a green-copper roof that looks like a place you'd keep a fairy-tale princess. A French Provincial fairy-tale princess. We taste in a tall room inside the tower. One wall is mostly stained-glass window with a scene of three wine muses, and the room has two tasting bars, a stairway up the side of the tower, and it's got Alan Arnople, the Yodel Meister. That's what his card says. Yodel Meister.

Alan is slim with thinning blondish-gray hair. He's a longtime Napa musician, and has been working at Peju more than a decade. Alan is also a piece of work.

We've got a group of about ten people standing at his tasting bar—those huge stained-glass wine muses looking over our shoulders—and Alan starts simply enough. He pours a round of 2003 Sauvignon Blanc, says we might pick out some grapefruit flavors, and that it goes well with shellfish. He waits while we taste. Then he yodels. Or maybe it's shrieks. He does something that makes a pitchy, wavering sound, which must be a yodel cause that's what it says on his card. We're all a little stunned. Alan keeps moving. The 2003 Provence, a red blend, is next.

"This wine is so unique," Alan says, "the term 'totally radical, dude' applies." He explains it more in surf-dude talk. "It's like, sooo a blend. It's got, like, Merlot, Cab Franc, and Syrah, and dude, there're whites in there. Like Sauvignon Blanc. Radical."

We go to a 2001 Napa Valley Syrah. Alan starts making noises with his lips. Kind of sucking and spitting to a beat. Alan is starting to Rap. A foursome from Los Angeles is swaying with his rhythms. I think he's describing the wine, but honestly, I'm lost.

The 2002 Napa Valley Zin gets more rap, though, if you want to get technical, I think it's closer to hip-hop. He says something about a Zinfandel being a Croatian grape. Or crushin' great. Something, anyway. A tall, blond woman to my right is not down with Alan. She's wrapped herself in her arms and is more rolling her eyes than the wine across her tongue. The rest of the crowd loves him.

In a Caribbean-like sing-song, Alan says, "We have one more wine that proceeds the buying frenzy," then stops and does his Arnold Schwarzenegger/Hans-and-Franz imitation, "I want to stock you up." The woman next to me can't wait to leave. Most people laugh. I can't remember what the wines taste like.

There is, indeed, a buying frenzy. Some people also buy a CD from Alan's band, California Zepher. As we walk out, Hank says, "Great show. Maybe we should go back and taste the wine sometime."

THE RUTHERFORD GRILL IS A CLASSIC Napa Valley spot. It's on the corner of Highway 29 and Rutherford Crossroad. I've never driven by without seeing people hanging out all over the place, looking like they're having, really, more fun than me. We need to be a part of it for an evening. It's got good food, a nice-but-casual air, and—this part is huge—no corkage fee.

We're staying around the corner at Rancho Caymus, a snug, little two-floor hotel that combines a Western laid-back air with a European inn–feeling courtyard full of flowers and fountains. We walk to the Rutherford Grill and the outside terrace has, as always, all those people having fun. Inside, the tables are busy, but we're heading for the bar. The restaurant has big booths, tall ceilings, and lots of light. Huge ovens in the back fill the place with the whiff of mesquite smoke. There's the amiable feel of a room you could walk around and visit people at other tables.

But the bar is the spot. It's like Bounty Hunter in Napa town, or the bars at places like Martini House in St. Helena, the Calistoga Inn, and, from what everyone says, Bistro Don Giovanni, where locals hang out and mix easily with travelers. The air is lively, a bit wine-oriented, and people feel like friends at a party, not pickups or angry drunks, though I'm sure this place has seen its share of angry drunken pickups.

Rutherford Grill's bar, shaped like a speedway oval, is in the middle of the restaurant and lit brightly with warm overheads. We find spots down on Turn Two. Hank has a bottle of the just-released 2004 Provenance Rutherford Sauvignon Blanc we got today. He puts it on the bar, but I feel kinda cloddish about that because I think we're supposed to buy drinks as the excuse for eating there.

The bartender, a guy named Barry Cothran, sees the bottle and wanders over.

"Great wine, huh," he says. "I just bought a case of it. That got released, like, last week. You want me to open it?"

I ask if it's impolitic to bring our own to the bar.

"Look around," he says.

Three guys on our left in jeans, dark T-shirts and worn Caymus hats are drinking a bottle of that Belle Glos Pinot Noir we can't get. Clearly, Caymus guys. To our right, two men in slacks and linen short-sleeve shirts have a bottle of BV's Cab-Syrah blend called Dulcet. Across the bar, two twentyish women in professional clothes are sharing the Miner Family Natural Yeast Chardonnay, probably my favorite Chard of all the great Chards we've tasted. These people know how to drink wine.

"We don't carry any of those," Barry said. "Good wines, though."

I'm feeling good that our humble Sauv Blanc holds up in the illustrious bring-your-own company around us. We order—Hank gets the grilled salmon, I have the roasted chicken because the mesquite wood smoke has me ready to kill for anything from that grill—and Barry wanders back to chat. He has settled into his rhythm, a night guy, a restaurant guy as full of energy as his bar.

Barry's the wine buyer and bar manager here. He asks if we're local. We say, these days, almost. We tell him about our Quest.

"Cool," he says. Cool. That's the Napa response. Not, why? Or, what the hell is wrong with you boys? Cool. Because, basically, who wouldn't go to every tasting room if they could?

"So, where have you liked?" Barry asks. OK, that's everyone's question. Kind of everywhere, we say. We tell him about some of the happy Rutherford surprises for us, Piña, Rutherford Grove, and Sawyer, for instance—I particularly liked Sawyer's six-foot stuffed bear. He was wearing a waiter's apron and holding a tray of wine and glasses. I'm a sucker for ironic cuteness. We tell him we always like Cakebread, St. Supéry, and, especially, Provenance. We don't mention the Yodel Meister. Our jury is still out on him.

By now, the guys drinking BV's Dulcet have left. A woman named Rosie is sitting there. She's about our age with long blond hair. She orders a martini.

"I've been drinking wine all day," she tells us, almost apologetically. Rosie worked in the valley for years, moved to Santa Barbara, and is back catching up for a few days. "I'll have a glass with dinner," she promises.

A couple comes up behinds us. We've been seeing them all day. They're Andres and Tasha Delgado and they manage a restaurant in Rancho Mirage near Palm Springs. They're on a sort of busman's holiday, trying wines and chilling in the valley.

"If you're stalking us," I tell them, "we can have Barry here toss you guys."

Barry meanders back and eventually asks how they're liking their visit.

Great, beautiful, relaxing. All the Napa descriptions. We all talk about what we've tasted and liked, and all come back around to Provenance, and not just because their tasting room floor is made from the barrel heads of their first vintage—a 1999 Cab. They make a bunch of rich, interesting Merlots and Cabs. I say their Sauvignon Blanc isn't bad, either, since we've been drinking it with dinner, and everyone nods. But we get right back to their reds.

Barry's the one who notices and gives me a shrug. I ask how come no one talks about great whites?

"Funny, huh," he says. "I sell a lot of whites, probably more whites by the glass than reds. But reds, man, big, hunky Cabs, those are the wines that get attention. They get the scores and the big bucks. That's how you get a reputation, make a great, monster red."

After Robert Mondavi, Sutter Home White Zinfandel, and the national Chardonnay infatuation, the next big step in Napa's, and America's, modern wine progression came all at once, in a single, sudden evolutionary leap. It was a fall night in 1991—November 17, to be exact, because they remember in Napa and around the wine world. The venerable TV newsmagazine, *60 Minutes,* aired a report by Morley Safer that said, in essence, drinking red wine can help you live longer. Drink wine. Be healthy. No downside there.

Safer called it the French Paradox. The French smoke, barely exercise, and mostly eat like crap. They might as well take butter injections. But they have a lower incidence of heart disease than we diet-obsessed, treadmill-hugging Americans. The French live relatively healthy lives, Safer said, and not just because they're too mean to get sick.

Turns out, some of it's the wine. Studies show that moderate consumption of red wine does all kinds of healthy things. Some come from the flavonoids—which function as antioxidants—that are found in the seeds and skins of grapes, and some might come from the alcohol itself. Researchers found red wine cuts the stickiness of blood platelets, cells that sometimes get it in their little cell heads to cling to fat deposits and start blood clots. It can increase HDLs, the good cholesterol that removes fat from the walls of blood vessels like little scrubbing bubbles. And it might even fight cancer by slowing the growth of tumors.

How good was this? More wine. Fewer heart attacks. Maybe fight cancer. You could hear corks popping across the country. In the month after the *60 Minutes* story, red wine sales blasted up with nearly a fifty percent increase over 1990, a jump of about 2.6 million bottles. The French Paradox story grew and spread, and the myths around it grew, too—the French, it turns out, eat fairly healthy food besides the butter and probably get more fruits and veggies than we do—but research confirmed the fundamental truths. Red wine drinking went nuts.

"I had guys coming in like they had script from their doctors," Hank says. "They were going, 'My doctor says I need to drink more wine.' I think a lot of those guys missed the second point about moderation."

Wine and moderation have never been comfortable together. Why start now? The French Paradox fever came just as many Americans were beginning to explore more reds, anyway. For Napa, like in most wine regions, there was an immediate and consistent spike in red wine sales over the next few years. The first wave jacked up Merlot.

Despite the scorn from the film *Sideways,* Merlot can be a powerful, opulent wine, but it can also be smoothed out—dumbed down, the *Sideways* guys would say—to make it fruity, almost sweet, and very easy to drink, though that leaves the wine with the depth and character of your average politician.

Mass producers were pumping out smooth, simple Merlots in the early 1990s. Napa had to follow or lose a huge chunk of the market. This was when people ordering a glass of red at the bar really meant Merlot, the way ordering white meant Chardonnay. American wineries everywhere adjusted. No matter how sophisticated their top-end wines, and no matter what kind of complex, Bordeaux-like Merlot they produced, most wineries also pumped out easy little Merlots and pumped in easy big bucks.

But wine tastes progress, even without TV. Many American wine drinkers began to want something more. They wanted better Merlot, different reds, wines that left an impression. Wines with heft. And the timing was right. This was the mid-1990s, there was an economic boom. Lots of wine drinkers could afford wines with heft. The demand for better and better wine, for bigger, deeper—but still approachable—reds mushroomed. And there is no finer place in America, maybe in the world, for big, lush, drinkable red wine than Napa Valley.

There was one more force giving energy to this big red shift in American wine. His name is Robert M. Parker Jr. He is, by all accounts, still the most influential man in the wine world. Not always the most popular, at least not in some circles—particularly in Europe—but there's no doubting the impact of the man who taught millions about fine wine, and who even changed the way many wineries make wine.

Parker was a lawyer with a wine Jones until 1978. That's when he started what he still considers a consumer advocate newsletter called the *Wine Advocate.* Parker made himself a champion of the wine shopper, and generally tried to stay as incorruptible as a self-described hedonist could be. He built a reputation as a man playing it straight.

Parker also seems to be blessed with a superhuman sense of smell, a discerning palate, and a spectacular memory. He has a Midwestern work ethic, solidly American tastes in wine—Parker wines are ripe, concentrated, in your face—and an equally American disregard for tradition. He was the perfect critic for the emerging New World wine devotion.

Parker's reputation for consistency, thoroughness, and a democratic approach was also New World. Either the wine was good or it wasn't. Didn't matter who made it. Little Napa guys got the same treatment as big French guys, though some French complain little Napa guys got better treatment. And yet, Parker's first coup was predicting the quality of France's 1982 Bordeaux before anyone else—even as some critics disagreed—and making that a record-selling vintage, in the U.S. and in France.

All of that matters a lot. All of that distinguishes Parker. But most of all, what made him a critic for his time, what made him The Man for American consumers and a massive force in wine, was his point scale. Parker knows the wine language. He writes with clarity and power. But for most wine drinkers, for the extreme majority who can barely tell their tannins from a tennis ball, descriptions are just vague, ethereal ideas. Most Americans have one simple question: Buy the wine or not? Parker answered them. He gave them something definite. He gave them numbers. Hard, solid, easily assessible numbers.

Parker's scale starts at fifty—trust me here, no one wants a fifty; a good Listerine would go better with roasted chicken than a fifty—and runs to 100. Middle-to-high eighties are very good, low nineties are outstanding, high nineties extraordinary. More to the point, Parker measured and quantified something that has mystified mid-pack, everyday wine drinkers forever. He calculated quality. Put it on a one-to-one scale, with grade-school simplicity. No more dark cherries vs. ripe cherries vs. Bing cherries. No more frickin' cherries. It's ninety vs. eighty-five. Can it be more clear?

The wine world jumped on that train. Everyone needs guidance, particularly the vast middle of the market, where people take long stares at wine lists and store shelves, then just guess. Wine is such a mystery, even to its fans. Maybe you know a winery, but what about the varietal, the appellation, the vineyard, the vintage? Or was that even the right winery? You went wine tasting, the guy was great. What the hell were you drinking? Upper-end buyers know more, but they still get lost. There are so many styles, so many influences, so much goddamn wine. But when Parker gives it a ninety-five, that means buy.

There's a well-told, everyone-swears-it's-true story about a guy in a California wine shop who bought a case of wine, drank one bottle, and returned the rest the next day. He didn't much like it. He came back in a week or two and bought another case of the same wine. Why? "Parker gave it a ninety-five," the guy told the owner.

Point scales are everywhere now. After Parker, the *Wine Spectator* magazine—the other huge voice with wine consumers—went with fifty-to-100 in the mid-1980s. Everyone followed: competitions, newsletters, websites, and blogs. There are so many ratings now, wine aisles can look like a math department.

People in Napa say Robert Parker is much more than just a numbers guy. They say he considers himself a dogged consumer advocate, and is a nice man, a wine lover, and above all, someone who wants the world to be full of great wine. But his enduring impact is that point scale—and the kinds of wines that do well on it. By the mid-1990s, whether they knew it or not, many, many American wine drinkers were under the influence of Parker, because they weren't the only ones looking for big numbers. Wineries were, too.

A big score from Parker or the *Wine Spectator* is worth big bucks to vintners. Hank sees people walking down his aisles with lists of ratings. Jo Ann Truchard told us about their fax machine spitting out orders before she knew anything. She just assumed they'd scored well somewhere and she was right.

Lots of wineries, even in France, changed their style in recent years, made their wines more ripe, more intense, more Parker-like, to get big scores. But in Napa, it didn't take much doing. Those wines come so naturally here with the valley's soil, mild winters, and bright, Northern California sunshine. Napa always made Parker wines. Napa always made other, more subtle, less up-front wines, too, but it was easy for vintners here to catch a big piece of that new, emerging, ratings-oriented market.

That market was growing for another reason: People had money to spend on luxuries like wine. In the mid-1990s, the economy was strong throughout the country. Even bigger for Napa was the high-tech boom and the dot-com gold rush centered in Northern California.

Some of those suddenly flush dot-comers were determined to drink great wine—because, mostly, they could—but they only had vague ideas about what that would be. But Robert Parker knew. So did the *Wine Spectator*. And the wines getting big scores were the kinds of wines that beginning connoisseurs tend to like, too: powerful, intense, subtlety-be-damned wines.

So here's what was happening. Top-end wines, mostly those mammoth reds, were soaring in price because there were people paying those prices. And some tiny wineries, many of them with hillside vineyards producing concentrated fruit but in small amounts, were getting big scores and big attention. The *Wine Spectator* called them "cult wines." Most of these places—like Colgin, Bryant Family, Harlan Estate, Araujo, Dalla Valle, Screaming Eagle—produced only a few hundred or maybe a few thousand cases. Great ratings, impossible to get, that's the definition of expensive. Prices jumped even more on the cult wines. And if you made Opus One or Caymus or Joseph Phelps Insignia, and you thought your wine was just as good, you hiked your price, too, or you'd look lesser.

Wine prices are like gas, they expand to fill their container. When the price of top wines blasted off, there was room for all the tiers to follow them up, though not quite as steeply. The only silver lining for consumers, if there was one, showed up in the everyday wines. The market had space for lines like BV Coastal, Robert Mondavi Private Selection, or Beringer Founder's Estate—$8 to $12 wines with a consistency and name recognition that made mid-market consumers feel comfortable paying more for everyday wine.

By the new century, the dot-com money had dried up, the economy slowed, and post-9/11 spending on luxuries was thinner. But America had developed a taste for better wine, for those big reds and more complex blends, and there was no going back.

"The downside to all that booming is that wine's pretty expensive," Hank says to our little group. "Most of what I sell is in the $8 to $15 range, and people really look at price and at the markdown."

Don't I know it. Half the time, that's how I buy. I go to the store figuring I'm going to spend, say $15. Then I look for the wine marked down the most to get to $15.

"On a good day, I'm spending $15 but getting a $22 wine," I say. "It's got to be way better than just a regular $15 Cab."

"Unless Parker hates it," Hank says.

"You know," Barry says, "one thing about Parker and those ratings is they got everybody—even the French—trying to make the same kind of wine to get the scores. You worry that eventually, things won't be that interesting. There'll be just one style."

We hit a pause after that. Almost a moment of silence in loving memory of diversity in winemaking.

"But not just yet," Barry says. He reaches under the bar and comes up with a Rosé, then pours us a freebie.

"I always have one Rosé off the list," he says. It's something I've never heard of, a Rosé from Caymus called Pinot Noir Blanc. It's light but full of those Pinot fragrances and flavors. It's wonderful. I ask again why no one really brags about wines like this.

"For every winery," Barry says, "whether you're Mondavi or BV or someone making 5,000 cases and selling out of your tasting room, what makes you stand out is your high-end stuff. You get the press and you get the scores. Everything flows down from that. If your best Cab scores in the nineties, people assume everything you make must be pretty decent."

After the Rosé, we wander out. Barry is off chatting up a group at the far end of the bar. Andres and Tasha head for their hotel. Hank and I walk down the road in the cooling night air. We can smell the fog crawling up the valley. I'm thinking about how many good evenings we have at Napa restaurants and bars, talking wine, making momentary friends, maybe learning a little or tasting something radical. This was a typical night. A good night.

"I think," I tell Hank, "I'd rate tonight a ninety-five. Maybe a ninety-six. I'd do it anytime."

THIS MORNING IS WARMER. THE FOG'S gone early and all that's left is a moist haze that softens the light. The lush greens of the vines blend with the darker green trees and the browning mountains around the valley. The sun is just warm enough, we can smell the vineyards and dirt, and the day is feeling like summer in Eden.

We are visiting some old friends today, still thinking about the night at Rutherford Grill's bar. We go next door to Beaulieu Vineyards and its redone, octagonal tasting room, then make a right turn—notice: a right—and head up Highway 29 to Franciscan and its big, square, high-ceilinged room. These are two wineries that have always been good to us, and particularly Hank, not just with their wines, but with hospitality over the years. Franciscan has an outstanding Bordeaux blend called Magnificat that's priced at $40. BV's Georges de Latour Private Reserve Cabernet—the first "reserve" wine in Napa, by the way—is one of the longest-lived, most-respected and most-collected wines in America. It sells for $80.

Both often get scores in the nineties and have shown they're consistently special. Why, then, the relative bargain prices? Hank has no answer. We aren't the only ones confused. Let me quote a guy who ought to know. "One might wonder why Franciscan's Napa Valley Cabernet (price: $25) sells for a fraction of Opus One when their vineyards are only separated by a road," wrote Robert Parker. See, he doesn't get pricing, either.

At Honig Vineyard and Winery, a midsized, family-run winery, owner Michael Honig is telling us the same thing, that in Napa, and particularly for a winery in the heart of Rutherford, image and price meld together into a high-stakes, unfathomable puzzle.

"Nobody wants to be perceived as being cheaper," he says. "We all want to make a reserve-style wine. You sort of need to show that you can play at the $70 price point.

"But we all walk a line. You can't be greedy. The market is a pyramid. As you go up in price, you get less and less real estate. And you want financial momentum. If you start backing up (in price) people smell blood. Truthfully, though, some of it is, 'If my neighbor charges $50, and my wine is better, I'll charge $60.'"

Honig's 2001 Stagecoach Vineyard Cabernet goes for $65. Their 2002 Napa Valley Cab sells for $33. I like them both. The Stagecoach has this mouth-filling chocolate thing going on that makes the price seem pretty good from what I've seen.

"In the context of the world, we are expensive," Michael says, "In the context of Napa, we're a bargain."

Michael Honig is slim, with slightly sharp features and dark brown hair. He wears jeans, work boots, and a gray V-neck T-shirt. He's in his mid-forties and took over the winery in 1984 when he was twenty-two. His grandfather, Louis, bought the sixty-eight-acre ranch in Rutherford in the 1960s and, until he died, kept it mostly as a farm, vineyards, and a country-gathering spot for the family.

Now, it's the winery itself that's become a gathering point for the family. Michael and his ex-wife, Elaine, manage the place and other family members have gotten sucked in, including Michael's brother, Stephen, who's a friend of Hank's and one reason we're here talking to the winery owner.

Michael, though, would talk to anybody. Jose Rodriguez, the cellarmaster, walks past covered with grease. "What have you been doing?" Michael asks.

"Working on a pump," Jose says.

"Isn't some of the grease supposed to stay on the pump?" Michael says.

Jose and his brother, Alberto, were kids with grade school educations when their parents worked at Honig. Michael and his family hired teachers for them and, as they've grown up, promoted them through the winery company. Alberto is training to be an assistant winemaker.

"We all think of this place as the legacy of our family. I'm just trying to be a caretaker. We want everyone who works here to feel like they're part of that, part of the family," Michael says. Then he gets a cheeky grin. "I tell my family they have to work hard."

We're sitting at a table outside Honig's recently opened tasting room. The vineyards are a few feet away and the day is spectacularly pleasant: sunny, light breeze, mid-eighties. An August day that's close to heaven, unless you own a winery. This summer, this temperate, inviting, gentle summer, is becoming a little nerve-racking for wine people.

Cabernet grapes need a decent number of solidly warm-to-hot sunny days—eighty-five to ninety degree temps are perfect—to reach the sugar levels that winemakers and growers like Michael want. Maybe as many as 100 days like that. But July and August have been cool, though not disastrously miserable, but rarely hot, so this has been a season of slower growth.

There are pluses and minuses to that. More time on the vines—

hang time, they call it—usually translates to more flavors, more characteristics of the varietal, simply because the grapes get time to mature. But the cooler temps can also mean lower sugar levels—the Brix—because the vines and grapes need sunlight and decent heat to produce the sugar.

There are also a couple of risks involved. The longer growing season brings more risk of rain, which can devastate a crop with mold. Or it could end up that Honig and others will leave money lying on the ground.

If the grapes are growing slowly, vineyard managers often drop fruit—they cut off some bunches and let the vines concentrate on the grapes that are left. Someone told us to think about it as if each vine has 100 units of flavor to dish out. If there are 100 grapes hanging there, each grape gets one unit. If there are fifty grapes, they get two.

That's not the technical explanation, but it's more or less the operating principle for the vineyard guys at Honig.

"When it's cooler than usual, you drop as much crop as you can, so what's left gets the flavor profile you want," Michael says. "If it gets hot and the sugars spike, you've left more grapes on the ground than you'd want to. But if you leave more to set, you either need it to get hot, or you have to hold on until October and risk rain and mold."

Hotter than usual has its own set of problems. Too much heat dries out the grapes or it slows their development, too.

"They're kind of like humans," Michael says, "too cold and they shut down, too hot and they shut down."

Honig crews also opened up the canopy of vines, to give the grapes a little more direct sunlight, but only morning sun so the little buggers don't burn or shut down or, who knows, just turn around and flip off the entire Honig clan.

This conversation is another reminder for us that farming is never easy, and that growing wine grapes is farming at the graduate level. Michael is saying he's pretty confident the quality will be good, possibly outstanding, this year, though the quantity may be down.

Scarcity and quality, I say. Sounds like a formula for a price hike.

He laughs at me. "We don't want to put the product on a pedestal," he says. "We're just nice people trying to have fun and sell wine."

Pause.

"Of course, it's a lot easier to sell when it's good wine."

EIGHT

St. Helena

BUSY KITCHEN.

Ten women with wineglasses bunch around the small, white center island. Some sit, some lean, some stand. All talk happily and sip wine. Off to one side, three couples hold glasses and wait for lunch. Behind them, by the door, five more people just walked in. Hank and I are flattened against one counter, trying to stay the hell out of the way.

Technically, this is not a kitchen anymore. It's now the ordinarily peaceful, converted tasting room for Arger-Martucci Vineyards, all windows, bright colors, tall ceilings, sunlight, and—at the moment— all people. What we've got this Saturday is a rush.

In the middle of the upheaval, dashing, talking, juggling wine and glasses and food, putting on one stellar display of hustle, is Katarena Arger. She's the winery manager, the director of sales and marketing, and the tasting room boss. Clearly, Katarena can multi-task.

She rings up a sale, stuffs crystal wine glasses into a dishwasher, cuts up rosemary bread, pours dipping oil, scavenges high up on shelves for clean glasses, rushes into a back room for more tasting notes. She's says "hi," pours us a rich, melon-y 2004 Viognier, promises to be back, laughs at a joke, wraps a couple bottles for travel, greets the people at the door, and tells the lunch group she'll get them seated outside by the pool really, really soon.

Hank and I watch in awe.

"Wow," I say.

"Notice," Hank says, "she hasn't spilled a drop of wine."

"Talent," I say.

"It's something you're born with," Hank says.

The phone rings. Katarena gets it and listens for maybe four seconds. "I love you, too," she says and hangs up. The room almost stops. We all look at her. "My boyfriend," she says. "He works at Del Dotto. He knew I'd be busy today." Most everyone goes, "aaaaawww." Hank and I try to look appropriately, but still masculinely, impressed.

Katarena might be crazed at the moment, but she is not unhappy. These ten women buy a ton of wine, nearly three cases among them, and they have fun. They're saying on their way out that they love this place, love the wine, love Katarena. When we see them later that day at another room, they're talking about Katarena and Arger-Martucci.

That is Word-of-Mouth 101. It's huge for a small winery in Napa, really, for all the wineries, but especially important if you're not one of the big boys. The valley gets more than five million visitors a year, but the vast majority knows only a few names, maybe a dozen wineries or so. Get a handful of people talking about you, get them spreading the word about your wines and your affable Napa hospitality, and that'll bring you a tiny percentage more of the Napa tourist traffic—which translates to a colossal leap in winery business and wine sales. For a place like Arger-Martucci, which makes 5,000 cases of wine and sees fifteen or twenty people in the tasting room on many days, one daily group like those ten happy women can make a serious difference.

After Katarena seats the lunch people under an arbor outside, she comes back and explains the chaos.

"We're not usually like this," she says, as if we thought a human could survive that regularly.

Katarena's mid-twentyish, tall and thin with long, dark hair and deep, dark eyes. Even running around crazy, there's a calmness about her. She says the women who just left are on a limo tour with one of the drivers who repeatedly bring clients to Arger-Martucci for the wine, the taste of something smaller, and, we're guessing, for Katarena's energy.

The people eating merrily outside bought a tasting-and-lunch package at a charity auction, something Arger-Martucci offers a lot. Katarena made the lunch last night at her house. It's easier to cook here, but she doesn't want the smells messing with the tasting room wines. (Lunch included a fresh mozzarella-basil-tomato salad, couscous with more fresh squash and tomato—most veggies are from her garden—and a shrimp and corn salad dish. "I put the corn on a barbecue grill to give it a roasted flavor," she tells us.)

Arger-Martucci's wines are very good, solid top to bottom, and occasionally quirky. Katarena lets us taste a Wild Yeast Pinot Noir Rosé that sparkles with cherry and strawberry. She says they only recently started charging for tastings because giving people a good experience was worth way more when they were starting.

"Everyone knows Beringer or Sutter Home," she says. "They'll go there just on their names. We don't get many people who just walk in here on their own. Almost always, someone else told them to come here because they liked us."

That's why the limo tours are so important to a small winery. They're like an outside sales force. And it's reciprocal. Drivers love to take clients off the beaten path and make them feel like Napa insiders.

I say we've heard some griping about the limo tours, and we've seen a few tipsy groups pile out and overwhelm small tasting rooms.

"It's like watching a plague in action," I say.

"They eat everything down to roots," Hank says.

Funny, she says.

"I'm glad to get a call from a driver who wants to bring a group here," Katarena says. "I know it's a pain for some wineries if a big bunch just shows up, but a lot of drivers call ahead, and it's really good for us."

There's a more direct effect beyond just name recognition, too. Tasting room sales are the simplest, and most-profitable for wineries. By a lot. There are no distribution costs, no packaging costs, no trying to keep distributors supplied. It's pure profit.

"We sell about seventy percent of our wine out of the tasting room," Katarena says. "We'd love to sell more, but not all. We want some of our wine in stores and going to restaurants, because we want people to know about us."

As we talk, Katarena pours us the 2002 Dulcinea, a dessert wine that's a blend of Sauvignon Blanc and Sémillon and has some bright acid, so it finishes sweet and crisp. One man from that group of five wants to buy the Dulcinea, and six new tasters have settled in, eagerly holding out glasses. Katarena's handling them all, and spooning the smoky-corn-shrimp dish onto plates when the phone rings.

"Uh-huh, sure." she says. "Yup, sure, five minutes. See ya."

Katarena gives a single clap and looks at us. "Great," she says, deadpan. "There are thirteen more on their way."

IF THERE IS ANY PLACE THAT is ground zero for the boom in the popularity of Napa Valley, it is St. Helena, the narrow end of the funnel for all those cars and all those people rolling through on August weekends like this. St. Helena is where the traffic backs up—though, I'm telling you, not if you use Silverado Trail. It's where you find names like Louis Martini, Beringer, Sutter Home, and Charles Krug. And it's where the valley tapers and pushes everyone onto a few blocks of wineries, restaurants, shops, and charming, if way busy, wine country.

Tourism is hugely important for Napa. It's also hugely contentious, has been for decades. All those people mean sales, reputation, and money. They also mean construction, cars, smog, and all those damn people. Seemingly everything in this industry, and in this paradise of a valley, involves some kind of trade off, and surely one of the biggest, most public butting of heads involves tourism.

Most wineries, and the restaurants, shops, and inns that have moved in alongside them, need the out-of-towners to stay alive. The big places, the wineries with corporate owners or hundreds of thousands of cases in production, need the visitors for their tightly drawn bottom lines. But no one likes the traffic. The exhaust can't be good for grapes. Longtime residents feel overrun. The roads, sewers, and water supply are only so big. And even the businesses who crave visitors will tell you that at some point, those tourists, all those damn people, will be too much.

Outsiders—like me and Hank—are caught in the tangle. We love Napa. We love coming here, tasting, eating, and wandering around, stealing a little of the wine life for ourselves. We bring enthusiasm and money, but we bring a car and our bodies crowding out someone else. This is the kind of knotted little quandary that pops up in vacation areas and scenic regions around America. Can you, or should you, close a door behind you? If so, when? And what happens when you do?

Those kinds of questions are all the more complicated in a place like Napa, that, for all its sophistication, is still a farming valley. It's competing against world wine markets yet trying to preserve its rural, countrified charm, not to mention its vineyards. You get to points where the logic doesn't track, where some Napa people want to stop vineyards to save vineyards, to keep visitors out so they can sell wine to visitors.

Over the years—and never easily—Napa County has taken some shots at protecting everything, and, of course, often made people here more angry than happy about them. In 1968, the county classified much of its land as an agricultural preserve. That meant vine-yards, and any farmland, can only be sold in lots that are at least forty acres, and it's, basically, one house per lot. It could be a winery and a house, but the one house is key because there's not a lot of development pressure for homes on forty-acre lots. It was a huge blow against urbanization, and as controversial as it was in 1968, the ag preserve, as they call it here, is now the most generally beloved move in county history.

Other restrictions or planning attempts have been less universally popular. Probably the most far reaching, and the law most directly affecting tourism, was the 1990 ordinance that defined what wineries could and could not do. In simple terms, new wineries opened after 1990 have pretty tough restrictions, including the "appointment only" tasting room requirement—that we hate—and severe limits on things like selling food and staging big events. (Unofficially, Napa County is pretty loose on the "appointment only" thing and on restrictions against picnics. Unofficially.)

When you're here, it seems the valley has struck a decent balance so far. Some days are too crowded, some days are quiet. Some places the traffic almost stalls. And so you wait five more minutes to get to the next winery. Some places you just roll right along. Some wineries are packed, some would love a crowd.

At Corison Winery on Highway 29 a few blocks south of St. Helena proper, they wouldn't mind a couple more visitors now and then. This place, with its old-school building and sophisticated, classic wines, somehow escapes much of the tourist traffic, which is too bad for a lot of tourists.

The barn-like, gray and green winery with dormers and white trim looks like it belongs in the New England countryside, and the long driveway running off the highway feels like a country lane. We're pretty proud of ourselves for ditching the mainstream here. Except we can't decide where to park. It's empty, wide open, and still we can't figure out where to put our car. We get that way sometimes. Mostly it's me. Hank says we can probably park anywhere.

With some hesitation, we drive to the back and park near a cement pad and winery equipment, but also looking straight out at vineyards stretching west to the mountains. There's a new bench out-side the building. Looks like a visitor spot. We knock on the big win-ery door. Nothing. We knock on the office door nearby. Nothing. Back to the big door.

"I think I hear someone in front," I say.

We jog around the building and rap on the large white front door. No answer. We wait, then knock again.

"I'm telling you," I say, "there's someone in there."

Then I hear a door open out back. We jog around again. No one. We try knocking on the back door once more.

"Hank," I say, "Now I hear something out front, I swear to God."

"OK," he says. "So, this is a ghost winery with real ghosts?"

This time we get in the car and drive around the front. For sport, we knock on the front winery door one more time, wait a bit, then bail. "Too bad," Hank says. "They make good wine."

Driving down the little driveway road, I look back and see the front door open.

"Whoa, whoa." I say. "A ghost."

The ghost is Bob, a thin middle-aged guy with dark hair, who works here some weekends. Usually, the front door is open, but he was trying to take a rest room break.

"Every time I headed for the bathroom," he said, "someone was banging on another door."

Hank's right about their wines. Corison and its owner/wine-maker Cathy Corison specialize in Cabernet. They're the kind Hank pushes and are a bit rare in these days of fruit-forward, big-scoring reds. They're slightly lower alcohol, balanced, and structured, what Hank calls a real expression of the fruit.

Bob tells us Corison is regularly open for visitors, aside from the occasional bathroom break, but they're officially "appointment only." He says it with air quotes.

He sees the problems and the compromises—turning left out of their driveway can be a pain—but Corison gets twenty-five to thirty visitors a whole day, and four people at once is a rush.

"I doubt we would create a traffic pileup if we had the permits to be open without appointments," he said.

And by the way, we ask, where should we have parked?

"Oh, anywhere," Bob says.

WE MAKE A RUN THROUGH TAYLOR'S Refresher at the south edge of St. Helena for lunch. It's been around since 1949 and is a big, classic drive-in, except that it's in Napa and it's so much more.

Taylor's has all the usual, the burgers, the bacon double-cheese-burgers, shakes, fries, and chili cheese dogs. But there's also a light summer salad—baby greens tossed in a lemon-Dijon vinaigrette, topped with cherry tomatoes, fresh Parmesan, and, naturally, toasted pine nuts—and there's fried calamari, fish tacos with jalapeño-cilantro sour cream, and a whopping good ahi tuna burger seared rare. Their wine list is impressive. It includes Cakebread Sauvignon Blanc, Rombauer Chardonnay, and a Shafer Cab. And they have a corkage fee. It's only $5, but Taylor Refresher may be the only drive-in in North America with a corkage fee.

Then it's back down Highway 29 a bit for us, to Prager Ports. Neither of us has seen it before. Judging by the jolly, unruly tasting room, we may be the only people in Napa Valley out of the loop. The place is hopping. And it's everything you would not expect from a producer of fine Port wines.

Prager Winery and Port Works is a block off Highway 29, virtually behind Sutter Home Winery in a big, century-old, ramshackle wood building that was once part distillery. The packed and bustling tasting room is through the yard, inside a small door behind some stairs, down a narrow aisle crowded with barrels, and in what looks like an unfinished rumpus room, which, winery manager Jeff Prager tells us, it basically is.

The walls are simple wood, covered with money from around the world—or from monopoly games, in some cases—all left by visitors. Jeff says he's not really sure how it started but it's way cheaper than painting.

Jeff, one of the four kids of founders Jim and Imogene Prager, is a barrel-chested guy with a white goatee. He's wearing a work shirt, jeans, and worn boots. He's running the tasting room today, and he's sitting on a stool when you walk in, like the bouncer at a speakeasy. I'm about to say Leroy sent us, but Jeff sticks glasses in our hands almost before he says hi.

He's there with the vineyard manager, Richard Lenney, another big guy, though more tall than wide, with messy brown hair and an untucked shirt. They both look like they should be riding Harleys, not pouring smoking-jacket-and-pipe Ports.

Their Ports, however, are mesmerizing. Either that, or I've become a full-on Port guy. Possibly both. Their Ports are clean and smooth, and Hank and I both bond with a 2001 Aria White Port, another thing neither of us has seen before. It's named after one of Jim and Imogene's grandkids, like a lot of their wines. They have twenty-two grandchildren total, so there's not much danger they'll run out of wine names anytime soon.

Prager also makes unfortified, regular ol' wine, which maybe they don't take quite as seriously, because the tasting notes for the 2002 Merlot say, "The fruit was grown on our Calistoga vineyard and blah, blah, blah, blah . . . It has developed a wonderful blah, blah, blah, blah . . . and a hint of blah, blah, blah, blah."

The room has a couple wood chairs and a table, but mostly people just stand around and chat, read the money walls, and keep getting more Port. Jeff and Richard regularly find us right on time with our next pour, and they manage to keep track of where we are on the list, which is impressive considering the commotion.

We ask Jeff about the room, and if it's always busy.

"Pretty much," he says. "We sell most of our wine here, which is great. Honestly, I'm not sure how we got popular. It's not like we put a lot of sweat into this room."

He points to an Oriental rug on the floor. "That's only the second rug we've had since we opened in 1981," he says. "It's great, because when it gets worn out, you just turn it over." Jeff looks at his room for a second, pulsing with people in clumps of threes and fours, holding glasses, reading the walls, looking at bottles, and generally laughing. "We somehow never finished our tasting room," he says. "I guess we don't really need to now."

IT IS AFTER 5 P.M. AND WE'VE joined the throng crammed into the simple, right-on-the-road tasting room for Milat Vineyards. Milat's a respectable little winery. It's a longtime operation from a family that's been growing grapes here for more than half a century. Plus, they have a solid list of estate-grown wines that are positively cheap by Napa standards. Whatever. That's not why the place is stuffed.

Milat is right on Highway 29. Even better, it's open until 6 p.m. There aren't many wineries open this late. Milat's the last oasis. It's doubtful many of the couple dozen people shoe-horned into the small room came for the balance and complexity of Milat's Cabernet.

"Are you chewing gum?" the tall guy serving the wines asks a woman at the bar in full-on, mock disgust. "You think that's the reason the Chenin Blanc tastes like bubble gum?"

We hear that from far away. We're stuck in the back of the crowd. We watch two attractive women, one dark, one blond, both overdressed in spaghetti-strap tops, tight skirts, and heels, knife through the pack like speedboats on a calm lake. On their way back out, I ask the dark-haired woman how she did that.

"C'mere," she says. She takes my hand and heads back into the chaos. The seas part for her and she takes me to the bar, Hank following in our wake. Then she gives my hand a pat.

"Try the Zinfandel," she says. "It's great."

I turn but the crowd has swallowed her. I look back at the server behind the bar.

"Was she real?" I ask him.

"Those two have been coming in here every day for almost a week," he says. "She just buys a glass of Zin. Her friend just gets a Cab. I guess it's easier than going to a bar."

If you handle crowds like they do. Or like Cliff Little. He's the tall guy behind the tasting bar. Cliff's a nephew of co-owner Mike Milat and the latest in a line of family members to run this tasting room since it opened in 1986. He has light brown hair, a half-smile etched into his face, and is six-foot-four and built like a tight end, a useful size with an end-of-the-day crowd.

Hank and I ask if there's a spit bucket and Cliff, who's still pouring about a million tastes and explaining how the Rosé is lower alcohol because not all the sugar was fermented, reaches into an office behind the bar and comes back with two coffee cups.

"These OK?" he asks. "We don't see a lot of guys spitting at 5:30. That's more the morning crowd."

On his trips back to us, Cliff says he tended bar for a bit, which helps him here, and he's learned to deal with people differently at different times.

"In the mornings, or on weekdays, people want to talk about the wine," he says. "It definitely gets harder as the day goes on. I feel like I don't get to tell them about the wine or the family.

"But the end of the day is more about the fun and the experience. I've learned not to worry if a glass is empty for a minute. And if people have a good time, they'll remember us even if they don't remember what they tasted."

Cliff gets interrupted by a phone call for a second. Then he calls out to the room.

"Hey, everybody, listen up a sec," Cliff yells. "The Highway Patrol has a checkpoint down the road by Mondavi. If you've been drinking a while, you might not want to go that direction." Pause for a moment of sanity. "If you've been drinking a while, you might not want to be driving in any direction."

Cliff is a mountain of good cheer, and the room is a happy place. It's not entirely on image for Napa. It's not that low-key, wine-country gracefulness. Milat is at the crossroads where wine tasting and tourism meet happy hour. A few months later, they would quiet things—a bit—by pushing their closing time to 5:30 p.m., but right now, this is all energy, laughter, some flirting, and, of course, a dose of alcohol. It's pretty fun.

"I like that guy," I say to Hank. "The man can tend bar."

We hear someone in the crowd ask Cliff if he has any dinner recommendations.

"Oh, yeah," Cliff says. "Don Giovanni. It's phenomenal."

"You still like him?" Hank asks me, innocently as always.

"It is possible," I say slowly, measuring my words, "I may be wrong about Don Giovanni."

HANK IS IN GERMANY. HIS ACTUAL job takes him to places like that now and then, to see their vineyards and learn their wines. I find it vaguely disloyal to Napa, but mostly because I'm jealous. Whatever. The bastard.

Since our rules for the Quest require team visits, I have some time to fill in gaps on a couple of powerful forces in Napa: White Zinfandel and bocce ball. They are unrelated. I start with White Zin.

Let me just say this. I went to a party a few years back—possibly, it was a *Miami Vice*–watching party. What can I say?—carrying a bottle of wine that I knew, absolutely knew, was The Cool Bottle. I've never been that sure since. It was Sutter Home White Zinfandel. Twenty years later, for millions and millions of people, it's still the cool wine. Maybe not in Napa, but more than one out of every ten bottles of wine sold in America is White Zinfandel.

When White Zin exploded on the market in the early 1980s, it gave a rocket boost to the American wine industry. It provided an easy introduction to wine in real bottles when the country was guzzling beer, sweet drinks with vaguely sexual names, or stuff like Blue Nun, Almaden, and Lancers. Often mixed with soda. White Zinfandel also turned Sutter Home Winery into an industry monster and powered its parent company, Trinchero Family Estates, toward becoming one of the biggest wine companies in America, producing more than nine million cases a year.

And it was all a mistake.

That's what Bob Trinchero, the winemaker who invented the stuff, is telling me. It was bad execution of a bad idea in the first place. He loves that. Trinchero, in his sixties, is now CEO of the company, and you'd think he'd be tired of the story. We're sitting in his comfortable-but-modest office with vineyards outside that's part of a huge administration, winery, and warehouse complex. This is all across Highway 29 from the Sutter Home tasting room and the pale green Victorian that is one of the most recognizable landmarks of Napa Valley.

"I like the story," he says. "I'd still be working in that little tasting room across the road if it hadn't happened."

OK, first off, Sutter Home's tasting room is massive. But the point stands.

Bob's father, Mario Trinchero, bought the then-dormant, extremely run-down Sutter Home Winery in 1947, and moved his family to Napa from New York. Like the dozen or so Napa wineries then, the Trincheros produced a couple hundred, then a couple thousand cases of wine. And like most Italian winery owners, Bob said, they made dozens of different wines.

Bob took over as winemaker in 1960 and started thinking about change. "I wanted us to be like the châteaux of France," he says, "I wanted us to make just one wine."

Trinchero is not particularly big, but he has thick hands and a healthy, stocky build that shows his life's had some physical work in it. He seems generally bemused, like he knows he hit the jackpot in his life and he shouldn't take himself too seriously. When Bob talks about his châteaux plan, he's rolling his eyes. "We finally got our wine drinkable by the late 1960s," he says.

In the 1960s, a friend named Darrell Corti, a Sacramento grocer and a respected wine guy, helped Bob find the Deaver Vineyards near the California Sierra foothill town of Plymouth, where they grow spectacular Zinfandel grapes.

"The '68, '69, '70 wines were delicious," Trinchero says. "Suddenly, we were in fine wine magazines. I said, 'Dad, this is it, we're just gonna make Zinfandel.' My dad was Old World Italian, but he was adaptable. He said OK, as long as the number of cases didn't drop."

There were only a few big-time Zinfandel producers then, and they were trying to out Zin each other with big, gutsy wines. In 1972, Trinchero tried a common trick: He bled off some of the Zinfandel juice before it fermented. That left less juice for the same amount of skins, and gave the wine deeper flavors. Trinchero removed thirty gallons of juice per ton of grapes, then let the rest ferment and turn to Zin.

And since he had this leftover juice, he added some yeast and fermented that, too. It had no skin contact, so it was still white.

"The '72 Zin was great: big and tannic, and it's still good," Bob says. "And I had this leftover stuff. It was bone dry. It was white. I didn't know what it was, but we had about 220 cases of it."

Corti offered to take half of it off Trinchero's hands to sell as a curiosity. Corti wanted to call it Oeil de Perdrix, French for Eye of the Partridge.

"I said, 'If you want to buy half of it, I don't care what you call it,'" Trinchero says.

Problem: The Bureau of Alcohol, Tobacco, and Firearms, which still regulated wine labels then, wouldn't let them label a wine without an English description of what the hell it was. Trinchero and Corti figured, fine, call it White Zinfandel.

"It moved like manhole covers," Bob says. The name meant nothing to buyers. Corti didn't know whether to put it with the whites or the reds. It just sat on shelves.

Back then, the winery was producing about 7,000 cases, half of them regular Zin. Roger Trinchero, Bob's brother and the money guy at Sutter Home, didn't let Bob just toss the White Zin, so they kept bottling it, and it kept going nowhere.

Then in 1975, the White Zin fermentation stopped early. Maybe it ran out of nutrients or got too hot or something, but the yeast didn't convert all the sugar to alcohol. Trinchero never knew why. It just happens sometimes in winemaking, particularly to a wine you're mostly ignoring.

"This was not exactly a priority," Bob says. "We didn't check back for a couple weeks. It was slightly sweet, because there was some sugar left—it had maybe two or three percent residual sugar—and it was pink. I might've left some skins in. And it was pretty good."

The Trincheros tried it on friends, who loved it. They tried it on customers, who loved it, too. Bingo. By 1978, they figured out they wanted it pink and slightly sweet on purpose. It sold out. They doubled production. Sold out again. The demand was multiplying faster than yeast in sugar.

White Zinfandel was an entry wine for millions of people, an easy wine for millions more. It was the first mass-market, upscale wine America had seen. By 1987, it was the most popular premium wine in the country, brought tens of millions of new customers to the wine industry, and it made Sutter Home a tourist attraction.

These days, Sutter Home sells 4.8 million cases of White Zinfandel, nearly a quarter of the twenty million cases sold throughout the country, and it is still The Cool Place for thousands and thousands of tourists who wander through Napa and know only that name.

The various wineries of Trinchero Family Estates make some top-of-the-market wines, including a Deaver Vineyards Zinfandel for Montevina Winery, which Trinchero owns. But, despite those high-end wines, despite the sleekly restored Victorian (bought in 1986; Mario Trinchero couldn't afford it in 1947), and despite the boost it gave to Napa wines and tourism, Sutter Home's legacy will be that once-premium, now decidedly lower-market, very American pink wine.

That is fine with Trinchero. He's something of a populist anyway. We talk about how much Napa has changed since that tasting room across the road really was little, and how Napa's enormous popularity changed tasting rooms and the entire valley.

Trinchero says the difference is staggering from those still-recent years when there were a couple dozen wineries and a few hundred people wandering up and down the valley on a weekend. But he's not complaining about the traffic, the growth, the prices, and the people—nor should he, since they helped make him rich. But Trinchero's right when he says there's a natural trade-off when your livelihood involves selling both a product and an image to the public. You can't, then, tell the public to go away.

"Napa is a unique place," Bob says. "It's an experience here, the food, the wine, the beauty of it. As long as we remember this is still a valley with agriculture.

"I don't mind the traffic, I just plan for it. When I have to go somewhere on the weekends, I just make sure I don't have to turn left. Even if it means going a couple miles out of your way, always turn right."

That's what we say, I tell him. Turn right. That's our standard plan, go in one direction and always turn right.

Heading out the long driveway back to Highway 29, I'm thinking all it takes is a little planning. I'm also thinking I need to get better at it, because when I get to the road, I need to turn left.

I LIKE MIKE SMITH. I LIKE him because he's a fun, easy guy. And because he's introducing me around, and 'cause he owns Sunshine Foods in St. Helena, a great small supermarket and possibly the best place to stock a picnic on the planet. But mostly, I like Mike right now because he's got a magnum of 1999 Caymus Special Select Cab.

Mike is at Crane Park, on the western edge of St. Helena. He's here, along with nearly 100 other people, to play bocce ball. Bocce ball. The national sport of Napa.

Everywhere we go, people in wineries, in restaurants, in stores, tell us they play competitive (so to speak) bocce ball at this park, and now I can see why. It's an energetic, eclectic crowd, a wild scene that's part sporting event, part community picnic, and part wine festival. There are six decomposed granite courts inside a wooden fence and surrounded by wood tables. Right now, the flat top of the court's flat fence is lined with water bottles, Sprite, Coors Light, Stella Artois Lager, Sierra Nevada Pale Ale, and lots and lots of wine.

This is the last night for the Wednesday summer league—there are leagues on every night but Saturday—then play-offs start, which, someone tells me, just ups the caliber of wine.

"Everyone is out here for the food, the wine, and the friends,"

Mike says. He's in his forties, with wavy dark hair, wears shorts, very old loafers, and a worn, Oxford blue shirt with "Stinky Oaks" stitched over the pocket. "The bocce ball is sort of an afterthought."

There are teams from Sutter Home, Chateau Montelena, Silverado Brewing Co. (motto: "It takes a lot of great beer to make good wine."), but mostly these are just mix-and-match friends.

"You don't have a clue," says Mel Juler, the head groundskeeper at Chateau Montelena, "who out here has a million dollars and who doesn't have crap."

Well, maybe a clue. I see a guy from one of the tasting rooms. I meet Jim Regusci, the owner of Regusci Winery. I'm introduced to some very nice men who everyone calls the Millionaire's Club. I get ribbed by two tall, well-dressed sixtyish women who look like money and act like happy kids. And I meet Jim. Jim's lived in St. Helena all his life, and often comes out to the bocce courts even when his team isn't playing. He wears a blue T-shirt and jeans—almost always, I'm told—drives an old truck and only drinks Budweiser.

This is the Napa Valley that Hank and I are getting to know: friendly, surprising, full of life. The valley has certainly changed in recent years, but whatever its conflicts, we're learning that its image and its reality have some genuine connections. This is a mix of folks united by the fact they live in a great place and work in, or around, or simply like, the wine world. Except Jim. He's a Bud guy.

I'm feeling a little guilty being here without Hank because I know he'd love this scene. But he's in Germany, getting entertained and fed and introduced to all kinds of good wines. Poor him.

Mike Smith's team is called Accounti-Obi-Denti because it was started by an accountant, a dentist, and an OB/GYN doc named Bruce Scarborough, who, legend has it, helped deliver a baby via cell-phone during a bocce match. "He wasn't on call that night," Mike says, as if that explains everything.

For the record, I made friends with them before I knew Mike had that magnum of Caymus. When I walked up, they were drinking Artesa Carneros Pinot Noir—not exactly swill—courtesy of the "Accounti," Tim O'Leary, who's the controller at Artesa Winery and the nominal team captain. He's got a slightly unkempt beard, a gray T-shirt, and jean shorts, and looks more like one of Mel Juler's doesn't-have-crap guys.

Not that O'Leary seems to care. He doesn't strike me as your stan-dard, take-things-seriously accountant. I ask him if they have a game strategy. "Oh, sure," he says. "We yell, 'Throw it close.' And we try to keep the wineglasses full."

Full wineglasses seem to be key.

Bocce ball—something of a cross between shuffleboard and curling—has been in Napa Valley for decades, which is what you'd expect from an area that is home to a bunch of families with deep Italian roots. The insanity is more recent.

About fifteen years ago, a group of semi-retired guys, blue collar workers mostly, wanted to build some bocce courts and asked St. Helena if they could have a bit of park space. Smart cities don't turn down free construction and St. Helena gave then a nice stretch of Crane Park behind the high school. The recreation director, Kathleen Carrick, also found some city money for lights.

Still, for a long time the major rec league sport in St. Helena, like in most towns, was softball. But in 1997, a fire damaged the elementary school where the city softball leagues played, and school officials stuck temporary classrooms on the softball field. The locals migrated to bocce ball. Once the damage was fixed and the field reopened, everyone kept playing bocce.

Now, there are more than seventy-five teams and 700 players from all over the valley for the summer league. There are also spring and fall leagues, there's an indoor winter league in Napa town, and they have two bocce ball federations. Two. And it seems every winery in the valley has, or is building, a bocce court.

But, and this is important, it isn't about the bocce.

"This is the only sport I can do holding a wineglass," says Dan Dolen, who owns a wine-country tour company. He's there with Jack, his black Labrador puppy. Jack occasionally romps across the court and no one seems to mind, though I'm guessing Jack would get a serious reprimand if he knocked over any wine. He seems to know that, too.

Katie Parks, now a mainstay on team Accounti-Denti-Obi, discovered bocce ball four years ago, when she was working for Sutter Home. She was new to the area and a friend dragged her to Crane Park.

"We found out where the locals hung out," she says, almost conspiratorially. Katie is blond, trim, and like many of the women here, she's wearing jeans, a short-sleeve shirt, and sandals. "We didn't learn how to play till that Wednesday night. We came here two hours early and practiced."

Now it turns out, she's pretty good at this. "It might be natural," she says, "I'm Italian."

"Red wine helps," says Mike.

Accounti-Denti-Obi is locked in a fierce battle—which is to say the match is close, but they still share food, beer, wine, and some trash talk—with the Hardballers. The Hardballers captain is Ken Mee, who owns Silverado Brewing Co. He, Tim, Mike, and a lot of the guys are friends back to high school.

The Hardballers are in first place. ("It's the first time, ever," Ken says. "There's so much responsibility.") Accounti et al. is mid-pack— Tim and Mike think fifth out of twelve but aren't entirely sure—and they're offering to throw the match for some of Silverado's ribs.

But they want Ken to sweat, too. Things have stopped for a moment, then everyone looks at Katie, who's off the court, talking to some friends when it's her turn.

"Katie," says Mike, seriousness dripping from his voice, "you gotta get your head in the game. Just for a minute." She gives him an oh-like-you've-never-done-that look, and steps back on the court. Before she can roll, Mike stops her to pour wine in her glass. This is not a team that's going to let a possible win get in the way of, actually, anything.

Katie plays the break on the court just enough to knock a Hardballers' ball out of the way and score for her team. She gives me a shrug. "See," she says, "Italian."

Mike has a break, so he goes to another group and gets a blue plastic cup for me to try the Pinot. I like that Mike. I also want to talk to him about Sunshine Foods. I love that market. I loved it before Mike started pouring me wine.

If there is any downside to Sunshine, and I'm not saying there is, it's that choosing a lunch can be hard. Too many options. I was in earlier today and got stymied by the enormous sandwich lineup and the deli possibilities, not to mention the guy making fresh sushi.

The ready-to-eat foods included orange garlic halibut, house-grilled salmon, barbecue spare ribs, vegi deep-dish pizza, roasted chicken, smoked salmon, smoked trout, anchovy fillets, tubs of calamari, mussels and octopus (I was not thinking octopus), shrimp salad, spring pasta, salmon couscous, corn and avocado salad, mango cucumber salad, stop me before I eat myself silly. There's a huge cheese section, a great vegetable aisle, shelves of fresh breads, even the wine aisle is fun because it's grouped by winery instead of varietal and that works in wine country when you're looking for something you tasted on tour.

For the record, my grilled chicken garlic Caesar sandwich rocked.

Mike says he took over Sunshine Foods from his dad, who started it in 1975. He added the hall-of-fame deli in the 1990s when he realized he would get killed trying to be a straight-up supermarket market. It's still a market, it's just so much more. He has two chefs besides the sushi guy and a cheese man.

And he's found the perfect test market for new deli dishes. He uses bocce ball's one-and-all picnic atmosphere.

"I just set it on a table and see what happens," Mike says. "If it disappears, I go back and tell Angel (one of the chefs) to keep making it."

These teams are into a slow game two—each match is best two out of three—and Mike decides it's time to open the Caymus. People in the area just seem to sense it, the way dogs know when food is opened across the house. They wander over and Mike happily pours for them.

"Wine is to be shared," he says. And he pours for me, too. Caymus Special Selection Cabernet Sauvignon in a blue plastic cup. Kind of a cool moment.

One guy who wanders over is Michael Weis, the winemaker at Groth Vineyards. Mike pours Caymus into his glass.

"Oh, darn it," Weis says. "OK, I guess I can drink this."

Weis, it turns out, also has a bocce ball Jones. His team is called the Quatro Stupidos. They, apparently, don't take themselves seriously, either.

I tell him we were at Groth in June when people there were worried because they'd gotten so much rain. I was wondering how the fruit was developing in this cool summer.

"We had to drop a lot of fruit, but I think it's going to be a great year," he says. "These kinds of summers give us real balanced wines, as long as it doesn't rain before we pick. Last year, we saw a lot of sunburn. We're not seeing it at all this summer.

"I tend to anthropomorphize the vines," Weis says. "I don't like the hot weather, and if it's a nice year for me, I think it's a nice year for them."

Anthropomorphize. Don't let anyone tell you winemakers don't read.

By game three, the Hardballers have taken command. Tim and Katie are trying to tell Ken they're throwing this game and he owes them ribs, and Mike's about finished pouring the Caymus. A friend of Katie's, Morgan Taylor, who plays for Sutter Home, wanders by and scores some wine.

"We get laughed at by our friends around the country for playing bocce ball," Morgan says. "They go, 'It's so Napa Valley.' Then we tell 'em what we're drinking."

HANK'S BACK FROM GERMANY AND TALKING Riesling. It's the other white wine. In Germany, it's light, lower alcohol but with good acids, so it seems almost delicate. Some are a bit sweet but the good ones all finish with crispness and snap. A lot of early winemakers in Napa, particularly some of the original German immigrants, made Rieslings here, but they were rounder and not as subtle or as crisp, because it turns out Napa's weather is too kind. Rieslings need a long, fairly cold growing season to get that acidity. A few Napa wineries make Rieslings, but they aren't German.

Hank is telling me some of this when we're at V. Sattui, which makes a dry and an off-dry Johannisberg Riesling—one of the names Americans call Riesling—not to mention just about every other wine, including a sparkling, Chardonnay, Sauvignon Blanc, Gewürztraminer, a dry Sémillon, a dry Muscat, and a Napa Valley White blend, just among their whites.

All that, and we're here mostly for lunch. That's no knock on the wine—their top end is well-regarded—it's just that if there is one name-brand picnic spot on Highway 29 for tourists, it's V. Sattui's two acres of grass, trees, and tables. V. Sattui opened in Napa in 1976, and clearly, it has the permits to traffic with tourists.

The buildings are picturesque replicas of a European country winery, with thick stone walls, square towers, and heavy wood beams. And there is a vast tasting room wing that's built for volume.

This is an early Thursday afternoon a few days into September, and we count maybe fifty people and a dozen servers spread along the large, L-shaped tasting bar. It seems half-empty. The servers cover the crowd easily and our guy, a trim, middle-aged man named Ernie, is not shy about telling us how many medals the wines have won, and, by the way, they've won a ton of medals. Tasting is free. The wines are fine. Ernie is selling hard, almost like he's got a script, but he's kinda fun. What the hell. A guy's gotta earn a living.

The room itself is a bit less charming, more like a wine warehouse, with large displays and cases stacked six feet high. V. Sattui makes 60,000 cases a year and sells every bottle out of its tasting room, club, or website, so it *is* a wine warehouse and store.

What's really impressive is the deli. Man. It's not Sunshine Foods—what is?—but it's something to see. There's an enormous gourmet cheese counter with scores of cheese wheels. There are sandwiches on demand, and stacks of pre-made sandwiches. They stock a bunch of pastas, salads, pasta salads, fruit combos, spreads, loaves of breads, and piles of chocolates. Picnicking is both art and industry here. Like the tasting room, the deli can handle a crowd.

I get a multi-Italian meat sandwich that includes, I'm fairly sure, every cold cut ever made. Hank gets a huge roast beef–on–focaccia sandwich. Paying for them is something, too. There are six registers inside and four more right outside if needed. Today, they only need five total to whisk us through. We ask the young woman ringing us up how busy they get.

"I'm pretty new," she says, then calls to the dark-haired woman at the next register. "Hey, Ann. How many people do we get in here on a weekend?"

Ann laughs. It's not all amusement. "I dunno," she says. "Pick a number."

TODAY WE ARE ON PLAN. MOSTLY. We're heading north, turning only right. Traffic's not that bad, anyway. Heitz Wine Cellars and Louis M. Martini Winery are both sort of opposites of V. Sattui, though they, too, are bedrocks of Napa's wine industry and have been here long enough for most permits. Tasting at Heitz is also free, like at V. Sattui, but there are only four people in the contemporary, cabin-like tasting room, and the feeling is unhurried and quiet. At Martini, the neat tasting room is small and modern, a bit like a new restaurant bar, and during the week, when the crowds are thinner, you sit at the tasting bar or at tables. Martini also has a little brick courtyard trimmed neatly with grass, flowers, and trees, and it's another great picnic spot. It's empty. We ask why, as stupid as that seems.

"I don't know," the woman serving us says. "It's pretty out there, isn't it? Maybe we should make a bigger deal about it."

We drive past Charles Krug for a moment, because we're saving it. In the little neat tasting room at Ballentine Vineyards, we talk with Guido Greggi, and get to chatting about the vagaries of tourist traffic. He says Ballentine works hard to get people into their tasting room, but they clearly aren't a hot spot.

"People just sail by here," he says. "We're kind of in a bad place because it looks like we're part of Markham (just south of Ballentine). And we don't have gardens or anything. That could be our slogan: 'No gardens, just great wine.'"

Guido has dark hair and looks like he's in his twenties, but he says he's been working in the valley a few years, and he's seen the different kinds of crowds the various wineries get.

"The people that come in here, come because they know about our wine," he says. "I worked at Sutter Home for a while and that was a little different. We got tons of people in there and all they knew was White Zin. Sutter Home was like a royal name to them.

"Some of them tried, I'll say that. People would get a White Zin and ask, 'What am I looking for in this wine?' What are they looking for? It's White Zin. You're looking for the buzz."

NOW IT'S TIME FOR CHARLES KRUG. By our calculations, this is tasting room number 100 for us. We've hit triple digits on our Quest. We figure Charles Krug is the perfect place for this milestone. It's not that it's the oldest winery in Napa, or that it's part of the Mondavi connection, or that they helped pioneer innovations like cold fermentation, vintage dating, and fermentation in small oak barrels. That's all wonderful. Not our reason. We're celebrating here because Charles Krug Winery had the first public tasting room in California, opened in 1882. Couple years before Napa County imposed restrictions.

The visitor's center now is surprisingly simple, just an unfussy wood building under trees, with windows looking across a big courtyard at the huge, old stone winery. Candice Dunham, who's pouring for us, says they're planning a new tasting room in the old winery, but while that building is being redone, they've suspended winery tours and their tasting room traffic has dropped some, too.

Candice is tall and blond, wears a dark blue Charles Krug shirt, jeans, and boots. She's like so many people we've been meeting, a transplant to Napa after spending, in her case, twenty-five years working in the San Francisco Bay Area with an information technology company. She got a job for a while as a wine buyer and then came to Charles Krug.

We say, well, even if the tourist crowd has thinned, this is still a special place for us. We tell her about our Quest and that Charles Krug is number 100. Candice isn't particularly impressed.

"How charming," she says.

"We've been doing this since March," I say.

"Way to go," she says.

"No, see, we're going to all the tasting rooms in Napa. We planned it so this would be a landmark," I say. I hear my voice getting pitchy. "So it's a landmark at a landmark. And we actually planned it out right."

"You must be so proud," Candice says.

OK, got it. Candice is yanking our chain. She laughs and toasts the trip with us, pours herself a little of the Zinfandel Port that I've already fallen for.

"Good luck the rest of the way," she says. "If you get lost, let us know."

I'm still pretty sure she's not impressed.

AT BERINGER VINEYARDS, THERE'S RARELY A shortage of tourist traffic. It's one of the monuments of Napa. And if Disneyland made a Wine Country USA, it would look exactly like Beringer. I say that with admiration.

Everything about the winery is idyllic and perfect, the gardens, the trees, the stone walls, the fountains. Everything looks the way you'd want it to, no burrs, no rough edges, no rogue leaves. There is nothing out of place, just like in Disneyland, though the wine's much better here.

Technically, this is not a winery, that's across the road. This is officially a historic district, as designated by the National Register of Historic Places. It's got the old carriage house, which functions as the entrance to this park—they even give out amusement park–like maps and sell tour tickets. There's the old winery up on a hill with the tasting room for current releases and mid-priced wines. There are the old caves, an 1850s farmhouse, there's a gnarled oak tree circa 1787, and there is the most-Disneyland of all the attractions, the dark stone, sharply steepled, fairy tale–looking Rhine House.

Beringer was started in 1876 by Frederick and Jacob Beringer—Jacob first worked for the original Charles Krug, and surely would have impressed even Candice—and they had the seventeen-room Rhine House built in 1884 to re-create the family home on the Rhine River in Germany.

These days, the Rhine House, with its heavy stone facing, steep roof, and wraparound dark-wood porch, is where they taste reserve wines. We go there because the house is so cool—inside, the light comes through tons of stained glass, and there's a glossy, hardwood staircase and more tall panels of polished wood—and because this is where they pour the good stuff. Beringer has a lot of that.

We wander into the narrow, elegant tasting room. Before we get to the bar, there's a guy calling, "Hank. Yo, Hank."

His name is Mike Glasney and he knows Hank because he worked for a wine distributor for years who sold to Nugget Market. Now he pours for Beringer.

This happens now and then, people recognize Hank as a pro, and here it's good news for us. Our rules for this Quest are that we explore the valley as tourists, normal wine guys—or as normal as I can manage. We don't ask for the special treatment that buyers like Hank usually get, because, we just decided not to. Our rules, however, allow for people to recognize Hank on their own, which still lets us sample some choice wine. Yes, it's arbitrary. They're our rules.

Mike is hustling to keep up with everyone at the tasting bar, but he let's us cherry pick the reserve list, which ranges from a vibrant 2001 Bancroft Ranch Howell Mountain Merlot, to a bright 2002 Stanly Ranch Pinot Noir, to Ports of Cabernet Sauvignon and Cabernet Franc, both more wine-like and fruity than a lot of Ports.

Then Mike goes back and pours us the 2001 Private Reserve Cab, Beringer's best wine. One of Napa's best, maybe. They offer the Private Reserve for tasting, but I'd like to think Mike poured a little heavy for us.

We wander outside the tasting room onto the wood deck. There's a young couple in one corner, pretending we're not here. We tiptoe past and move to the front of the Rhine House. In front of us is a perfect combination of trees, flowers, a fountain in the distance, and grass manicured so smoothly Tiger Woods could putt on it.

It's just starting to turn into evening. The light is cut by long shadows. The air is still thick with summer, but the late sunshine has a softer gold to it, almost a glow. Autumn is not so far away. We stand there, just soaking in this impossibly faultless mix of green and gold, holding glasses of great wine.

"You can start to see," Hank says, "why people want to come here."

NINE

North Valley

"**THIS COULD BE** it," the amiable guy at Benessere Vineyards is saying. "The vintage of the century."

You hear that a lot in wine country. Every couple years: Vintage of the century. Usually it's hype, or over-excitement, or someone who's drunk. On the other hand, since this century is, what, six years old, the competition is a little less fierce. Either way, he's not letting up.

"There are some crazy flavors out there right now," he says. "This year is going to be epic."

Truth is, other people have been saying that sort of thing, too. Just not as emphatically. Mr. Emphatic is Andy Gridley, the sales manager for Benessere, and he's working the tasting room on this bright Sunday morning. He's got a goatee, some gray at the edges, a friendly, round face, and a smooth voice. He's a low-key guy, really, it's what he's saying that's raucous.

"The weather has been weird. For a while there, it was killing us," Andy says. "But now we've had this long growing season and a lot of hang time. Not big-sugars, high-alcohol hang time. Big flavors. We're seeing it all over the valley."

It's September and the valley is pregnant with grapes, hanging everywhere in big, dark bunches at the bottom of the vines. This bounty of fruit seems limitless. There are rows and rows of it, along the roads, in the flats, winding up the hillsides and mountains. There are so many grapes, such an awesome mass of purple clusters, it is overwhelming.

Hank and I are proud of the grapes. They've grown so strong. We knew them when they were tiny buds, when the vineyards were just thin lines of stalks, posts, and wire. Now the grapes are plump and inviting. We feel we've got a stake in their well-being. I think of them as family. Hank says I probably have too much of a connection.

The fruit is thick around Benessere, a small winery in the middle of the valley floor, halfway between St. Helena and Calistoga. It looks like a white country cottage, surrounded by flowers and the vines. The world around it is so pretty, it looks fake.

This is where Napa Valley narrows to maybe a mile in width. The mountains are close and frame every curve and rise in the terrain. Here, everything is closer: the steep knolls, the small, soft hills, the open spots on the valley floor. They're more palpable, more dramatic and striking. The landscape has so much texture it feels alive. It's our favorite part of Napa.

The area is also the warmest in the valley, Andy says. That means the sugar level can get pretty high, pretty fast, which makes for big reds but not necessarily for nuance or a real sense of the fruit, unless you handle it right. The key is to keep the sugars down long enough for the grapes to evolve and develop those flavors.

"When the grapes are part of the vine longer, they pick up so much of the varietal's characteristics," he says. "That's what we're getting this year."

We ask about the screwy spring, about the late rains and mild summer, and how it's all meshing together for Andy's epic vintage.

"That late rain had everything growing insane," he said. "It was like the vines were on steroids."

Benessere, and everyone else, dropped a lot of fruit. They cut grapes off the vines—more than double the usual amount—and they trimmed and adjusted the canopies to control the growth. Too much fruit dilutes the flavors because, basically, the vine can't support all the grapes, so the nutrients—and the flavor—are spread thinner. Less flavor per grape equals thin wine.

Too much wild vine growth has its own set of problems. If the grapes are always shaded, they'll be under-ripe and taste more vegetal. Worse, they could get mold, not a great wine taste. The vines need to be pruned enough to let in some air and sun, but, of course, not too much sun, because that gets you grapes that are too ripe and prune-y.

Vine growth is a balancing act for another reason. When grapes are stressed, they develop thicker skins—the flavor's in the skin. Just like people, when grapes have to work a little, they develop character. If the vines, those solar feeding panels, make life too easy for the grapes, they get plump and have less taste, also like people.

Andy says once vineyard managers got the steroid-like growth under control, this even, mild summer let the fruit mature slowly, develop some acids and tons of flavor and character. And because there were few heat spikes, the Brix stayed down, so the alcohol levels won't be through the roof. The result should be balanced, complex, flavorful wine.

"We're always talking about the vintage of a lifetime," Andy says. "I'm telling you, this could be it."

Andy's enthusiasm is contagious. We're getting excited. We ask if we should be putting in orders now for cases of '05s.

"Maybe," Andy says. "It could rain."

Because the fruit is growing slowly, most vineyards probably won't even start harvesting reds until early October. Maybe later. Rain brings mold and all kinds of problems to mature grapes. In Napa, a rainy October is against the odds, but it happens. Maybe one year in four or five. Enough to make people nervous, particularly on a vintage of the century. Stupid rain.

"I'm not kidding. You are going to love the '05s," Andy says. "Unless it rains. Then we're screwed."

I'VE GOT MY NOSE DEEP INTO a black wineglass, trying to figure out the smell. I know it. It's common. What the hell is it?

"What'd you get for number five?" I whisper to Hank. "Just gimme a hint."

We're standing at a table in the middle of the open tasting room at Ehlers Estate, a pretty winery in a square, stone building that looks like an old country church. Inside, century-old stone and heavy wood beams are mixed with new wood, comfortable couches, and glass tables set on barrels. It feels like they should serve espresso.

Our table has eight of those black glasses. Each has something in it we're supposed to identify by smell. This is Ehlers's "fun" sensory evaluation test that I think I'm flunking. Hank's been whizzing around the table, taking quick notes. I've got a lot written down, but the only answer I'd bet on is cinnamon. Who can't identify cinnamon? On this last one, I'm struggling and looking for help.

"You're asking me to cheat?" Hank says.

"This isn't grad school," I say. "Just a hint."

"It would be wrong," Hank says.

"I know. Tell me."

"Fine," he says. "Think the holidays."

"Oh, God. That one's not cinnamon."

"There are other spices for the holidays."

"Pumpkin pie? Chocolate? Peppermint?"

"Jesus," he says. "It's nutmeg."

"That's what I thought."

We bring our answers back to the tasting bar and the patient woman who sent us over for the test. Her name is Emily Bell, she's in her twenties, pretty in that fresh-scrubbed way, and clearly someone who's serious about wine. She quit a thriving sales job, sold her house in Florida, and moved to Napa in 2004. Now she's studying at the Culinary Institute of America and trying to develop as a wine writer.

"The point of the drill," she tells us, "is to pay attention."

"Say, what?" I say. To her credit, Emily forces a smile.

Hank got seven out of eight. He only missed maple syrup. He called it coffee.

"That's very good," Emily says. "Above average."

I had coffee, too, for the syrup. And cumin for what was dirt, and leather for what was white pepper. "That's close," Emily says, though I can't figure how. I hope I never put leather on my eggs.

"Five out of eight," she says. "You're almost normal."

"Thanks," I say. "'Almost normal' is better than I usually hear."

<hr />

WE MOVE DOWN THE ROAD TO Frank Family Vineyards, another winery in the middle of this narrow stretch of valley. We're standing at a tasting bar in the outer room. The floor show is about to start. The tasting rooms here are nothing special. They're in a simple, wood-frame building with ratty carpet and, you know, who cares? It's all about that show.

Behind the bar is a big, slightly round guy, maybe fifty, with a well-trimmed beard, wire-rim glasses, not much hair, and a subdued purple Hawaiian shirt. His name is Jeff Senelick and he'll be our server and comedian this afternoon. Jeff, it turns out, is also a man with some abilities.

"Where you from?" he asks us.

"Sacramento," Hank says.

"That fits," Jeff says.

"What?" I say. "You happen to know people from Sacramento are idiots?" Bad self-effacing humor. It's all I've got.

"No, no." Jeff gives me a half laugh, like, actually, in this case, maybe yes. But, really, he's got a formula: Mid-week, three-out-of-four people tasting wine in Napa are from more than two hours away. They're staying in the valley, or in San Francisco or Sacramento, but are out on a longer trip. Fridays and Saturdays, it's an even split. Sundays it's three-fourths local. It's Sunday. We're on pattern.

Two more guys walk up.

"Where you from?" Jeff asks.

"The City," one guy says. In Northern California, that's San Francisco. Capital "C."

Jeff gives me and Hank a nod with raised eyebrows that says, "ain't I smart." Next is a foursome.

"Kentucky," they say. Jeff shrugs at us. More people dribble in.

"Boston."

"New York."

"L.A."

"Orange County."

"Cincinnati."

"Salt Lake City."

"You guys allowed to taste wine?" Jeff asks them. "See," he says to me and Hank. "What'd I tell ya?"

Funny guy. Here's what we know already. Jeff will not be deterred, and tasting wine at Frank Family Vineyards is not for the delicate. This isn't a particularly reverent place, you don't get to stand quietly at a bar and get served, and it will be loud. On the plus side, you get the show, and it's still about the wine. Here, they group you, move you around, and bombard you with good humor, some of it even funny. Mixed in is some wine education. It's easy to like this place.

Our group has grown to twenty. Jeff starts serving glasses of sparkling Blanc de Blancs that's yeasty and dry, and gives some instructions. "This is the orientation," he says. "Then we'll go back to another room. That'll be the disorientation."

"By the way," he says, "my name is Jeff. If you like me. If you don't like me, it's Enrique. En-ri-que."

He stops handing out glasses for a moment.

"This is 'wine tasting,'" he says. "Two sips is what I ask of you. Take one sip, let it coat your tongue and sit there for a few seconds. When you're done with that, wait a bit, like thirty seconds, and take a second sip. Two sips; takes about a minute. Any more than that, and it's 'wine drinking.'"

Since most of this bunch is off Jeff's blueprint and on vacation, they're here for wine drinking. Jeff knows two guys in our pack and tells everyone they're from Charles Krug. They're spitting, like me and Hank. We're the only ones.

Jeff moves the pack into a back room and calls out as we walk. "It's OK to dump what's in your glass. It's not going to waste," he says, talking loud over everyone's heads. "It all goes into the spit bucket. Then we ship it over to Charles Krug."

"Thanks, Enrique," one of the Krug guys says.

Jeff lines us up in a room full with Marilyn Monroe posters, paintings, and memorabilia. There's a six-foot-tall Marilyn portrait, a series done by Andy Warhol, framed pictures of Marilyn drinking wine. This winery has a long history, starting as Larkmead Winery in 1884, then it became Hanns Kornell Champagne Cellars in 1938—which explains both the sparkling wines and Marilyn Monroe. She used to come here in the 1950s and hang out with Hanns, sipping bubbly, occasionally greeting stunned visitors. Current owners, Rich Frank, a former Disney television executive, and Koerner Rombauer, owner of Rombauer Vineyards, bought the place in 1992 and figured Marilyn's memory was not a bad touch.

Jeff has moved us along to the 2004 Napa Valley Chardonnay. "We taste it unchilled here," he says. "Is that gonna scare anyone? We think you can taste more of the wine's qualities when it's room temperature. Now watch this. I'm gonna do this in one shot."

Jeff lines up twenty wineglasses. He uncorks a new Chard and starts pouring quickly. The amounts in each glass look identical, the wine levels lined straight like they were measured with a laser. Jeff's getting down to the end of the line and the end of the bottle. Same perfect amounts. People are cheering. Last glass. Bottle's empty. Exactly perfect. Our group goes nuts. I go nuts.

"We go to school for that," Jeff says.

The wine is good. Smooth and soft. There's apples to it and caramel and a sense of the crust from a fruit crisp. It's hard to tell what it would taste like cold, but it's got the long, crème brûlée finish Jeff was advertising.

The 2003 Zinfandel is huge. Maybe too ripe for Hank. There's lots of jam and some spice. It's the kind of Zin I always fall for and feel guilty about it. We ask what the alcohol percentage is.

"The bottle says 15.2," Jeff says, "but it's more like sixteen . . . cough . . . point . . . cough . . . five. We don't advertise that. It's so high alcohol, we call it LPR. You know what LPR is?" He waits a beat. "Liquid Panty Remover." Jeff points to a blond woman who's part of the group from Kentucky. "If you guys want to put more in her glass, I won't stop you." The guys look embarrassed. She laughs brightly.

It goes like this for a while. There are some details about the wine, some insults, some history of the place. Jeff quotes from a sign. "I live in my own little world," it says. "It's OK. They know me there."

He wraps it up with the usual plug to buy the wines here, but his line is a bit unusual.

"If you choose to buy nothing, that's OK," he says. "It's not your job to buy, it's my job to sell." He says that as people start to leave the tasting room and move toward the sales room in front. "But you'll be missing out . . ."

We talk to him when it's quieted down. He says he tries to read each group to decide how silly to get. This gang was a tourist bunch; they wanted less wine talk and more silly.

We mention to him what Andy at Benessere was saying. We're wondering if he agrees.

"He may be right," Jeff says. "People always think this is gonna be The Year. You know, the last couple years have all been pretty good. We've had these milder late summers and good, later harvests. There's a lot of really good wine in the valley right now waiting to come out of barrels.

"But that kinda makes me worry. We've dodged a lot of weather bullets in the last few years. We still have a long way to go before we start picking this year, and with all those good grapes out there, I'm getting nervous that this is the year we crap out."

WE'RE HANGING ON SILVERADO TRAIL TODAY on a mid-September Sunday. At Duckhorn, we get a sit-down tasting in what could be the dining room of a luxury summer resort. There's a big white porch outside with some comfy-looking chairs, and beyond that, vineyards and hills. Inside, it's pale wood and lots of light, and the tasting is sort of luxury resort style, too.

We're seated at tables, restaurant style, then servers come to pour like waiter-folk. Each wine gets a new glass and they talk lots of details. The tall, fiftyish guy who seems to be running the room checks in with us, so we ask about this vintage-of-the-century thing. He doesn't scoff.

"Some people are saying that," he said. "And some people think we might not get enough of the flavors."

We tell him about Andy at Benessere. He says Andy could be right. "And it could be he's right about just their grapes. This has been an odd one," he says.

The people at Cuvaison, with its lively little tasting room on a short rise above Silverado Trail, are talking about lots of grapes from the heavy spring rains. And, possibly, not enough heat for them all to mature.

"No one irrigated until August," our server tells us. "There may be too much fruit out there. Some people are a little worried."

At Casa Nuestra Winery and Vineyards, a bit south of Cuvaison, it's another story. It's another world, really, of cheery and slightly droll folk who seem to be unstressed about the harvest, and about pretty much everything.

That's the image, anyway, and we have no reason to doubt it. Casa Nuestra is off Silverado Trail, down a dirt road that owner Gene Kirkham fights to keep unpaved. The tasting room is in a rickety-looking yellow farmhouse behind some large, ancient oaks and past a lawn, a shed, and a livestock pen. The word *rustic* comes to mind.

Inside the open, eclectically scruffy room, the word is *throwback*. There's a fireplace, psychedelic posters, peace signs, photos of blues and folk musicians, and a wall that's a shrine to Martin Luther King Jr. and Elvis Presley. Elvis stuff is everywhere.

As we walk to the tasting bar, a guy with a bright short-sleeve shirt and a thick head of slightly graying hair is laughing into the phone.

"Appointment?" he says. "We can, if you want. Or, we're open 10 to 5 every day. Can you make that?"

His name is Bailey. Steven Bailey, actually, but his card just says "Bailey." He's also a caterer and used to do that in Hollywood for the film industry until he got tired of insane people. Now he's in wine country and, in contrast, things seem positively stable.

"Welcome to our hippie museum," he calls the room.

We tell him we've been flying past the sign out on Silverado Trail for years and barely noticed the place. Hank says he's not sure he's even tasted their wines.

"It is never too late," Bailey says, "for enlightenment."

He is right about that. Everything we taste is good. Their 2004 Dry Rosado has all those cherries and strawberries of a good Rosé, and it finishes crisp and clean. Their 2004 Meritage is rich and complex. And their 2003 Tinto Classico is bright and mouth-filling and spicy with all kinds of flavors in there. That last wine is a bit unusual, Bailey tells us.

The Tinto comes from vineyards in Oakville that the family of Gene Kirkham—who, for the record, calls himself the Happy Farmer—has owned since 1956. The wine is a field blend in the Old World style, so the nine different varietals growing there all get picked and ferment together.

We ask what kind of varietals.

"God, I dunno," Bailey says. He starts ticking them off on his fingers. Zinfandel, Petite Sirah, Carignan, Mourvèdre, Pinot Noir, Cabernet Pfeffer, Alicante-Bouschet. "Stuff like that."

I've never heard of the last two.

"They're actual grapes," Bailey says. "Everything was mostly planted in the 1940s. I'm not sure anyone's figured out exactly what's out there. We take it all in and it makes pretty good wine."

"Oakville?" Hank says. "That's expensive land for a field blend."

"I know," Bailey says. "It's, like, right next to Harlan Estate and pretty close to Martha's Vineyard. They probably hate having us heathens out there."

But he can't sell us any because they're almost out of it. What's left is for tasting and to make us want it more next year. How much do they make? I ask.

"1,500 cases," Bailey says.

"Of the Tinto?" I ask.

"Of everything," Bailey says.

Robert Conrad, a young, burly guy with a red beard and nearly buzzed hair is also working the tasting bar and he's laughing at the conversation.

"1,500 cases," he says. "It's part of our plan for world domination."

"Do you guys ever run out of wine?" I ask.

"Often," Robert says.

I'm liking this place. Robert's card says "One of six." Their wines are too good for them to really be this casual about everything, but the atmosphere feels like we're in a bar on a river somewhere, and we should all be hanging out drinking beer. Or Tinto Classico, if they didn't run out. We figure the Elvis pictures, clocks, and toys are just part of a kitsch streak. Turns out, he shot a couple scenes from the movie *Wild in the Country* out back in the early 1960s. Casa Nuestra's fields played a swamp.

We get Robert and Bailey serious enough for a moment to ask about the grapes and the weather this season. They have no specific answer. Some places are getting high yields. The cooler hillside vineyards seem to be thinner. Some people love the quality, some aren't so sure. Everyone expects a late harvest. Everyone's hoping it doesn't rain.

"This is the kind of year that the vineyard manager and the winemaker have to work for a living," Robert says.

Bailey walks out the door with us and we look at this pretty country scene, the grass, the oaks, a couple picnic tables on a redwood deck, and a pair of goats in the little corral. "Is this a working ranch, too?" I ask.

Bailey laughs again. "Uh, no. They're our weed abatement crew," he says. "City people. You see a pen and two goats and you think it's Animal Farm."

WE'RE CONFUSED. IT'S NOT AN UNCOMMON feeling for me. Hank's less used to it, at least when it comes to wine. This is where we are: Could be a great year. Best wine ever. Or maybe it'll suck. Yields are high. Yields are low. Yields are right in the middle. To clear things up, Hank gets us some chat time with Vince Bonotto, the director of vineyard operations for Diageo Wines.

Diageo is one of the big boys in the valley, the corporate owner of nearly two dozen wineries, including Sterling, BV, Provenance, and Acacia. Bonotto looks after nearly 2,220 acres of vineyards in every piece of Napa, from Carneros to Calistoga, and in mid-September, with mild day after mild day and his grapes growing oh-so-slowly, "stressed" describes Vince more than his grapes.

"We're in neutral right now," he says. "We're waiting for the light to change. And while we're sitting here, we could get hit by a truck."

Vince is waiting for a bit more maturity and flavor in most of his reds. He's worrying about the storms starting to form out in the Pacific. They're heading far north of Napa Valley for now, aimed at the Pacific Northwest. But if one or two gets off track and dives for Northern California, Vince, and every other vineyard manager in Napa, will have a mess.

It's mid-afternoon and Vince is back in his office inside a simple set of buildings. They're tucked against the hill below Sterling Vineyards' white, Mediterranean-looking winery and fortress. He walked vineyards much of the early day, tasting Chardonnay and Merlot grapes in Carneros and lots of mid-valley Cabernet fruit.

"We're seeing full berry clusters, so the yields look good," Vince tells us. "But they're not meeting the flavor profile we're looking for."

OK. Now I'm more confused. What about those crazy flavors all over the valley? Does this really look like a landmark year, or are we hearing standard vintage-of-the-century hype?

Vince is, fundamentally, a working stiff, though the maps, soil reports, and rolls of charts spread around his desk and on shelves make his large, simple office look like it belongs to a geologist. He's another guy with the healthy, stocky build of a man who works hard. He has a dark goatee and dark hair and wears a peach-colored short-sleeve shirt and his sunglasses up in his hair. Vince has been running around vineyards nearly twenty years, starting his career managing the vineyard at Fresno State when he was a student. He worked his way to better and better spots until he landed at Sterling and Diageo. He's not the kind of guy to blow great-vintage smoke, unless it's real.

"There's lots of potential," he says. "We're not there, yet."

He says, more or less, what everyone else says. They're getting good acids. The sugars are getting there. The flavors are coming. The pieces are gathering for great wine, they just need to get the right balance, now. Because of the relative cool summer, everything is behind the usual cycle.

There is plenty of upside to the moderate summer months. There weren't many heat spikes that cause those sudden rises in sugars and make the grapes ready for picking before all the flavors have developed. If you wait for those flavors and don't pick, the high sugars and dehydration turn the grapes into raisins on the vine. Or, sometimes, the summers are so hot, with days regularly over nintey-five degrees, that the vines shut down and nothing develops.

"I'm looking at it as having the potential to be a really great vintage, if it stays dry and we get the hang time," Vince says. "The advantage in a year like this is that when the grapes do reach the flavor profile we're looking for, it's due to the natural course of things, and you get much more of the flavor of the fruit and the varietal characteristics."

The downside, we're figuring out, is it makes guys like Vince, and pretty much everyone in the valley, crazy waiting for the damn things to come around.

Most wineries in Napa have started picking some grapes by now. They're taking in their whites, like Sauvignon Blanc and Chardonnay, and some Pinot Noir and other cooler weather grapes. But there's still a lot of Chard out there, particularly on the hillsides, where it's generally cooler anyway and cycles tend to run a couple weeks behind the valley floor. And the heat-seeking reds, like Cabernet and Syrah, might still need to hang around their vines for as much as another month.

That worries Vince, and everyone, because one or two rainstorms could bring calamity. The thin-skinned grapes, like Chardonnay and poor old delicate Pinot Noir, absorb the rainwater through their skins, swell, and burst, letting in all sorts of mold spores to ruin what's left of the crop. Heartier reds won't burst but if they sit in moisture very long, they'll develop mold on their skins and absorb the taste.

Just as bad, if the ground gets a good soaking, the fields become muddy swamps. The harvesters and tractors can't get in there to get the grapes picked.

"If we get a shot of rain, then it dries up and gets warm, that's OK," Vince says. "What happens after the rain is just as important."

Oh, but there's more. Even if there's no rain, even if not one cloudy day darkens the skies, the grapes could have troubles. First off, each day deeper into fall there's less and less sunlight and a shorter growing period, so each day the grapes and vines get less work done. And as the nights get colder, the naive vines start thinking maybe it's full-on autumn. Time to shut down and take a long winter's nap. Then everything stops progressing.

"If we see storms coming, or if it just gets cold, we have to decide if this is it, if it's not going to get any better," Vince says. Beneath his steady voice, we can hear the dread. "Maybe we'll have to make the call that it's as good as it's going to get."

They've also got piles of contingency plans before a coming storm, which include picking their best fruit—the grapes they don't want to risk—or picking some of everything from everywhere just in case the storm is a catastrophe. "But our tendency is to try to wait it out," he says.

It's a little weird to be talking disaster plans on a day like this. The Friday afternoon has reached the high seventies, and the soft sun is filtering through trees outside Vince's windows, making his office into a cheerful greenhouse. It is exactly days like this, months like this, that have filled the comfortable deck up at Sterling with visitors to Napa. It's weather a lot like this in September and October, exactly the consistent, sunny, and dry weather Vince and the grapes want, that makes Napa Valley such a paradise for wine.

Is it really such a worry, all these scenarios of doom? I ask.

"There is nothing that's happened to indicate this can't be a great vintage," he says. "That's one reason we're nervous. We might have something big here.

"And it's been slow. We keep waiting and waiting. It's kind of mind-boggling to last this long. It would be nice to see some hot weather come along, like eighty-eight or ninety. That would be perfect."

If the weather continues to track dry with these high seventies and low eighties, Vince says they'll pick Pinot grapes in Carneros next week, and maybe some Merlot.

"Those Cabs are going to stay out there a while still," he says "We'll heave that sigh of relief when the last load comes across the scale. Until then, it's really nerve-racking."

Now Vince has racked our nerves. We head for Sterling proper and ride the little aerial tram 200 feet up to the winery. Sterling has the flat-out best walking tour in Napa for seeing how to make wine. It's logical, goes through the steps with video screens, even explains how different barrels, and different levels of toasted wood in the barrels, can affect the texture and taste of wine. We don't care. We both need a drink.

Tasting at Sterling is in an airy, wood and glass room with tall ceilings, or out on a big stone deck looking through trees down to the valley floor and north to Calistoga. We head for the deck. The wine list is OK, but the view and atmosphere are spectacular.

It is Friday nearing 5 p.m. The air is warm and still, and most people around us are done tasting wine. They are, as Jeff at Frank Family Vineyards would say, getting down to drinking it. Why not? It's happy hour leading toward a sunny, mild weekend in wine country. They've got tastings and picnics, cafes and great restaurants ahead of them. They may end up drinking some of the best wine on the planet. They surely are in one of the prettiest places it's grown.

It makes us happy to see all this. It makes me think maybe doom is not just one rainstorm away. This blissful party atmosphere is a relief from yet another reminder that, for all the romance of it, for all the serious talk and simple fun involved, making wine starts with farming. And farming is always hard and risky.

IT'S THE FIRST WEEKEND IN OCTOBER and we're back on Big Tree Lane at Tudal Family Winery, just across some vineyards from Benessere and emphatic ol' Andy. At the moment, we're up on a two-story metal catwalk, looking down into a large steel tank at 2,000 gallons of fermenting wine. It looks like the chunky filling of a blueberry pie.

Ron Vuylsteke, Tudal's winemaker, is up here, showing six of us around on a tour. "That's it, right there," Ron says. "Baby wine."

Ron's not that serious a guy. Nobody around here seems to be. Ron's casual about the tour—"That's where we make it. That's where we drink it," he tells us. "What do you want to see?"—and seemingly as casual about some of the details of his winemaking. Truth is, he goes more by feel and taste than by formula.

Those big tanks will be fermenting for at least a week. Ron will taste the baby, then adolescent, wine a few times every day to monitor its progress. And tasting was how he decided when to start picking the grapes, eight tons of which are in that one tank now.

"You have to go out in the field and taste the berries," he says. "We pretty much throw away the numbers. You want that mix of acidity and sweetness. Not coated in sugar. Not really fruity. Not too tart. You want that balance."

Ron's been in the business thirty-five years, and comes from an Oregon family that made wine, too. He looks like a middle-aged surfer dude, with a slightly ruddy face, and with moppish blond hair starting to get a little gray into the mix. He wears an untucked, worn orange T-shirt and black jeans.

As we all climb down the metal stairs, Ron tells us he's pretty thrilled to have that baby wine in the tank. It was a long wait this year. We wander over to some knotted and knobby vines still holding onto grapes that will become their Old Vine Cabernet. "We'll probably pick these next week," he says. "That will be the last of it."

It's been three weeks since we talked about the potential for ruin with Vince at Diageo. We've checked back and Vince's crews have been picking away, though they still have more to do. But Ron and everyone at Tudal are about to heave that sigh of relief that comes when you get the crop in. There are plenty more grapes still hanging in Napa, loads of them up the cooler hillsides, but the weather has taken a turn.

There was a short bout of rain a week ago, just a harmless sprinkling from a tropical storm that ran through Southern California. The sun popped right back out and the temperatures went up, climbing into the mid-eighties, not so hot to make everything ripen at once, but enough to get things moving.

"This is perfect right now," Ron says. "It was tense there for a while. The whole year made us nervous."

It also turns out that yields were huge. Tudal brought in maybe fifty percent more grapes than they were expecting. Ron says it's hard for small operations to do more than guess at the tonnage in the vineyards.

"There's no way we can really tell," he says. "There are spots in the vineyards that are heavier and lighter. You take samples, look at cluster weights, but it's all approximate. Some of the big guys have better ideas what they've got, but for us it was a pleasant surprise. We were scrambling to find places to put it all, but we've got it under control."

I'm thinking it's about time. Everything in Napa is showing signs of fall. Tudal Family Winery—a collection of low ranch buildings, Western-style dark-wood fences, and friendliness—is in that narrow stretch of valley with the Vaca Mountains a quarter mile to the east and the Mayacamas range a mile away to the west. The vineyards running to both ridges don't look their freshest. The greens are pale, the vines have some yellow creeping in, the grass on the eastern hillsides is a thin brown, and gold is starting to show in some trees. The sense of autumn is palpable.

Ron takes us back to the winery, and pours barrel samples of the 2004 Cabernet. This tour turns into a merry little bull session. Arnold Tudal, the owner, has come over from his house on the property to join us in the crowded office.

That's because two of the visitors, Ben and Patricia from the Hamptons in New York, fell in love with Arnold when they visited years before, and try to say hello whenever they're here. He was happy to come see them, and to give Ron grief. Arnold's not a serious guy, either.

He started this winery in 1974 after already spending twenty-seven years farming vegetables in Alameda, east of San Francisco. Arnold is eighty-two and fighting Alzheimer's now, so he spends some time in a wheelchair, which doesn't seem to make him any less cheery, or any less of a wiseass.

"You're seeing Ron dressed up today," Arnold tells his old friends as he nods toward Ron's semi-ratty T-shirt. "He's usually sloppy."

"He's as good a storyteller as you are," Patricia says.

"Can't have that," Arnold says. "I'd dump him but he makes pretty good wine. I've laxed in this business. I'm too henpecked to keep up."

"You can tell Alma [Arnold's wife] is in Virginia," Ron says.

There are pictures of Joe DiMaggio, who was a longtime family friend, with a much younger Arnold. We ask how often Joltin' Joe visited. "A lot," Arnold said. "He used to date my wife. Cost him $50. He told us some stories about spring training I can't repeat even when Alma's not here."

It goes on like this for a while, this general silliness with its underlying affection. Arnold treats Ron like a son. He chides him, kids him, and never lets him forget he is proud of how Ron has taken over.

Even on this warm Saturday afternoon, Arnold wears pressed gray slacks and a gray-blue sweater. Annabelle, a black cat with splatters of tan and white, brings a fuzzy ball into the room and bats it around, scurrying between legs to get it. She spends a lot of time under Ron's chair, then dashes out to chase her ball. Arnold bends over to pet her. Judging from Annabelle, and the pictures on the walls, Arnold's a cat guy.

I ask about the framed White House menus hanging in the middle of those pictures showing Tudal wines served at a lunch and a dinner. Arnold gets a genuine look of humility on his face. It's about the only time he's close to serious.

"That was nice," he says. "I guess we figured out how to do this winemaking."

So it seems. For all the country gee-shucks around here, little Tudal has a big rep for Cabernets. When Arnold bought the place, he planned to grow walnuts on his ten acres, but his neighbor, a guy named Louis P. Martini, convinced him he owned top-grade Cabernet land. Tudal has always made Bordeaux-style Cabs, which means slightly less alcohol that some of the big-fruit, big-points monsters, but more balanced, more timeless wine.

They thought about raising the price for the 2002 Cab to $45, Ron tells us, for the preposterous reason it would sell better. "People are laughing at us at $35," he says. "A lot of collectors can't imagine how our wine could be all that great at that price. I have a friend who just spent $3,100 on a bottle of wine. That is an insane, ridiculous amount for any bottle.

"Anyway, we decided to keep it at $35. We still think it's good."

It is. It's got berries and chocolate and some mint in it. It's very drinkable now, but Ron says it will sit fine for eight or ten years if you want.

Tudal also makes three unusual red blends called Tractor Shed Red, Flat Bed Red, and Rag Top Red. Arnold keeps the old family tractor from the Tractor Shed Red label under a tree by the winery. Around a corner is an ancient-but-functioning flatbed truck, and there's a cherry red 1964 Chevy Impala convertible parked by the house.

Actually, Arnold says, the wines are all tributes to farmers. The tractor represents their hard work, the truck's for bringing in the crops, and the rag top, he says, "is for going to town and foolin' around."

There is something about the way Arnold said that, part playful, part earnest, full of admiration, not just for his own work, but for Ron's and his field crew's and for all the crews and farmers up and down the valley. It stops me.

By now, our group has spread to the gravel driveway outside the office. Most everyone is standing around with wineglasses, Ron petting Annabelle the cat, Arnold sitting in his wheelchair laughing, his old friends touching his shoulder now and then. Around them are the remains of the growing season, the last of the grapes on the vine, earthy autumn colors creeping in, the big tanks with "baby wine" fermenting away.

I'm standing to one side. I realize I've got the dopey grin I get when I wander into sentimental territory. Hank's seen it a lot through the years and walks over.

"These are people you root for," he says.

"Yes, they are."

It's people like Arnold Tudal, a hardworking man and a buoyant soul, who brings people across the country—from Ben and Pat to Joe DiMaggio—to seize a little more of the wine country essence they find when they see him. It's people like Ron Vuylsteke, with winemaking in his genes, with an innate connection to the land and the process. It's this small winery with memorable wine and a big, light heart. They are, together, the image of Napa, the real picture that goes on every book cover. They are the spirit of the place. They are why it's not just the wine that stays with us when we leave.

TEN

The Mayacamas Mountains

WE'RE INSIDE ONE of the midnight blue Hess pickup trucks, bouncing along a dirt road on the side of Mt. Veeder, nearly 2,000 feet up and looking at vineyards that drop off like ski slopes. The truck barely fits the road. I'm in the back seat, with my head out the window, eating dust so I can gawk down at a rippling mountainside of vines and out across the bottom of Napa Valley. I can see low fog sitting on San Francisco and its bay.

"This is awesome," I say, as if Hank and Richard wouldn't notice without my help.

Richard is Richard Camera, the director of vineyard operations for the Hess Collection Winery. He's taking us along on his rounds checking vines and grapes on 360 acres spread over a couple miles of Mt. Veeder's notches, meadows, and peaks. Hank pulled some strings—yeah, that violates our Quest rules—because we want a sense of what's happening on the hillsides.

Richard is our man. He's been at Hess since 1993, taught hillside viticulture at Napa Community College for eight years, and, most importantly as far as I'm concerned, he can get this truck to go anywhere.

At the moment, we rock our way up to a ridge that seems to be on top of the planet. To the south, the vineyards plunge down, running off at different angles, then gathering again to hit a distant line of pine trees. Beyond them is Napa, Atlas Peak across the valley floor, Mt. Diablo and the San Francisco Bay to the south. Hank and Richard have wandered into the vineyards. I'm staring into space.

I catch up as they stop to taste grapes. These will go into the Hess Collection Cabernet and they surprise me. They're sweet. Sweeter, even, than grapes from a store. I don't know why, but I thought they'd be tart, or slightly acidic like some grapes we'd tasted earlier this year. Or maybe they'd taste like Cabernet. Instead, they taste like grapes.

"They're sweet," I say.

Hank and Richard are polite. They both just nod.

"We're not tasting for sweetness," Richard says. "The sugars are there. The last thing we're waiting for is the acids to drop. It's all about getting everything to match."

He spits the small seeds into his hand. There's still a little green in them. "We're a couple weeks away," Richard says. "The seeds should be all brown."

Richard is tall and high shouldered, like he might have played basketball in another life. He's in his early fifties and looks twenty years younger in a Hess baseball cap, white T-shirt, tan jeans, and work shoes. His reddish beard and red-blond hair are showing what might be hints of gray.

He is also a smart guy, which is something we find a lot among vineyard managers and winemakers. Apparently, this business requires some brain power.

"I have a dumb question," I say.

Richard, to his credit, doesn't give me that "no question is dumb" crap. We've been rolling around in his truck for more than an hour already and he knows I'm completely capable of very dumb questions. He looks at Hank, who gives him a "just go with it" shrug.

"How long have the grapes been sweet?" I ask.

"That a pretty good question," Richard says. I think he's trying to keep the surprise out of his voice.

He says it helps to understand vineyards if you think of grapes as the reproductive part of a vine. It is how they spread their seed. Literally. Birds eat the grapes and scatter the seeds in their waste.

"The vine wants the grapes healthy, and it wants them independent," Richard says. "But it doesn't want birds eating the grapes until the seeds have matured." So the grapes are sour for most of the season—they have low Brix and high acid—until the vine is ready to have the birds chow down. That's why, when the sugars rise in grapes and the acids drop, it's usually time to pick.

This year, Richard says, they've been waiting forever.

"We were done at this time last year," he says. "Done. We finished on October 18. Over just two years, it's a very different viticultural experience."

We're three weeks into October. They're nearly done on the valley floor. Down on the flats, most of the vines look light without their grapes, and yellows, golds, and reds are moving into the fields and across the landscape. Up on the hillsides, everything is a few weeks behind. The cooler days make the season run as much as a month behind, so the vineyards here are still mostly green and the harvest has at least a couple weeks to go.

"If we stay dry through to November, it'll be a fantastic year," Richard says. "The acids are changing, the tannins are changing. It's almost like a cold soak there on the vines. Everything is softening and melding. What we really need is the weather to play with us.

"We're gambling right now. If you farm in the hills, you have to be a gambler."

What they're risking in the hills is the longer season and more vulnerability to bad weather. What they want as the payoff seems odd: stress. If everything goes well, their poor little grapes will put some hard effort into growing up.

Farming grapes for fine wine is not like growing wheat or corn, or grapes for the supermarket. Give most crops good sun, rich soil, and buckets of water, and they'll grow as high an elephant's eye. Wine grapes, on the other hand, you torture. Make the suckers work.

In simple terms, the more stress a vine is under, the more it will channel its energy into surviving and reproducing, so everything goes to the grape. The result isn't big, plump grapes, it's smaller, denser grapes with thick skins and loads of nutrients. That translates to deep flavors and complex wine.

Winegrowers learned to stress the vines by planting them close together and making them fight for their water and soil. Or by planting vines on hillsides, with thin soil, lots of rocks, and gravity naturally drawing water down the mountain and away from the roots. That doesn't mean you just plant the vines and walk away. They need even more careful tending in the hills.

"Pruning is still the most important thing you can do to a vine," Richard says. "It keeps it virus free, gets the right canopy, gives us more ability to keep things uniform and to control the yields and the quality."

To that end, Richard has created for Hess what he calls a "digital heritage." He's computerized the record keeping for every scrap of info about the season. That includes details of growing patterns, irrigation amounts and grapevine clones, and data from moisture sensors, weather stations, and even satellite infrared photography.

"We put all this work into it," he says, "we might as well have some record of what it does. And that helps us make decisions for the next year."

We rumble out of the vineyards and down the mountain to the winery. Donald Hess, the owner of the place, actually rents the main winery building—on a ninety-nine-year lease—from the Christian Brothers, who are no longer in the wine business. Hess came to Napa from Switzerland in 1976 looking to expand his mineral water company. He decided Americans would never go for bottled water, but showed he wasn't entirely bereft of vision when he saw the potential for these Mt. Veeder vineyards.

He took over what was the former Mont La Salle Winery in 1983, and by 1989, opened a dramatic tasting room and art gallery—three sleek stories of open space, white wood, and glass—built around the original stone walls of the 1903 winery.

The 13,000-square-foot gallery houses Hess's collection of contemporary art, and it features some big-time international names, including Frank Stella, Francis Bacon, and Franz Gertsch. The piece that resonates with me is by Argentine Leopoldo Maler. It's an old Underwood typewriter with flames shooting from it. I have no idea what it really means, but as a guy who writes for a living, I'm thinking it has something to do with pain.

Richard leads us to the tasting room, with its oval, polished maple wood bar inside the native stone walls. Hess has a large portfolio of wines. Its reserve line, called Hess Collection, is strong and, if you go by me, underpriced. My favorite is the 2002 Mountain Cuvée, a Bordeaux-like blend except it also includes Syrah. I'm getting layers, starting with, I think, cherry then turning to pepper, and it's rich and earthy, too.

Richard tells me that winemaker Dave Guffy can have a seemingly endless number of choices for the Cuvée or any of the reserve wines, because of all the elevations, angles, microclimates, and exposures of their vineyards.

"With all the nuances," he says, "when we start blending, we probably have 100 different lots off the mountain. Winemakers, they have a lot to think about, too."

WE ARE WINDING EAST ON MT. Veeder Road, which runs parallel to the valley floor, a couple hundred feet above it to the west. Hank is talking about the irony of it all. In the old days, vineyards got planted on hillsides to save the fertile flatlands for more valuable crops. They put the vines where nothing else would grow.

That's about opposite from Napa now. Hillside vineyards have become primo territory for the small-production, highly stressed, hugely priced wines. All those cult reds, like Colgin Cellars, Bryant Family, or Screaming Eagle, those big, intense reds with big, intense reps—and tiny, impossible-to-get releases—come from the hills.

It's also true that the mountains on both sides of the valley are the only places left for new vineyards and wineries, and that's turned them into a battleground. Some locals have fought and even sued to stop new vineyards in the hills, which on first blush sounds absurd because not so long ago environmentalists, as well as Napa County, pushed vineyard growth, figuring vineyards and wineries would keep developers from building houses and shopping centers on some of America's most precious agricultural land.

Napa County passed a hillside ordinance in 1991 that requires permits, erosion control, and environmental reports—at the least—to put in new hillside vineyards, but it all remains a tangle here, with splits among environmental groups and constant political intrigue.

Meanwhile, even replanting your own hillside vineyard can be slow and expensive. That explains the acres of unplowed, bare dirt in front of the main buildings at Mayacamas Vineyard, a small winery built inside one of Mt. Veeder's volcanic craters. I ask if it makes anyone there nervous to live inside a volcano. They say Mt. Veeder's been extinct for about a million years, so it's probably pretty safe.

There are other qualities special to hillside wineries, starting with the scenery. On the way to Chateau Potelle, we're heading up a long road through trees when we turn a corner and pop out to sunlight, a wide slope of grapevines, and a view halfway to Bordeaux. Up the road, the tasting room feels like a snug mountain cottage, with a little tile counter, wood paneling, and a wood-burning stove in the corner. It would make a great cozy breakfast spot or, I suppose, a nice place to taste wine.

It's also a room with some good gags. "Up here, we have a lot of time to think," says Tony Bartolomucci, the tasting room manager, do-everything guy, and general ambassador for the place.

There are small signs above the bar with suggested questions to ask Tony, like "How high up are we?" (1,500 feet; their vineyards go to 2,100); "Where does the name Chateau Potelle come from?" (It's an estate in France. There's a picture on the wall. It's somewhat larger than the Napa version); and "What does VGS mean?"

VGS is what they call their reserve wines—which for the record, are spectacular and internationally known. If you ask the Alcohol and Tobacco Tax and Trade Bureau, which approves wine bottle labels, it means Vintner's Grand Selection. Ask Tony, or Hank, or anyone who knows, it means Very Good Shit. Hard to argue. The 2003 VGS Zinfandel about takes my socks off. It's got a huge, juicy nose and rich fruit, but not the hot alcohol of some big Zins.

Actually, they're pretty good at naming wines, here. They have a Once in a Blue Moon Late-Harvest Chardonnay, which needless to say, does not come out every year, and they own some steep mountainside vineyards on California's Central Coast that go by the Gravity Hills label. There's one stretch of vines planted on a forty-four-degree slope that gave them such fits with their heavy equipment, they called the wine Tumbling Tractor Syrah.

We head outside and take sandwiches we stowed away over to some picnic tables under the trees. We're looking down the hillside out at forever. Tony's got an empty tasting room, so he brings his lunch out and sits with us. He's followed over by Mimi, a gray and black Border collie. Mimi has big-time begging skills. She sits at my feet, looks up at me, and rests her chin on my knee.

I tell Tony I'm impressed.

"She's an amateur," Tony says. "You should meet Opus." Opus is their dalmatian, who's off with the owners today. We tell him we've heard of Opus. He gets national press from wine writers who stop here and have lunch.

"Opus may be the sweetest dog in Napa," Tony says, "but he doesn't like other dogs, except Mimi. Even if you leave your dog in the car, Opus will stand there and bark. He's scratched up a few paint jobs." He says they are serious about the sign on the road that says, "No pets allowed. Ours get jealous."

Chateau Potelle, like so many small wineries, is a place with a good back story. It was founded by Marketta and Jean-Noël Fourmeaux, who worked as official wine tasters for the French government and visited California in 1980 on a mission to see what was going on here. They came to Napa, looked around, and sent a telegram back to France. "Looks good," it said. "We stay."

They moved their family here and in 1988, bought the 202 acres that is Chateau Potelle. Marketta is the winemaker. Tony says the philosophy is to make wine with a minimum of intervention, which includes using gravity to move the wine into tanks and barrels, and to let the grapes for all the VGS wines ferment with wild yeast—the yeast that's naturally on the grapes from the fields. The benefit, he says, is the wines keep all the textures and flavors from the vineyard. The risk is that the fermentation is a lot harder to control.

"We're gamblers here," he says.

We tell him we hear that a lot in these hills.

WE REACH SMITH-MADRONE BY DRIVING five miles up Spring Mountain Road, hanging a right at the county line, and backtracking down a bumpy, potholed road I have to admit they warned us about. When we called Smith-Madrone for directions, they also said, when in doubt, turn right, which is not 100 percent accurate because at least one right leads to a dead end, but we're not complaining because we've navigated our way to a few dead ends on our own.

The winery itself looks like a wood barn sitting on a bluff about 1,800 feet above northern Napa. Hills of vines rise around it on three sides. To the east, toward the valley, the vineyard slowly drops away, and a road lined by trees follows the vineyard down.

We walk around the building to the cement crush pad facing that vineyard. A group of people and kids is milling on the pad, and a two-year-old boy is climbing into the open bottom of an empty steel fermentation tank.

"Is that OK?" I ask Hank. "Shouldn't he have to go through the stemmer first?

"It's a matter of choice," Hank says. "Some winemakers put everything in with their reds: stems, seeds, hats and pants, little shoes."

The boy turns out to be Davis, the two-year-old grandson of one of the owners, Stuart Smith. He crawls in and out of the tank for a while, trying to drag the older kids with him. Occasionally, one of the adults directs him away from the edge of the pad, but Davis mostly really likes the tank. This, we learn, is pretty much the style here. Casual, unaffected, and, if you want, anyone can play in the tanks.

Tours and tastings are run by either Stu or his brother, Charles, as is just about everything at Smith-Madrone. They are both tall, with white beards, athletic builds, and they wear jeans and work shirts. They look more like mountain men than winemakers.

We go into the belly of the winery, a large, garage-like room with a cement floor, big tanks along both side walls, and a long table at the back with wines, displays, trophies, pictures, and a work space with measuring equipment and scales. It reeks of family winery.

Charles pours our small group a hefty taste of the 2001 Napa Valley Cabernet and excuses himself. "We've got some grapes coming in," he says. "I have to measure the sulfur. We don't have much of a tour to speak of. Our approach is to pour you wine and let you wander around."

It's a good approach, though I'm lost for a minute in the Cabernet. It's got a floral nose and tastes like blackberries and lots of soft dark fruit. I snap out of my haze and see everyone has gone outside to the crush pad. Davis is no longer in the big tank. Instead, Stu is standing with a four-foot-high metal wagon filled with dark blue grapes. They look like marbles. In front of and below the crush pad is what looks like a white metal dumpster, except it has a large corkscrew running along its bottom.

That's a stemmer/crusher. It will gently take the grapes off the stems and break them open. Stu hooks his wagon to a winch that pours the grapes into the stemmer. Next, he sprinkles a bit of the white sulfur dioxide over the grapes. They are sliding along in the white stemmer, roiling forward, breaking up a little, looking like a deep blue and purple lava flow.

Stu is standing next to me as we watch the current. I can't contain myself.

"You're making wine," I say.

"It's what we do," he says.

"We've been bouncing around this frickin' valley for eight months," I say. "Finally, someone is making wine."

Stu Smith is a big guy. He was a star football player long before he started this winery in 1971. He came here via the Universities of California Berkeley and Davis, and he and Charles built this small winery with their sweat and persistence. He is also articulate and candid. Jeremiah Johnson with a master's degree.

Large, smart Stu Smith looks at me for a second. Then he looks down at the moving mass of grapes.

"It takes a while, doesn't it?" he says.

Of course it does. It's easy to forget for all the glamour of winemaking, that wine growing, and making it, too, takes patience. I have decided my new best friend is Stu Smith and I'm going to learn about winemaking from the man.

"So what just happened here?" I ask.

"That was one ton of grapes," he says. "It'll make almost 200 gallons of juice. We put the sulfur dioxide on it to kill the natural yeast on the grape skins. We'll add our own yeast so we can control the fermentation."

The stemmer/crusher removes the stems and drops them into what looks like a pile of wood pulp. Stu and Charles and their crew will put the stems/pulp into the bed of a battered, decrepit-looking, half-painted-over pickup truck with barely a grill and no back window. If Stu ever gets the truck started, the stems will be spread back out in the vineyards.

We can see the crushed grapes, the skins, the seeds, a few stem pieces, and a bee now and then—the mix is now called must—still flowing like purple lava, getting pumped through a hose, into one of those big tanks that Davis was playing in.

If this were white wine, say Smith-Madrone's near-legendary Riesling, the juice would be separated from the skins and everything else right now. It's the skins that give the grape juice/wine-to-be its color. So, instead of getting pumped into one of Davis' tanks, it would be pumped into a press, first, then the juice alone would go into a steel tank and get a dose of hungry yeast.

The red grapes, skins and all—the red must—just go straight into the tank with the yeast. The juice will be pressed out after it ferments.

It's in those tanks, with the mix of must and yeast, that we get the magic. Yeast are microscopic, single-celled fungi. That makes them related to mushrooms, but, and most people know this, you can't make wine with mushrooms. Yeast love sugar. In that, they are like people. Unlike people, yeast don't convert sugar to potbellies. Their tiny, single-celled metabolisms change it to alcohol, which they excrete. The reaction also creates carbon dioxide and heat. Voilà: fermentation.

It was Louis Pasteur who figured this out in the 1850s when he was more or less inventing microbiology. Before that, winemakers just knew if they crushed grapes and let them sit in a barrel, they'd get wine. They also knew the barrels gave off heat, so, back in the day, those barrels were open topped to let the heat escape. Sometimes, the carbon dioxide, rising with the heat, would overcome passing birds, and the birds would plop into the tanks, adding a hint of, well, bird, to the wine.

In this slightly more modern age, most tanks are closed, temperature controlled, and designed to let the carbon dioxide escape without putting a hit on the local avian population. And brewers, winemakers, and scientists of all stripes have bred scores of yeast strains to make the fermentation smooth.

This is the thing about winemaking. On one hand, the stuff makes itself. Put grapes in a barrel, leave them alone. You'll get wine. It won't be a medal winner, but it will be wine. (For a while. If it keeps sitting, it'll move on to vinegar.) But, winemaking is also endlessly complex, a Rubik's Cube of choices and possible combinations, starting from the beginning with picking the yeast. Unless you go with the yeast already on the grapes.

"There are so many different yeasts out there, it boggles the mind," Stu says. "It's like everything in winemaking, you chose through trial and error. It's literature, it's what your buddies and colleagues say, it's what worked before. You kind of make an educated guess, and use what works for you."

That means getting yeast that will eat all the sugar, convert it all to alcohol, and not poop out on you—and it needs to happen at the speed you want. Yeast may be almost everywhere there's moisture, but they have their limits when it comes to working conditions. They need the right nutrients. Too much heat will kill them. So, too, will too much alcohol. In other words, they are polluters. They poison themselves in their own waste. Also, if there's bacteria on the grapes or in the tanks, that could stop them. When any of that happens, it's called a stuck fermentation. Usually, that's bad, unless you're Bob Trinchero at Sutter Home and you're inventing White Zinfandel.

"You just want your yeast to work," Stu says. "I defy anybody to pick up a glass of wine and say, 'Ah ha, this was made with Champagne yeast or Steinberg yeast.'"

So the yeast and lava-like must go straight to the tank and it's money in the bank, I ask?

Not exactly. There are bunches and bunches of choices ahead for a winemaker.

First up: When to add the yeast. The grapes, with the natural yeast destroyed by the sulfur dioxide, are occasionally allowed to just sit in the temperature-controlled tanks. That's called a cold soak, and it can help meld some of the flavors together and get a softer, slightly fruitier wine.

Since there's no yeast involved yet, there's no alcohol in the mix to extract the tannins from the skins and seeds. Tannins—part of a class of compounds called phenols—are what give wines a slightly bitter or astringent taste, and they show up as a mouth-drying, wind-parched feel after you swallow. They also give wine firmness or body or heft, and without them, you have jug wine or alcoholic punch. But they need to be balanced, and a cold soak is one way to extract some flavors without too much tannin.

Stu says he's not a huge fan of cold soaks and like everything else, that's just his preference. Oddly enough, Smith-Madrone used to cold soak its Rieslings for maybe eight to ten hours, maybe overnight. That's white wine juice left with the skins. They quit when they found that after seven or eight years—and another great thing about Riesling is that it's a white you can age—the wine turned a bit darker.

"We never really knew why," Stu says. "We just stopped doing it."

OK, so either cold soaked or not, the wine goes into the tank to ferment. Now it's time to think about times and temperatures, and it gets to another one of those counter-intuitive pieces of winemaking. You'd think that reds—big, brawny, macho reds—would take the longest to ferment. Takes a while to break those boys down and extract everything into the soup. But, of course, no.

The thing is, the lighter the wine, the cooler you keep the temperature when it's fermenting. The cooler the temperature, as with most reactions in nature, the longer it takes. Winemakers control the temps and fermentation speed with refrigeration and with their choice of yeast—whites get dainty, slow eaters; reds get gluttonous, Homer Simpson yeast that chow.

Stu says they let their Chardonnay ferment in a range of probably fifty-five to sixty degrees and it can take three weeks. Their Cabs generally ferment in the high seventies but can get into the eighties and even the low nineties for a short time—they have to be careful not to kill the yeast—and need seven to ten days before all the sugar is converted to alcohol.

"Everyone does it differently," he says. "We ferment our Riesling in the low fifties or even the high forties, and they can sometimes take two and a half to three months."

While that's going on in red wines, the skins and seeds—and maybe that leftover bee—end up floating on the top of the wine-in-the-making, the way unstirred chocolate mix floats on top of hot chocolate. That is called the cap. The carbon dioxide rising in the wine helps push it to the top, too. (Whites have no cap because they're in the tanks without the skins.)

But all the flavors and tannins and generally interesting stuff— excluding that damn bee—are in the cap, which can be a foot or two thick to almost half the tank. Winemakers want it back in the mix, and broken up as much as possible, so the fluid will have total contact with it and the growing level of alcohol, which acts as a solvent, can dig out the flavors.

This is the fun part; it's called punching down the cap. You need to smash it up and stuff it back down into the tank. In the good ol' days, that was the occasion for dancing around barefoot in the wine. We're a bit more advanced now, unless someone is making an episode of I Love Lucy.

Stu shows us the simplest punch-down technique. They have a 400-gallon open tank in the middle of the winery that's about chest high. There's a pole with a flat, solid metal piece at the end turned an angle from the pole. He gives it to Hank, who uses it to shove down on the cap. It mostly stays down.

"I punched down the cap," Hank says to me.

"Cool," I say. "What's it like? How thick is it? How hard is it to get down?"

Stu has the patience of a parent. He lets us burble. The cap on this tank was about a foot thick and put up some resistance. But Hank won the fight. For now.

"We have to do that two or three times a day," Stu says.

There are other, more mechanical techniques. The most common is called a pump over. The juice gets drained from the bottom of the tank and pumped up to a sprinkler system at the top, which sprays it over and through the cap. Other tanks have punching devices built into their tops that shove the cap down.

After the fermentation and all the punch downs, winemakers have a new set of choices before putting the wine into barrels. One possibility for reds, is what they call extended maceration, or extended skin contact, which translates to letting the wine sit with all the skins and the rest of the mess for a few days or even a couple weeks.

It's another way of softening tannins and extracting more flavor, but it's also a risk. It can create unwanted flavors in the wine or take some muscle out of it. The wine is so young, deciding if or how long to leave it with skin contact takes a sophisticated palate.

"It's a dicey deal," Stu says. "The wine can go backward. It's slightly dangerous, but if done well, it's part of the arsenal a winemaker uses."

After the fermentation, and, maybe, the extra days or weeks on the skins, the red wine gets pressed into juice and heads for the barrels. It also heads for a second reaction. There is generally still bacteria left in the wine—a friendly bacteria in this case—that will change the malic acid in the mix to lactic acid. That's called malolactic fermentation, or, as they say around the tasting rooms, ML, as in "This wine went through heavy ML."

Malic acid is tart. Think green apple. Lactic acid is the softer, smooth acid found in milk. Think milk. ML makes wine rounder, richer, and full-bodied. All reds go through this because crispness is not an ideal quality for a red. If ML doesn't happen naturally, winemakers will induce it.

With whites, it's a bigger decision. Wines that thrive on that crisp acidity, like say, a Sauvignon Blanc, or Smith-Madrone's Riesling, don't want ML. But Chardonnays are all over the map. If you're going for a smoother, buttery style Chard—the kind of Chardonnay that helped kick off America's wine boom—you want that lush lactic acid.

Smith-Madrone's Chards go through some ML, but they still keep a decent amount of acidity. Some winemakers prevent it entirely. They stop the ML with either another tiny dose of sulfur dioxide, or by keeping the temperatures down low enough to prevent the reaction. Chardonnays that do go through ML not only get softer, they develop a compound called diacetyl. That's what gives it that buttery flavor. Diacetyl is also the stuff added to margarine and other spreads so we won't believe it's not butter.

ML or not, whites also generally get cold stabilized at this point. The idea is to keep the wine from developing little crystals when it's bottled and refrigerated later, so winemakers develop the crystals now then dump them. The wine is chilled to a point just above freezing. That causes the tartaric acid left in the wine to turn into little snowflakes—and yes, Stu says, there does seem to be an endless supply of acids, compounds, and general junk popping up in wine. Those tartaric crystals eventually settle and get removed before the wine is bottled. And that bottle in the fridge? Nothing but wine.

Most of that ML and cold stabilization happens after the wine has gone into the barrels. Not always, but mostly. This brings up possibly the most complicated word in winemaking: oak.

"Oak is like a winemaker's spice rack," Stu says. "You can do little things with it and big things. Every wine reacts differently. And every winemaker has a different approach."

Oak barrels, on the average, hold about sixty gallons of wine—roughly twenty-five cases, or 300 bottles, or approximately 1,200 glasses. Couple fewer if you pour big. What the oak does to the wine depends on how the barrel was made—that's called the cooperage—where it came from, how old it is, how much it was toasted, and, you know, everything.

If you look at winemaking tables, oak can add variations of vanilla, roasted nuts, caramel, chocolate, spice, tea, tobacco, coffee, pretty much every flavor on the planet including, of course, oak. But that's just the start.

Aging in oak can add tannins or soften them, it can add complexity, depth, and texture. It can make the wine a bit sweeter or bigger or more balanced. And it can overcome all the varietal and regional characteristics and get you a bottle of toast-y, vanilla tree. The handling is everything.

The newer the barrel, the more intense the impact from the oak, and the wood is generally considered to be tapped out and neutral, meaning the flavors are kaput, after five or six years. French oak—barrels from trees in French forests and made by French coopers—has a more understated, some would say refined, impact on wine than American oak, which tends to be stronger and more vanilla-like, when it's not waving flags and chanting, "USA, USA." French oak can cost up to $800 a barrel. Good American oak goes for about half that.

I ask Stu how the oak impact actually works. Surprisingly enough, he says, they're still doing research on it.

Here's what we know. Oak and the barrels breathe a bit. They allow alcohol out and oxygen in, just enough so there can be some evaporation from the barrel, and so the oxygen can slowly transform the wine. Also, the alcohol, solvent that it is, extracts tannins and other compounds from the woods. Over time—and, yet again, every winemaker thinks differently on this—the wine, the wood compounds, the oxygen, the remaining gunk at the bottom of the tank that includes the dead yeast (called the lees) all meld together a little and change the wine.

And how long should that take? And how much should the wine change? God knows, Stu says. There's no formula. Lighter reds like Pinot Noir might be in barrels a year, big Cabs could go two to three years, depending on the winemaker, hefty reds like a Barolo might need four years. Oaked Chardonnays usually stay in the barrel a few months to maybe a year or more.

"You just never know," Stu says. "You have to taste. We anticipated bottling our '99 Chardonnay in less than a year. We tasted it in August 2000 at eleven months and the wine just hadn't developed, so we canceled the bottling. We tasted it again in January, that's at fifteen months, and it was coming around, but it wasn't there yet.

"We finally bottled in April '01, after eighteen months of oak aging and it ended up winning four gold medals. It was just a late bloomer. People were telling us, 'It's so nice you don't over-oak your wines,' and we'd say, 'You've probably never had a Chardonnay with more oak.'"

And because this is wine, there's yet another counterintuitive piece to the oak puzzle. Wines fermented in oak, with all the heat and the bubbling and the helter-skelter yeast action, are actually less oak-y than wines only aged in oak. That's because during the fermentation, the tannins and other compounds get absorbed by the soon-to-be dead and removed yeast—the lees—and actually get taken out of the wine.

Removing the lees, and whatever else might be in there, is done through what's called racking the wine. Every barrel gets racked, though some more than others. That can be a simple process. You let the solids, including those tiny yeast corpses, settle to the bottom, then pour or pump the clear wine into another barrel. Some winemakers believe using pumps for anything hurts the wine and takes away a bit of its native flavor and characteristics. So they let gravity do the racking. They just open the barrel and let the clear wine pour into another barrel below it.

There's even a bigger range of ideas when it comes to fining and filtering, which is done—if it's done—while the wine is sitting in barrels. Fining is a way of getting some solids or tannins out of wine. Filtering removes other particles and some bacteria.

Opinions are all over the map. Maybe it helps the wine. Maybe it destroys some character. Maybe there's a middle ground. Maybe this can drive you crazy if you think about it too much. Even Stu admits his choices are partly arbitrary.

To figure this out, he says, you need to start with the clarity of wine. There are three technical levels for that: "brilliant," "clear," and "cloudy." "I believe wine is visual, too, and white wine should be 'brilliant,'" Stu says. "We think fining and filtration are necessary for whites. I'm not so picky about reds, so 'clear' is OK with me."

At Smith-Madrone, as at many wineries, they fine white wine by dropping a clay coagulant called bentonite into the barrel that globs onto proteins and other solids in the wine—essentially the molecules bond together—then settles to the bottom. The globs are left behind when the wine is racked. For red wines, some wineries use the older method of dropping egg whites in, which act as a coagulant like the clay.

Filtering involves pouring or pumping the wine through a porous fabric or pad. The tighter the fabric, the more the wine is filtered, which can include removing tiny particles that give the wine some taste, smell, or body.

Most winemakers fine their whites, and most filter them, too, Stu says. Fining and filtering reds is more a matter of style and taste. If you ask three winemakers about this, as the saying goes, you'll get five opinions.

"I have a double standard," Stu says. "I'm not sure if filtering really hurts red wine, but we don't do it. And, frankly, it gives us a little sales pitch to say we don't filter our reds.

"We think—and it's just our guess—but we think filtration is more detrimental to reds. If you ask me why, I'd say, 'Not a clue.'"

I'm a little dumbfounded by all this. I've heard a lot of it before in pieces—on tours or from Hank. But put all together, it's staggering how complicated this little trick of letting nature take its course really is. How does anyone comfortably make all those decisions, particularly when there's a business and a reputation and, for God's sake, a year of wine at stake?

Stu gets this brief faraway look on his face when I ask. You can tell he's thought about this before.

"That's really a philosophical question," he says, "and I think that gets to why Napa has done so well in such a relatively short time."

Stu, like many wine folk in Napa, spent some time in Europe, watching the people who've been making wine for generations and for centuries. "It was the mecca," he said. "But we also found it was very regimented. People made wine just like their father made wine. It's tradition. No innovation accepted."

Stu got his master's from U.C. Davis—"We were a bunch of little wine geeks," he says—and he was taught to think critically, to try things, to question every move. No one said change just to change; they did say you might discover improvements.

"So when all of us little winemakers went out in the world, we were saying 'Why not?'" Stu says. "We all went through a lot of trial and error, and we learned that either tradition or science only takes you so far. You have to do what works for you. It's like a jazz pianist has to learn the classics, then play to his own ear and heart."

I like that. I like the adventurous, jazzy, slightly quixotic notion of winemaking. It's the way Hank talks. Wine is complex and ever-changing and different for everyone. That's part of its lure. Making a great wine is science and art and a giant, unpredictable, unstable puzzle. It should be hard.

That's also why it's endlessly fascinating and confusing. It starts with such a cleanly simple concept—good grapes + good handling (+ luck) = good wine—and spreads to staggering layers of detail and complexity. Most of us will never completely understand it all.

"Wine is like sex," Stu says. "People don't want to admit they don't really know anything about it."

SPRING MOUNTAIN ISN'T A REAL MOUNTAIN as a much as a 2,600-foot-high series of ridges in the Mayacamas range between Mt. Veeder to the south and Diamond Mountain on the north. Its name comes from the springs running off the hillsides, dumping into the little gorges that drop to the valley.

Spring Mountain Road runs west up the hill out of St. Helena. We're leaving town on a bright, late October morning. The air is crisp and still. As we're getting to the mountain road, we see these sudden round bursts of artificial colors straight over the car. Napa's hot air balloons are always a shock—their colors and shapes and designs are an explosive contrast to the landscape, particularly in this golden fall. The balloons are bright yellow, purple, green, and red, their colors painted in jagged patterns across the balls of the balloons. They are huge in the sky over our car, then we move into the trees on Spring Mountain Road and they're gone, just like that.

It was a stunning little moment. Neither of us knows what to say.

"Was that real?" I mumble.

"Was what real?" Hank says.

We're visiting Spring Mountain Vineyard, an intense experience in its own way. The winery is just outside town, at 400 feet elevation, but its 850 acres sprawl up to 1,800 feet. It's an unusual and impressive tour, less for the winemaking—though their wines have become first class—than for the walk through the plantation-like grounds, for the European-looking winery building and caves, and for the mansion.

The mansion was designed in the late 1800s by architect Albert Schroepfer for a French orchard owner named Tiburcio Parrott.

Schroepfer also designed the Rhine House on the Beringer estate and the mansion at Inglenook for Gustave Niebaum. Parrot ordered his house to be bigger.

Schroepfer built him a spectacular home of spires, stone towers, and staircases. He also put in a stained-glass parrot window. Tiburcio would probably not be thrilled with what happened to his window in the 1980s. CBS producers used the winery and house as the setting for the prime-time soap *Falcon Crest* that aired from 1981 to 1990 and they decided the bird was really a stained-glass falcon.

The *Falcon Crest* era is something they downplay at Spring Mountain Vineyards. I asked Brian Hawkins, who was pouring for our group inside one of the mansion's dining rooms—and for the record, the 2003 Syrah is intense, a little smoky, and mesmerizing—how it was that in the ninety-minute tour, no one said the words "falcon" or "crest" once.

Truth is, Brian says, Spring Mountain isn't particularly proud of its winemaking during that period, and they are now. "We want wine people coming here," he says, "not TV people. We think wine people will love what we're doing. TV people will want more flash."

I'm kinda both, and I like the place. Not sure what that says about me. After we've tasted, our group trundles out the front to stand on the grass and stare down at the valley. One woman in our group is turned around, looking back at the house. "I've been trying to figure out why this looks so familiar," she tells me. "Wasn't this where they made *Falcon Crest?*"

WE FIND ANOTHER, YOU WANT TO say "freaky," place up the mountain. It's Terra Valentine and it's at once extravagant, dazzling, and, yeah, freaky. It's part stone and concrete Gothic mansion, part 1960s retreat, and, when you get down to it, it's a place you have to see.

Terra Valentine was restarted in 1999 by its current owners, Angus and Margaret Wurtele, and their winemaker, Sam Baxter. Their wine, particularly their Wurtele Vineyard Cabernet, has been getting raves. But it's the original owner who gave this place its freaky quotient. And I say that with admiration.

It was founded by Fred Aves, the definition of a Renaissance man. He's the guy in the 1960s who invented license plate holders with advertising on them. He invented the little joystick for moving your side-view mirror. And he's the guy who invented those springy curb feelers for big cars. He made a ton of money from those things. This is the winery built by curb feelers.

Aves moved to Napa in 1970 and began building this place. He called it Yverdon after the Swiss town his mother lived in. He wrote, took up winemaking, and learned how to work with stone, cement, brass, copper, wrought iron, stained glass, and, probably, the space-time continuum. The result was a 17,000-square-foot winery and shrine to free thinking.

There's a glass wall with a stained-glass scene of Dionysus and dolphins that leads to a stunning balcony with a view through the trees. There's a plush oak-paneled sitting room, with two fireplaces and a stained-glass rendition of St. Genevieve de Paris, patron saint of winemakers. There are massive, arched, wooden doors, held on by three-foot-long wrought-iron hinges in the shape of grapevines. There's a stained-glass jungle scene on one set of floor-to-ceiling windows, and the leopard's round, open mouth is a cat door. There are grape clusters everywhere, in glass, metal, and cement. There are statues and columns. There's polished stone and carved wood. And there are the door handles, all of them some ornate metal fish.

Our guide is Elizabeth Pryor, a young woman with long, curly, dark hair, high cheekbones and an athletic bounce to her. She said for a while, people thought Aves made those handles because he was a Pisces. Then his son, who lives in St. Helena now, visited the winery and explained. "It turned out," Elizabeth tells us, "he just liked fish."

Aves also put in what is my single favorite winery feature in Napa. In a corner of what's now the office, there's an over-sized wood barrel—maybe a 1,000-gallon barrel—standing on end. It has a door cut into it. You open the door, and there's a circular, wrought-iron staircase leading down to the barrel room. It's not just handy, it's a slick *Get Smart*–style escape hatch.

Aves died in 1998, but he stopped making wine thirteen years earlier, in 1985, partly because he was ill for a while, and partly because he was a full-on recluse. Elizabeth says most people in the area, including those on Spring Mountain, never knew the place existed until the Wurteles took it over. Aves even posted a sign on the driveway that said "Trespassers will be shot on sight."

Hank says he's stayed in the guest house out on the ridge when he was here on an industry visit. Elizabeth says it was where Aves lived.

"We've heard it's haunted," she says. "Did you see anything?"

"Maybe," Hank says. "We couldn't get the heat to turn off."

ROBERT KEENAN WINERY IS THE CLOSEST winery to Terra Valentine geographically, but it is a different world in feel. It's based in a century-old, simple stone building, and when we walk into the wood-paneled loft that houses the tasting bar, we feel like we've just joined a party in a mountain lodge.

There are sets of easy chairs around the front of the room, a huge rectangular wood table with six people taking just half of it, and the tasting bar under warm lights in a back corner. We're greeted by pretty much everyone in the place: other visitors, the tasting room manager, Laura Marcel, and Laura's black Lab-mix, Scrappy. Her other dog, Scooby, normally Scrappy's co-greeter, has gone home down the road because he's hoarding a rawhide treat.

By the time we've gone through the wines—another impressive lineup and we're starting to think people know what they're doing on Spring Mountain—Laura decides to move the party.

"C'mon downstairs," she says. "Let's check out what we've been crushing today."

Robert Keenan, like everyone on the mountain, is still bringing in grapes. And they're finding the yields are good quality and big. Almost too big. Laura tells us everyone's calling around, trying to find tanks for their wines.

"We're at full crank now," she says. "We need tank space, so we're putting wine in the barrels that's still fermenting. We'll compensate by racking it a little sooner."

There are six of us visitors walking around the outside of the building, plus Laura—who's short, has brown hair and the cheery energy of a woman running a happy pub—and, now, both dogs. Scooby, a Lab-golden mix, has joined the party and looks happily chewed out.

We all walk into the barrel room, and Laura is scooting the dogs away so she can show us a barrel on its side with a cheese cloth over a small open plug. The wine's fermenting in there and the cloth lets the carbon dioxide and some heat escape without letting flies and bees in.

"Put your ear to the hole," Laura says.

I hear the ocean. Actually, it sounds more like the snap and crackle of breakfast cereal, a constant, substantial fizzing and popping. That's the yeast chowing on the sugars, doing its magic act. It sounds like a party in there.

Laura fills wineglasses with juice from a big fermentation tank holding grapes that just came in today. Eventually, the juice will become 2005 Napa Valley Merlot, but right now it's a milky blue-pink. There are pieces of skins and seeds floating in it. It doesn't taste like Merlot. It tastes like a grape smoothie.

"This is great," a tall, dark woman in stylish jeans tells Laura. "You should sell this stuff."

"We do," Laura says. "We call it wine."

WE'RE ON THE REDWOOD DECK AT Barnett Vineyards. It's nearing the end of the day. The sunlight is especially sharp, it's still warm, and we're sitting high at the top of the world.

In a region of dazzling vistas and mountain wineries, this place may be the best. The deck is a couple dozen yards away from the little winery building, out a path through vineyards, and up one last hill. The sight from here is so breathtaking, so full and rich and expansive, it's hard to take in. Even Tyson Ducker, the sales manager at Barnett who is here every day, stops to stare. Only Ruby, the gold cat, is immune. She walks along the rail out in space, then jumps down to the deck and curls herself to sleep inside a coiled hose in a corner.

The deck looks over some of Barnett's impossibly steep hillside vineyards—the vines widely spaced and looking like they'll roll down the mountain—then out at ridge after ridge of trees, down 2,100 feet to the valley floor. The dramatic folds of Diamond Mountain are to the north, and beyond that, the cone shape of Mt. St. Helena. Straight out, seemingly miles below, is Sterling's Three Palms Vineyards. We can tell because Tyson tells us it's Three Palms. Now we're sure we can see the three trees.

We're here for the last tasting of the day, sharing the deck and the wine with a group of four from El Paso, and we've already tasted through the list, which includes the world-class 2002 Rattlesnake Vineyard Cabernet Sauvignon, a dark, layered Cab that seems to change as it goes through the palate. Tyson's no longer working. He pours everyone more of the terrific-if-less-rare 2002 Spring Mountain Cabernet, then pours himself a glass, too. We talk about the charms of sitting nearly a half-mile straight above the valley, about Napa, and about wine.

"You know what Napa needs?" Tyson says. "Maps. We would love to get one decent map. Those crappy maps with their mystery dots are terrible. Half of them are in the wrong place and half the wineries aren't even on them."

We say mapping our Quest has been like a scavenger hunt. No one map has every winery, and some maps only list wineries that belong to the right organization, or bought advertising, or, I guess, have the right horoscope sign.

"Here's what bugs me," says Tom Alost, an El Paso orthopedic surgeon, here with his wife and two friends. "People who hoard wine."

I've been liking Tom since we met his group on this deck. He's got that surgeon's confidence, but he's happy to say he isn't much of a wine expert—like me—and he loves learning about it—like me. Unlike me, I suspect he can afford a pretty good class of wine to learn about, but with him it's not about status. He drinks what he likes.

"I don't get the idea of buying wine and never drinking it, then trading it for more wine you never drink," he says. "That's not aging, that's hoarding. If you hide wine like a rare commodity, it's like those guys who buy great art and keep it from the rest of the world. I hate those guys."

I mutter some version of "here, here."

At that point, as if cued by a director, Tyson pours more of the Cab for us. No hoarding for Tyson. Tom and I try to decide what we're tasting. Tom says he gets jam and dark cherries, but he always seems to get dark cherries. I say I get chocolate, but I'm always looking for chocolate.

"This is why you share wine," Tom says. "This is what you're supposed to do. Swirl it, stick your nose in it, taste it. Talk about it. You share the whole experience and you're educating each other. What grapes went into this? How will it age? Why are some grapes here still on the vines? I just love all of it."

As we're talking, a tall, lean, curly-haired guy who might be thirty, walks onto the deck with two of his friends. Tyson introduces him: Nile Zacherle. His name is on the Cabernet bottle. He's the winemaker.

Maybe it's because we've been drinking, surely it's because of what we've been drinking, but when Nile gets introduced, the visitors, all six of us, start clapping. We're like extras in a cheesy movie. We applaud, then get out of our chairs and give poor Nile a standing O.

He looks embarrassed. Nile gives us an "aw shucks." We're guessing he's dealt with loopy Barnett fans before. He's just finished a day of getting freshly harvested grapes into tanks and his long hands are stained blue.

"I'm so over grapes," Nile says, "I won't buy them at the store."

We ask what we consider simple questions. To Nile, they're probably awkward. "Why are you so good at this?" I say. "How'd you learn to do this?" Tom asks.

Nile does another "aw shucks." He jokes some, downplays it more. "I'm just a steward to the grapes," he says. "Mother Nature is in control."

Partly to let Nile off the hook, we get back to drinking the Cab, chatting, and staring at the view. Hank is talking to Tyson about distributing Barnett wines. One on one, Nile gets a little less self-effacing and, really, a little more honest. Nile is a modest guy. He's not entirely comfortable talking about himself. But he's also sure of his judgments, of his tastes, which is a requirement for his job.

He tells me about a dinner where everyone loved the wine. "I didn't say anything," Nile says, "but I thought it was a little thin in the mid-palate and the back fell off. Maybe it was just me, but that's the job of a winemaker, to make judgments. We all have our own perspective, we all react differently when we look at a piece of art or take a bite of food. Ultimately, it's my job to decide what I like and don't like."

Taste. That's everything. Funny as it sounds, it's a talent and a skill. It's something you can train and develop. You can learn to pay attention, learn to identify smells, textures, and spices. A tasting palate is something you develop over time, Nile says. But some people will be better at it than others, and that's a key ingredient to producing great winemakers.

Nile has been at it since 1995, when he was a student at U.C. Davis, though his first focus was beer. He decided wine was more interesting and did what lots of young winemakers do, went to Australia and France for a while. Back in California, he worked for Jim Klein at Navarro Vineyards and Bo Barrett at Chateau Montelena, and came to Barnett in early 2004.

I ask about the judgments he makes. How often does he have to uncork that palate? He gives me a straight answer despite the lame pun. I'm noticing another trait of winemakers is patience.

The answer is, constantly. It starts in the vineyard. He walks the blocks, tastes the grapes to decide when to pick and which grapes are best for which wines. "You have to really chew the skins," Nile says. "That's where the flavor comes from."

That continues all the way through. It's one reason why winemaking is so individual and can be so varied. Every choice along the way affects the next choice, and, as Nile says, it can be personal.

"It's kind of a touchy-feely thing," he says, sounding a bit metaphysical. "In winemaking, as soon as you've made a decision about something, that's it. That's the direction you've chosen. And everyone has their own direction."

For instance, his direction, he says, is that he thinks filtering reds is not necessarily a bad thing. "It's bad when it doesn't need to be done," Nile says. "That's an incredibly horrible thing. Or if you over filter, you'll damage the wine."

But in some cases, it's like cleaning a window to get a more clear view. Taking out the leftover yeast and particulates, in essence, removes barriers between you and the wine.

"The clarity and focus of the wine is what you're buying," he says. "You're paying for the essence of the vineyard. You don't want to taste something else.

"To me, I can taste wines that are unfiltered. I can taste it on the back palate. It gives it a rustic edge. That's great for some winemakers, but I don't like my wine with too many edges. I want it to be polished and elegant. I don't want it to catch me on the way out the door."

Talk with a guy like Nile, and you get a sense of what it's like playing in the big leagues. There are thousands and thousands of winemakers around the country, either producing good wines for wineries or homemade wines for themselves. But people like Nile, and like all the winemakers around Napa making great wines, they have talents and skills we can't imagine. It's like baseball. Most of us played it. It's pretty simple, until you see a fastball at ninety m.p.h. That's lightning. An impossible-to-hit streak of air. Then throw that to a pro, it's cream-puff slow. He'll hit it into the seats.

Nile and the other top winemakers read the fastball us mortals barely see. They pick up the tastes and textures and all the nuances that make for great wine. That is how they can manage what seems to me to be impossible alchemy: the decisions to blend different lots and varietals to finish the wine.

The '02 Spring Mountain Cab, for instance, is seventy-seven percent Cabernet. It's also sixteen percent Cab Franc, six percent Merlot, and one percent Petite Verdot. One percent. How do you decide something needs one percent of anything?

That's what winemakers do, they blend tastes to get better tastes. Some great wines are from a single vineyard, but that's rare, and even then, the winemaker could be choosing among blocks. Mostly, unless the soils are special and really diverse in a small area, a one-vineyard wine won't be particularly interesting, Nile says. Blending blocks and varietals fills out a wine and allows a winemaker to construct the depth and character.

"A blend lets you layer a wine," Nile says. "You can go through multiple zones of tasting different elements."

OK. So how? Here's a surprise: Every winemaker is different on this.

Nile says he looks at all the wines that might go into the Spring Mountain Cab as separate entities. He ferments and barrels each wine first on its own. He also looks at them as one entity, tries to think how they'll blend. His approach is to incorporate them together as soon as possible so they can coalesce and build on each other. But that still might be a year into the nearly two years of barrel aging.

"That year allows me to see those wines develop to where I might see something that wasn't there before," Nile says. "Maybe it's more herbal or more vegetal than it first seemed. Maybe it developed into something more complex."

After he blends the first time, he still holds a little back in case he needs to tinker. "You want it to be a percent of this or a percent of that at the end," he says.

A percent. How do you know it needs a percent?

"You can taste it," he says.

And I can hit a ninety m.p.h. fastball.

Nile says winemaking should be individual. Wines should have their own personalities because of their winery, their winemakers, and because, most of all, where they came from. He's not the first person to tell us he's worried the art of winemaking is getting dulled because of what sells right now and what scores big points from influential critics. It's not that he dislikes those kinds of wines, Nile says, it's just there should be lots of kinds of wines.

"There are people holding their ground," he says, "making wines the way they feel they should be made. That's what makes winemaking special. It's what makes wine special.

"The intrigue of wine is one of the great things about it."

Hank and Tom have joined the conversation by now. The three of us are nodding with Nile, doing everything but shouting "you go guy," because he's saying what we were saying, except, well, better. We're glad to hear a pro thinks about the mystery and vastness of the wine world with a little of our starry-eyed marvel, too.

"At the end of the day, when you want a cold beer, you just want a cold beer," Nile says. "You want it to be good, but you don't sit there and analyze it. Wine is so much more alive. It goes through a series of evolutions from every decision you make. All those decisions, from one end of the spectrum to the other, lead you to more choices and different paths. That's why winemaking is so dynamic.

"That's why we like talking about it so much. Each stage of a wine is different, each choice made it different. You can taste that. Tasting it, thinking about it, talking about it, that all puts you more in contact with where it came from. It puts you in contact with the people who grew it and made it. It puts you in contact with nature."

Nile says his goodbyes and goes to talk with his friends. He leaves me and Hank and Tom a little overwhelmed. We sit silent—which is something for me and Tom—looking at the view. The light has gotten soft and changed the scenery. It's now more about the colors, the autumn yellows and reds, the still-green mountain trees, the golden sunlight. It's like looking out at a shimmering, earth-toned ocean.

We just sit. Finally, it's Tom who speaks.

"Nice guy," he says.

"Heck of a guy," I say.

"Great guy," says Hank.

ELEVEN

Calistoga

WE'RE SITTING ON the patio at the Calistoga Inn. It's the end of November and the weather is still warm. You gotta love California. It's mid-afternoon, but the sun is about to drop behind the Mayacamas range, which slope right to the edge of town. We're doing an early happy hour. We think we've earned it.

All around Napa Valley, the wine is in fermentation tanks and storage barrels. This wine season is over, at least the front end of it. We've seen bud break, watched pin-sized grapes grow up, seen them change color, turn sweet, and get picked and crushed. Most of the big action is finished. Now, the wine will sit for months or years, and become, we all hope, something a little magic.

It was a great harvest in the valley, good fruit and tons of it. Throughout Napa—at Truchard, at Groth, at Honig, Tudal, and Sterling, and up in the hills at Hess, Smith-Madrone, and everywhere else—all the places we heard the early worries, they picked quality grapes and in huge amounts. Maybe Andy at Benessere Vineyards was right, maybe this vintage will be epic.

We'll know for sure in a couple years. In the wineries, right now, there's more to do. Barrels are being racked, wines are being clarified, and some fermentation tanks still have yeast doing their alcohol-making voodoo. But me and Hank, our work is done. We've been to more than 140 tasting rooms, sampled this valley from bottom to top, tasted maybe 1,000 wines, everything from Rosés to sparkling wines to monster Cabs. We've walked on mountain sides, wandered through vineyards, poked around in caves, stared at barrels, and stood at more polished wood and granite bars than Dean Martin.

"So what have we learned?" I say.

"You can spit," Hank says. "Sort of."

"Almost," I say. "I still get a drop on the chin. What else? That was nine months roaming this valley. We must've learned something important."

"OK. We know there're lots of dogs and cats in Napa."

"See, there's one. That's good."

"And we know half those 'appointment only' signs are fake."

"That's major," I say. "That's as big as anything. How many people go sailing past all those great tasting rooms?"

"And the picnic spots," Hank says. "We found a ton of picnic spots."

"We never need to go to V. Sattui again," I say.

"Good cheese, though," Hank says.

"Sunshine Foods," I say. "Grilled Chicken Caesar. I'm telling you."

"Yeah," Hank says, "that was good."

We are just sitting, in no real hurry for the first time since bud break in March. Around us, the patio is busy. The black metal tables are filled with people on the same poky schedule that we have today. We're sitting under an open, white trellis, surrounded by trees in various states of undress. Despite the warm day, you can sense winter is not far away.

Our Quest is complete. And, in all honesty, we've surpassed our goals. We wanted to learn about Napa, to get to know this beautiful valley, to absorb a little of the wine life. We got all that. And we got an enormous appreciation for the passionate world of growing and making wine, for the variety of ideas and tastes, for the hard, careful work involved, and for the spirit of so many people here. Plus we drank some astounding wine.

"I don't want to leave," I say.

"You never want to leave," Hank says.

This is true. Nine months of methodical stomping around. Years of casual visits. There has never been a day, never a moment, when I was ready to go home. Driving down the highway, standing outside a winery, crossing a street in Yountville or St. Helena, I'm always a bit aware I want more time here.

Now we're in Calistoga, probably my favorite town in Napa,

though maybe because I know it best. This is the top of the valley where the mountains come down to both ends of the main street. You can sense them around you. It feels like a Western outpost or a high Sierra town. Many of the two-story buildings on Lincoln Avenue—Calistoga's main drag—have wood awnings extended over the sidewalks to add to the notion.

Calistoga is a throwback to old Napa, the home of hot mud and spas, a generally slower pace, and a simpler feel. And there is something vaguely adventurous and romantic here, from the closeness of the mountains, to the smaller wineries in the area, to the look of the land and the town. And something heartening. Watching people in a café in the morning, seeing groups head out for some wine tasting or a picnic, or breathing in the evening scene of the bars and restaurants, it all just makes me happy.

"If there were ever a town that should be in wine country," I tell Hank, "this is it."

"You say that everywhere," he says.

"True. But I really mean it here."

Even the name has an old wine connection. Or more accurately, a drinking connection. The town's founder was Sam Brannan, who learned in the mid-1800s about the region's thermal waters. One night, he was telling friends his plan to build a resort for rich San Franciscans that would mimic Saratoga in New York, and ol' Sam was drinking. We romantics like to think he was drinking wine, but the odds are against it. Either way, Sam transposed some letters and announced he would build the "Calistoga of Sarafornia." Then he passed out. At least, that's one version. The name stuck, and the story also explains why there's a Cafe Sarafornia in town which, by the way, serves an impressive breakfast.

Calistoga and this end of Napa have an almost timeless sense to them. Part of that's because there are still a handful of family wineries nearby, as if the notion of owning a winery, of making your own wine and living the life, was not such an ethereal, unreachable fantasy these days.

There is Zahtila Vineyards, a little house, winery, and rose garden just past the end of Silverado Trail. Laura Zahtila, a former technology sales rep, bought the small facility and the vineyards in 1999. Now she runs her homey little winery and tasting room like a Main Street boutique.

There's Vincent Arroyo Winery just north of town. Vincent Arroyo was a mechanical engineer in Silicon Valley until he bought twenty-three acres here in 1974, and for years worked the place alone with his family. He now has eighty-five acres and such a following he sells all his 7,000 cases by reservation or out of his tasting room—though, frankly, we think J. J., his black Labrador, who climbs barrels, catches tennis balls, and has her own wine label, helps draw customers big time.

And there's Calistoga Cellars, a winery that grew out of a friendship among college fraternity brothers. Two decades ago, they started pooling money to buy vineyards, and now there's thirty-eight partners, a facility that makes 9,000 cases a year, and a classic ranch house they take turns visiting.

That partnership, naturally, has given Hank and me some idiotic ideas about doing something similar. Not that we have a plan or, you know, a clue how to set up something like a winery partnership. But we're talking about it enough to make our wives nervous and to have friends and family seriously avoiding us.

That's the thing about spending any time in this valley. It's magnetic. You start devising schemes so you won't have to leave, so you can become a part of it. Wine country around California, or anywhere, is almost always beautiful. Vineyards add drama and subtlety to landscapes that start off relatively scenic on the natural. But Napa is special. The hills and mountains that made this soil so precious for growing grapes also make the light, the countryside, and simply the feel and the sense of place here spellbinding.

"What about your boss?" I say to Hank. "You think he'd want to own a piece of a winery."

"Great idea," Hank says. "Why don't I save the middle steps and just fire myself now."

"OK. That's a maybe."

On my little fantasy planet—population: me—we would have a place like Schramsberg Vineyards, a short way up in the hills above Calistoga. It has everything for the perfect Napa dream. There's a classic, restored Victorian with a giant porch, a rebuilt nineteenth-century winery, hillside vineyards, gardens, and a general idyllic feel to the property.

There's also a pond between the house and the cave entrance that's got a metal statue of a frog in a tuxedo holding a sparkling wine bottle and flute. It's a tribute to Ramon Viera, who's been riddling bottles—the process of rotating them to clear sparkling wine—in Schramsberg's cellars and caves for thirty years. The frog is holding his flute up to the moonlight to check for clarity in the wine. Who wouldn't love a winery that pays tribute to its people with a frog?

Schramsberg, started by Jacob Schram in 1862, was the first hillside winery in Napa. It hit rough times during Prohibition, and went through years of neglect. In 1965, Jack and Jamie Davies restarted the winery when it was one of the few new—and decidedly risky—ventures in the valley in decades.

The Davies kept the original name, but they took another risk by making Schramsberg the first American winery to focus on sparkling wines, and to make them in the French method—*méthode champenoise* on the bottle—that has the secondary fermentation occur inside the bottle, which, among other things, requires the services of a riddler like Ramon.

Schramsberg is the quintessence of modern Napa, because of its history, because of the Davies' story, and because of the essence of the place. You can feel the respect for their roots here, and the work that went into everything. And you can feel the simple, powerful allure of the setting.

That's something else I like about this piece of the valley around Calistoga. There are also a couple bedrocks of Napa winemaking.

Besides Schramsberg, there is Chateau Montelena. Its history goes back almost as far as Schramsberg—to 1882—but its impact is more current. It was a 1973 Chateau Montelena Chardonnay that was the top-scoring white wine in that now-mythic 1976 Paris Tasting. Between the '72 Stag's Leap Wine Cellars Cabernet Sauvignon and the Chateau Montelena Chard, it was a sweep for the Americans, and for Napa. Besides the figurative face slap to the French, that tasting rocked a Euro-centric wine world, and sent the message that Napa Valley, and American wine in general, could play in the big leagues.

The Paris Tasting also made Chateau Montelena early royalty in Napa, and more than three decades later, its reputation hasn't faded. Neither, some people argue, has its royal attitude.

Hank and I have been among those people. We like their wines, respect their winery, happen to know they have a gorgeous lake sitting behind the old stone building. But Chateau Montelena may have been the single tasting room we most dreaded.

The last time I was there—which to be fair, was a few years back—the experience was an exercise in they-were-cool-and-I-was-not. Can't say I'd argue the point even now, but still, you want people to be nice.

Hank, too, had a not-great experience there, and in the wine world, anyway, he's plenty cool. On this Quest, we asked lots of people for favorite and least-favorite tasting rooms, and Chateau Montelena was a solid contender for "least." Though they all said it had been a while.

Hank and I are nothing if not open-minded. When we walked up to the tasting room entrance a couple weeks earlier, the crowd milling around the stone gate looked, frankly, over-dressed for a Saturday afternoon wine tasting—the men had slacks and expensive shirts, the women had too much jewelry. I'm not saying we were intimidated, but it did look like Snoot City.

"This is gonna suck," I said open-mindedly.

Inside, the bar was mildly crowded. I sulked. The room is not large, and with a dark wood bar backed by a stone wall from the old winery, it feels like a big, warmly lit cave. We stood at the back of the cave. A tall red-haired woman behind the bar saw us, smiled, and waved us over. She sort of danced the tasting menu across the bar playfully.

"Hey guys," she said. "Great day out there, huh."

Well, yeah, it was pretty outside. Since she brought it up.

"Can I get you started with the Riesling?" she asked.

Sure, why not, we mumbled.

Her name was Denise Dumond. She opened a new bottle of the 2004 Potter Valley Riesling, poured a splash into a glass, swirled and tasted. "You'll like that," she said. "It's perfect for a day like this. We should all be outside sipping Riesling."

OK, she's very nice. And unassuming. And not pushy. She was right about the Riesling, too. It started a tiny bit sweet but finished clean and crisp. While we tasted, our new friend excused herself and moved down the bar to help another group. I saw some tasting notes on the Riesling that said floral tones. "Floral?" I said, sort of to Hank and sort of just talking. I do that.

"Oh yeah," said another server behind the bar, a smiling, dark-haired guy. "Some calla-lily and tulip and there's sunflower, daisy, and maybe camellia."

OK, again. That's kinda funny. I even know that camellias have no smell. Fine. He's friendly, too.

Another woman stepped up to serve us our next wine. She was blond, a bit short, and had a comfortable smile. "Oh, you made it to the bar," she said. That implied she'd seen us earlier and was worried about us. What the hell was going on here? Where'd all these likable people come from?

It went like that. Amiable servers, just silly enough to be fun. They were attentive, informed, and casual. A well-dressed guy came in who the servers knew, and who was probably important, judging by the way his posse treated him. He hung in one corner of the room. The serving crew took turns stopping by to say hi, but they were quick about it and never abandoned the common folk at the bar. A young couple next to us seemed fairly new to wine, and Denise walked them through the tasting. She sounded like their kind big sister. I want a big sister like that.

Hank and I eventually wandered down a hall to a small display with the notes and scores from the Paris Tasting. We poked our heads into an elegant room reserved for the more expensive estate tastings. A trim, middle-aged man was putting glasses away. "Hey ya, guys," was all he said. No "get the hell out of here," no "show me your papers," just "hey ya, guys," and back to work.

On our way back through the tasting room and toward the door, Denise called out, "Enjoy the day."

We were outside and through the stone gate before either of us said anything.

"Well," Hank said, "that was disappointing."

"I know," I said. "They were so nice."

Sitting on the Calistoga Inn patio now, I'm thinking Chateau Montelena was sure another little lesson: Don't believe too many of the horror stories, even, I guess, if they're your own. Bad tales tend to get repeated more than the good ones. Sometimes, a guy just has a bad day.

"You know," I say to Hank, "I sure liked those people at Chateau Montelena."

"I wanna go back," he said.

When you think about it, considering how much serving-the-public gets done in this valley, this is a spectacularly civil place. In sheer numbers, every weekend is Christmas Eve at Macy's, but we found so few instances of rudeness on either side of the tasting bar it was unnatural.

There was, however, the woman "tasting"—in her own way—at Bennett Lane. Bennett Lane Winery is just north of Calistoga, and it's one of the cheeriest little rooms we went to. But this thirty-something woman gave them a test. She spent most of her time on her cellphone. Probably thought she was in a supermarket check-out line.

Jim May, the tasting room manager with the serenity of a kindergarten teacher, never stopped being patient and friendly with her, explaining each wine though she barely nodded at him. I seriously thought about tossing her phone in the spit bucket.

When she left, we asked how often that happens.

"Now and then," Jim said. "I don't get it. You spend all that effort getting here, you're in this great place, then you're on the phone the whole time. We try to be really, really nice because we don't want to let her ruin it for everyone else in the room, but, jeez, take it outside."

Jim is tall with a trimmed, graying goatee and he manages to be both lively and low-key at once. Great qualities for a tasting room manager. We asked what advice would he give visitors so they'll have a good time.

"Besides ditching the cellphone?" he said.

Most of it is obvious: Be friendly, they'll be friendly back. Move aside for other tasters. Don't let your kids trash a tasting room, and, really, what are kids doing in a tasting room? Take your time. Ask any question you have. Show a little interest and they'll probably pour you a couple extra wines on a slow day. Don't be a smarty pants. That last one's good advice for life in general.

"And don't reach over and grab the bottle to pour for yourself," Jim said.

He was serious. People do that. Most often when they've been swallowing more than they've been spitting.

I asked how many people spit.

"Today, counting you guys," Jim said. "Two."

He said they do get plenty of serious wine people who spit, and who really try to experience the wine. But it's a smaller percentage, which is fine with him.

"Especially in tasting rooms, it should be whatever works for you," he said. Wine tasting is supposed to be fun and social, and it's generally done on vacation. There doesn't need to be a lot of demands on people. Except maybe, no talking on the damn cellphone, I said.

There was another thing Jim said that stuck with me. He tries to tell people—gently—about the tools of wine tasting. He suggests people sniff the wine for a bit before drinking, or that they suck some air in with their wine. Or just hold it in their mouth for a few seconds and let it cover their tongue. But he can't convince too many people it's worth the effort.

I mention that to Hank now.

"People get embarrassed," he says. "They think it's just trying to look cool, or that they look dumb doing it. Some of it just sounds too wacky to be true."

"Like the glass tasting?" I say.

"Like the glass tasting," he says.

"I'm a believer," I say.

"That was amazing," Hank says. "I never knew it made that huge a difference."

No kidding. It was one of the most eye-opening encounters on our Quest, even for Hank, who knows wineglasses. More accurately, it would be called a glass comparison, but it was still something.

One of the more common points you hear about wine—without much real explanation—is that a good glass makes the wine taste better. And you'll hear there's a right glass for different wines.

In simple terms, larger, thin-lipped glasses are best, though sparkling wines ought to get flutes—the better to see the bubbles—

and whites get smaller glasses than reds. Those are the rules. You'll also hear don't pour too much into the glass—the rule of thumb is one-third of the glass for a red, one-half for a white, and three-fourths for a sparkling in a flute because of those bubbles. (Unless you're at a wedding. Then the bartender fills it up so you won't come back for a while.)

But is there really much of a difference in glasses? I am telling you.

On a day early into the Quest, Hank had business at Franciscan Oakville Estate, a winery we both have good feelings about because of their wines, their approach, and their generally chipper mood in the tasting room. So he arranged for a glass comparison that day. Our guide, so to speak, was Cory Strike, a thin, mid-thirtyish guy with a youthful exuberance.

Cory brought us into one of the small rooms off the comfortable main tasting center, and sat us at a table. We had five whites in front of us, each in a very different glass. And we had six reds, also in different glasses. There were the small, dense glasses you find at motels that you could hit with a hammer, and the semi-thick, rounded glasses fairly common in restaurants. The reds included a big bowl-like glass—a Burgundy glass—and a large, slightly straighter glass I now know is a classic Bordeaux glass.

"This is a blind tasting," Cory told us. "Here's a pad for some notes. Tell me what wines you think you're tasting and what you think of them." Then he left.

I was still learning my technique. I sniffed and swirled and sucked and gurgled and tried to spit gracefully. Hank was more nimble.

"I think one of these is a Sauvignon Blanc," I said. "The one in the big glass is definitely a Chard. I think. Maybe. It's white. I know that. I can't get a couple of the others."

"You know," Hank said, "I think he's messin' with us."

Of course he was. This was a glass comparison. Cory was going to pull some tricks. Every wine tasted unique. I thought that, and Hank thought that.

I need to say, Hank is good at this blind tasting. He and the crew that works for him at Nugget medal in competitions. We've been to dinners where Hank's nailed the varietal, winery, and vintage, partly because he'd tasted the same wine recently, but he remembered it exactly. That takes some skills.

In any case, we knew why we were there. We figured Cory was playing with our heads and taste buds. I thought the trick was three whites and three reds. Hank thought two or three. They all tasted very, very different. The only reasons we limited the number of wines was our suspicion. On my own, I'd have guessed five separate whites.

"So what'd you get?" Cory asked when he came back in.

We told him.

"In that glass," Cory said, pointing to the first white, "is our Franciscan Napa Valley Chardonnay. In that one is our Franciscan Napa Valley Chardonnay. In the third is Franciscan Napa Valley Chardonnay. Those two on the end had Franciscan Napa Valley Chardonnay."

The reds, all six stupid glasses of them, were Franciscan's Napa Valley Merlot.

"Whoa," I said.

"Whoa," Hank said.

"Makes a difference, huh," Cory said.

Hell, yeah. We re-enacted it with our eyes open. Cory dumped the glasses and poured the Merlot into the crystal Bordeaux glass, the all-purpose rounded lip restaurant glass, and the thick, little, you-can't-break-this-with-a-brick motel glass. Widely different in each. Spectacularly different. So different even I could tell.

"Why? How?" I said. "I mean, you know, what?"

"Yeah," Cory said, "people say that."

He explained it some. Mostly it has to do with smell.

To break it down too simply, remember that we only really taste a few basic flavors: sweet, salty, sour, bitter, and umami, or savory. But we pick up thousands of smells, which fill in the gaps and create what we think of as flavor. In simple, non-scientific terms: smell rules. So the main thing a good wineglass does, then, is let you smell the wine.

Oddly enough, that's why a thin rim helps. A thicker rim, particularly one with a roll on it, forces you to suck the wine in, sort of like when you gulp water. And that makes you suck the aroma straight into your throat and past your olfactory system—the nasal passages with your smell receptors. A thin rim lets the wine pour into your mouth, and the smells rise up more gently and into your nose.

But there is more. The smell from wine is, basically, the wine evaporating. The more surface area, the more evaporation. A glass with a wide bowl gets you lots of surface and lots of evaporation, so you'll take in more of what wine people call "volatiles" but we'll call smells. Swirling works by coating the glass with even more wine and getting you even more evaporation and smell.

The size of the opening matters, too. If the opening is too small to get your nose in, even a little, that's just wrong. On the good glasses, it's more complicated. For instance, the Burgundy glass—with the widest bowl—has a relatively narrow opening. That concentrates and intensifies the smell, which is why it's supposed to be good for Pinot Noir, a more delicate wine with a terrific-if-lighter bouquet.

A Bordeaux glass, for those powerful Cabernets, has a slightly smaller bowl and a slightly wider opening, so the Cab doesn't climb up your nasal passages and smack your brain with tannin.

Now here's where it gets hinky.

Lots of wine people will tell you the glass affects taste because of where it deposits wine on your tongue. True. And not true. Also, the classic old tongue map? Never mind.

First, the shape of the glass can indeed direct the wine to different parts of your tongue. For instance, the width of the opening changes your head position when you're sipping. A narrow glass, like a Champagne flute, makes you tilt your head back. A wide opening, like on a Bordeaux glass, lets you lower your head forward more.

But—and this is a massive "but"—you'll hear that the perfect glass for each wine directs it to the appropriate taste buds. So, say, a sharp Sauvignon Blanc will get steered to the front of your tongue. In theory, that's where your sweet receptors hang out. Also, in theory, it helps the acidic wine dodge the sour and bitter taste buds on the sides and back of your tongue. The better to avoid a pucker face.

In theory. Here's what Hildegard Heymann, a professor of Viticulture and Enology who runs the University of California, Davis', sensory research, says about that:

"It's crap. Total crap."

The reason: that age-old tongue map, with the sweet receptors in front, the acid taste buds on the side, and the bitter buds in the back, is also total crap. It's based on a misreading of some 1901 research, and though a variety of papers and scientists have debunked it, it still gets repeated. Sometimes by wineglass sales reps.

I called Heymann to get a grip on this. She said taste buds are spread all over the tongue, though not evenly, so there are, more or less, different zones. But here's the thing, and it's a big thing: It's different for every person.

"We all have places of varying sensitivity," she said, "but it's totally idiosyncratic."

And those glasses that aim the wine?

"I can't see how they'd work, at least not similarly for everyone." She says what would seem best for any wine is a glass that gets it to the middle of the tongue, where all your taste buds have a shot at it, and, more importantly, where your olfactory sensors can best pick up the vapors.

"It's all about the nose," Heymann said. There's two pieces to that, actually: the smell before you swallow, and a second, different impression after the wine goes down and the remaining vapors get pushed into your olfactory system. The second part—called retro-nasal olfaction, if you're cramming for the test—is actually more powerful, which is one reason why you're supposed to suck in some air and gurgle your wine. Or at least hold it in your mouth momentarily.

OK, here's what we know. Different glasses make the wine taste different. Hank and I are empirical, if-now-slightly-fanatical proof. And it's different for different people. "Different" is the operating word. "Better?" That's more complex. Those small, thick, you'll-never-smell-the-wine glasses? We know they suck. The Bordeaux glass vs. the Burgundy vs. the Chardonnay glass? That's harder. It probably depends on—and you knew this was coming—individual taste.

The biggest name in stemware is Riedel, an Austrian company that's generally regarded by winemakers, wineries, and just wine people around the world as the Cadillac of wineglasses. They have a glass for seemingly every grape on earth. They may also have glasses specifically for lefties or for wine drinkers with athlete's foot. They are thin-lipped and elegant, and they look damn cool. We liked the wine best in Riedel glasses during our glass comparison. So does pretty much everyone. So does Professor Heymann. I asked why.

"It's a combination of how they help what happens in your nose, and what the glass feels like in your hand," she said. "It just feels better. That matters."

And is there really the perfect glass for each kind of wine?

"Good question," she said.

Whatever the answer, I'm still kinda shaken about the tongue map. I hear a lot of people talking about it in wine country. One of the enduring discoveries of our Quest has been that this world of wine has its share of loose fables. I've decided you just can't take things for granted.

I need to put the Napa Valley Wine Train in that category. It was another surprise for us, and for me in particular. I was always afraid of the Wine Train. I thought it would be even more snobbish and upper-crusty than Chateau Montelena. Which, I guess, really isn't, either. Not the point. Wine Train.

Turned out, I had it backward. It's unpretentious, aimed at mid-level visitors, and pretty damn fun. The Wine Train is owned by Vincent DeDomenico, who also created Rice-a-Roni and owns Ghirardelli Chocolate Company in San Francisco. They sell Ghirardelli chocolates in the well-stocked, and well-priced, wine shop at the train station in Napa town. No Rice-a-Roni boxes, though.

The train started up in 1989, after a pretty good fight in Napa. The original plan called for regular runs up and down the valley like a commuter service, dropping people at wineries and crossing the highway regularly. Winery owners and the towns of Napa had no authority over the train—railroads are federal—but they fought back by prohibiting passengers from getting off the train onto their property.

Eventually, the compromise was two trips daily—one with lunch (brunch on weekends), one with dinner—and a three-hour, mostly sightseeing tour. Now, except for seeing the stately train moving up the valley along the vineyards, it's been a non-issue.

We went on a dinner trip and riding the train was, frankly, cool. It's part–Orient Express, part–rolling tasting room. The train has 1915 and 1917 Pullman dining and lounge cars, which have that classy, gilded-era look. And since there are two meal seatings for each out-and-back trip—we ate on the way home—we wandered around and found the wine-tasting car and Chrissy Werris. Chrissy, put simply, is a world-class wine geek, in every good sense of the term.

Her card says "wine educator," which we've seen a few times, but in Chrissy's case, "ardent" and "original" should be on there, too. She asked people questions about taste preferences—not wine tastes, but favorite tea or coffee style or fruit—then came out with wines that repeatedly had tasters swooning. If someone mentioned a winery or a wine, and she had a story—not an "I know everything" story, but things that were quirky or, here's a good one, interesting. She knew winemakers, history, some freaky things about the grapes.

So, it turns out, the wine train is about wine, which, when I say it that way, makes some sense. It's even better in the daytime when you can see the vineyards. Honestly, I don't know how I got the impression it was lame and snobby. Like I said, loose fables. There are plenty running around this valley and through the wine world.

"I have a resolution," I tell Hank now. "You will not catch me trashing any place until I've been there."

"What if you have been there, but you're wrong?" he says, all benign and innocent.

I know where this is going.

"This is gonna be a Don Giovanni reference, isn't it?" I say.

"I should make you drive down there and apologize to those people," Hank says.

He should. After all the chatter about Don Giovanni, after all the people talking it up and recommending it, and me talking trash, we had to go. The open-minded boys go to dinner. Plus our wives. Bringing Deborah and Tina to the good places was still standard procedure for the Quest.

Bistro Don Giovanni sits just off Highway 29, literally a few yards north of Napa's city limits. It may be the most generally popular restaurant in the valley, and surely, judging by what we've heard over the last nine months, the most heavily recommended.

I was not one of those recommenders, though I'd only eaten there just once and it was late, we were tired, and never mind all the reasons. Snap judgments are snap judgments.

So we gave it another try. A Saturday night. Seven-thirty reservation. Busy time. Make them play at the top of their game.

The restaurant building is sort of wine-colored, and from the road, it looks like it could be made of adobe. It has a deck with tables. That's also where people can wait for their tables—where we waited that late night, incidentally, for a good, long time. For the rematch, Deborah and I were meeting Hank and Tina there. Walking up, a few minutes early, the outside deck was packed. The waiting area also looked packed. "Here we go again," I said to Deborah, who, even more than Hank, has learned not to pay attention too closely to whatever I'm saying.

My cellphone rang. It was Hank. They'd gotten there early and were already seated. OK, there's one improvement.

The inside has a lively, boisterous café feel. The bar at one end of the big room looks over a little wall at the restaurant, there are windows into the kitchen, and the tile floors, high ceilings, and warm ceiling spots make the room almost feel like it's an outside patio. No complaints about the room.

As we were seated, our waiter, Tim, a dark-haired, middle-aged veteran, greeted us. Hank and Tina had already ordered a bottle of Honig 2003 Napa Valley Sauvignon Blanc.

"They started without you," Tim said. "I can reprimand them if you want." He said it was pretty busy right then, so if we couldn't find him, just hail anyone if we needed help. Damn. Tim's a good guy.

The wine list is huge and fun. The Honig Sauv Blanc, I noticed, cost $27. The prices weren't extravagant, though there were extravagant wines on the menu, up to a Screaming Eagle Cabernet for $1,200. We were probably not going to order that.

The food menu was just as fun. There was a quote at the top from Emily Post: "Nothing is less important than which fork you use." I was starting to think I may have misjudged these people. This was getting to be a pattern.

We got waves of busboys bringing water, bread, good humor. I had a Caesar salad that was light, garlicky, and terrific. I was almost twitching it was so good, and that was just the salad. Tim checked in, so I asked if they got many people ordering the Screaming Eagle. "We have three bottles in the cellar," he said. "We sell maybe one a month.

We used to sell two or three bottles a week when all the dot-com kids were coming through."

I took another bite of that salad. It was still terrific. I was feeling bad. I probably should not have bad-mouthed this restaurant.

We ordered a Saintsbury 2001 Carneros Pinot Noir with the main courses, which were even better than my salad. I had a risotto with wild mushrooms, Parmesan, and a red wine accent in it. It had a sweet, deep flavor, but not the cloying richness that some risottos have that wear you out. It was wonderful. It came with strips of flank steak skewered on rosemary sticks. Tina let me try her grilled pork chop. It was so good I wanted to roll in it.

Meanwhile, Deborah, who ordered a pan-roasted chicken served with Tuscan tomato and bread salad, was sitting there, not talking to anyone, maybe rocking a little and mumbling, "Mmmmmm." Another bite, slight rocking, "Mmmmmm." That was not her normal behavior.

After a time, she regained consciousness. "You . . . have . . . to . . . try . . . this," she said. The Tuscan thing-y was unworldly. The tomatoes were light and fresh, but still a bit roasted, and the bread with them had a deep, grilled, smoky taste. I rocked a little and said, "Mmmmmm."

Tim came by again. Just to say hi. It was his third or fourth trip during the main course. Always friendly, always unpushy. He never said, "How is everything?" Points right there. He did say, "Hope you guys are enjoying it." I would have been, except for what had become by then the deep, aching guilt. "I am such an idiot," I told our table.

"News flash," my wife said.

We were sitting there, looking around the room. It was a comfortably mixed and energetic crowd. A fun crowd. Some guys in Hawaiian shirts, some women in sundresses. Some people dressed for Saturday night. There was a large family here and there, a couple on a clearly hot date. There were groups just starting their evenings, and others making their meal at Don Giovanni that night's main course. It looked exactly the way a restaurant in wine country should look: cheerful, sociable, vibrant.

Then our bill came. It was only $17 more—for all four of us—than Hank and I had spent on just our dinner a couple nights earlier.

"I love this place," I said. "I love Don Giovanni."

"Has he been like this the whole trip?" Deborah asked Hank.

"Pretty much," he said.

"Sorry," she said.

"Guys," I said, "can we come back tomorrow?"

At the Calistoga Inn, a busboy drops bread and water on our table.

"Your waitress will be here in a sec," he says. "This warm weather has us slammed."

"No worries," Hank says. "We could not be in less of a hurry."

We both sit for a few moments, just absorbing the gold light hitting the eastern side of the valley. That's something we never do enough when we're here, simply absorb the place. There's always so much to get to.

"OK," I say. "Here's the real question. What wines stand out? Not the best, but the ones that, for whatever reason, you remember most."

"I knew you'd get to that," Hank says. "I've been saying this for a couple months: Opus One. Just for the sheer intensity of it. I don't know if I'd have it with food, but I still think about the concentration, the extraction. I just remember it's overall powerful image."

He gets no argument from me. That Opus One was something. "You know what I keep thinking about?" I say. "That Zinfandel Port at Jessup. Maybe it was the chocolate sauce, but I think I'm having recurring dreams about it."

"That was more you than me," Hank says.

"How about those Barnett Cabs?" I say.

"Both of them," Hank says. "Those were both really elegant, really polished."

"Really good, too," I say.

"I remember the Ehlers Cab," Hank says. "It had a true beginning, middle, and end. A really long end. It just kept going."

"Another one I keep thinking about was the Truchard Syrah," I say. "That white pepper was almost a shock."

"They had a lot of great wines," Hank says. "I loved their Tempranillo."

Since it was a Truchard Syrah that kinda got us started on this Quest, I like that we found another Truchard Syrah that was great. We both stop for a minute, thinking about the Truchards. Nice folks. And they sure can make wine.

"What else?" I say.

"The Cliff Lede Sauvignon Blanc," Hank says.

"I loved both the Honig Sauvignon Blancs," I say. "When we were talking to Michael Honig, I was losing focus. I just wanted to drink the wine."

We start to get going now. We both liked the wines at Robert Mondavi. Hank and our guide, Inger, almost spasmed over the Reserve Cab. I know I spasmed over the Oakville Cab.

And there were the wines at Piña. Even the barrel samples were loaded. Cardinale and Atalon were superb. There was the Trefethen

Chardonnay, the Hewitt Cabernet at Provenance, the Cab at Corison and their Acappella Zinfandel. The Domaine Carneros Brut Vintage. Suddenly, I'm a sparkling guy, though it could have been the deck out there.

"Miner Family Wild Yeast Chardonnay," I say.

"Robert Craig Howell Mountain Cab."

"Benessere Sangiovese."

"Cuvaison's Reserve Pinot."

"Hess Mountain Cuvée," I say. "I don't know why that isn't more popular."

"Prager's Aria White Port," Hank says. "That was different."

"So was Van Der Heyden's Late Harvest Cabernet," I say. "I'd never heard of that."

"Smith-Madrone's Cabernet," Hank says. "It seemed like everything we tried on Spring Mountain rocked."

"Silverado Vineyards," I say. "I don't remember which one. I know I liked the wine, but I really remember loving that place."

Silverado Vineyards, up a hill off the Silverado Trail in the Stags Leap district, has an Old World–style lodge, a huge open room, a happy atmosphere, and an incredible view up the valley for miles. Carrot juice would taste decent there. I can still viscerally recall holding my glass, standing on the stone deck, just inhaling the scene.

That right there is the power and the enchantment of Napa Valley. It's solid and ethereal and, maybe, airborne, but these thirty miles permeate with the feeling this is a special realm. It's the views, the vineyards, the people, the wineries, and the wine—the collective force of it all—and it makes the intensity of being here overwhelming and soothing and captivating. That's why just walking into a tasting room is magic every single time. You've opened a door into the kingdom.

We take that home when we buy wine here. We look for it when we drink wine anywhere. But the truth for visitors caught in the grip of the valley is, wine tastes better here. It just does. In a way, we get fooled a little. Some of the "Napa charm" comes from salesmanship—by the wineries, the restaurants, and the adorable little inns with vineyard views. The next Silverado Vineyards wine I taste won't be quite the same, because I won't be standing on that stone deck looking at miles of knolls and vines.

But it will still be good. And it will be special. That's because most of that charm is genuine, and it does indeed stay with anyone who encounters this singular place. It is undeniably true for us. The personality, the sensibilities, the soul of Napa are all imprinted on me and Hank now, because we spent so much time here and because we looked for it.

Napa has grown, just as the American wine industry has grown, and it's as much a commerce center and its own product as it is a farming region and a gracious countrified valley. Cross interests fight over streams and hillsides, over growth and traffic, over all the things people fight over everywhere. Napa is sometimes crowded, often expensive, and it's struggling with its reputation and its character.

And yet, more than anything, it is also extraordinary. We found that every dazzling day here. There were wet, late winter afternoons, with mists rising off the mountains in layers and the valley floor looking like a soft, gray pool you could swim in. There was early spring, with the intense, mind-bending green and the sticks standing skinny and bare in the vineyards. There was May and June, days when the vines were solid and defined, when the entire valley looked like something sketched in a line drawing. There were the lush, thick fields of summer; the single blanket the valley floor became in September; the electric yellows, reds, and golds of fall—of harvest time—and now, the slow turn back toward winter.

And we found that in people. They are extraordinary, too. There was Jo Ann and Tony Truchard, who built a winery and a life with heart and hard work. There was Nate Page in the tasting room at Steltzner, just wanting people to try his wine, or Vince Bonotto at Diageo and Sterling, worrying every grape out of the vineyards and into the tanks. We met Nile Zacherle at Barnett, so bright and intense about winemaking, Richard Camera at Hess, a cascade of wisdom about vines and hills and weather, Barry Cothran at Rutherford Grill, full of energy every night just talking wine. Karen Nielsen at Trefethen and Emil Bell at Ehlers left solid jobs to chase wine world dreams. Bonnie Zimmermann left Hollywood and found happy calm in the quiet of Pope Valley. Katarena Arger put off law school and seems happiest when there is no calm at her dad's winery. There was Sunshine Foods' Mike Smith, pouring astoundingly expensive wine at a bocce ball game, Michael Honig gathering his family through their winery, Arnold Tudal putting his legacy and his wine in the hands of Ron Vuylsteke. There were Stuart and Charles Smith, growing grapes and making wine on Spring Mountain for three decades, as stalwart and woven into Napa Valley as any Madrone tree on their property. When Robert Mondavi was talking up Napa Wine a half century ago, when he was telling the world it should take notice, it was these people, their passion, their wine he was envisioning.

That's why people come here. Because in Napa, the wine life is real. Because there is nowhere else in America, and only a few places on the planet, so utterly and energetically devoted to wine. And because this is where they make it great. There is something beautiful about a glass of wine. There's something graceful and fascinating in its production, and something compelling, almost primal, in the sight of the vineyards that grow it.

That's what makes Napa Valley a wonderland. Its land, its weather, its vineyards, its people. They are the heartbeat of American winemaking, and they're what anyone who picks up a glass wants to taste.

Hank and I talk about that now, about how much more tangible and pronounced all the parts of Napa feel to us, and about how much more we want to explore. It seems that in all things wine, every time you learn something, you also learn there's more out there. Maybe our work is not done.

Our waitress comes over, looking a bit more harried than she'd like to.

"What'll it be?" she asks.

Hank is a pro to the end. He says what wine people say after a long tasting trip.

"Beer, please," Hank says.

"Me, too," I say. "I'll have a beer."

"You know guys," she says. "We have a great wine list."

We look at each other.

"Give us a minute," Hank says.

the tasting rooms of napa valley

Tips for Wine Tasting

HERE'S THE THING we learned about tasting wine in Napa: It's incredibly hard not to have fun. If you go off plan, miss an appointment, or hit a crowd, so what? You're in Napa Valley. Just look around.

That's our first, most important advice: Relax, be in the moment, and go slow.

We do, however, have some tips for visiting the tasting rooms and the valley. If you ignore them all—as we sometimes did—no worries. Consider these a bonus, they're enhancements, hassle-avoidance advice, bits of guidance that will make it more fun. And we have this guide that describes the tasting rooms to help you choose.

The Big Things:

- **Don't try to do too much. Give yourself time to hang out somewhere you like, to explore someplace you discover, and to eat.**
- **Eat. Seriously, eat. You'll be drinking wine. Food is good when you're drinking, and it's great in Napa. High-end restaurants, small lunch spots, or places to stock a picnic are everywhere. (There's a list of the larger winery picnic areas below.) One note: There aren't many food spots on Silverado Trail, so either make time to cross to Highway 29 or plan to picnic.**

- **Drink water.** Same point. You'll be drinking wine. Hydrate. You'll feel better.
- **"Appointment only" does not always mean appointment only.** This one is huge. Napa County requires most wineries opened after 1990 to be appointment only—at least in name—but many, many tasting rooms handle it by letting visitors sign in for an instant appointment, and the county doesn't seem to mind. There are exceptions, however. As a general rule, tastings combined with tours require reservations, simple tastings don't. For complete listings, use this guide. We'll tell you if you need an appointment.
- **Carry a cooler.** Don't cook your wine. If your car gets over eighty degrees, you'll damage the wine. It wouldn't hurt to toss in an ice pack. If you're flying to Napa, or you forget, a Styrofoam cooler costs a few bucks at a market.
- **The busy times are summer and harvest season.** It gets busier as the week goes on, from Monday to the weekend, and as the day gets later. In busy times, assume the large wineries and the tasting rooms right on Highway 29 between Yountville and St. Helena will be packed by early afternoon. Better options include tasting earlier in the day (your palate is freshest in the morning, by the way), staying on Silverado Trail, and tasting during the lunch hour (when many people are eating) and lunching in the afternoon (when everyone is tasting). On those busy days, almost every winery gets jammed by 3 p.m., and on almost any day, the tasting rooms that stay open past 5 p.m. will be stuffed. For some people, that's a good thing; it's just more happy hour than wine tasting.
- **Consider the off season.** Early spring can be warm and dramatic, late fall is stunning for its color, and in winter, the tasting rooms get cozy with fireplaces. The tasting experience changes entirely when it's just you in the room.
- **Have a plan.** Yes, we said go with the flow, but it still helps to start with a plan. Just don't be obsessive.
- **Figure on three or four wineries a day, maximum.** Probably just one with a tour. And vary the day. For instance, try one big winery, one midsized name you like, then some place out of the way. Or just venture into wineries you don't know.
- **Turn right.** Sounds dumb, but left turns out of a winery's driveway on Highway 29 during busy times don't exist. If you can, plan to go in one direction—particularly by mid-afternoon—and stay on one side of the highway, so you'll always be turning right. If you absolutely insist on a left turn, here's what you do: Turn right anyway and go until there's a left turn lane (or a middle lane) where you can pull in somewhere, turn around and go right again, back the way you wanted. Yes, it's farther. Don't be stubborn. If you wait for that left from a driveway, you'll wait till nightfall.

Buying Wine:

■ Prices at wineries are generally a couple dollars more than at retail stores (unless there's a sale) because they don't want to undercut their frontline distributors. Our theory, however, is when you find something you want, buy it there. You'll forget later. You will.

■ Almost every winery has some wine sold only there. If you really like a wine, ask about distribution or buy it there.

■ Many wineries refund your tasting fee if you buy a bottle. Even if they don't do it automatically, it never hurts to ask.

■ Every winery has a wine club. They are generally good deals, and often get you access to wines you could not find otherwise. Here's how most work: It costs nothing to join, but you commit to a certain number of shipments for a year, generally a couple bottles every month or two, and generally totaling a case (twelve bottles) or two for the year. The price is always discounted. The real decision, then, is, do you want to commit to that case or two, and from the same winery? The payoff is discounts, some hard-to-find wines, and privileges at the winery—like free tastings and occasional wine club parties. The payout is the promise to buy.

The Little Things:

■ There are coupons everywhere for free or discounted tastings. Look in the free wine country magazines and maps piled around Napa. Ask in tasting rooms if they have coupons for other wineries they'd recommend. Check the websites of wineries you want to visit. (Many are listed in our guide.)

■ Share tastings sometimes. If you want the all-Cab flight, and your tasting buddy wants to try the whites, get one of each and share. Or if you're hitting a lot of wineries, share one at every place. (Sometimes, they'll end up pouring you both full tastings. But that's not really the point. We're talking variety.)

■ Ask questions. Most tasting room servers are wine people. They know a lot. If you have wine questions, ask away. If you don't understand a description or a winemaking term, ask. Ask about the winery, the vineyards, or if they have recommendations for other tasting rooms. They're full of good information. And, the more you engage, the more they'll engage back, and probably, the more wine they'll pour.

■ Don't take this personally, but don't be a smarty-pants. Don't lecture tasting room servers on wine. There is nothing in it for you. They already know wine, and they really know their wines because they taste them every day. You don't need to impress them. They'll treat you better if you're just nice.

■ If there's a picnic table or two, it's polite to ask about using it, particularly since they might have a permit problem. Often, even if they don't have all the permits, they'll let you hang out if you ask, especially if you buy a bottle of wine. (Our guide below tells you all the picnic tables that are open.)

- Don't feel you need to buy something every place you go. On the other hand, if a server is very nice and you like the wine, that's the time to buy.
- Rest your palate. Takes breaks with food or water or, honestly, beer. Winemakers drink a lot of beer.

Free Tasting Rooms:

August Briggs Winery
Caymus Vineyards
Elyse Winery
Frank Family Vineyards
Frog's Leap Winery
Heitz Wine Cellars
Mayacamas Vineyards
Milat Vineyards
Piña Cellars
Pope Valley Winery

Robert Craig Wine Cellars
Robert Keenan Winery
Rombauer Vineyards
Smith-Madrone Vineyards and Winery
Truchard Vineyards
Tudal Family Winery
Vincent Arroyo Winery
V. Sattui Winery

Great Views:

Artesa Vineyards
Barnett Vineyards
Bouchaine Vineyards
Catacula Lake Winery
Chateau Potelle
Diamond Oaks
Domaine Carneros
Graeser Winery
Joseph Phelps Vineyards
Kuleto Estate
Laird Family Estate

Monticello Vineyards
Pride Mountain Vineyards
Robert Keenan Winery
Rutherford Hill Winery
St. Clement Vineyards
Silverado Vineyards
Smith-Madrone Vineyards and Winery
Sterling Vineyards
Terra Valentine
William Hill Winery

Picnic Areas:

Alpha Omega Winery
Andretti Winery
Benessere Vineyards
Bennett Lane Winery
Bouchaine Vineyards
Casa Nuestra Winery and Vineyards

Catacula Lake Winery
Chateau Potelle
Clos Du Val
Clos Pegase
Cuvaison
Folie à Deux Winery
Freemark Abbey

Hall Wines
Laird Family Estate
Louis M. Martini Winery
Madonna Estates
Mahoney Vineyards
Monticello Vineyards
Napa Wine Cellars
Pine Ridge Winery
Pope Valley Winery

Regusci Winery
Rutherford Hill Winery
St. Clement Vineyards
Silver Rose Cellars
Smith-Madrone Vineyards and Winery
Summers Winery
V. Sattui Winery

Galleries or Contemporary Art Collections:

Artesa Vineyards
Cliff Lede Vineyards
Clos Pegase
Del Dotto Caves
Hall Wines
The Hess Collection Winery

Markham Vineyards
Mumm Napa Valley
Robert Mondavi Winery
St. Supèry Vineyards and Winery
Turnbull Wine Cellars
Vintner's Collective

DOWNTOWN NAPA TASTING ROOMS

Back Room Wines

974 Franklin Street
Napa, 94559
707-226-1378 or 877-322-2576
www.backroomwines.com
HOURS: 10–6 Monday–Thursday; 10–9
Friday; 10–7 Saturday

A small, unassuming wine shop whose owner, Dan Dawson, says he tries to stock the best small-production wines in California. The room is simply adorned but the range of wines is broad and eclectic.

ATMOSPHERE: It's a place for locals and wine people, but anyone feels welcome. Warm yellow walls, with one red accent wall, give off an avant-garde tone, but mostly the ambience is no-frills. The room is filled with wine racks and light comes from overhead fixtures. It doesn't feel shoddy; it does feel that it's all about the wine.

SERVICE: Dawson asks visitors what styles they like, then consistently nails it. He covers the small bar and brings wine to people sitting on a couch. He says each wine has a story, but he waits for you to ask.

TASTING TOOLS: Good, large glasses. Spit buckets, water, and crackers handy. Good light.

INTANGIBLES AND EXTRAS: This is a serious yet un-intimidating place for wine lovers. Tastings are available all day, but they conduct their special themed tastings every Friday night. All the tastings come with good descriptions of wines being poured.

WINE AVAILABILITY: This is a wine shop that specializes in small releases. Dan also says he knows his customers see a lot of Napa Valley wines, so he tries to keep a good stock from other regions. Prices are across the board. Wines opened for tastings often range from $15 to $50.

PICNIC PROSPECTS: None.

COST: Price varies on pours by the taste, half-glass or glass. Friday night tasting is $15 for six to eight wines.

DIRECTIONS: Downtown Napa. On Franklin just south of First Street.

RECOMMENDED FOR: Everyone but wine novices.

Bounty Hunter

975 First Street
Napa, 94559
707-226-3976 or 800-943-9463
www.bountyhunterwine.com
Hours: 11–10 Sunday–Wednesday;
11–1 a.m. Thursday–Saturday

This exuberant wine bar, pub, and bistro is one of our favorite places in Napa. It's got the energetic, friendly feel of a hot spot for people who don't go to hot spots. It is popular so there's a full house on most evenings, and daytime might be better for pure wine sampling. But this is a terrific place to end the day.

Created by Mark Pope, founder of the Bounty Hunter rare wine catalog, it offers a range of tasting flights, forty wines by the glass, and 400 wines by the bottle.

ATMOSPHERE: Comfortable, high-ceilinged room has glass walls on each end, oak posts, and lots of wood and brick. There are racks of wines along one wall. The medium-sized bar—one bar stool is a saddle—is an L near one entrance and there are tall community tables and smaller, cafe tables around the room. Most impressive, however, is the easygoing liveliness.

SERVICE: Although busy at night, bartenders are accommodating.

And they are wine people. They also understand hospitality. We watched one waitress chase two people outside to tell them a space had opened up at the bar. Servers taste their wines regularly to know the inventory.

TASTING TOOLS: Very good, large glasses. Good light. Detailed wine descriptions. No spit buckets, but this is a bar.

INTANGIBLES AND EXTRAS: Hard to imagine a better evening spot or bar in wine country. This is a place for wine lovers, but there is more. The bar has a long list of beers, and the full, bistro-style food menu is very good. Ask about the Beer-Can Chicken. Great room, great crowd, great energy.

WINE AVAILABILITY: They stock many hard-to-find wines, so it may be here or nowhere. Prices by the glass range from $6 to $20, and by the bottle from $16 to $400.

PICNIC PROSPECTS: None.

COST: Wine tasting flights range from $10 for Chardonnays to $18 for Cabernets. Wines by the glass or bottle are cheaper than at most similar bars and bistros.

DIRECTIONS: Downtown Napa near the corner of First and Main streets.

RECOMMENDED FOR: Everyone.

Copia

500 First Street
Napa, 94559
707-259-1600 or 888-512-6742
www.copia.org
Hours: 10–5 Wednesday–Monday;
    closed Tuesday

A sleek, modern, 80,000-square-foot center created with a big push from Robert and Margrit Mondavi, Copia opened in 2001 and pays tribute to the connections between food, wine, and art. It's named after the Roman goddess of abundance and the feel is part museum and temple, part food court, and part luxury mall.

ATMOSPHERE: The Wine Spectator Tasting Bar is a large, curved glass bar in an open, mall-like section on the first floor. A three-story glass wall throws natural light on the center's glass, metal, and pale-toned tiles. The tasting bar has an easy, walk-up casualness. Depending on the day, tasters range from wine authorities to first-time tourists.

SERVICE: This is a mixed bag depending on the day, because the servers are volunteers, unless they are winemakers pouring their own wine. Some volunteer servers are more like bartenders—friendly and pouring big, but lacking real wine background. Others are experts from the industry.

TASTING TOOLS: Very good glasses. Spit buckets and crackers handy. Water on request. Very good light.

INTANGIBLES AND EXTRAS: Copia is a high-end tourist destination with art, exhibits, films, and demonstrations related to food and wine. There's a full wine bar, a stylish restaurant, an upscale deli, and a museum store. It is lavish and expansive inside, and the tasting bar is a nice part of that. But it feels urban and contemporary, and is missing the sense it's in Napa Valley.

WINE AVAILABILITY: Varies widely, depending on what's served that day. Prices depend on what's being served.

PICNIC PROSPECTS: They have scores of tables outside under olive trees and along the three and a half acres of organic gardens. There's also space on the grass in a small amphitheater next to the Napa River.

COST: Entrance to Copia is $5; free tasting daily noon to 4; the full wine bar offers two-ounce pours ranging from $2 to $12 and full glasses from $4 to $24.

DIRECTIONS: Three blocks east of downtown.

RECOMMENDED FOR: People looking for a contemporary food/wine museum. Not recommended if you're looking for a Napa winery tasting.

JV Wine & Spirits

426 First Street
Napa, 94559
707-253-2624
www.jvwineandspirits.com
HOURS: 2–7 daily

This retail wine and spirits store says it has one of the five largest wine collections in California. The tasting bar is inside the store's smaller room for expensive wines.

ATMOSPHERE: It's simple but surprisingly winery-like, considering the location and grape-colored cinder block back wall. Spotlights on the tasting bar give warm light, and the racks of bottles nearby give a sense this is a place for serious wine tasting.

SERVICE: Efficient and professional—and patient, since the tasting list was twelve wines deep. The assumption was we knew what we were doing.

TASTING TOOLS: Good, large glasses. Spit buckets. Water and crackers on request. Good light.

INTANGIBLES AND EXTRAS: They have a large, innovative tasting list that rotates forty wines regularly. Servers offer everything that's behind the bar, sometimes including wines not on the list. The sense is this is where locals taste. Two wine distributors stopped to try a couple wines during our tasting. The Friday evening tastings—discounted to $2—feature winemakers pouring their own. The store also has wine consultants available.

WINE AVAILABILITY: This is a big store; you come here to buy. They also have a wine club and an online catalog. Prices our day ranged from $15 to $30, but the store carries wines of every level.

PICNIC PROSPECTS: None.

COST: $5 for ten to twelve wines. $2 on Fridays. Waived with purchase.

DIRECTIONS: Four blocks east of downtown. Just east of the Copia complex.

RECOMMENDED FOR: Anyone more interested in wine than atmosphere.

Napa General Store

500 Main Street
Napa, 94559
707-259-0762
www.napageneralstore.com
Hours: 10–6 Sunday–Wednesday; 10–8 Thursday–Saturday

Much more than a general store, this is really a small, upscale, indoor marketplace, with a wine bar, exposed kitchen, restaurant, and large deck over the river. Their large tasting list is intriguing and looks like lists from any good restaurant.

ATMOSPHERE: The airy, bustling, two-story room has brick, beams, exposed fixtures, wood trim, and a wood-burning stove around the open restaurant. Light filters through large skylights and the glass wall leading to the deck. Overhead spotlights add warmth to the tasting bar.

SERVICE: They're efficient, sociable, and professional, but this is a restaurant wine bar, not a real wine tasting spot. Servers know wine, but they don't have a lot of time for wine talk because they're working the room.

TASTING TOOLS: Good, large glasses. Spit buckets handy. No crackers. Water on request.

INTANGIBLES AND EXTRAS: This is a terrific room and it has a large wine list. The wine bar is part of the restaurant, so it offers good people-watching opportunities.

WINE AVAILABILITY: They pour a range of popular wines, all available in restaurants and markets. Prices range from $17 to $49.

PICNIC PROSPECTS: None, but this is a restaurant and deli. There is seating on the outside deck over the river.

COST: Wines by the glass range from $6 to $12.50.

DIRECTIONS: In a refurbished complex on Main Street at the river, three blocks south of First.

RECOMMENDED FOR: Everyone. But it's a cool restaurant, not a winery experience.

Napa Valley Traditions

1202 Main Street
Napa, 94559
707-255-8544 or 800-627-2044
www.napatraditions.com
Hours: Monday–Saturday 9:30–5;
  Sunday 11–4

This country store had the first tasting bar in downtown Napa, but they seem to have lost some enthusiasm and may end the tastings soon. The bar is a table deep inside the store and offers Bayview Cellars wines. They make Sauvignon Blanc, Chardonnay, Syrah, and Cabernet Sauvignon.

ATMOSPHERE: Casual only begins to describe it. The small tasting bar is in the back of the store and around a corner. There's room for a handful

of people and you don't get the sense anyone here takes this too seriously.

SERVICE: The store clerks are extraordinarily nice, and they obligingly hustle over to pour the wine. They're also conversant in Bayview's line and story, and very eager to make the tasting a good experience. But their real attention is on the store.

TASTING TOOLS: Small glasses. Spit bucket and crackers handy. No water.

INTANGIBLES AND EXTRAS: As much as the tasting bar here is an afterthought, they have endearing servers and a charming store. It's comfortable for beginners.

WINE AVAILABILITY: Only at the store or website. Prices range from $15 to $19.

PICNIC PROSPECTS: None.

COST: $5 for four wines.

DIRECTIONS: Downtown Napa, at the corner of Main and Pearl streets.

RECOMMENDED FOR: Beginners or downtown Napa shoppers.

Napa Wine Merchants

1146 First Street
Napa, 94559
707-257-6796
www.napawinemerchant.com
Hours: 10–5 Monday,
  Wednesday–Saturday; 11–4 Sunday

Twelve small wineries share this casual wine shop and collective tasting room. It's managed by the Gustavo Thrace wineries and the lineup includes Beaucanon Estates, Liparita, Chrichton Hall, St. Barthelemy, Croze Wines, Young Ridge, Waterstone, and Z-52.

ATMOSPHERE: It's one of the many casual, approachable wine shops in downtown Napa. Big windows and overhead spotlights give it a cheerful feel, and it's a tall room with high ceilings and light wood trim.

SERVICE: Casual and approachable, almost silly. They talk about the wines when asked and are well-versed on their inventory, but they mostly seem happy to have visitors. They talk about Napa and all its wine and doings, rather than just the wines.

TASTING TOOLS: Good, large glasses. Spit buckets handy. Variety of pretzels and mustards on a nearby table. Very good light.

INTANGIBLES AND EXTRAS: The servers' general happiness in being there made us happy to be there. And the unfussy air got everybody at the good-sized tasting bar comparing wines and talking with each other. Besides the mustards and pretzels, they have a bar for tasting olives and oils.

WINE AVAILABILITY: They handle mostly small wineries. Though some of the wines are well distributed, this may be the best place to find some of them. Prices range from $9 to $60.

PICNIC PROSPECTS: None.

COST: $5 for five pours from a long list (but servers were purposely undiligent in counting); free tasting coupon available on the website.

DIRECTIONS: Downtown Napa, at the corner of First and Coombs streets.

RECOMMENDED FOR: Everyone.

Robert Craig Wine Cellars

880 Vallejo Street
Napa, 94559
707-252-2250
www.robertcraigwine.com
HOURS: 10–5 Monday–Saturday by appointment

Robert Craig has been involved in Napa winemaking for years, including a long stretch as general manager at Hess Collection Winery. He started his own winery on Howell Mountain with its first vintage in 1992. The mountain site doesn't allow the general public, but they offer tasting in this small, charming, throwback room in downtown Napa connected to one of the first winemaking facilities in town. (The winery is still used for some small, independent labels.)

They make limited quantities of some very good wines, including Chardonnay, Syrah, Zinfandel, Cabernets from Mt. Veeder and Howell Mountain, and a Cab named Affinity.

ATMOSPHERE: This room is old school in lots of good ways. It's small and bright, with pale walls and a big table in the middle for tasting. It has a simple tile floor, straight-back chairs, windows that look across the street at a couple old Victorians, and an active, city feel—but a city in wine country.

SERVICE: Rachel Miller runs the tasting room as if it's her house you're visiting and it's her wines she's pouring. Visitors sit at a table and Rachel proudly pours, explains, and makes the tasting friendly and personal. She's a wine veteran who knows the valley and is full of good info—and good fun. She'll re-pour what you feel you need to taste again.

TASTING TOOLS: Good, large glasses. Spit buckets handy. No water or crackers. Good light.

INTANGIBLES AND EXTRAS: This feels like Napa before the boom. It's intimate and low-key and not at all showy. The tone here is very comfortable and the wines are big, luscious, and well regarded. Don't be bothered if Rachel has to leave for a moment to run an errand at the winery office a couple blocks away.

WINE AVAILABILITY: The wines can be found in some shops and restaurants, but are made in small quantities and the best bet is through the winery or website. Prices range from $22 to $50.

PICNIC PROSPECTS: None.

COST: Free.

DIRECTIONS: Downtown Napa on Vallejo between Yajome Street and Soscol Avenue.

RECOMMENDED FOR: Everyone except first-timers who might be intimidated by a small sit-down tasting.

Vintner's Collective

1245 Main Street
Napa, 94559
707-255-7150
www.vintnerscollective.com
HOURS: 11–6 Wednesday–Monday;
Tuesday by appointment only

Downtown's most upscale tasting room. It's in a historic stone building that was once a brewery, then a saloon and brothel. It's a collective tasting room for eighteen small, premium winemakers including Judd's Hill, Ancien, Richard Perry, Gregory Graham, Patz & Hall, Melka, Mi Sueno, and Phelan.

ATMOSPHERE: The inside is fashionable, with a small art gallery and a serious, dark tasting bar framed by blond wood. They advertise themselves as no frills, no views, and they clearly are serious about wine, but the room is definitely high-end. Servers, however, are welcoming and unstuffy.

SERVICE: Very knowledgeable, very descriptive service, which is expected in a room with a good range of high-end wines. Servers are willing to talk small details about winemakers and wines, but they start as comfortably broad as you need. Despite the expensive air and the quality wines, the servers and the room don't have a sense of self-importance.

TASTING TOOLS: Good, large glasses. Spit buckets and water handy. Tasty crackers. Good light.

INTANGIBLES AND EXTRAS: This is a strong lineup of wines all in one place. Winemakers pour their own on Saturdays. Altogether, it's a satisfying tasting experience for serious wine people.

WINE AVAILABILITY: Most are found in fine shops and restaurants, but the store or website are the first places to look. Prices range from $18 to $75.

PICNIC PROSPECTS: None.

COST: $15 for Vintner's Tasting (four wines); $25 for Luxe Tasting (four premium, hard-to-find wines).

DIRECTIONS: Downtown Napa, on First between Pearl and Clinton streets.

RECOMMENDED FOR: Serious wine people. Not for wine novices.

Wineries of Napa Valley

1285 Napa Town Center
Napa, 94559
707-253-9450 or 800-328-7815
www.napavintages.com
HOURS: June–October: 11–6
Monday–Thursday; 10–7:30
Friday–Sunday; November–May: 11–6
daily

This storefront tasting room and wine shop under a purple awning is managed by Goosecross Cellars and houses a collective of small wineries, including Bourassa Vineyards, Burgess Cellars, Girard Winery, and Baldacci Family Vineyards.

ATMOSPHERE: It's an unpretentious, bright room with a glass front, light woods, and a well-lit tasting bar. The feel is part sales shop, part cafe, part wine bar. There's plenty of room at the blond wood bar and a handful of tables around the room.

SERVICE: Because they are next door to the Visitor's Center, servers have a gentle touch with beginners and make tasters feel safe asking the most basic questions. They are knowledgeable enough for experienced wine drinkers, but they only push info as far as tasters seem to want to go.

TASTING TOOLS: Good, small glasses. Spit buckets, crackers, and water handy. Very good light.

INTANGIBLES AND EXTRAS: Hard to imagine a more approachable tasting room, particularly for beginners or newcomers to Napa. They offer free wine education and concierge services, and broadband internet and Wi-Fi connections for wine bar customers. Opened bottles are sealed in a nitrogen gassing system to slow oxidation. You can also buy a glass of wine and sit at the sunny tables out front.

WINE AVAILABILITY: These are all small wineries and the wine shop or website are the best bets, though many of the wineries here have some wines available in restaurants and markets. Prices range from $15 to $52.

PICNIC PROSPECTS: Two sunny tables, covered by umbrellas, out front. The view is a walking mall, but the tables are surrounded by cheery plants and flowers.

COST: $5 for five tastes (from a list with more than a dozen wines). Wines by the glass range from $4.25 to $13.50.

DIRECTIONS: On the walking mall in downtown Napa, at the corner of Clay and Randolph streets. Next to the Napa Valley Visitor's Center.

RECOMMENDED FOR: Everyone, particularly beginners.

OAK KNOLL DISTRICT TASTING ROOMS

Andretti Winery

4162 Big Ranch Road
Napa, 94558
707-261-1717 or 888-460-8463
www.andrettiwinery.com
HOURS: 10–5 daily

This mid-valley winery, established in 1996 by race car driver Mario Andretti, sits on fifty-three gorgeous acres of valley floor and is designed as an Italian countryside villa with just a hint of Disneyland.

The tasting room is through a stone-tiled piazza and past a Renaissance-style fountain. Their current star is a mid-priced Sangiovese, and their large wine list includes Pinot Grigio, Chardonnay, Pinot Noir, Merlot, and Cabernet Sauvignon.

ATMOSPHERE: The good-sized tasting room, like the winery, is painted with warm Tuscan yellows and mustards, and the back wall of French doors looks out to a garden patio, a guest house, and rows and rows of long vineyards beyond that. It's so pretty here and the room so charming, it almost has the artificial feel of a Disney's wine country exhibit. We mean that as a compliment.

SERVICE: Servers are definitely not Disney employees. They know wine, talk it up, toss away bottles that just hint of being corked, and deal smoothly with the crowded moments. When things are quieter, a bit of interest in their wines gets them pouring more not on the list.

TASTING TOOLS: Good, big glasses. Spit buckets and water handy. No crackers. Good light.

INTANGIBLES AND EXTRAS: It's a spirited, high-energy place. The polished Tuscan feel works, partly because it doesn't cross the line and partly because it's such a beautiful spot. Pictures and memorabilia from Mario's racing days sit in one understated corner. Wine classes, winemaker dinners, and tours are available by reservation. Mario shows up occasionally, particularly for new releases.

WINE AVAILABILITY: Most wines readily found in restaurants and stores. Prices range from $16 to $50.

PICNIC PROSPECTS: Small tables in a stunning little patio surrounded by flowers, with an expansive view of vineyards and hills. One of the great small picnic spots in the valley.

COST: $8 for four tastings (or $12 and you keep the glass); $10 for three reserves.

DIRECTIONS: On Big Ranch Road two and a quarter miles north of Napa and a half mile south of the intersection of Big Ranch Road and Oak Knoll Avenue.

RECOMMENDED FOR: Everyone, especially people looking for a bit of escapism.

Darioush Winery

4240 Silverado Trail
Napa, 94558
707-257-2345
www.darioush.com
HOURS: 10:30–5 daily

Darioush became an instant landmark in 2004 when they opened the regal 22,000-square-foot winery building and visitor's center. It is meant to resemble a Persian palace, in tribute to owner Darioush Khaledi's roots, and is fronted by a long, tree-lined driveway, matching sets of low fountains, and sixteen free-standing stone columns, each eighteen feet high.

Khaledi and his wife, Shahpar, grew up in one of the world's first wine regions, in an Iranian town called Shiraz, and left Iran for California in the 1970s during the Islamic Revolution. They built a grocery business in Southern California, then started the winery here in 1994. They're drawing praise for a range of wines, and especially their Bordeaux varietals. Their list includes Viognier, Chardonnay, Pinot Noir, Merlot, Cabernet Sauvignon, and a Bordeaux blend.

ATMOSPHERE: The tasting room is the size of a major hotel lobby and looks like a sleek, though well-lit, nightclub. In the center is a square, crinkled-glass bar with tall chairs and lots of room. It sits among stone columns and under a large skylight. Contemporary droplights hang over the bar. Low, black couches are around the outside of the room, which also has a varied collection of art on its walls. All of it looks at a twenty-foot-waterfall wall. Upscale, thy name is Darioush.

SERVICE: Given the nightclub feel, you half expect standoffish club attitude, but servers are easy and approachable, and know their wines. They seem to understand visitors will want to spend some time in the place and do not rush you.

TASTING TOOLS: Good, large glasses. Spit buckets, water, and crackers handy. Very good light.

INTANGIBLES AND EXTRAS: The ultra-modern building is rare in Napa and the architecture is worth seeing. Darioush Khaledi's fondness for his homeland and his wine is apparent, which adds to the experience.

WINE AVAILABILITY: Generally small releases make the wine sometimes hard to find outside the winery or website, but they are on many upper-end restaurant menus. Prices range from $24 to $68.

PICNIC PROSPECTS: A handful of tables in front of the winery look across a large lawn to stone columns on one side and out to vineyards on another.

COST: $20 for four Signature wines.

DIRECTIONS: About two and a half miles north of Napa on the east side of Silverado Trail. About a half mile south of Oak Knoll Avenue.

RECOMMENDED FOR: Everyone but first-timers or people looking for a more countrified experience.

Del Dotto Caves

1055 Atlas Peak Road
Napa, 94558
707-256-3332
www.deldottovineyards.com
HOURS: 11–5 daily

One of Napa's first wineries, this stone building was constructed in 1885 for the Hedgeside Winery, and laborers hand dug a 350-foot cave into the low, limestone hillside. After Prohibition, the building spent decades as a scotch distillery, then was abandoned.

In 1997, David and Yolanda Del Dotto restored the building and caves, and started specializing in premium, accessible reds. They make Sangiovese, Merlot, Petite Sirah, Cabernet Sauvignon, and a handful of red blends, including their flagship, called The David.

ATMOSPHERE: One of the unique tasting rooms in the valley, because you feel the heavy stones of the building and the depth of the caves. You walk in and immediately sense the solidness around you. The tasting room, which has high ceilings, recessed lighting, and a medium-sized bar, opens up to the barrel room and caves dug into the hillside. Art is plentiful and jovially eclectic: Renaissance Italian sculpture, Mardi Gras–like masks, a four-foot-tall Asian urn and bright, modern paintings.

There's happily odd art and sculpture in the barrel room and in front of the caves, too. And altogether, the place is a mix of sturdiness, elegance, and playfulness.

SERVICE: Servers are friendly, unfussy, and passionate about their wines. This slightly out-of-the-way site keeps the crowds down and lets servers treat visitors as if they're friends. They pour big and often add a couple wines to the tasting list so you can compare vintages.

TASTING TOOLS: Good, large glasses. Spit bucket, water, and crackers handy. OK light.

INTANGIBLES AND EXTRAS: When the room is slow, servers take you through the barrel rooms and over to the caves. There is something special about the old stone building and the caves, especially mixed with the playfulness of the decor. The timelessness of it, the feel of the barrels and the limestone, the overall setting, and the strong line of wines make tasting here a terrific experience.

They offer cave tours and barrel tastings ($40) by reservation.

WINE AVAILABILITY: Some can be found in shops and restaurants, but most are sold at the winery or through the website. Prices range from $39 to $75.

PICNIC PROSPECTS: None.

COST: $10 for five wines; $20 for eight wines and barrel tasting.

DIRECTIONS: On the west side south of Atlas Peak Road, about a quarter mile north of Monticello Road/Highway 121. Look for the stone building right on the road, covered with ivy behind an old wooden water tower. A small sandwich-board sign says "Del Dotto Caves."

RECOMMENDED FOR: Everyone. Except, probably, serious claustrophobics.

Hagafen Cellars

4160 Silverado Trail
Napa, 94558
707-252-0781 or 888-424-2336
www.hagafen.com
HOURS: 11–4 Sunday–Friday; closed Saturday

Hagafen is a small, premium winery founded in 1979 by Irit and Ernie Weir, and they produce impressive kosher wines served on occasion at the White House. They moved into the Mediterranean-style winery on Silverado Trail in 2000 and opened the charming, stand-alone tasting room in front of the winery in 2002.

Almost all their wines draw good reviews. They include White Riesling, Sauvignon Blanc, Chardonnay, Pinot Noir, Merlot, Syrah, and Cabernet Sauvignon.

ATMOSPHERE: The little stone tasting room has windows on all sides and you feel like you're standing in a hut in the vineyards. The tasting bar is midsized and the room can get crowded, but servers are adept, bouncy, and capable. The big, white winery looms behind the room and reminds you this is a working operation, too.

SERVICE: Smart and easygoing servers field questions about the vineyards and about making wines kosher. Like at so many wineries, they give off a sense of being genuinely happy to work here.

TASTING TOOLS: Good, large glasses. Spit buckets and water handy. Crackers (and matzo during Passover) also handy. Very good light.

INTANGIBLES AND EXTRAS: One of those surprising finds. They make terrific, award-winning wines and have an inviting spot right on a main road, yet they're barely known to most visitors to Napa. Because of the image of thick, sacramental wines, they don't push the point about being kosher, but they'll explain it all if you ask. Tours are conducted daily at 11 a.m. by appointment.

WINE AVAILABILITY: They have a limited production, but their wines are distributed widely. Still, the winery or website are the safest bets. Prices range from $14 to $40.

PICNIC PROSPECTS: None.

COST: $5 for four tastes in a choice of white, red, or library wine flights.

DIRECTIONS: On the east side of Silverado Trail about two and three-quarter miles north of Napa and about a half mile south of Oak Knoll Avenue.

RECOMMENDED FOR: Everyone, particularly people looking for a find.

Backstage Vintners
5225 Solano Avenue
Napa, 94558
707-299-3930
www.backstagevintners.com
HOURS: 10-5 daily

There's a rustic, quiet feel as you drive up to this small winery, even though it's maybe 200 yards from Highway 29. It is, like many smaller spots in Napa, off the beaten path but, really, right on the road.

This winery was Koves-Newlan Vineyards until 2006, and now it is a collective of 15 small labels. Winemaker and general manager Craig MacLean oversees about half of them, but they all get grapes from different vineyards and make a range of styles, so this is a great spot to sample the wide variety of Napa wines. Wines include Sauvignon Blanc, Chardonnay, Pinot Noir, Merlot, Cabernet Franc, Zinfandel, Syrah, Cabernet Sauvignon, and an assortment of blends.

ATMOSPHERE: The new tasting room is planned as a lounge-style spot with comfortable chairs, a fireplace, and jazz and blues playing. The idea is for visitors to hang out, nibble cheese and crackers, and get comfortable as they sort through a long wine list.

SERVICE: The casual feel is intended to make visitors feel like insiders, and to help them be at ease asking about the small label wines and different style or just hanging around until they find a wine that speaks to them.

TASTING TOOLS: Good glasses. Spit buckets handy. Cheese and crackers.

INTANGIBLES AND EXTRAS: The "lounge style" combined with the you-belong-here attitude, makes visitors feel like Napa insiders. The winery also has plans for small concerts and events open to the public.

WINE AVAILABILITY: Most wine is sold at the winery or through the website, but some is available in restaurants or shops. Prices range from $15 to $100.

PICNIC PROSPECTS: Tables out back are under trees and look west across vineyards at the Mayacamas Mountains on the valley's rim.

COST: Tasting flights are $5–$10.

DIRECTIONS: About three and a half miles north of Napa, just off Highway 29. Turn west on Oak Knoll Avenue, then a quick right on Solano after crossing the train tracks. It's almost one mile north on Solano.

RECOMMENDED FOR: Everyone but large groups.

Laird Family Estate

5055 Solano Avenue
Napa, 94558
707-257-0360
www.lairdfamilyestate.com
HOURS: 10–5 daily; appointments encouraged for large groups

Longtime vineyard owner Ken Laird had been selling grapes to some of the best wineries and winemakers in Napa for decades. Then in 2000, he opened his own winery inside a large, modern-looking, high-tech facility used as a shared winery—called a custom crush—by many of Napa's top wineries.

The tasting room is inside the glass-enclosed front of the new winery that sits on a small pyramid above man-made caves. It has expansive views of vineyards all around and looks toward the mountains at the south end of the valley. They make Pinot Grigio, Chardonnay, Syrah, Merlot, and Cabernet Sauvignon.

ATMOSPHERE: The airy, contemporary tasting room gives the feel of floating over vineyards with wide views on three sides. The room is mostly glass with copper trim and some blond wood. The medium-sized tasting bar is curved glass. The sense is very modern and the lines are clean, uncluttered, and natural.

SERVICE: Knowledgeable, friendly, and a nice mix of unpretentious atti-

tude with pride in the facility and the wines.

TASTING TOOLS: Good, large glasses. Spit buckets, water, and crackers handy. Very good light.

INTANGIBLES AND EXTRAS: Few tasting rooms have such complete, open vineyard views. Also, we came near closing time and our server was friendly, unrushed, and generous. She charged half the fee because one wine was missing from the list.

WINE AVAILABILITY: Small lots mean they encourage buying at the tasting room or through the website. Some wines are found at restaurants and markets. Prices range from $16 to $80.

PICNIC PROSPECTS: Good-sized metal tables sit on patios on both sides of the tasting room, all with great views. On one side, you see only vineyards; on the other, there's the large working winery and the hills behind it. During harvest and crush in the fall, there's plenty of noise and activity from the winery, but the view is always there.

COST: $10 for eight current releases.

DIRECTIONS: About two and a half miles north of Napa, just off Highway 29. Turn west on Oak Knoll Avenue, then a quick right on Solano after crossing the train tracks. It's almost immediately on your left.

RECOMMENDED FOR: Everyone.

Luna Vineyards

2921 Silverado Trail
Napa, 94558
707-255-5862
www.lunavineyards.com
HOURS: 10–5 daily

Luna was started in 1995 by two Napa veterans, George Vare and Mike Moone. (It's Moone's name that gave them the idea to call it Luna.) Moone also is an investor in a La Quinta restaurant with Arnold Palmer, so Palmer invested in Luna, which explains the Arnold Palmer Chardonnay and Cabernet.

Luna specializes in Italian varietals with an approachable California feel, and features Pinot Grigio, Sangiovese, Merlot, Petite Sirah, and two flagship blends, a white called Freakout and a red named Canto.

ATMOSPHERE: The winery and tasting room are Tuscany-inspired but feel classic Californian. The recently refurbished, adobe-colored building has plenty of windows, is topped with a bell tower, and is surrounded by a tiled porch.

The tasting room is modern, open, and uncluttered, with a square, wood tasting bar in the middle of the room under a rim of spotlights. Light comes through doors and windows, and you see the working winery and vineyards around you. There is a buoyant energy to the room. In cold weather, a fireplace in the corner is lit.

SERVICE: On quiet days, this is a great place to talk wine, because the Italian varietals offer a contrast to much of Napa and servers know the details. On busy days, this is a place to have fun. The servers still explain the Italian flair, but they know the location makes it a popular late stop and they have a knack for keeping the cheer going while still talking wine.

TASTING TOOLS: Good, large glasses. Spit buckets, water, and breadsticks handy. Good light.

INTANGIBLES AND EXTRAS: This is a very comfortable, generally upbeat place to taste, and their wines are fairly unique in Napa. They suggest visitors take their glasses up to the

open, three-story bell tower and look out over their vineyards.

The Arnold Palmer wines are reasonably priced—at $15 each—because Palmer always seemed a regular-guy golfer, and he wanted to be a regular-guy vintner.

WINE AVAILABILITY: Their mainstream wines are generally available in stores and restaurants, but reserves can be found only at the winery or on the website. Prices range from $18 to $50.

PICNIC PROSPECTS: The building is surrounded by a veranda with a handful of small, metal tables. The view looks at the winery, olive trees, and some fields, but also some parking lot.

COST: $5 for four current releases; $10 for six reserves.

DIRECTIONS: The first winery north of Napa on Silverado Trail, about one and a quarter miles up (at the intersection of Silverado Trail and Hardman Avenue). Two miles south of Oak Knoll Avenue.

RECOMMENDED FOR: Everyone. Large groups should make appointments.

Monticello Vineyards

4242 Big Ranch Road
Napa, 94558
707-253-2802
www.corleyfamilynapavalley.com
HOURS: 10–4:30 daily

Monticello is modeled after the Virginia home of Thomas Jefferson, one of America's founding wine connoisseurs. The buildings are, they say, one-third the size of the originals, and it's all in a grove of trees in one of the valley's dazzlingly beautiful spots with vineyards on all sides.

The winery was started by Virginian Jay Corley in 1980, and continues to win awards, particularly for its Cabernets and Bordeaux blend. Their range of wines also includes Rosé of Syrah, Chardonnay, Pinot Noir, Merlot, Cabernet Franc, and a sparkling wine.

ATMOSPHERE: This is a surprisingly quiet tasting room, considering the beauty of the spot. The room is good-sized, lit with bright overhead spots and framed in dark wood, with the bar along one wall. It looks across a courtyard at a brick replica of Jefferson's home. Two large glass doors also look into a cask room.

SERVICE: Very professional and welcoming; more cordial than congenial. They have an interesting wine list and know it well. Because this place does not get packed, they go slow and often add wines to the tasting.

TASTING TOOLS: Good, large glasses. Spit buckets, crackers, and water handy. Good light.

INTANGIBLES AND EXTRAS: It starts with the view: It's simple and all on the flats, but it is overpowering. You are surrounded by vineyards and see them rolling off in every direction toward the mountains. Add the quality wines and the likelihood the tasting room will be quiet—which means plenty of individual attention—and you get a vastly underappreciated winery.

They also offer one-and-a-half-hour food-and-wine-pairing sessions ($25) and vineyard tours ($15 with tasting) that often include barrel tastings, both by appointment.

WINE AVAILABILITY: These are mostly limited-release wines, so though they can be found in markets and restaurants, the winery or website are the best bets. Prices range from $26 to $75.

PICNIC PROSPECTS: Terrific. Tables sit on the grass under large trees, looking across what feels like miles of vineyards. Traffic is light on the road past the winery. It's one of Napa's hidden gems.

COST: $10 for six to eight wines; returnees are free.

DIRECTIONS: On Big Ranch Road two and a half miles north of Napa and a quarter mile south of the intersection of Big Ranch Road and Oak Knoll Avenue.

RECOMMENDED FOR: Everyone, particularly people trying to get off the main roads.

Reynolds Family Winery

3266 Silverado Trail
Napa, 94558
707-258-2558
www.reynoldsfamilywinery.com
HOURS: 10–4:30 daily; appointments are a good idea, but if there's someone behind the bar, they're happy to pour

The small family winery was founded in 1994 by Steve Reynolds, a deep-sea diver turned dentist turned winemaker. Steve, his wife, Suzie, and their kids live in the house at the front of the property, by the "Slow, Kids at Play" signs. The winery is beyond the house and next to a small pond.

Their first vintage was released in 1999. They make Chardonnay, Pinot Noir, Cabernet Sauvignon, and a red blend called Persistence.

ATMOSPHERE: The tasting room has a modern, Mediterranean feel, and is bright from windows looking up at a hillside of vineyards and from French doors opening onto a deck over a small pond with a fountain.

SERVICE: This is a small winery and the room is often quiet, so they will take plenty of time with visitors. Often, the more you like their wines, the more they will bring out to taste.

TASTING TOOLS: Good, large glasses. Spit buckets, water, and crackers handy. Very good light.

INTANGIBLES AND EXTRAS: This genuinely feels like a family winery built by people who wanted to be in the wine business. Their Persistence red blend is named, they say, after the effort it took to get started and the effort it takes every day to make good wine. There's a nice sense of being somewhere undiscovered.

WINE AVAILABILITY: Their wines are mostly found only at the winery or on the website, though some make restaurant wine lists. Prices range from $30 to $89.

PICNIC PROSPECTS: Tables on the deck look at the little pond and up at the vineyards and hills. The sound of the fountain is soothing, but the tables can get hot in the summer.

COST: $10 for six to eight wines.

DIRECTIONS: On the east side of Silverado Trail, two miles north of Napa and just about a mile south of Oak Knoll Avenue. (It's just south of Soda Canyon Road.)

RECOMMENDED FOR: Anyone who wants to try a small winery.

Signorello Vineyards

4500 Silverado Trail
Napa, 94558
707-255-5990
www.signorellovineyards.com
HOURS: 10:30–5 daily; Ignore the "appointment only" signs, they are happy to see you

Raymond Signorello Sr. and Jr. started buying vineyards and selling fruit in the 1970s, and by the mid-1980s they liked their grapes so much, they wanted to make their own wine. Their first vintage was 1985 and they began building this Italian-looking, hillside villa and winery in 1986. Raymond Sr. passed away in 1998, but Raymond Jr. still lives there at times and uses the kitchen in the tasting room to entertain.

They make Chardonnay, a Sémillon-Sauvignon Blanc blend, Pinot Noir, Merlot, Zinfandel, Syrah, Cabernet Sauvignon, and a Bordeaux blend, Padrone, named in tribute to Raymond Sr.

ATMOSPHERE: The big, high-ceilinged room has large, light-wood community tables, a tile floor, and a restaurant-caliber kitchen. The colors are Mediterranean earth tones and light comes from high windows and small bright lights over the long bar. You get the sense this is the recreation room for the villa when it's not open to public. There's often a mix of bluesy rock playing in the background, which adds to the feel of walking into an open house party.

SERVICE: They encourage visitors to explore different ways to taste and they're enthusiastic without being pushy. Like at many small wineries, the people working here have a strong connection to the place, and they talk proudly about their vineyards and winemaking style.

TASTING TOOLS: Good, large glasses. Spit buckets, water, and crackers handy. OK light.

INTANGIBLES AND EXTRAS: Servers can take you through a spirited course of Wine 101 if you're interested. It's a lively place that makes you want to stay for the party, because there just has to be a party.

WINE AVAILABILITY: Their larger releases make it to restaurants and markets, but small lots mean buying at the winery or through the website is the best bet. Prices range from $25 to $50.

PICNIC PROSPECTS: None.

COST: $10 for six current releases or one taste of reserve Padrone.

DIRECTIONS: Three miles north of Napa on the east side of Silverado Trail, just south of Oak Knoll Avenue.

RECOMMENDED FOR: Everyone.

Trefethen Vineyards

1160 Oak Knoll Avenue
Napa, 94558
707-255-7700
www.trefethen.com
HOURS: 10–4:30 daily

The historic rust-and-redwood-colored wood winery, built in 1886, is one of the classic buildings in the valley, designed by Hamden McIntyre, who also designed Far Niente, Inglenook (now Rubicon Estate), and the building housing the Culinary Institute of America at Greystone. It sits in a grove of 100-year-old oaks and is surrounded by a square mile of vineyards.

Trefethen Vineyards is one of the classic wineries of Napa. It started as Eshcol in the nineteenth century, struggled through phylloxera and Prohibition, and closed in 1940. Eugene and Catherine Trefethen bought the property in 1968, reopened the winery in 1973, and almost immediately won international acclaim, particularly for their Chardonnay. They make an array of wines including Dry Riesling, Viognier, Pinot Noir, Merlot, Cabernet Franc, and Cabernet Sauvignon and a lively Bordeaux blend called Double T Red.

ATMOSPHERE: Surprisingly simple and country casual for such a historic building. The tasting room has two small bars and is lit by warm, overhead spotlights. It's paneled in light, simple woods, and has the feel of the lobby of a country inn. There's a nook in back that sells books, fabrics, and ceramics along with wine items.

SERVICE: The service also is country casual and relaxed. They hand everyone a glass of Estate Dry Riesling when they walk in. They have a distinguished history and a prominent reputation—which they know and are happy to talk about—but it's more about making tasting here a friendly experience.

TASTING TOOLS: Good, large glasses. Spit buckets, water, and crackers handy. Very good light.

INTANGIBLES AND EXTRAS: The overall feel of the room and the winery is that it's established and dug into the valley. The building is simple and beautiful, and you can wander into the barrel room or down to the wine library room, a big space with heavy wood furniture, leather sofas, a fireplace, and a bar that gives a hint of what the good life was like a century ago. Free thirty-minute tours are by appointment, but on slow days you can often sign up when you get there.

WINE AVAILABILITY: Trefethen wines are widely distributed, but some reserves are only available through the winery or website. Prices range from $18 to $75.

PICNIC PROSPECTS: None.

COST: $10 for four current releases; $20 for three reserve and library wines.

DIRECTIONS: Three miles north of Napa, just east of Highway 29.

RECOMMENDED FOR: Everyone.

Van Der Heyden Vineyards

4057 Silverado Trail
Napa, 94558
707-257-0130
www.vanderheydenvineyards.com

HOURS: 10–6 daily; ignore the "appointment only" signs, they just mean you sign the guest book

There may not be a place in Napa that more fits the words "family winery," or that is a more unique tasting experience. The small, funky tasting room is a converted carport, and to get to it visitors have to pass the house and navigate kids, dogs, and farm equipment. If it weren't for the vineyards, the place would feel like a kitschy antique yard.

It was started by Andre and Sande Van Der Heyden, and their first vintage was 1984. They make Chardonnay, Merlot, Petite Verdot, well-aged Cabernets, and what they swear is the world's only Late Harvest Cabernet Sauvignon.

ATMOSPHERE: The tasting room continues the homey kitsch, and you can tell it was once a carport. The small bar is a faded wooden counter, and it's crowded with bottles and chocolates for sale. It can fit three people. All around are old shelves, plants, travel posters, figurines, and pleasant silliness like "Wino Crossing" traffic signs. It's cheerfully cluttered and anti–big winery.

SERVICE: The server often is Andre Van Der Heyden, and he's an engaging teacher and pleasant company. In a slightly goofy, fully accepting style, he explains the wines and their styles, quizzes tasters on the process, and draws visitors into enthusiastic conversations. Extremely knowledgeable. Extremely casual.

TASTING TOOLS: Good light from windows on all sides. Small, thick glasses. You have to ask for the spit bucket or water. No crackers. Very good light.

INTANGIBLES AND EXTRAS: This is a one-of-a-kind stop. It's a chance to meet people who built their winery, to learn from them, and to have a good time. The energy and quirkiness are a joy, and there are few wineries with a more merry, laid-back air. Warning: The restroom is an outhouse along the driveway.

WINE AVAILABILITY: Only at the winery or through the website. Prices range from $18 to $50.

PICNIC PROSPECTS: They have three tables under awnings outside the tasting room at the end of the driveway. You can see vineyards and the little working winery, but it feels more like a friendly backyard.

COST: $10 for five wines.

DIRECTIONS: On the west side of Silverado Trail about two miles north of Napa and just north of Soda Canyon Road. About one mile south of Oak Knoll Avenue.

RECOMMENDED FOR: Everyone with a sense of humor, but only in small groups. Not recommended if you're looking for elegance.

William Hill Winery

1761 Atlas Peak Road
Napa, 94558
707-265-3024 or 866-522-9463
www.williamhillwinery.com

HOURS: 10:30–4 daily; ignore "appointment only" signs, everyone is welcome, anytime

Hill is a major California landowner who started making wine in 1978, then built the modern winery on a rise looking over the rolling hills of the lower Napa Valley. Since then, the winery changed hands a few times and now is owned by Beam Wine. They put a vine leaf on their bottles that is from the same varietal as the wine inside.

Besides these vineyards in southern Napa Valley, they also own Atlas Peak Vineyards, and sometimes serve their popular Sangiovese in the tasting room along with William Hill wines that include Chardonnay, Merlot, Malbec, Cabernet Sauvignon, and a Cab/Malbec blend.

ATMOSPHERE: Outside, wavy hills of vines seem to ripple away from the winery. Inside the remodeled, slightly retro tasting room, you can still see the vineyards, or look through large windows into a vast barrel room below that's so big it almost looks fake. The sleek, black-topped bar sits under small hanging lights and is both modern and comfortable.

SERVICE: They are slightly off the main roads, plus they're stuck with the official "appointment only" notice required by the county, so they rarely get swamped. Servers seem genuinely happy you came. They're professional but casual.

TASTING TOOLS: Good, large glasses. Spit buckets and crackers handy. No water.

INTANGIBLES AND EXTRAS: This is one of those terrific spots that seem to get ignored. They have a nice range of wines, an approachable air, and that view of vineyard hill after undulating vineyard hill. It's a wonder it's not busier. They also offer a food-and-wine pairing ($20) by appointment—real appointment.

WINE AVAILABILITY: Many of their wines are well distributed. A handful can only be found at the winery or on the website. Prices range from $16 to $38.

PICNIC PROSPECTS: None, but hang out a while with the view.

COST: $5 for five current release wines; $10 for four reserves. Two-for-one coupon on website.

DIRECTIONS: Atlas Peak Road runs north off Monticello Road/Highway 121 east of Napa town. William Hill is on a hill on the east side of Atlas Peak, past the entrance to the Silverado Country Club, and a half mile north of Hardman Avenue.

RECOMMENDED FOR: Everyone.

Acacia Vineyards

2750 Las Amigas Road
Napa, 94559
707-226-9991 or 877-226-1700
www.acaciawinery.com

HOURS: 10–4 Monday–Saturday; 12–4 Sunday; officially "appointment only," but they welcome walk-ins (except on Sunday when you do need an appointment)

One of the mainstay wineries of the Carneros region, the winery is a modern, but not overly industrial, complex on a bluff over hills that roll down to San Pablo Bay. And, like so many sites in the Carneros area, the place feels more wide-open and coastal than the upper Napa Valley wineries. The tasting room is under a small, green awning on the side of the building.

Acacia was founded in 1979 and after a couple ownership changes is now part of Diageo Wines, which also owns Sterling and Beaulieu Vineyards. Their reputation for classic Carneros Chardonnay and Pinot Noir has not changed, and over the years they've branched out to sparkling wines, a Viognier and a Chardonnay Brandy.

ATMOSPHERE: The pleasantly snug, simple room looks through glass doors into a huge warehouse with large storage tanks. Bright, slightly pale light from the front windows has the feel of being near a wide body of water. There's space at the tasting bar for maybe a half-dozen people, yet, because of light, the room feels almost airy.

SERVICE: They are pleasant, unhurried, and experienced servers, and many have been with Acacia a long time. They often add a wine or two to the tasting list when you ask about them. With dogs walking in and out and the general attitude, it feels like it's still a family winery.

TASTING TOOLS: Good glasses. Spit buckets, water, and crackers handy. Good light.

INTANGIBLES AND EXTRAS: It's a comfortable place with friendly service, but this tasting room is all about the wines, and what makes Acacia really stand out is its high-quality Pinot Noir.

WINE AVAILABILITY: Many are found in markets and restaurants, but limited releases are available only at the winery or through the website. Prices range from $20 to $60.

PICNIC PROSPECTS: None. (The tables near the tasting room are not for the public.)

COST: $10 for three current releases; $15 for five single-vineyard wines.

DIRECTIONS: Follow Highway 12/121 west for about two and a half miles past the junction of 12/121 and Highway 29. Turn left at Duhig Road—at the twenty-foot-tall gate and where Domaine Carneros sits on a hill. Take Duhig about two miles to Los Amigas Road. Acacia is on that corner.

RECOMMENDED FOR: Anyone looking for a smaller tasting room with great Pinot Noir.

Artesa Vineyards

1345 Henry Road
Napa, 94559
707-224-1668
www.artesawinery.com
HOURS: 10–5 daily

One of Napa's destination wineries for its architecture and soaring views, Artesa sits high on a hill above Carneros and you see it, and its fountains, from more than a mile away. The style mixes ultra-modern and art deco, and it's dug into the top of the hill, a black glass obelisk covered by grass. The view looks down on vineyards rolling every which way, then out across the northern San Francisco Bay.

Its owners are connected to the Codorníu family of Spain, the second-oldest wine-owning family in the world (dating back to 1551), and it started in 1991 as Codorníu Napa, making only sparkling wines. They renamed it Artesa in 1999 and began producing award-winning still wines, too, including Chardonnay, Pinot Noir, and Cabernet Sauvignon.

ATMOSPHERE: Think European/contemporary, with modern art, lots of space, and trimmings in glass, metal, and wood. It feels more like a popular nightclub than a winery tasting room. The crowd, often young and stylish, sometimes seems more nightclub than winery. As terrific as the room and the views are, this can be a busy place, particularly on weekends, and could be intimidating for visitors looking for a quieter, more casual stop.

SERVICE: Friendly and efficient in the way of servers at a busy bar. Servers know their wines and offer tidbits and advice, but on weekends they need to keep moving.

TASTING TOOLS: Good, large glasses. Spit buckets are hard to reach when the bar is crowded. Water handy. No crackers. Good light.

INTANGIBLES AND EXTRAS: This winery and its tasting room—with skylights, lots of tables, an indoor courtyard around a pool, floor-to-ceiling windows, and a panoramic view —is popular for a reason. It is simply a great space: energetic, original, and polished. The deck outside is a stunning spot to sit and drink a glass, or a

bottle, of wine. Don't be in a hurry here. Free tours daily at 11 a.m. and 2 p.m. The store in the visitor's center sells some unique art besides the usual wine-related books and items.

WINE AVAILABILITY: Most wines are available in stores and restaurants. Some sparkling wines are found only through the winery or website. Prices range from $15 to $50.

PICNIC PROSPECTS: None, but if you pull out some crackers with your wine on the deck, they won't complain.

COST: $8 for six wines; the tasting menu changes daily.

DIRECTIONS: Follow Highway 12/121 west for two miles past the junction of 12/121 and Highway 29, turn north on Old Sonoma Road then left on Dealy Road. Bear left as Dealy turns into Henry Road. Artesa's driveway is about a half mile past that.

RECOMMENDED FOR: Everyone, particularly for people looking for a view. Weekends get busy.

Bouchaine Vineyards

1075 Buchli Station Road
Napa, 94559
707-252-9065 or 800-654-9463
www.bouchaine.com
HOURS: 10:30–4 daily

The oldest continuously operating winery in the Carneros region sits like a huge redwood barn in the low hills around it. The winery began producing in the mid-1880s as Boon Fly Ranch, changed hands a few times, then in 1981 Garret Copeland, of the Dupont family, and his wife, Tatiana, bought the winery, refurbished it and re-created it as Bouchaine. The buildings were renovated in 1995, and that redwood facing came from the wood of old casks.

The small, charming tasting room

is in the smaller building across the driveway from the main winery. They specialize in Carneros varietals—Chardonnay and Pinot Noir.

ATMOSPHERE: Casual and comfortable, with a touch of luxury. The tasting room has a stirring view through large glass doors toward a redwood deck and vineyard-covered hills. The medium-sized tasting bar has simple, country elegance with flowers and pale colors. The filtered light from windows, skylights, and glass doors reminds tasters they're near a bay and the Pacific. Their small fireplace is lit on cooler days.

SERVICE: Very friendly and welcoming. The people here are veterans of the winery and the region, and they treat visitors like locals. They make reservations for you at other wineries, riff on themselves, and add wines to the tasting list. When we asked about the region, one server took us down the hall to see old photos, then out to the deck and the vineyards to see the grapes.

TASTING TOOLS: Good, Burgundy/Pinot Noir–style glasses. Spit buckets and water handy. No crackers. Good light.

INTANGIBLES AND EXTRAS: This is a winery almost at the end of the road, and the servers seem to know that and make the experience a pleasure. We left feeling like we made friends. The terrific view from the room, and even better, the deck, is open, stunning, and different from much of Napa. Besides the vineyards, you see pastures and the bay in the distance, and it feels wide open instead of the more snug sense in the valley. They offer catered picnics with a bottle of wine on their deck ($60 for two).

WINE AVAILABILITY: Many are available in markets and restaurants, but smaller releases are found only at the winery or through the website. Prices range from $12 to $40.

PICNIC PROSPECTS: One of the hidden little gems of Napa, particularly for picnics. The terrific deck and patio are covered by a trellis, and have redwood tables and that expansive view. You also smell the freshness of the wetlands and marshes just over a hill. You have the choice of a catered picnic or of bringing your own. (They suggest you call on weekends to make sure no events are scheduled, but they'll try to find you space.)

COST: Free.

DIRECTIONS: Follow Highway 12/121 west for about two and a half miles past the junction of 12/121 and Highway 29. Turn left at Duhig Road—at the twenty-foot-tall gate and where Domaine Carneros sits on a hill. Go about two miles to the first left, which is Los Amigas (and site of Acacia Vineyards). Take Los Amigas about one mile to Buchli Station Road and turn right. Bouchaine will be the big complex on the right.

RECOMMENDED FOR: Everybody. Ideal for first-timers and for Napa veterans who haven't been to Carneros.

Mahoney Vineyards

1285 Dealy Lane
Napa, 94559
707-253-9463
www.mahoneyvineyards.com
HOURS: 10–5 daily

This little winery has been producing since 1972 and is now owned by Michael Mondavi, but it's still home to the wines of founders Francis and Kathy Mahoney. They say their Pinot Noir is the official wine of the Irish city of Cork.

The cheerful yellow tasting room is across the parking lot from the simple, barn-like winery. The tasting room was built in 2001 and looks like a large country home. Like many others here, they specialize in Pinot Noir and Chardonnay.

ATMOSPHERE: The two-story room has high windows and overhead spotlights that give it a spacious, bright feel. The pale walls, blond-wood-trimmed windows and doors, tile floor, and large, dark granite tasting bar all make it a clean, modern country place without feeling slick. Lively music playing in the background adds to the relaxed feel. It's an easy room for wine novices to walk into.

SERVICE: They are chatty and unpushy here, as if they're glad you made it. Servers know their wines, winery, and the Carneros region, and, like at some other Carneros wineries, offer to make you reservations at other wineries.

TASTING TOOLS: Good, large glasses. Spit buckets and water handy. No crackers. Good light.

INTANGIBLES AND EXTRAS: The large room could handle crowds but is generally less packed than some Napa wineries. You feel the Carneros region here, the proximity of water and open spaces instead of the upper valley's more tucked-in feel.

WINE AVAILABILITY: Many are available at restaurants and markets. Smaller releases are only available at the winery or through the website. Prices range from $12 to $25.

PICNIC PROSPECTS: The tables under trees in front of the winery building offer a quiet, distinctly Carneros spot. The view looks at those low Carneros hills with vineyards on them in every direction.

COST: $10 for five wines. Waived with purchase.

DIRECTIONS: Follow Highway 12/121 west for two miles past the junction of 12/121 and Highway 29, turn north on Old Sonoma Road then left on Dealy Road. It's about three-quarters of a mile up the road on the left.

RECOMMENDED FOR: Everyone. A comfortable spot for wine novices.

Domaine Carneros
1240 Duhig Road
Napa, 94559
707-257-0101 or 800-716-2788
www.domainecarneros.com
HOURS: 10–6 daily

The winery, owned by the Taittinger family—one of France's premiere Champagne producers—was built in 1989 and immediately became a Napa Valley landmark. The brick, wrought-iron, and terra-cotta building is modeled after the family's eighteenth-century country château in Champagne and looks like a movie set. It is one of the valley's spectacular places to visit.

Not surprisingly, Domaine Carneros specializes in sparkling wines, but since 1992 it's also made premium Pinot Noir.

ATMOSPHERE: Tastings are done sitting at tables in the graceful salon surrounded by Old World furniture and under opulent chandeliers, or—and even better—outside on the sunny stone-and-brick terrace that looks over gardens, a pond, a graceful staircase, vineyards that roll up to the terrace, and seemingly, the regal Old World where words like elegance and refinement still mean something.

There's also the view to the north, looking across the highway at Winery Lake and the wooden sheep, including one outcast black sheep, grazing on the hillside.

SERVICE: Tasters order at their table, choosing among flights of sparkling wine or Pinot Noir, or from wines by the glass. Cheeses, pâtés, and crackers also are available. The servers mix California friendly with a bit of that Old World refinement and politeness. This is a busy winery that gets a variety of visitors, but there are plenty of servers and the attention feels personal.

TASTING TOOLS: Small tasting flutes for the sparkling wine, good, large glasses for the Pinots. Spit buckets on request. Crackers and water available, along with some other food. Very good light.

INTANGIBLES AND EXTRAS: One of the genuine treats of Napa. It's easy to feel transported to the Champagne region because of the building, the views, the service, and the wine. All that's missing is a carriage and powdered wigs.

Tours with tastings daily at 11 a.m., 1 p.m. and 3 p.m. ($25). Reservations suggested but not required.

WINE AVAILABILITY: Domaine Carneros is well distributed, but their still wines and some sparklings are hard to find outside the winery or website. Prices range from $19 to $55.

PICNIC PROSPECTS: None.

COST: $13 to $14 for tasting flights. Wines by the glass range from $6 to $10.

DIRECTIONS: Follow Highway 12/121 west for about two and a half miles past the junction of 12/121 and Highway 29. Turn left at Duhig Road and the twenty-foot-tall gate. You cannot miss it from the highway.

RECOMMENDED FOR: Everyone, but don't be in a hurry. Great spot for beginners to try sparkling wines.

Madonna Estates

5400 Old Sonoma Road
Napa, 94559
707-255-8864 or 866-724-2993
www.madonnaestate.com
HOURS: 10–5 daily

Owned by the Bartolucci family, one of the oldest winemaking families in Napa, Madonna Estates was founded in 1922 in the north of Napa, then moved to Carneros in 1970. They built this California/mission–style tasting room in 1977.

Madonna uses organically grown, dry-farmed grapes from the Carneros region and specializes in Chardonnay and Pinot Noir, but they make a range of wines including Pinot Grigio, Merlot, Dolcetto, and Cabernet Sauvignon.

ATMOSPHERE: The simple room has old wood counters, linoleum floors, and slightly faded pictures that show it's been around since the 1970s. The light is OK from overheads, but you don't get much feel of a sunny day outside. It seems as much a casual highway stop as a wine country tasting room.

SERVICE: Friendly and knowledgeable, and at times downright goofy. But when one of the regular bus tours of fifty people comes in, the room gets stuffed and it's reduced to feeling like an amusement park show with the tour guide shouting instructions on how to taste.

TASTING TOOLS: Good glasses—reserve tasters get large Burgundy/Pinot glasses. Spit buckets handy. No water or crackers. OK light.

INTANGIBLES AND EXTRAS: It's a convenient, pretty spot and the winery and family have eighty-plus years of history. But they get six bus tours each day, and those can overrun drop-in tasters.

WINE AVAILABILITY: Only Estate Chardonnay and Pinot Noir are sold in stores. Everything else is exclusive to the winery or website. Prices range from $20 to $55.

PICNIC PROSPECTS: Tables are in a corner of the lawn under vine-covered trellises. It's close to the high-way, so you'll hear cars, but the pleasant view is of the winery and the vineyards.

COST: $5 for four tastes; $15 for six reserves.

DIRECTIONS: At the intersection of Highway 12/121 and Old Sonoma Road. About two miles west of the junction of 12/121 and Highway 29.

RECOMMENDED FOR: Anyone who wants to try Madonna wines. Not recommended for people looking for an elegant wine country experience or when there is a tour bus in the parking lot.

Truchard Vineyards

3234 Old Sonoma Road
Napa, 94559
707-253-7153
www.truchardvineyards.com
HOURS: Tours and tastings by appointment

Tony and Jo Ann Truchard started buying land and growing grapes in Carneros in 1974, when Tony was a doctor in Reno driving 200 miles each way to work his vineyards. They eventually moved to Napa and began producing their own, stellar wines in 1989.

They own 400 acres and make a range of wines, all from their own grapes. They're often nationally recognized for their Chardonnay and Syrah, and get raves for their other wines that include Roussanne, Pinot Noir, Zinfandel, Merlot, Cabernet Franc, Cabernet Sauvignon, and Tempranillo.

ATMOSPHERE: This is a family operation, so the tours are small and personal. They're often led by Jo Ann Truchard. They start and finish in a "tasting room" that's one corner of the wooden barn/office/barrel room. Visitors start with some wine,

wander up the hill and into the vineyards to look back over the rolling property, then go into the 11,000-square-foot caves.

SERVICE: Visitors get to pick the wines to taste, and the tours continually stop by the tasting room to get another wine. Because these tours and tastings are often guided by the owners, it's impossible not to feel treated well. Both the Truchards are genuinely attentive to their visitors, and since it's their wine, they can break out as much as they chose to pour.

TASTING TOOLS: Good glasses. Spit buckets handy in the tasting room. No water or crackers. Light depends on where you are.

INTANGIBLES AND EXTRAS: It's always a treat to have the people who planted the vineyards and started the winery tell you their story, and the Truchards are genuinely solid, interesting people. Besides tasting some very good wines, the tour leaves you feeling as if you understand a bit more about making wine in Carneros.

WINE AVAILABILITY: Many of their wines are found in shops and restaurants, but some are only available at the winery or through the website. Prices range from $25 to $50.

PICNIC PROSPECTS: None.

COST: Free.

DIRECTIONS: At the top of Old Sonoma Road (about three miles north of Highway 12/121 and about one and a half miles west of Highway 29) where it turns from north-south to east-west and where tiny Congress Valley Road runs into it from the east. Look for the driveway on the north side of Old Sonoma Road.

RECOMMENDED FOR: Everyone, but call ahead.

YOUNTVILLE/STAGS LEAP TASTING ROOMS

Chimney Rock Winery

5250 Silverado Trail
Napa, 94558
707-257-2036 or 800-257-2641
www.chimneyrock.com
HOURS: 10–5 daily

The white, South African–style Cape Dutch building is modeled after a seventeenth-century church, and its flowing, rounded edges and curved steeples sit back in the vineyards and blend against rounded hills. The sight from the highway and up the access road is graceful and stunning, and could make even golfers forget that owner Sheldon (Hack) Wilson plowed under nine holes of a golf course when he bought the land in 1980, then in 2001, with co-owner Anthony Terlato, turned the back nine to vineyards, too.

They're known for their Cabernet Sauvignons and a Bordeaux blend called Elevage—all the grapes come from these Stags Leap District vineyards—plus they make a Fumé Blanc and a Rosé of Cabernet Franc.

ATMOSPHERE: The medium-sized tasting room feels like an airy British pub—or more properly, a South African pub. It has high wooden beams, a square, medium-wood tasting bar in the middle of the room, and lots of light from big windows and glass doors. You feel the clean, white winery around you, with its curves and soft arches, and you see the gardens and the small, neat courtyard through all the glass. They also proudly display high ratings from wine critics on large banners.

SERVICE: Efficient and professional, which is needed for a generally busy stop. The servers are unfailingly polite, and tell stories of the winery and the district with the comfortable, if restrained, air of people used to dealing with crowds. They never made us feel hurried or unappreciated.

TASTING TOOLS: Good, large glasses. Spit buckets and water handy. No crackers. Very good light.

INTANGIBLES AND EXTRAS: The feel in the tasting room is more pub-ish than most, and it blends well with the building's style. The courtyard is charming, and though they do not allow picnics, it's a good spot to sip wine and just breathe. They also sell ceramics and glass art, and for people traveling with large rolls of bubble wrap, enormously oversized Riedel crystal glasses.

WINE AVAILABILITY: Most wines are available at restaurants or markets. Older vintages are found only at the winery or through the website. Prices range from $16 to $100.

PICNIC PROSPECTS: None.

COST: $10 for five current releases; $20 for five big reds.

DIRECTIONS: On the east side of Silverado Trail one and a half miles north of Oak Knoll Avenue and about three miles south of Yountville Crossroad.

RECOMMENDED FOR: Everyone.

Cliff Lede Vineyards

1473 Yountville Crossroad
Yountville, 94599
800-428-2259
www.cliffledevineyards.com
HOURS: 10–5 daily

Canadian businessman Cliff Lede and his wife, Cheryl, bought the S. Anderson winery in 2000 that had been here making sparkling wines since 1971. They kept the S. Anderson label for vintage dated sparklings and created the new Cliff Lede and Poetry lines.

Poetry, which is also the name of a luxury inn they run on a nearby hillside, is the theme here. They translate it to mean "free, exciting, fun-loving, soulful and unexpected" and that's a pretty good way to describe the feel of this place. It's both lighthearted and open to the valley around it. Besides the sparkling wines, they make a surprisingly strong line of wines including Sauvignon Blanc, Chardonnay, Merlot, Pinot Noir, Petite Sirah, a Claret, and their Poetry Cabernet Sauvignon.

ATMOSPHERE: From the road, the craftsman-style building looks like a contemporary lodge. Inside, the tasting room feels more like a large, well-done family room, or maybe the mingling area at a non-snooty country club.

It has slate and earth tones, and a long wall that's all sliding glass door and open to the deck and sculpture garden. There are tables with displays of books, decanters, and wine art in the middle of the room, and a few wicker chairs around the sides. The slate-colored, long, L-shaped bar has space for more visitors than the room usually gets.

SERVICE: The optimistic sense of liveliness extends to the well-versed staff. They change glasses from white to red, and make sure visitors entering the room are made to feel comfortable. On a day celebrating the release of their 1997 Diva Prestige Cuvée, the women wore little tiaras and handed them to anyone who wanted their own.

TASTING TOOLS: Good glasses, changed for whites and reds. Spit buckets, water, and crackers handy. OK light.

INTANGIBLES AND EXTRAS: This is one of the unheralded-but-terrific places to visit, and to hang out a bit. The back deck has comfortable wicker furniture and connects to an open sculpture garden with a vaguely Southwestern feel that has vineyards running up to its edge. There's also a contemporary art gallery on the property. Altogether, it hits that target of making this a place, as they'd say, with that wine-art-life joie de vivre. For the record, it's pronounced Cliff Lay-dee.

WINE AVAILABILITY: Their wine list is long and well distributed, but some wines sell out and others are available only through the winery or website. Prices range from $18 to $120.

PICNIC PROSPECTS: None, but they'll let you hang around the deck and garden as long as you want.

COST: $10 to $15 for four or five wines, depending on what's available that day.

DIRECTIONS: On the south side of Yountville Crossroad about one and a half miles east of Highway 29 or a quarter mile west of Silverado Trail.

RECOMMENDED FOR: Everyone.

Clos Du Val

5330 Silverado Trail
Napa, 94558
707-259-2225
www.closduval.com
HOURS: 10–5 daily

Clos Du Val is French for "small estate in a small valley," and the idea of it began in 1970 when John Goelet, an American with family roots in French winemaking, teamed with young French winemaker Bernard Portet and sent Portet to look for a new place to make great wine. Two years later, Portet found these 150 acres and the two began making some of Napa's most respected wines, including Chardonnay, Pinot Noir, Zinfandel, Merlot, and Cabernet Sauvignon.

The winery looks like a European monastery sitting off in the vineyards and against the hills. It also is the long-established home of hundreds of swallows. They nest in the forty-foot-high eaves and return every March 19—leap years included—just like their more famous cousins in San Juan Capistrano. Visitors bombed by the little birds get a free tasting.

ATMOSPHERE: Inside the enormous wood doors and under the twenty-eight-foot ceiling, the large, fairly simple tasting room feels classic and timeless. The walls are nearly the same reddish brown as the wine labels, there's a long wooden bar, and the light comes from windows looking out to the vineyards. It feels like a place where people could have been tasting wine for centuries.

SERVICE: Servers are approachable and confident without being pushy, as if they know you'll like their wine. They poured four extra wines for us when we asked about them.

TASTING TOOLS: Good, medium-sized glasses. Spit buckets and water handy. No crackers. OK light.

INTANGIBLES AND EXTRAS: One of Napa's cornerstone wineries, this place has the feel of deep roots and ties to centuries of winemaking. It's also a big, unhurried room and it's comfortable taking your time here.

WINE AVAILABILITY: Most wines are available in restaurants and markets. Prices range from $21 to $95.

PICNIC PROSPECTS: Tables are spread around the grounds, some under olive trees along the driveway, some on grass next to the winery. The best spot is on the grass out front of the winery, looking over the vineyards that run right up to the tables.

COST: $5 for four wines, plus whatever your server decides; free if the swallows hit you.

DIRECTIONS: On the east side of Silverado Trail one and a quarter miles north of Oak Knoll Avenue and about three and a quarter miles south of Yountville Crossroad.

RECOMMENDED FOR: Everyone.

Domaine Chandon

1 California Drive
Yountville, 94599
707-944-2280
www.chandon.com
HOURS: 10–6 daily May–December;
11–5 January–April

When Champagne makers Moët-Hennessy founded Domaine Chandon in 1973, it was the first infusion of French wine money in the valley—old French money, because Moët-Hennessy was established in 1743. The visitor's center here opened in 1978 and mixed French tradition with California spacious styling. The result is a sumptuous place to visit and to taste some outstanding sparkling wine.

There's a lot going on just walking around here. Coming in from the parking lot, you go over bridges and pass fountains and ponds and a garden of two-foot-tall stone mushrooms. This is a spectacular, lush property—more for the grounds than vineyard views—and you feel pampered just walking around it. Besides nearly a dozen sparkling wines, they also make Chardonnay, Pinto Noir, and Pinot Meunier.

ATMOSPHERE: The main entrance is under huge trellises and it leads into what looks like an opening for caves. That brings you in at the gift shop level. The tasting room is at the top of a large, curved staircase (across from the restaurant), and it's airy and modern with a long, polished-wood bar. Behind the bar, a wall of windows is wide open to rolling grass knolls and hills beyond that. The room also has dozens of tables, and leads to a deck with plenty more tables under umbrellas and old oak trees. This is a big place, so it looks more like a restaurant than a tasting room, but the feel is open and nonchalant.

SERVICE: They offer a range of tastings and wines by the glass, plus appetizers to pair with the wines. You can taste a flight at the bar, or buy a glass or a bottle to sip at a table.

Walking in, it may not be clear whether to take a table or go to the bar. All orders for wine and food are taken at the bar, but for people who prefer to sit at a table, once you get your wine, they will bring you your food. When it's busy, it can feel overwhelming because of the size of the room, but they're adept at handling crowds at the bar.

The mood is cheery and easygoing. They will talk about their wines or let you sit around as long as you'd like.

TASTING TOOLS: Very good flutes. Spit buckets and water handy. Food can be ordered. Good light.

INTANGIBLES AND EXTRAS: Like all the sparkling wine houses in Napa, this is a spot to go slow and enjoy the setting. It's a luxurious feeling to drink sparkling wine and sit on the sunny deck. One caution: Like at many wineries, they get packed on summer weekends and there's not the same easiness.

They have a range of tours and tastings including one on the hour ($7) that is the most popular (the groups can be more than a couple dozen people), and a smaller guided tour and tasting ($20). Domaine Chandon also has large, sleek gift store and its four-star restaurant is one of the top eateries in Napa.

WINE AVAILABILITY: Many Domaine Chandon sparkling wines can be found in shops and restaurants. But the still wines and some sparklings are only available at the winery or on the website. Prices range from $22 to $55.

PICNIC PROSPECTS: Tasting on the deck here is like picnicking, but you can't bring your own food.

COST: Tasting flights range from $10 to $20; a glass of wine ranges from $5 to $13.

DIRECTIONS: Take the Yountville exit off Highway 29 (where the highway becomes a raised overpass) and go west toward the mountains. That street is California Drive. Cross the railroad tracks and turn right onto the entrance road.

RECOMMENDED FOR: Everyone.

Elyse Winery
2100 Hoffman Lane
Napa, 94558
707-944-2900
www.elysewinery.com
HOURS: 10–5 daily; they like you to phone ahead, but welcome walk-ins

This small, excellent winery was started by owner and winemaker Ray Coursen and his wife, Nancy, in 1987 as a 200-case-a-year operation using rented space. They bought the winery facilities in 1997.

Elyse is named after Ray and Nancy's daughter. For the sake of domestic peace, they added a second label, Jacob Franklin, named after their son. They also love their animals here, which explains the lively red blend, Nero Misto, named for their gray cat, who sits behind visitors in the tasting room and waits to be petted.

They make a range of wines, including Sangiovese, Syrah, a crisp, food-friendly Rosé, and Pinot Noir, but their focus has been their top-notch Zinfandel, Cabernet Sauvignon, and Petite Sirah.

ATMOSPHERE: Simple, clean room with tile floor, small wood tasting bar, and warm bright light from overhead spots and windows. Through the glass front doors you see the large wine storage tanks. The feeling is both casual and professional, though the cat and the dogs move through regularly to make sure tasters remember this is a family winery.

SERVICE: Efficient and exuberant. Servers seem genuinely excited about the wines and pour a range of them, even going back and re-pouring earlier wines so tasters can compare. The small bar makes it easy for them to give everyone personal attention.

TASTING TOOLS: Good crystal glasses. Big spit buckets. Water cooler in a corner. No crackers. Good light.

INTANGIBLES AND EXTRAS: They proudly sell no hats, T-shirts, or corkscrews because they want the experience to be about their wine. But it is still an unstuffy, enthusiastic experience about the wine, and they welcomed a group of beginners

with the same energy they gave a tour of Italian wine tourists.

WINE AVAILABILITY: Many are found in restaurants and wine markets, but most are available only at the winery or through the website. Prices range from $15 to $65.

PICNIC PROSPECTS: None.

COST: Free.

DIRECTIONS: About one mile south of Yountville, Hoffman Lane intersects Highway 29 and the frontage road (Solano Avenue) that runs parallel along the west side of highway. Turn west at Hoffman and go a bit more than a half mile. Elyse is on the right. If there's a dog or two at the gate, they're very friendly, though they may beg for a scratch behind the ear.

RECOMMENDED FOR: Everyone. Great place for animal lovers.

Goosecross Cellars
1119 State Lane
Yountville, 94599
707-944-1928 or 800-276-9210
www.goosecross.com
HOURS: 10–4:30 daily

Dictionary definition of a family winery. Visitors park alongside the house, walk across a patio, between some tanks, possibly past winemaker (and homeowner) Jeff Gorsuch fiddling with something, and into the tasting room. Jeff took over from his parents, who started it in 1985. Jeff's partner, David Topper, met public relations director Colleen Tatarian Topper at the winery and got married on the grounds. Pamela Topper, one of David's sisters, runs distribution and sales. Family winery, we're telling you.

Goosecross, by the way, is a translation of the family name, which in Old English means something like "goose who crosses the stream." They make a range of good wines, including an estate Chardonnay, Viognier, a red blend called AmeriTal, a Howell Mountain Cabernet Sauvignon, and their top-of-the-line Cabernet, AEROS.

ATMOSPHERE: The tasting area, crammed inside the barrel room and next to a small business office, is done in gentle blond wood and warm lights, and has a country-store feel to it. Winery folk drift through and stop to chat, or sometimes push a wine they like, and the sense is happily informal enough that you feel like visitors in their house.

SERVICE: They mix that familiarity with a solid knowledge of their wine and of Napa, and toss in some goofiness for people who want it. The server kept adding new wines to our tasting and got us trying to pick out the varietal. He told stories abut the winery and tales of the people who run it, while a few of them stopped by just to give him grief.

TASTING TOOLS: Good crystal glasses. Spit bucket and crackers handy. No water. OK light.

INTANGIBLES AND EXTRAS: This is one of Napa's out-of-the-way gems. The experience—from the wines to the servers to the winery folk floating through—is comfortable and friendly, and leaves you feeling a bit like an insider. You leave feeling you've made some friends. They also have a free wine education class on Saturdays at 10:30 a.m. (Reservations needed.) And besides the usual clothes and knick-knacks, they sell snacks, cheeses, mustards, and wine bottles dipped in a half-pound of chocolate.

WINE AVAILABILITY: Some can be found in shops and restaurants, but many are available only through the winery, the website, or at the Wineries of Napa Valley tasting room in downtown Napa. Prices range from $18 to 62, except in years when the rare Aeros Cabernet is released. It sells for $128.

PICNIC PROSPECTS: None.

COST: $5 for five wines, and how many others they feel like serving up.

DIRECTIONS: Take Yountville Crossroad and turn north on State Lane. The winery is about a half mile up on the left.

RECOMMENDED FOR: Everyone. Terrific for anyone looking for a spot off the beaten path.

Havens Wine Cellars

2055 Hoffman Lane
Napa, 94558
707-261-2000
www.havenswine.com
HOURS: 10–4:30 daily; appointments preferred but walk-ins are welcome

Michael and Kathryn Havens started their winery in 1984 based on their love of wine at the table, something they discovered in Europe when they were also falling in love with each other. They make Northern Rhone– and Right Bank Bordeaux–style wines (meaning more Merlot than Cab based), and have earned international reputations for their Syrah, Merlot, and Cabernet Franc. They also make Borriquot (a Cab Franc–Merlot blend), and Albariño, a Spanish white varietal.

They only recently opened their little tasting room, which is why it feels more like a foyer than an official wine-tasting spot.

ATMOSPHERE: The tasting here is a bit different because the small room has no tasting bar. There is just a glass wall on one side looking into the winery and, on the other side, a large, wooden buffet with a white counter and bright lights. The wines sit on the buffet's counter and visitors might have to wait a moment for a server to come out and greet them. With no tasting bar between you, it feels like a private tasting among friends.

SERVICE: Standing face-to-face to taste makes it both informal and personal. Servers are accommodating and friendly without being solicitous. When our server couldn't answer a question, she tracked down the winemaker for a response.

TASTING TOOLS: Good crystal glasses. Spit bucket handy. No crackers or water. Good light.

INTANGIBLES AND EXTRAS: The individual attention and range of high-quality, often unusual, wines made for a unique experience. And it makes it easy to believe them when they say they pay attention to details.

WINE AVAILABILITY: Some wines can be found in restaurants and wine shops, but the winery or the website are the only guarantees. Prices range from $24 to $45.

PICNIC PROSPECTS: None.

COST: None.

DIRECTIONS: About one mile south of Yountville, Hoffman Lane intersects Highway 29 and the frontage road (Solano Avenue) that runs along the west side of the highway. Turn west at Hoffman and go about a half mile. Havens is on the left.

RECOMMENDED FOR: Anyone looking for a quieter, more personal tasting. Probably not good for large groups.

Jessup Cellars

6740 North Washington Street
Yountville, 94599
707-944-8523
www.jessupcellars.com
HOURS: 10–6 daily

Jessup Cellars started in 1996 with vineyards in the Pope and Wooden valleys of Napa County. But owner and winemaker Mark Jessup had no tasting room until they opened this neat storefront on the main street in Yountville in 2004 where the town jail once stood. They make Merlot, Zinfandel, Cabernet Sauvignon, and Zinfandel Port.

ATMOSPHERE: The tasting room is modern California/Western style and has pale walls, high ceilings, wood trim, square windows, and a light marble bar. It has a wood-framed front with a couple barrels by the door, and you half expect to see a horse tied to a post out front.

SERVICE: The room is staffed by people intimate with the winery, including, often, family members, so they give the tasting a casualness, an air of authority, and sometimes some good bits of gossip.

TASTING TOOLS: Good, large glasses. Spit bucket, water, and wafers handy. Good light.

INTANGIBLES AND EXTRAS: This is a comfortable, stylish room and maybe a chance to meet the family members running the winery. They offer their terrific Zinfandel Port for tasting with shortbread cookies dipped in a Zinfandel Port chocolate sauce. Be warned: The pairing is so good, it's been known to drive people to madness.

WINE AVAILABILITY: Jessup is just beginning to get their wines more widely distributed, so the winery and website are the best shots. Prices range from $24 to $60.

PICNIC PROSPECTS: A two-block walk away is the city's Yount Park, with plenty of tables. It's a good-sized grass field surrounded by trees and looks up at vineyards and the Mayacamas to the west.

COST: $10 for four or five wines and the Port.

DIRECTIONS: On the east side of Washington Street—the main drag in Yountville—at the north end of town, a block below Madison Street (the street that connects to Highway 29).

RECOMMENDED FOR: Everyone, especially if you have lunch or dinner plans in Yountville.

Paraduxx Winery

7257 Silverado Trail
Napa, 94558
707-945-0890 or 866-367-9943
www.paraduxx.com
HOURS: 11–4 daily; officially, they are appointment only, but not really, you can walk in anytime

Paraduxx is a spin-off label—and since 2005, a spin-off winery—of Duckhorn Vineyard. The label was first introduced in 1994 and it's still a one-wine winery, for now, that makes a proprietary red blend founded on Zinfandel. In most years, it's been Zin mixed with Cabernet Sauvignon, but they occasionally include Merlot and other varietals. They're considering adding a Zinfandel-Syrah blend and a reverse Paraduxx that would be more Cabernet than Zin.

ATMOSPHERE: Not including the sparkling wine houses, Paraduxx has one of the few restaurant-style, sit-down tastings in the valley, where you find a spot, then get table service. This wide-open, contemporary tasting room makes it feel like a modern-but-comfortable hot spot. It's done in polished cherry wood, with peaked ceilings, exposed rafters and skylights, and lots of windows that let in light and views of a large courtyard with stone walls and ancient oaks.

There actually are two rooms to pick from. One feels like a restaurant bar, with a large community table, small individual tables with tall chairs, modern easy chairs around coffee tables, and cushioned window seats. The "dining room" has sets of tables for eight and one wall that is entirely windows looking into the courtyard.

SERVICE: After you pick your spot, they bring your wines on a tray, with detailed tasting notes on the back of oversized Paraduxx labels—which always show, say it together, a pair of ducks. Because they make only one wine, you get a vertical tasting of three consecutive vintages. This is a new winery and it's staffed by wine people. When it's not jammed, they will talk as much wine detail and trivia as you want, though when it's busy, they are making the rounds. Still, the overall feel is relaxed and pampered, and even when they're packed, there's no pressure to hurry out.

TASTING TOOLS: This is one of the few rooms in the valley using stemless crystal glasses. They'll bring spit buckets on request. Small water bottles and crackers on the table.

INTANGIBLES AND EXTRAS: This place has a young, almost nightclub vibe, and the service is a style that's different from most tasting rooms. It can get less personal when they're packed, but they still let you take your time and enjoy the wine and the setting. And because it's on Silverado Trail in the lower half of the valley, it doesn't often get overly busy.

WINE AVAILABILITY: Paraduxx is generally distributed. Prices range from $45 to $65.

PICNIC PROSPECTS: None.

COST: $10 for three wines.

DIRECTIONS: On the west side of Silverado Trail about a quarter mile north of Yountville Crossroad or about one and a half miles south of Oakville Crossroad.

RECOMMENDED FOR: People who want a slower, sit-down tasting of a unique wine.

Pine Ridge Winery

5901 Silverado Trail
Napa, 94558
707-257-4742 or 800-575-9777
www.pineridgewinery.com
HOURS: 10:30–4:30 daily

Named after their ridge with, of course, the big pines, these cozy grounds feel out of place for the Stags Leap District and more like they belong in the high mountains. Even the well-manicured, grassy picnic grounds and the small experimental vineyards in front of the winery have a high-country feel.

Pine Ridge was founded in 1978 and earned an international reputation and spots on top-100 wine lists with its line of Cabernets, including Cabs from Rutherford, Oakville, Stags Leap, and Howell Mountain. They also make Chardonnay, a Chenin Blanc-Viognier blend, Merlot, and a handful of Bordeaux blends, including Andrus, which is named after founders Gary and Nancy Andrus.

ATMOSPHERE: Designed to feel like a mountain lodge, all that's missing is a ski lift and a pickup lounge. Instead, the modern tasting room has a stone floor, wood trim, and a black tasting bar. A glass door leads to the barrel room, and you half expect to see a giant wheel from the machinery of a mountain tram.

SERVICE: Their big-time reputation for major-league reds, plus the charming grounds, draw consistent crowds ranging from wine novices to experts. Servers are affably patient with beginner questions and knowledgeable enough for big-red aficionados, but if you want to ask questions on a busy day, find a spot near the middle of the tasting bar.

TASTING TOOLS: Good crystal glasses. Spit buckets, water, and crackers handy. Good light.

INTANGIBLES AND EXTRAS: The array of great Cabs mixed with the unpretentious feel of the room makes this an accessible place to try some special wines. They offer a variety of tastings and tours: Winery and cave tours ($20) start daily at 10 a.m., noon, and 2 p.m., elegant barrel room tastings ($30) are daily at 11 a.m., 1 p.m., and 3 p.m., and they have a two-hour, food-wine pairing/cooking demonstration ($40) on Sundays at 11 a.m.

WINE AVAILABILITY: Many wines are available in stores and restaurants, but the high-end reds can only be found at the winery or on the website. Prices range from $13.50 to $95.

PICNIC PROSPECTS: A handful of shady tables are spread along the lawns surrounding the winery and look across a narrow valley of vineyards to the steep, pine-covered ridge. They just ask that you check in with the tasting room before starting a picnic. No check-in necessary to use the swings.

COST: $10 to taste four current releases; $20 to taste four Cabernets.

DIRECTIONS: On the west side of Silverado Trail a bit less than two miles south of Yountville Crossroad and a bit less than two miles north of Oak Knoll Avenue.

RECOMMENDED FOR: Everyone. Good place to splurge on a more-expensive big-red tasting.

Regusci Winery

5584 Silverado Trail
Napa, 94558
707-254-0403
www.regusciwinery.com
HOURS: 10–5 daily; although the signs say reservations only, they're just there to keep away tasters looking for happy hour; anyone can walk in

The three-story, heavy-stone buildings sit on a low hill above Silverado Trail and it's one of Napa's "ghost wineries"—original wineries built in the 1800s then later closed and abandoned. This simple-but-graceful, country-style structure was once the Grigsby-Occidental Winery built in 1878. It was decimated by phylloxera and shut down around 1900. Gaetano Regusci bought it in 1932, but used the land to farm and raise cattle. It was re-established as a commercial winery when his son, Angelo, and grandson, Jim, crushed their first vintage in 1996 and reopened in 1998.

They make elegant Chardonnay and estate Merlot, Zinfandel, and Cabernet Sauvignon from Stags Leap vineyards.

ATMOSPHERE: The large, old-winery tasting room sits inside the original hand-cut, two-foot-thick stone walls, and under tall ceilings bolstered by heavy wooden beams. Only the tasting bar, under bright, hanging spotlights, looks modern. The room is filled with old winemaking equipment and fairly reeks of Old World and stability. One wall is the dark wood tasting bar and the other has big windows looking out at an expansive view of the valley.

SERVICE: Very friendly, very casual, and yet very serious about wine. They leave the reservation-only sign out to slow down the traffic in the tasting room, because they want visitors to spend some time with their wines. They are not, however, wine snobs, and are happy to answer basic questions or chat about the wines and winery. They just want the experience to be a wine tasting, not a crowded party.

TASTING TOOLS: Good crystal glasses. Spit buckets and bread (with custom olive oils they sell) handy. Good light.

INTANGIBLES AND EXTRAS: There's a throwback feel here, more quiet and earnest than busy, and there's a sense of calm about the grounds. This is a place where tasters feel comfortable talking about the intricacies of wine. Regusci also sells its own olive oils and offers them with the tasting.

WINE AVAILABILITY: Most can be found in restaurants and some stores. As with many smaller wineries, supplies can run low, so the winery or website are the safest bets. Prices range from $28 to $48.

PICNIC PROSPECTS: They have a few tables on a small lawn in front of the winery shaded by olive trees. These are not—in theory—public tables, but they won't throw out someone sipping their wine with a bit of food.

COST: $10 for three or four wines.

DIRECTIONS: On the east side of Silverado Trail one and three-quarter miles north of Oak Knoll Avenue and about two and three-quarter miles south of Yountville Crossroad.

RECOMMENDED FOR: More serious tasters.

Robert Sinskey Vineyards

6320 Silverado Trail
Napa, 94558
707-944-9090 or 800-869-2030
www.robertsinskey.com
HOURS: 10–4:30 daily

A lot of wineries talk about marrying food with wine. These people took it another step in 1991, when owner Rob Sinskey wedded star San Francisco chef Maria Helm Sinskey. But that's just part of it. They produce wines in the Old World style, with a bit higher acid and good balance, to make them go well with food. And inside the stone-and-redwood, ranch-style winery built in 1986, the tasting room includes a sleek, professional kitchen where they make snacks to pair with the wines being sampled.

They make a range of terrific wines, including a Stags Leap District Cabernet, Chardonnay, and Pinot Blanc, but they're most recognized for a good-acid, food-friendly Merlot and their Pinot Noir, one of the most versatile food wines.

ATMOSPHERE: The tasting room is narrow and tall, with thirty-five-foot-high cathedral ceilings and long hanging spotlights that give the room the feel of a modern, comfortable bistro. There's enough glass to feel the trees and wisteria around the outside of the winery. Behind the bar, a glass wall looks into a large wine tank room. At the far end, the professional kitchen adds to the sense this could be an eatery.

SERVICE: When it's busy, the servers are swamped pouring and trying to be friendly—which they manage as well as you can expect—but as soon as it slows, you can feel their enthusiasm for Sinskey's wine-with-food philosophy as they pass around the snacks and talk about their wines. This tasting room has space for a lot of people, but, like with many popular wineries, it can get crowded on weekend afternoons.

TASTING TOOLS: Good glasses. Spit buckets and water handy. Food for pairing with wine. OK light.

INTANGIBLES AND EXTRAS: The food-and-wine notion is vibrantly alive here, and the food they serve is very good. The focus on Pinot Noir and slightly more unusual Bordeaux styles is a change of pace for a Cab-heavy stretch of Napa. They also offer a variety of cooking and food-wine pairing classes, and stage a Pinot release party in late spring every year.

As you'd expect from a winery big on food and wine, they sell a number of cookbooks and sauces. Then there's the barrel of "Mystery Wine," half-bottles of some kind of wine wrapped in brown paper bags that sell for $12 and you take your chances.

WINE AVAILABILITY: Many are found in restaurants and stores. Some reserves are available only at the winery or website. Prices range from $18 to $65.

PICNIC PROSPECTS: A handful of tables on a deck looking over the valley are, like many, theoretically only for finishing your tasting, but they won't mind if you eat a few of your own snacks.

COST: $15 for four mainstream current releases; $20 for four reserves.

DIRECTIONS: On the east side of Silverado Trail a quarter mile south of Yountville Crossroad.

RECOMMENDED FOR: Everyone.

Silverado Vineyards

6121 Silverado Trail
Napa, 94558
707-257-1770 or 800-997-1770
www.silveradovineyards.com
HOURS: 10:00–4:30 daily

There's an urge to gush about tasting at Silverado Vineyards, and we're giving in to it. The stone-and-tile, European-style winery and visitor's center look majestic from below. When you get up there, the grounds and large fountain feel almost Disneyland-perfect, which fits because the winery is owned by Disney heirs who bought vineyards in the mid-1970s and built the winery in 1981. (The only overt sign is the one window with a stained-glass Mickey Mouse.) Even more wonderland-like is the enchanting view from the winery and its stone terrace.

On top of everything, Silverado makes some world-renowned Cabernets, plus Sauvignon Blanc, Chardonnay, Sangiovese, and Merlot.

ATMOSPHERE: The large tasting room has the air of a classic Old World hotel bar, with a fireplace on one end, a heavy wooden tasting bar running the length of the room, and thick, 100-year-old beams crossing the high-peaked ceiling. But dominating it all are the floor-to-ceiling, wood-frame windows that look out on that stunning view up Silverado Trail, across the crags and knolls of the Stags Leap District, to the top of the valley.

SERVICE: Servers are easy and honest and clearly happy to be in such a great spot. "I love my office window," one told us. The large bar can handle sizable crowds, but like many popular Napa tasting rooms, it gets crowded on weekend afternoons. Servers poured a handful of wines not on the list, and their website even advertises that you never know when someone will uncork a great library wine for everyone in the room to try. (Our suggestion: Bring up this point.)

TASTING TOOLS: Good glasses. Spit buckets, crackers, and water handy. Very good light.

INTANGIBLES AND EXTRAS: The view alone is worth a special trip, but the room and the atmosphere fit the mood. If they aren't swamped, servers encourage tasters to sit on the terrace and gaze across the valley. The top-notch wines are almost just a bonus.

They offer a public tour and tasting ($15) 10:30 a.m. and 2:30 p.m. daily by reservation, a vineyard tour and tasting with snacks ($50) by reservation weekdays at 10:30 a.m., and a library wine tasting ($75) that includes four older vintages paired with food, Friday through Monday at 3:30 p.m. by reservation.

WINE AVAILABILITY: Most are available at stores and restaurants, but limited reserves are only at the winery or on the website. Prices range from $16 to $100.

PICNIC PROSPECTS: None, but take your time sitting on the terrace. They won't attack if you break out some crackers.

COST: $10 for four (or possibly more) wines in Estate tasting; $20 for five (or more) in Premier tasting.

DIRECTIONS: On the west side of Silverado Trail just over one mile south of Yountville Crossroad and about three and a half miles north of Oak Knoll Avenue. Go through the stone gate and up the road to the top of a steep hill.

RECOMMENDED FOR: Everyone. One of the truly scenic spots in the valley.

Stag's Leap Wine Cellars

5766 Silverado Trail
Napa, 94558
707-944-2020 or 866-422-7523
www.cask23.com
HOURS: 10–4:30 daily

This winery is a piece of Napa's hallowed ground, not just because its roots go back a century, but also because a wine from here, a 1973

S.L.V. Napa Valley Cabernet Sauvignon, was named best red at the epic 1976 Paris tasting that told the world Napa produces wines as good as any on the planet. It's also because Stag's Leap is still run by epic winemaker Warren Winiarski, who made that wine and who worked for Robert Mondavi Winery when it started in 1966. In 2000, the Smithsonian Institution chronicled a year in the life of Stag's Leap.

As you'd expect, the winery still produces an array of world-class Cabernets, topping out with the Cask 23 Cab. Stag's Leap also makes White Riesling, Sauvignon Blanc, Chardonnay, Merlot, and Petite Sirah.

ATMOSPHERE: Nothing special. Seriously. You'd expect a church-like reverence for wine or maybe shrines to Winiarski and the Paris Tasting. Or something. Instead, there's a straight-up working tasting room with polished concrete floors, a couple enormous storage barrels, and a display of vineyard photos. There are three counters, two for the mainstream tasters and one for club members and visitors going the more expensive reserve route.

SERVICE: This is a place that gets busy, and they station a greeter at the front door to help you along. On the downside, a weekend crowd can almost overwhelm the servers, who try but don't always get to do much more than tend bar.

TASTING TOOLS: Good glasses. Spit buckets handy, even when crowded. Water available. No crackers. OK light.

INTANGIBLES AND EXTRAS: Even when it's busy, this is a special spot. There are some places you need to visit just because of who they are, and for wine people, Stag's Leap is one of them. The wine is good, too.

WINE AVAILABILITY: Most wines can be found in shops and restaurants worldwide. Some reserves are found only at the winery or on the website. Prices range from $18 to $150.

PICNIC PROSPECTS: None.

COST: $15 for four-wine Portfolio tasting; $30 for four-wine Estate tasting that includes top-end Cabs.

DIRECTIONS: On the west side of Silverado Trail two and a half miles north of Oak Knoll Avenue and about two miles south of Yountville Crossroad.

RECOMMENDED FOR: Everyone, but best on weekdays or early on weekends.

Steltzner Vineyards
5998 Silverado Trail
Napa, 94558
707-252-7272
www.steltzner.com
HOURS: 10–4:30 daily; appointments aren't really necessary, just fill out a card when you arrive and get an immediate "reservation"

One of the many terrific, semi-under-the-radar wineries in the region, Steltzner has a Mediterranean-style building built in 1992 with a three-story observation/clock tower looking over a beautiful notch in the valley. Owner Richard Steltzner has been growing grapes on this land since 1965 and began making his own wine with the 1977 vintage.

They make a range of quality wines, including Sauvignon Blanc and Chardonnay, the unusual South African red, Pinotage, and their classic Stags Leap Merlot and Cabernet Sauvignon.

ATMOSPHERE: The window-lined, square tasting room feels more like a friendly cafe than a winery, with French doors, a stone floor, and a big, soft couch. The room looks out on a terra-cotta patio, vineyards, and some of those sharp Stags Leap knolls. Steltzner plans to eventually move the tasting room to the entrance of their 710-foot-long cave.

SERVICE: Casual, energetic, and good-humored about their status. Servers were eager to expand the six-wine tasting list or chat about the wide world of wine at the drop of a question. The room never got too packed, even on a holiday weekend.

TASTING TOOLS: Good glasses. Spit buckets and water handy. No crackers. Good light.

INTANGIBLES AND EXTRAS: It's a beautiful spot surrounded by hills and knolls, and the winery is surprisingly quiet for its location on Silverado Trail. The feeling inside is that everyone is there because they're friends. Tours are scheduled by appointment.

WINE AVAILABILITY: Many wines are available at shops and restaurants; however, this is only a midsized producer, so the winery or the website are the best bets. Prices range from $16 to $75.

PICNIC PROSPECTS: Theoretically, none. But they'll let you sip your wine and snack on the small patio.

COST: $10 for six wines—and whatever else they decide to pour.

DIRECTIONS: On the east side of Silverado Trail about two miles south of Yountville Crossroad and two and three-quarter miles north of Oak Knoll Avenue.

RECOMMENDED FOR: Everyone.

OAKVILLE TASTING ROOMS

Cardinale Estate

7600 St. Helena Highway
Oakville, 94558
707-948-2643 or 800-588-0279 or
800-224-4090
www.cardinale.com and
www.atalon.com
HOURS: 10:30–5 daily; just sign in
when you get there, appointments
taken but not needed

The Cardinale building looks like a stone-and-earth monastery and, though it's on only a short hill, it has dazzling views of the vineyards running right to its doors on all sides. Just as dazzling are the wines served here.

Owned by Jess Jackson of Kendall-Jackson, this room offers two related labels: Cardinale, which, in the Bordeaux style, produces a single red blend (of Cabernet and Merlot from top-grade hillside vineyards) that regularly scores premium ratings from critics, and Atalon, a sister line with fruit from a handful of name vineyards, which produces Merlot and Cabernet Sauvignon.

ATMOSPHERE: The monastery feel goes away when you enter the spacious entryway (where they ask you to sign in for your "appointment"). The walls are pale and clean and trimmed in light wood, and the handsome tasting bar is in a narrow, middle room with blond wood, a marble floor, and a bright feel from recessed lighting. It's next to a large, open dining room with windows and vineyard views all around, and it leads to a small, second-story deck.

SERVICE: The room is slower-paced than many, and they combine graciousness and a sense that their wines are special with enough casualness to not be intimidating. These are, indeed, special wines and they do not hurry you through them.

TASTING TOOLS: Good, large glasses. Spit buckets, crackers, and water handy. Very good light.

INTANGIBLES AND EXTRAS: It's a classy place with classy wines that does not put on airs. The views from this knoll in the middle of Oakville are quintessential, beautiful wine country.

WINE AVAILABILITY: All are available in good wine shops and restaurants. Prices range from $25 to $120.

PICNIC PROSPECTS: None, but stand on the outside deck for a while.

COST: $10 for three Atalon wines; $25 for four vintages of Cardinale or $7 per taste.

DIRECTIONS: On the east side of Highway 29 about two and a quarter miles north of the Madison Street light on the highway in Yountville, or three-quarters of a mile south of Oakville Crossroad. Look for the small sign on the road and follow the driveway in and around to the top of the hill.

RECOMMENDED FOR: For anyone who wants a quieter experience and a taste of some of Napa's outstanding big reds.

Cosentino Winery

7415 St. Helena Highway
Yountville, 94599
707-944-1220 or 800-764-1220
www.cosentinowinery.com
HOURS: 10–5 daily

This is one of those wineries that will depend entirely on when you come. The neat, Old World–looking building has a small, classy little tasting room, a large portfolio of wines, and can be positively charming when it's slow. But, because it's next to Mustards and just outside Yountville, during busy times, it may have as many visitors per foot of floor space as any tasting room in Napa.

Cosentino was started by former golf pro Mitch Cosentino, which explains the golf balls and knick-knacks sold in the tasting room. Not that he's a hacker with wine. He started making it in 1980 in California's Central Valley. Ten years later, he moved his operation to Napa Valley and now makes three labels: Cosentino, CE2V, and Crystal Valley Cellars. They're proud enough of their wine to present tasters with long lists of scores and reviews. They make more than twenty wines, including Pinot Grigio, Sauvignon Blanc, Viognier, Chardonnay, Pinot Noir, Cabernet Franc, Sangiovese, Merlot, Zinfandel, Cabernet Sauvignon, and upper-end white and red Meritages.

ATMOSPHERE: The room is modern and a bit cozy, with light wood, a jagged, sleek bar, and nifty displays that include books and golf souvenirs. It's got a low roof and only a few windows, but recessed overhead lighting fills it in. When it's slow, it's a comfortable place. When it's busy, it can be overwhelming.

SERVICE: Servers are young and energetic, and they know the details of the nearly two dozen wines on their list, plus the stories of the winery and the people. On a busy afternoon, they can't tell you much of that. On a slow morning, they're an education. Even when it's packed, they recognize more serious tasters and are likely to offer wines off the list.

TASTING TOOLS: Good glasses. Spit bucket handy. No water or crackers.

INTANGIBLES AND EXTRAS: This place is such a mixed bag. Its location makes it very accessible, and very busy. Tasters in the room can be just killing time before lunch, or there to check out some of the high-end wines. The best advice about visiting is, use common sense and it'll be worth the time.

WINE AVAILABILITY: They are widely distributed and Cosentino wines can be found in many shops and restaurants, but because they make so many wines, some of their smaller productions are sold only through the winery or website. Prices range from $18 to $100.

PICNIC PROSPECTS: None.

COST: $5 for four new releases; $10 for three reserves.

DIRECTIONS: On the west side of Highway 29, one and a half miles north of the Madison Street light on Highway 29 in Yountville and a bit more than one and a quarter miles south of Oakville Crossroad. Next to Mustards Grill.

RECOMMENDED FOR: Everyone—but not on busy summer afternoons or weekends.

Diamond Oaks

1595 Oakville Grade
Oakville, 94562
707-948-3000
www.diamond-oaks.com
HOURS: 10–5 daily

Diamond Oaks is one of those slightly out-of-the-way wineries that's more than worth the effort. It's a short way up the Oakville Grade, has stunning views, a fun little tasting room, a picnic area surrounded by ancient oaks, and a solid line of wines.

This winery, under the names Vichon and La Famiglia di Robert Mondavi, was part of the Mondavi family holdings until longtime vineyard owner Dinesh Maniar bought it and released the first Diamond Oaks vintage in 2001. They produce Chardonnay, Pinot Noir, Merlot, and Cabernet Sauvignon.

ATMOSPHERE: Diamond Oaks feels like it's miles from the main roads and up in the mountains. The tasting room has a mural across the full back wall showing an Italian countryside that is the only holdover from the old owners. The rest is a nice mix of contemporary wood and glass. They opened up the wall behind the tasting bar with windows, and visitors see a dramatic hillside layered with vineyards.

SERVICE: This is not one of the busy, busy tasting rooms in the valley, so the servers have some time to spend with you. It's a low-key place and they know in the tasting room that visitors will want to hang around awhile.

TASTING TOOLS: Good, large glasses. Spit buckets and water handy. No crackers. Very good light.

INTANGIBLES AND EXTRAS: The area is peaceful, with a view that looks over half of Oakville. They ask that you buy wine to use the picnic area—but, truthfully, they don't push it—and you can make a reservation ($30) that gets you a tablecloth and a bottle of wine and stemware.

WINE AVAILABILITY: Their wines are distributed to stores and restaurants, but this is still a small producer and the winery or website are the best bets. Prices range from $16 to $39.

PICNIC PROSPECTS: The picnic area is on a flat under enormous oaks, and because of the trees, it's one of the few spots around the grounds that doesn't have the soaring views.

The property rolls in both directions and a more adventurous picnic would be to follow the stone wall down and sit where you like the view.

COST: $7 for five wines.

DIRECTIONS: East on Oakville Grade from Highway 29 about one and a quarter miles—about a quarter mile after it starts climbing—and it will be on the left.

RECOMMENDED FOR: Everyone.

Far Niente
1350 Acacia Drive
Oakville, 94562
707-944-2861 or 800-363-6523
www.farniente.com
HOURS: 10–4 Daily; tastings only with tours and by appointment

The main building here is one of the spectacular structures of Napa Valley, a large, European-style stone house with a slate- and copper-trimmed roof. It was built in 1885 by Hamden McIntyre, the architect who designed, among others, the Inglenook winery (now Rubicon Estate), Trefethen, and the Culinary Institute of America at Greystone. The house and property were abandoned for sixty years, from the start of Prohibition until the late Gil Nickel bought and began refurbishing it all in 1979. He found, chiseled into a stone wall, the words "Far Niente," part of the Italian phrase "dolce far niente," loosely meaning "it's sweet to do nothing" or "without a care."

Nickel was a former missile analyst, who, with his family, built one of the largest commercial landscaping companies in America. Both his touch at landscaping and his fondness for renovating classics is evident everywhere. The winery building, on a small rise that looks over the vineyards of southern Oakville, has a fairy-tale polish to it, and so do the thirteen acres of gardens and trees surrounding it.

Gil Nickel died in 2003, but his wife, Beth, and their family and partners continue producing premium Chardonnay and Cabernet Sauvignon. Under a separate label, they also make a highly regarded dessert wine called Dolce, that comes from late-harvest Sémillon and Sauvignon Blanc grapes.

ATMOSPHERE: The grounds, with stone-lined gardens and acres of flowers, are manicured and astounding. The view of Oakville is mesmerizing. The house is meticulously restored—elegant but still comfortable—and the tour goes through the large carriage house that holds a collection of more than two dozen vintage cars and motorcycles from Italy, Germany, Britain, and America. There is a wonderland feel here, and you walk around a bit in awe.

SERVICE: Far Niente only opened to the public in 2004. Because this is an expensive tour, they understand visitors expect a lot from the experience and the wine. The tastings are done after the tour, sitting at a table, generally in the large, central dining room that has a wall of windows looking east across the valley. They go as slowly as you'd like and treat visitors in that same elegant-but-comfortable style the house exudes.

TASTING TOOLS: Very good glasses. Spit buckets handy. Water, crackers, and cheese on tables. Good light.

INTANGIBLES AND EXTRAS: Everything here is high-end, including the wines, the property, and the tours—but visitors do pay for the privilege ($50). It is a chance to see the luxury class of both old and new Napa, to sample some distinct wines, and, for

car buffs, to see a 1961 Corvette Roadster and a 1951 Ferrari 340 America, considered, they say, one of the most beautiful Ferraris ever built.

WINE AVAILABILITY: All their wines are sold in fine wine shops and restaurants. Dolce is not produced every year, and in off years, the winery or website may be the only shot. Prices range from $52 to $135.

PICNIC PROSPECTS: None.

COST: $50 for the tour and tasting five wines. Waived with purchase of six bottles.

DIRECTIONS: West on the Oakville Grade from Highway 29 about nine-tenths of a mile. Turn left into a long, tree-lined driveway—on the road there's a tall pine on each side and a small sign that says "1350/1360 Acacia Drive." (If you start up the hill very far, or hit Diamond Oaks Winery on your left, you've gone too far.) Follow the instructions at the gate.

RECOMMENDED FOR: People who don't mind the fee and who want an indulgence, or the chance to see a rare, interesting place.

Groth Vineyard and Winery

750 Oakville Cross Road
Oakville, 94562
707-944-0290
www.grothwines.com
HOURS: 10–4 Monday–Saturday;
appointments required

Judy and Dennis Groth almost went somewhere else. They were ready to buy over the hills in Sonoma to the west, then in one last check of the region, looked at these 121 acres for sale in Oakville. That was in 1981. Groth Winery and Vineyard was founded the next year, and by 1985, Dennis had left Atari, a company he helped found, and moved with his family to Napa.

Their rose-colored, mission-style winery has a Moorish influence, with a rounded bell tower, a tile fountain, and graceful stairs leading to the over-sized rooms, and is one of the most recognizable wineries in the valley. Even more notable is their prized Cabernet Sauvignon, one of the top-tier Cabs in Napa, and their Reserve Cab, which they did not make from 2000 to 2003 because they had replanted the vineyards and didn't think the young grapes met their standards. They also make Sauvignon Blanc and Chardonnay.

ATMOSPHERE: The visitors' rooms inside the winery are light and open. The front tasting area has high ceilings, huge windows, pale walls, bright paintings, and an arched window looking into the barrel room. On the other side of a central fireplace is a roomy, light-wood dining room that feels like an art gallery because of the energetic modern paintings by Dennis and Judy's daughter, Suzanne. Outside, a deck looks north across a world of vineyards.

SERVICE: Tastings are by appointment and they try to keep it very personal. The staffers tell the winery story and the details of the wine, and also give off an almost conspiratorial air that makes visitors feel they're part of the insider group as they get shown around.

TASTING TOOLS: Good, large glasses. Spit buckets and water handy. No crackers. Very good light.

INTANGIBLES AND EXTRAS: The building is striking inside and out, and the feel here is unassuming considering it's been a premier producer for years.

WINE AVAILABILITY: Their wines are well distributed, though the Reserve Cabernet, when it is made, is produced in limited amounts and may best be found through the winery and website. Prices range from $17 to $55

PICNIC PROSPECTS: None.

COST: $10 for three wines, waived with purchase.

DIRECTIONS: On north side of Oakville Crossroad about one and three-quarter miles east of Highway 29 and about three-quarters of a mile west of Silverado Trail.

RECOMMENDED FOR: Everyone.

Miner Family Vineyards

7850 Silverado Trail
Oakville, 94562
707-944-9500 or 800-366-9463
www.minerwines.com
HOURS: 11–5 daily

The winery was founded in 1998 by Dave and Emily Miner along with his parents, Ed and Norma. Their label connects to the family's roots in Assyria with the image of a winged sun god representing the life and energy the vines need. It also is a nod toward the prosperity the family has enjoyed.

Their winery is up on a rise looking over the flats of Oakville. They make more than a dozen wines, including Sauvignon Blanc, Viognier, Chardonnay, Rosato, Pinot Noir, Syrah, Zinfandel, Petite Sirah, and their biggest stars, a Wild Yeast Chardonnay, a consistently high-scoring Cabernet Sauvignon, and a Bordeaux blend called Oracle.

ATMOSPHERE: The tasting room is up a set of stairs (or an elevator) and feels a bit like the lobby of a small, contemporary wine-country hotel. The big doors open into a wide space with a display table and a Persian rug. The light-wood bar is on one side of the room, looking out windows with a view across the flats of Oakville.

SERVICE: There is something bouncy about the room and the people. Servers are genuinely welcoming, and seem to like their wines. They're one of the few rooms using stemless wine glasses. Although the bar is small, they generally don't get packed, so servers have time to talk about the wine.

TASTING TOOLS: Good stemless glasses. Spit buckets handy. No water or crackers. Good light.

INTANGIBLES AND EXTRAS: They have a good display of books and sell a range of cigars in addition to the usual wine souvenirs. Outside, the small deck is up high enough that you can sit in comfortable chairs or at a table, sip your wine, and look across more than two miles of vineyards.

WINE AVAILABILITY: Many of their wines are found in shops and restaurants, but some are only at the winery or on the website. Prices range from $15 to $50.

PICNIC PROSPECTS: None. (You can sip your wine and break out some crackers on the deck.)

COST: $10 for five wines, including their best.

DIRECTIONS: On the east side of Silverado Trail about a quarter mile north of Oakville Crossroad.

RECOMMENDED FOR: Everyone.

Napa Cellars

7481 St. Helena Highway
Oakville, 94562
707-944-2565 or 800-535-6400
www.napacellars.com
HOURS: 10:30–5:30 spring and summer; 11–5 fall and winter

Considering its location and wine, this is a surprisingly under-the-radar tasting room. It shouldn't be. This venture was started in 1996 by Koerner Rombauer and Rich Frank, and is now owned by Trinchero Family Estates, and is in a neat, six-sided building with a good tasting room. It's not that they don't get traffic, it's that people accidentally find it when they should be intentionally looking for this place.

Napa Cellars makes a line of quality, generally well-priced wines including a Vin Gris Rosé, Sauvignon Blanc, Chardonnay, Zinfandel, Merlot, Syrah, Cabernet Sauvignon, and Fié Doux, a late-harvest Sémillon wine.

ATMOSPHERE: The softly lit tasting room has a big, six-sided bar in the middle with the wine glasses hanging over it, restaurant bar–style. One wall is windows and glass doors looking at their shaded picnic area. It's an unpretentious, approachable place.

SERVICE: These are unimposing but intelligent people who still try to educate. They treat novices with respect, but they certainly know wine and the valley well enough for the wine geeks. One motto here: Don't be intimidated, it's grape juice.

TASTING TOOLS: Good glasses. Spit buckets, crackers, and water handy. OK light.

INTANGIBLES AND EXTRAS: This is a fun, lively place to taste and to learn about wine. The combination of wines, service, and a pretty picnic spot make this a can't-miss. One exception is late on peak days. Like many Highway 29 rooms, they get very busy mid-to-late afternoon.

WINE AVAILABILITY: Napa Cellars is found in many stores and restaurants as well as through the winery and website. Prices range from $15 to $32.50.

PICNIC PROSPECTS: Their tables are in a pretty spot along the side of the building on grass under trees. They look west across vineyards but do have highway noise right behind them.

COST: $5 for four, or sometimes more, wines; waived with purchase.

DIRECTIONS: On the west side of Highway 29, a bit over one and a half miles north of the Madison Street light on Highway 29 in Yountville, and about one and a quarter miles south of Oakville Crossroad.

RECOMMENDED FOR: Everyone. Comfortable place for wine novices.

Napa Wine Company
7840 St. Helena Highway
Oakville, 94562
707-944-1710 or 800-848-9630
www.cultwinecentral.com
HOURS: 10–4:30 daily; 10–5 weekends

The operation here started in 1877 as Nouveau Medoc Winery, and has "Bonded Winery No. 9" painted on a large wall outside, which translates to the ninth permit to make wine issued in California. It has become Napa's largest custom crush facility, a place where winemakers rent space and equipment and can make wines without having to build their own winery.

Napa Wine Co., which also calls itself Cult Wine Central, houses more than sixty labels, including its own, and some prestigious names like Volker Eisele Family Estate, Phalmeyer, Mason, Joel Gott, Falcor, and Marilyn Merlot.

ATMOSPHERE: The square, open room has a tile floor, a medium ceil-

ing, and two long marble tasting bars. It feels a bit like a cross between a friendly wine shop and a library, with a very approachable tone.

SERVICE: They offer tastings of twenty-four different labels, and try to mix and match to help visitors. This is a place staffed by proud wine geeks, and because of the range of labels and winemakers operating here, they have stories about wines and personalities throughout the valley. The tone is amiable and unpretentious.

TASTING TOOLS: Good large glasses. Spit buckets, water, and crackers handy. Good light.

INTANGIBLES AND EXTRAS: This is an often overlooked place, and it's a different kind of tasting room because they have such a range of wines to offer. It can be a chance for a little different wine education because this also is a different kind of winemaking operation from most. Or it can be just a comfortable room to taste some wines you may not know.

WINE AVAILABILITY: With sixty-plus wines, it runs the gamut. The Napa Valley Wine Co. brand is available at some stores and restaurants, and all the wines offered for tasting are available through the winery websites and through links from Napa Valley Wine Co.'s site. Prices also run the gamut.

PICNIC PROSPECTS: None.

COST: $10–$20 for a handful of wines, depending on the day.

DIRECTIONS: On Oakville Crossroad at Highway 29. The tasting room is under an awning that says "tasting room."

RECOMMENDED FOR: Everyone, especially people looking for smaller or unique labels.

Nickel & Nickel

8164 St. Helena Highway
Oakville, 94562
707-967-9600
www.nickelandnickel.com
HOURS: 10–3 weekdays; 10–2 weekends; tastings only with tours and by appointment

Nickel & Nickel was started in 1997 by Far Niente's owner, the late Gil Nickel and his partners, who wanted to make single-vineyard wines. They decided a good place to start was this nineteenth-century Oakville ranch and its thirty acres of vineyards directly north of Opus One and straight across the road from Robert Mondavi Winery.

As they did with Far Niente, Nickel and his team carefully restored the charming buildings here, including the 1882 white Queen Anne–style ranch house and the barns. They also landscaped the grounds and built a winery building in the same 1880s style. It's all bordered by olive and oak trees, gardens, and a heavy, three-rail white fence that also encircles a corral for the horses in front.

Their wine requires at least as much care as the facilities, because it's all 100 percent single-varietal and single-vineyard, and their nearly two-dozen wines are among Napa's most interesting and distinctive. They make Chardonnay, Merlot, Syrah, Zinfandel, and Cabernet Sauvignon.

ATMOSPHERE: The faithful restoration and farm feel makes this a cheerful and intriguing place. The tour goes through the 30,000-square-foot cellars under the winery, and the Gleason Barn, another pre-

cisely restored building—this time from 1770s New England—that uses heavy wood and posts and creates a stunningly comfortable and airy feel inside. The big Sullenger house (named after original nineteenth-century owner John Sullenger) is tall and square and bright with windows. Tastings are done either in a long dining room in the house or out on the back porch.

SERVICE: Visitors get a small glass of wine and wait in a warm, country drawing room for the tour to gather. This is a terrific property to tour, because of the buildings and the skill in restoring them, and because of the unique winemaking style that demands almost constant attention, even when the wine is in barrels. (Single vineyard, 100 percent varietal, means no blending, so adjustments have to be more subtle.) They convey it all, but keep it in the casual tone of the setting.

TASTING TOOLS: Very good glasses. Individual spit buckets. Water and crackers handy. Very good light.

INTANGIBLES AND EXTRAS: This winery makes wines with a clear sense of place—of terroir—and they can explain how it works.

In some ways, Nickel & Nickel is the quintessence of Napa's charm, with painstakingly restored country property, distinct winemaking, an intense feel of vineyards all around, and a genial spirit. This is an expensive tour and tasting, but it feels worth the cost.

WINE AVAILABILITY: All Nickel & Nickel wines are distributed to shops and restaurants, but production is not large on any one wine—and it varies year to year—so the winery and website are the safest bets. Prices range from $40 to $125.

PICNIC PROSPECTS: None.

COST: $30 for the tour and tasting five wines.

DIRECTIONS: On the east side of Highway 29, a half mile north of Oakville Crossroad.

RECOMMENDED FOR: Anyone who wants to treat themselves.

Opus One
7900 St. Helena Highway
Oakville, 94562
707-944-9442
www.opusonewinery.com
HOURS: 10–4 daily

Opus One may have been the most high-profile winery opened in Napa, a joint venture between Robert Mondavi and Baron Philippe de Rothschild of the premier Bordeaux winery, Château Moton-Rothschild. And this was in 1979, when the French had even less regard for American winemaking and American grapes than they do now.

It wasn't just the combination of Mondavi and Rothschild, it was the state-of-the-art winery, the design by Johnson, Fain & Pereira—the architects of San Francisco's Transamerica Pyramid—and the $27 million poured into it. They called Opus One a mix of French tradition, American technology, and Napa Valley flair. The first two vintages, the 1979 and 1980, were released together. Both lived up to the billing. Opus One remains one of the premier wineries in the valley, making one of Napa's most distinct and powerful wines.

In the style of the great French chateaux, they produce just one main wine called Opus One, a Bordeaux blend based on Cabernet Sauvignon. In some years, also like the French houses, they make a sec-ondary wine called Overture if they have enough fruit.

ATMOSPHERE: The winery building, opened in 1991, a dozen years after the wine was born, is described by its architects as an inverted jewel. From far away, more common descriptions are spaceship and sanitation plant. But when you get close, that changes. It feels more like a temple for wine.

There's a grassy rise surrounded by cream-colored limestone walls. Graceful stairs lead to a courtyard that is simple and handsome with olive trees and colonnades. The entrance is a tall, polished wood door. Visitors sign in with the concierge and can wander around the outdoor hallways before finding the tasting room.

Inside, it's open and tall, and mixes the pale tan and cream stone with redwood and stainless steel. The sitting rooms have odd combinations of modern art, contemporary styling, and ornate, old-European furniture. The entire top of the winery is a trellis-covered terrace that gives visitors a view of the vineyards in the heart of Oakville.

SERVICE: They are restrained and gracious, and you can explore the building without tasting. The room itself is small and modern like the rest of the winery. You get one two-ounce pour—for $25—and most people take their wine to the rooftop terrace or out to the courtyard.

TASTING TOOLS: Good, large glasses. Spit buckets, crackers, and water handy in the tasting room. But, seriously, are you going to spit here?

INTANGIBLES AND EXTRAS: This is a singular place, for the architecture, the openness, the history, and the powerful wine. Tours of the hypermodern, gravity flow winery are just as interesting and given daily at 10:30 a.m. for free by appointment, but they often fill up weeks ahead.

WINE AVAILABILITY: Opus One is distributed to wine shops and restaurants. Overture is found only at the winery and not on the website. Opus One is $145. Overture is $45.

PICNIC PROSPECTS: None, but if you broke out some snacks on the rooftop terrace, you probably wouldn't be bothered.

COST: $25 for one two-once pour.

DIRECTIONS: On the east side of Highway 29, a quarter mile north of Oakville Crossroad.

RECOMMENDED FOR: Anyone who wants to invest in an unusual visit and who wants to taste Opus One wine.

PlumpJack Winery

620 Oakville Crossroad
Oakville, 94562
707-945-1220
www.plumpjack.com
HOURS: 10–4 daily

PlumpJack is not a church-of-wine place. The company and the winery are named after Shakespeare's Sir John Falstaff, a rogue whose nickname was Plump Jack and whose impish, rascally spirit seems to live in the winery and tasting room.

It is part of a group of PlumpJack businesses, including PlumpJack Cafe and Balboa Cafe in San Francisco, that was founded by San Francisco Mayor Gavin Newsom. The winery still uses part of the original 1883 winemaking facility here, and this is where Villa Mt. Eden operated until the early 1990s. PlumpJack's first vintage was 1995, and the Cabernet immediately scored major league points from critics. They also make

respected Chardonnay, Merlot and Syrah, but their Cab remains one of Napa's elite wines, which is why they added to their irreverent image in 2000 when they started producing half the Cabernet in bottles with screw tops.

ATMOSPHERE: The relatively small tasting room is half Renaissance Faire and half goofy roadhouse pub. It has a round, metal-trimmed bar, French doors leading to a tiny deck, and slightly off-kilter shapes to everything. With the mellow earth tones, bright light, and windows all around, in part, you feel like you're in the vineyards. Or, with the goofy-looking shields and swords mixed with modern art all over, you could also be in a tasting room in Cartoon Town.

SERVICE: No one takes themselves too seriously, and there is a young energy to the room. But the servers are serious wine people, too, and if you get them going, they'll give fiery and detailed arguments for putting screw tops on prized wines. However, if you insist, they will still sell you wine with corks.

TASTING TOOLS: Good, large glasses. Spit buckets handy. No water or crackers. Good light.

INTANGIBLES AND EXTRAS: There's a lot to like here, and much of it's a bit unconventional. The mood and liveliness are infectious, the deck and a couple picnic tables are right against vineyards that back up to short, cozy hills, and the freshness of their approach is invigorating. On top of that, they make great wine.

WINE AVAILABILITY: Their wines are generally available in shops and restaurants, but they often sell out some of their lines and the winery or website are safer bets. Prices range from $36 to $160.

PICNIC PROSPECTS: None, but you can hang out at the tables or on the deck as long as you'd like.

COST: $5 for four wines (if they haven't sold out).

DIRECTIONS: On the north side of Oakville Crossroad about 2 miles east of Highway 29 and ½ mile west of Silverado Trail. Look for medieval-style shields with a jaunty, almost comiclike scrawl and follow the driveway a couple hundred yards in.

RECOMMENDED FOR: Everyone, unless you are fairly stuffy.

Robert Mondavi Winery

7801 St. Helena Highway
Oakville, 94562
707-226-1395 or 888-766-6328
www.robertmondaviwinery.com
HOURS: 10–5 daily; reservations suggested for tours

This is ground zero for modern Napa wine. There are other wineries with longer histories, but Napa Valley's twentieth-century resurgence —and American wine's growth— got so much of their early force from this place and from the zest for excellence, the curiosity, the spirit and the communicable enthusiasm of Robert Mondavi.

Mondavi was an innovator and an ambassador for Napa. He also is the living embodiment of building a good wine life. But most of all, he's always been a cheerleader for his winery, for Napa, and for American wine.

This winery is among the most visited spots in the valley, but it's far from the flashiest. Its long, tan, mission-style building with the tower and arch almost look cliché now, because there are so many long, low, mission-style wineries in Napa and around California. But this was the first.

The sense of the place, and of tasting and touring here, is of being among vineyards, which you drive along coming in. When you walk through the arch, you see the vines running a mile back to the Mayacamas Range. They make a vast line of wines including Sauvignon Blanc, Fumé Blanc, Chardonnay, Merlot, Pinot Noir, Zinfandel, Syrah, Cabernet Sauvignon, and Sauvignon Blanc Botrytis.

ATMOSPHERE: They have the usual straight-up tastings here, or you can buy a glass of wine in one of two comfortable tasting rooms, but they steer you toward one of their many tours that have multiple tastings at the end. This personifies the Mondavi legacy of spreading the word and pushing a little wine education.

The most popular is the 75-minute To Kalon tour and tasting ($25) that starts on the hour and wanders along the edge of the famous 550-acre To Kalon vineyard. They have "talking areas" that are shaded benches grouped among the vines, where the guides stop to tell you the Mondavi story. Then you wander through the huge winery and end up in a small dining room with ranch-elegant wood furniture and a sit-down tasting of a handful of wines.

SERVICE: The tone is always a mix of educational, and of the notion that wine plus art plus grace equals a good life. They want you to know about Mondavi and all of Napa, and why wine can be fun. They get a lot of Napa first-timers here, and the guides can be gentle with pretty much any question, but they also are good teachers.

TASTING TOOLS: Good, large glasses. Spit buckets, crackers and water on tables. Very good light in most rooms.

INTANGIBLES AND EXTRAS: This is a place Napa visitors have to see at some point, because of its role in American wine, because of its array of intriguing tours, and because there is such a visceral vineyard feel here. It is not the most plush or coziest tasting experience in Napa, but you end up feeling like you understand more about the notion that wine, art, and food should be an enlightening, communal experience.

The tour/tasting possibilities include small-group tastings that explore the palate and sensations of wine (ranging from $50 to $65), a wine and cheese pairing ($50), and three different tour-and-lunch tastings that include the chef pairing wines with your meal (from $75 to $105). All require reservations.

WINE AVAILABILITY: Robert Mondavi wines are as well distributed as any in America, but there are still a few reserves that are hard to find outside the winery or website. Prices range from $17 to $125.

PICNIC PROSPECTS: None, in theory, but there are plenty of benches around out front where you won't be bothered.

COST: $10. Wines by the glass or reserve tasting flights $8–$30.

DIRECTIONS: On the west side of Highway 29 about ¼ mile north of Oakville Crossroad.

RECOMMENDED FOR: Everyone. Comfortable and educational place for wine novices.

Silver Oak Cellars

915 Oakville Crossroad
Oakville, 94562
707-945-1220 or 800-273-8809
www.silveroak.com
HOURS: 9–4 Monday–Saturday

There is probably no wine in Napa with a more fanatical following than the Cabernet of Silver Oak. People camp out twice a year for the Woodstock-like festival that comes with the release of each new vintage. (The Alexander Valley Cab comes out in late July, the Napa Valley version in early February.) And if you want to impress your average wine consumer with a high-end wine, this is your horse.

Ray Duncan and the late Justin Meyer started Silver Oak in 1972 on the site of a dairy farm, and they moved into this Gothic-looking, stone winery in 1982. The square-topped water tower on the label is nearby, and, considering the reputation and the site, you get a sense you're entering a country church.

ATMOSPHERE: Inside, you lose the church feel. It's more like a simple store, done in medium-dark wood, and almost a disappointment. The middle of the square, plain-tiled room has T-shirts and books on a table, and the lighting is a bit dim. There are three small tasting bars under brighter lights in the back. One glass wall looks into a barrel room and, in the only real bow to that church of wine thing, a glass door looks into an elegant room of library wines.

SERVICE: Friendly and accommodating, but often pressed. They serve two wines, their Alexander Valley and Napa Valley Cabs, and considering the $60–$100 retail price, give fairly generous pours. When it's busy, which is often, tasters get their wine and move away from the bar to make room.

TASTING TOOLS: Good, large glasses. Bread, water, and spit buckets on tasting bars (but that sometimes means fighting through a crowd). OK light.

INTANGIBLES AND EXTRAS: You are here for the Silver Oak wine. That's what you get. Tours are offered Monday–Friday at 1:30 p.m. by reservation.

WINE AVAILABILITY: Despite the reputation and demand, both Cabs can be found in many restaurants and stores. Price ranges from $60 to $100.

PICNIC PROSPECTS: None

COST: $10 for two wines.

DIRECTIONS: On the south side of Oakville Crossroad, a bit more than 1 mile east of Highway 29 and about 1½ miles west of Silverado Trail.

RECOMMENDED FOR: Any fan of Silver Oak.

Turnbull Wine Cellars

8210 St. Helena Highway
Oakville, 94562
707-963-5839 or 800-887-6285
www.turnbullwines.com
HOURS: 10–4:30 daily

The name, they say here, goes back to the 1300s, when Scottish king Robert the Bruce's life was saved by a member of his court who turned away a charging bull. The king dubbed his subject "Turnbull" and, though the winery has changed hands a few times since its founding in 1979 by the late William Turnbull, they still honor that pretty cool legacy with their label and its bull with his head turned.

Their wines include Sauvignon Blanc, Viognier, a White Meritage, Merlot, Cabernet Sauvignon, and a couple red blends called Old Bull Red, and their top-end proprietary blend, Black Label.

ATMOSPHERE: The simple, modern tasting room fits about a dozen people at the medium wood bar. It's got pale walls and glass doors leading to a small, brick patio with a view of vineyards and the vintage red Ford truck that's become a mascot for the place.

SERVICE: Casual and unpushy. There are no huge flourishes here, and this is one of the smaller tasting rooms on this stretch of Highway 29, so when it's not a peak time, it can be comfortably personal.

TASTING TOOLS: Good glasses. Spit buckets, water, and crackers handy. OK light.

INTANGIBLES AND EXTRAS: Winery owner Patrick O'Dell stocks an art gallery in the building with works from his personal collection. You can take a free self-guided tour on weekdays by appointment, and they do a gallery tour and reserve tasting ($10) on Saturdays by appointment.

WINE AVAILABILITY: Turnbull is available in many shops and restaurants, and through the winery and website. Prices range from $16 to $75.

PICNIC PROSPECTS: None, but you can sit on the peaceful deck and sip.

COST: $10 for three wines, waived with purchase.

DIRECTIONS: On the east side of Highway 29 about ½ mile north of Oakville Crossroad.

RECOMMENDED FOR: People looking for a straight-up, simpler tasting in a busy stretch of the valley.

Catacula Lake Winery

4105 Chiles Pope Valley Road
St. Helena, 94574
707-965-1104
www.cataculalake.com
HOURS: 11–4:30 Monday–Friday by
appointment

Catacula Lake Winery is part of the 1,025-acre Bar 49 Estate that owner Edward Keith bought in the 1960s and ran for decades as a summer camp for kids. In the 1970s, the Keiths planted their first vineyards, but didn't produce their own vintage until 1999.

The huge, modern, mission-style winery on a rise above Catacula Lake opened in 2002. The scale of the red-roofed building is impressive and it includes 15,000 feet of caves and a 245-foot-long mural showing the history of Chiles Valley. They make Sauvignon Blanc, Zinfandel, Cabernet Sauvignon, a rich Cab-Merlot blend they call Rancho Cuvee, and a late-harvest Sauvignon Blanc.

ATMOSPHERE: The tasting room is enormous, with a sixty-five-foot, L-shaped, pale granite bar, all of it backed by sixty-five feet of windows that look out at a large patio then down to the lake. The floor is earth-tone tile and the walls and vaulted ceiling are trimmed in blond wood. With the open space, light colors, and huge windows, the overall impression is of being on a vast terrace over the lake.

SERVICE: Informal, unfussy, and fun. The size and beauty of the setting, the enormous tasting room, and a sense of quirkiness about the winery makes it an unusual stop. This is also a family-run place and the people serving visitors know the wine and the history well.

TASTING TOOLS: Good glasses. Spit buckets, crackers, and water handy. Excellent light.

INTANGIBLES AND EXTRAS: Both the size of the winery and the great views of the lake and the mountains make Catacula a memorable stop. This also is a winery with a respect for history and a sense of place. The Keiths have deeded the Bar 49 to the Napa Valley Land Trust to preserve the ranch.

WINE AVAILABILITY: Although they make just 6,000 cases, most wines can be found in markets or restaurants and, of course, at the winery or its website. Prices range from $12 to $25.

PICNIC PROSPECTS: The stone terrace is a picturesque, quiet setting with a dozen tables looking over a meadow that runs down to Catacula Lake. On both sides, mountains frame the lake. All that's missing are deer, but there is a modern deer sculpture just off the deck in the meadow. For small groups—generally ten or more—they also offer a box-lunch-and-wine picnic ($30) by reservation.

COST: $5 for five wines, waived with the purchase of two bottles; a discount coupon is available on the website.

DIRECTIONS: Six miles north on Chiles Pope Valley Road from where it splits off Highway 128. The large winery sits by itself against a hill and is impossible to miss.

RECOMMENDED FOR: Everyone.

Kuleto Estate

2470 Sage Canyon Road
St. Helena, 94574
707-963-9750
www.kuletoestate.com
HOURS: Tours and tastings
Monday–Saturday at 10:30 a.m. and
2:30 p.m. by appointment

Restaurateur Pat Kuleto bought 761 dramatic acres on a mountaintop east of the valley and Lake Hennessey in 1992, and built what amounts to a ranch, winery, and fantasyland. The views sweep off at every angle, of vineyards, of mountains, of sheer drops to the valley below. The modern, gravity-flow winery and home are finished with stone and wood, and it's all far above Highway 128, a mile up a narrow road, so Kuleto Estate keeps its own fire truck and team ready.

The first grapes were planted in 1993, and the multiple angles and exposures for the ninety acres of vineyards, and the range of elevations between 800 and 1,450 feet, lets Kuleto grow a variety of grapes, including Chardonnay, Sangiovese, Pinot Noir, Syrah, Zinfandel, and Cabernet Sauvignon.

ATMOSPHERE: It's a dazzling mix of mountain lodge, Italian villa, and those astounding views. Inside the winery, the rooms are over-sized, with heavy wood but lots of light from windows. Outside there are stone decks with comfortable wooden furniture, trellises, and flowers.

There's a larger-than-life feel to the entire winery, because of the setting, because of the way the buildings fit the landscape, and because of the sheer scale of the mountain.

SERVICE: This is not an inexpensive tour and tasting, and Kuleto steps up with plates of cheese, fruit, and bread to go with the wines, plus a thorough look at the grounds and the winery. They know it takes some effort getting there, and they reward visitors for that.

TASTING TOOLS: Good, large glasses, specific to the varietal. Water and spit buckets handy. Snacks served with the wine. Very good light.

INTANGIBLES AND EXTRAS: The atmosphere is both natural and luxurious, and the personalized tours are rare and unhurried, so visitors can sit on the deck and soak in the place. But the real specialty of the house is the view.

WINE AVAILABILITY: Many wines are available in shops or restaurants—particularly those associated with Pat Kuleto—but some are only at the winery or through the website. Prices range from $15 to $60.

PICNIC PROSPECTS: None.

COST: $25 for the tasting and tour.

DIRECTIONS: Go about six and a half miles east up Highway 128 from where it meets Silverado Trail, and look for a gate on the left.

RECOMMENDED FOR: Everyone with the time and money, but the drive up the road could be a bit harrowing.

Nichelini Winery

2950 Sage Canyon Road
St. Helena, 94574
707-963-0717 or 800-938-2783
www.nicheliniwinery.com
HOURS: 10–5 Saturday–Sunday; weekdays by appointment

This is the oldest winery in Napa continuously run by its original family. Anton Nichelini founded it in 1890 in these hills east of the main valley because the area reminded him of Switzerland, where he grew up. But it looks more like you've found the Old West when you turn the bend in the highway and see the century-old family house and the dark-wood winery.

The Nichelini family and their winery have survived phylloxera and Prohibition, and make a range of wines, including a slightly sweet Sauvignon Vert, and a Chiles Valley Red blend of Zinfandel and Petite Sirah, besides old reliables like Merlot, Cabernet Sauvignon, and an Old Vine Zinfandel from grapevines planted in 1929.

ATMOSPHERE: Tastings are done outside an old barrel room on a stone terrace against one masonry wall of the century-old winery. There's a small wooden tasting bar, usually with flowers on it, and you're surrounded by trees and, often, the winery cats. In mornings, there's dappled sunlight coming through the trees. In afternoons, the tasting bar is in shadows.

In bad weather, the tastings move inside the barrel room, but either way it adds up to a country casualness, and a feeling of being thrown back to the time when there were only a handful of wineries around Napa.

SERVICE: Can't get much more personal than this. Usually one of the family members is doing the pouring, and they'll take you through the Nichelini history and the lineup of wines. And as much as they know their back story, this is a family that's been making wine for more than a century, so they know their wines, too.

TASTING TOOLS: Good glasses. Water and spit buckets handy. No crackers. Good light.

INTANGIBLES AND EXTRAS: The history here is palpable and there's a simple, old-fashioned hospitality. The site, on a bluff over a creek, is covered with trees and is a peaceful

spot for a picnic, some bocce ball, or just being calm.

WINE AVAILABILITY: Some are found at markets and restaurants. The quirkier wines are only at the winery or on the website. Prices range from $12 to $30.

PICNIC PROSPECTS: Lots of tables are scattered around the wooded grounds. The best are in a grove of trees below the winery on a small bluff, and on the grass along the creek. A couple others are down a hill next to the shaded bocce ball court.

COST: Free.

DIRECTIONS: About nine miles east of Silverado Trail on Highway 128. Some parking is available in front and more is at turnouts a few yards down the road.

RECOMMENDED FOR: Everyone.

Pope Valley Winery

6613 Pope Valley Road
Pope Valley, 94567
707-965-1246
www.popevalleywinery.com
HOURS: 11–5 daily; appointments suggested on weekdays

The country winery was founded in 1897 by Swiss immigrant Ed Haus, who built the three-story, gravity-flow building over a tiny creek, and took nine years to hand-dig caves into the mountainside. The winery went quiet when the last heir died in 1959. Then in 1998, a group of longtime Pope Valley residents bought the small, charming estate and brought it back to life.

They still use the old winery and those caves, and produce about 4,000 cases a year of Chenin Blanc, Sangiovese, Zinfandel, Merlot, Cabernet Sauvignon, and a Blue Port.

ATMOSPHERE: The sunny little tasting room is a converted—and cleaned—chicken coop and tack room, and it mostly feels like you're tasting on their porch. Besides the usual wine-related items in the small room, they sell small craft items made by locals. The crafts double as decorations in the room.

The wooden bar is small and neat, and there are windows all around that look across a small meadow at the century-old farmhouse.

SERVICE: You can't say casual and unpretentious enough to describe the feel—you summon the winery folks by ringing the bell hanging from an old oak tree in front of the winery—but that doesn't mean they aren't serious about their wine. Bonnie Zimmermann, the winery manager and server, will tell you the details of the wine or the century's worth of eccentric history of the place, including the sad story of the founding family. (Haus, basically, married the wrong sister. Let Bonnie tell it.)

TASTING TOOLS: Small glasses. Spit buckets and water handy. No crackers. Good light.

INTANGIBLES AND EXTRAS: A walk around the grounds and through the old winery and blacksmith shop is a reminder of how hard people worked a century ago to carve out a life. For all the sweat—and apparent gloom—of the founders, there's a happy feel about the winery. It's a hospitable, country setting and an all-around friendly place in a beautiful little notch in the hills.

WINE AVAILABILITY: Most are sold at the winery or through the website. Prices range from $10 to $25.

PICNIC PROSPECTS: A handful of tables are out in front of the winery in a casual, rural setting. They encourage visitors to bring kids and dogs and stay a while.

COST: Free.

DIRECTIONS: About two miles north on Pope Valley Road from the "town" of Pope Valley. That's where Howell Mountain Road meets Chiles Pope Valley Road, and that road drops the "Chiles" from its name as it heads north.

RECOMMENDED FOR: Everyone.

RustRidge Ranch and Winery

2910 Lower Chiles Valley Road
St. Helena, 94574
707-965-9353
www.rustridge.com
HOURS: Daily by appointment

RustRidge Ranch and Winery started as a 400-acre thoroughbred horse ranch in the 1950s, but added the winery in the mid-1970s. It's also a bed-and-breakfast and a generally laid-back, Western-style escape where the dogs, horses, cats, and owners are very friendly.

Winemaker and owner Susan Meyer, and her husband (and horse trainer), Jim Fresquez, produce Sauvignon Blanc, Chardonnay, Zinfandel, and Cabernet Sauvignon.

ATMOSPHERE: To get to the winery, you go past the ranch house, the corrals, and the paddocks to a small barn set between some vineyards and a stand of trees. The tasting area is inside the working winery, between the barrel room and the storage tanks. The mellow winery dogs often lie next to tasters, and are proudly featured on the Sauvignon Blanc label.

SERVICE: Like every winery in the Chiles and Pope valleys, the service is personal and friendly. Don't let all the sociable animals and general amiableness fool you. They are proud of their wines here and will take you into as much detail as you want.

TASTING TOOLS: Good glasses. Spit bucket handy. No crackers. Water on request.

INTANGIBLES AND EXTRAS: Their blend of country casualness yet earnestness about the wines makes for a pleasant, approachable experience. The mountain meadow in this narrow stretch of Chiles Valley seems miles and years away from modern civilization. The bed-and-breakfast is decorated with a Southwestern flair, has four rooms, a pool, and, in the evenings, serves, of course, RustRidge wines.

WINE AVAILABILITY: They make only 4,000 cases but all the wines can be found outside the winery at markets and restaurants. The winery and website are the surest bet. Prices range from $18 to $30.

PICNIC PROSPECTS: There are a couple tables under trees and in a big grass field between the winery and some vineyards.

COST: $10 for five or six wines, waived with purchase.

DIRECTIONS: From Silverado Trail, follow Highway 128 east, past Chiles Pope Valley Road to Lower Chiles Valley Road (about ten miles east of Silverado Trail). Turn left and go north about three miles.

RECOMMENDED FOR: Everyone.

Beaulieu Vineyards

1960 St. Helena Highway
Rutherford, 94573
800-264-6198
www.bvwines.com
Hours: 10–5 daily

BV is one of the most venerable wineries in the valley and, even if just for the wines, it's one of the must-stop wineries in Napa. But its history is as significant as any winery in Napa for its impact on the valley and American wine. Beaulieu—which means beautiful place—was founded in 1900 by Frenchman Georges de Latour, who brought phylloxera-resistant rootstock that helped save what was left of Napa wineries at the time.

De Latour was producing world-class wines when most of Napa was making jug wine, and in 1938 he hired André Tchelistcheff, who overhauled BV's winemaking top to bottom, and, until his death in 1995, was the wise man of Napa, modernizing and changing winemaking and advising scores of winemakers and wineries. BV is one of the largest and most respected wineries in America, produces a vast range and style of wine, makes some outstanding blends like Tapestry, Dulcet, and Beauzeaux, and has one of America's most-collected wines in the Georges de Latour Private Reserve Cabernet Sauvignon.

ATMOSPHERE: The room is a tall octagon, with dark wood, soft spotlights, and a decent helping of windows. There are a handful of tasting bars around the outside and a winding stairwell down to the store in the middle, and the feeling is a bit like being in an enormous wine barrel.

BV also has an airy, quieter reserve room open to everyone, and that's where visitors can slow down and try some of Napa's most renowned wines.

SERVICE: Visitors get a free glass of Sauvignon Blanc when they enter, and the servers are as casual or classy—or both—as you like. Everyone here knows wine and BV's extraordinary history, and they'll tell you if you ask. Or, they'll just add new wines to your tasting lineup, even if you don't ask.

TASTING TOOLS: Good crystal glasses. Spit buckets, water, and crackers handy. OK light.

INTANGIBLES AND EXTRAS: There's an energy here that comes from being in one of Napa's special wineries, and from all the history on the walls. The tour is impressive, partly because of the winery's size and partly because its import sinks in.

Besides the walk-in reserve room, BV also offers a variety of other tastings by appointment, including vertical tastings of the Georges de Latour Cab. The vast store below the tasting room has books, art, and all the usual wine clothes and knick-knacks.

WINE AVAILABILITY: BV wines are everywhere. Prices for current releases range from $10 to $110.

PICNIC PROSPECTS: None.

COST: $5 for four wines and a handful of others the server might offer up; $25 for the reserve tasting.

DIRECTIONS: On the east side of Highway 29, just a few yards north of Rutherford Crossroad and the Rutherford Grill.

RECOMMENDED FOR: Everyone.

Cakebread Cellars

8300 St. Helena Highway
Rutherford, 94573
707-963-5222 or 800-588-0298
www.cakebread.com
HOURS: 10–4:30 daily by appointment

Jack Cakebread began growing grapes and making wine in 1973, while he still ran a string of auto-repair garages in Oakland. He eventually decided wine was more fun than grease and moved full-time to running this winery that sits right off the highway.

It has the look of a modern, redwood-barn-and-ranch complex, and has grown to a good-sized operation, producing more than 50,000 cases a year. But it still has a mom-and-pop feel about it, because the family is still involved, because many of the employees have been there for years, and because there's a kind of exuberance to tours and tastings.

They make a range of well-regarded wines, starting with their beloved Sauvignon Blanc. There's also Chardonnay, Pinot Noir, Merlot, Syrah, and Cabernet Sauvignon.

ATMOSPHERE: Tastings are done at various spots around the winery, though the main tasting bar is in the middle of a large working room with wooden barrels stacked five high. Some tastings are done in vineyards; others are sit-downs with food.

SERVICE: They are big here on explaining grape growing, winemaking, and wine tasting, and have a cheerful energy about the business. They push the notion of tours—the basic tour-and-tasting is $10, the same as a tasting—and advise you to plan thirty minutes minimum even if you're only going to taste so they can explain their wines.

TASTING TOOLS: Good large glasses. Spit buckets. Water and crackers, depending on where you taste. Generally good light.

INTANGIBLES AND EXTRAS: They are almost abnormally dedicated to teaching about the vineyards, food and wine, and the joy of wine. They also have tastings dedicated to food-wine parings and to sensory evaluation ($20 for either) by appointment.

WINE AVAILABILITY: Many of their wines are found in stores and restaurants. Prices range from $21 to $95.

PICNIC PROSPECTS: None.

COST: $10 to taste five wines; $20 for food-wine pairing or sensory evaluation tastings.

DIRECTIONS: On the east side of Highway 29 about three-quarters of a mile north of Oakville Crossroad and a mile south of Rutherford Crossroad.

RECOMMENDED FOR: Everyone, particularly for people looking to learn more about wine.

Caymus Vineyards

8700 Conn Creek Road
Rutherford, 94573
707-967-3010
www.caymus.com
HOURS: 10–4 daily; tastings by appointment and limited to groups of ten; you often need to make reservations a couple weeks out

This is the home of one of Napa's top wines, Caymus Special Selection Cabernet, which has made repeat appearances on Top Ten lists everywhere. Given the stature, the winery is surprisingly low-key with the look of a small ranch.

It was founded by Charlie Wagner, whose family has farmed here in

Rutherford since 1906. In 1972, Charlie, his wife, Lorna, and their son, Chuck, started Caymus Vineyards, named after the original Rancho Caymus Spanish land grant for the region. Over the years, after Chuck took over, they created Conundrum, a proprietary white blend that now has its own winery on the Central Coast. The Wagner family also makes Belle Glos Pinot Noir, bottled in Sonoma County under its own label. In Napa, they focus on Cabernet and grapes from their sixty-acre estate.

ATMOSPHERE: The tasting room has a hacienda air, with a heavy, worn-wood table, a brick floor, thick walls, and wood-framed windows. There are old maps and photos and even a Bear Flag from California's early days. Each visitor has a place set at the table.

SERVICE: This is a sit-down, small-group, guided tasting, so you get lots of information about each wine and about pretty much anything you want. For a relatively formal approach, the tone is generally relaxed and low-key. Their theory is to pamper visitors but make it casual.

TASTING TOOLS: Good, large glasses, one for each wine. Small spit buckets, water, and crackers handy. Good light.

INTANGIBLES AND EXTRAS: First, they do not pour Special Select in the tastings. Second, they're fairly rigid about starting on time because they don't want to interrupt the experience for the group (so be punctual). Third, it's free, and they do pour their "lower-tier," $70 Cab. The point of it all is to have intimate, low-key tastings that are about the wine. Tastings also include Sauvignon Blanc and Zinfandel that

are made in small amounts and served only in the tasting room.

WINE AVAILABILITY: The Napa Valley and Special Selection Cabernets are widely distributed. Prices are $70 and $135. The Sauvignon Blanc and Zinfandel are sold only at the winery (not on the website). Prices are $25 and $36, respectively.

PICNIC PROSPECTS: None.

COST: Free, just be on time.

DIRECTIONS: From Highway 29, take Rutherford Crossroad (also Highway 128) east. It makes a T after one and a half miles. To the left, it becomes Conn Creek Road and stays 128. To the right (south) is Skellenger Lane. Turn right and Caymus is a few yards down on the left. From Silverado Trail, turn west on Conn Creek/Highway 128 and go about one mile. Go straight past Rutherford Crossroad, which would be a sharp right. Caymus is a few yards down on the left.

RECOMMENDED FOR: Anyone who can plan a couple weeks ahead.

Conn Creek Winery and Villa Mt. Eden Winery

8711 Silverado Trail
St. Helena, 94574
707-968-2670 or 800-793-7960
www.conncreek.com or
  www.villamteden.com
HOURS: 10–4 daily

The stucco, Mediterranean-style winery was built in 1979 for Conn Creek (which started making wine in 1973). Sister winery Villa Mt. Eden moved into the building in 1994. It's been remodeled into a modern-but-amiable room right on the highway, and is in a terrific spot on the valley floor where you feel the vines around you and the mountains that ring Napa.

They both produce a range of good and surprisingly reasonably priced wines (by Napa standards) from Sauvignon Blanc and Chardonnay to Zinfandel, Merlot, Cab Franc, Syrah, and Cabernet Sauvignon. Their upper-end wine is one of the best-named Bordeaux blends in the valley, Conn Creek's Anthology. There's also a bright Orange Muscat.

ATMOSPHERE: The tasting room is simple and open, done in rose and earth tones that make you think of Rutherford dust. The bar is marble and wood. Light from big windows comes in behind tasters at the bar, and the room opens behind the bar into a larger store and barrel room area. Two friendly orange winery cats, Simon and Sebastian, wander through regularly. Sebastian's the one the size of a wine barrel.

SERVICE: They have a lot of wines to get through here and they aren't shy about it. Our server poured more than a dozen, then continued bringing out wines off the list. She knew her wines, but was less fixed on the small details than on making sure we enjoyed the tasting.

TASTING TOOLS: Good, large glasses. Spit buckets handy. Water on the counter in wine bottles. Chocolate coins for palate cleansing.

INTANGIBLES AND EXTRAS: It's a comfortable place and, without overdoing it, severs want the experience to be fun. They also pour a ton of wine.

WINE AVAILABILITY: Most wines are available in stores and restaurants. Prices range from $15 to $50.

PICNIC PROSPECTS: None.

COST: $10 for ten to twelve wines. Free coupon on website.

DIRECTIONS: On the west side of the Silverado Trail, across from where Highway 128 meets the trail from the east and just south of where Conn Creek Road/Highway 128 hits Silverado Trail from the west.

RECOMMENDED FOR: Everyone. Good spot for wine novices.

Alpha Omega Winery
1155 Mee Lane
St. Helena, 94574
707-963-9999
www.aowinery.com
HOURS: 10–6 daily

This pretty little winery a few yards off the highway, with a redwood deck overlooking a small pond and some vineyards, was first Quail Ridge, then Esquisse. In 2006, long-time growers and vintners Robin Baggett and Eric Sklar bought the winery and renamed it to reflect their blending of Old World experience and New World, hands-on winemaking.

Winemaker Jean Hoefliger is passionate about the attention to detail here, which ranges from a variety of barrel-fermentation techniques to hand sorting the grapes. They make Sauvignon Blanc, Chardonnay, Cabernet Sauvignon, and a Bordeaux-style red blend.

ATMOSPHERE: The simple room has clean lines, a tile floor, and big windows behind the tasting bar that look out at the deck, lawn, and a twenty-foot-high water fountain in the pond. A more expansive, wood-framed room with high ceilings, larger bar, and lots of glass is in the works.

SERVICE: Zippy and enthusiastic. Servers seem to be happy to be at this new winery with ambitions to make world-class wine, but they are as unstuffy as you can get.

TASTING TOOLS: Good glasses. Spit buckets, crackers, and water handy. Very good light.

INTANGIBLES AND EXTRAS: There's an excitement here of an eager, growing winery, and people are genuinely proud of what they're producing. The deck and fountain make this a pleasant spot to just sit a while and be calm. Hourly tours with tastings cost the same $10 as just a tasting.

WINE AVAILABILITY: Mostly just at the winery or on the website, but Alpha Omega wines are beginning to show up in restaurants and some wine shops. Prices range from $24 to $60.

PICNIC PROSPECTS: There are a handful of umbrella-covered tables on the deck and bigger picnic tables under a tent next to the pond. More tables are planned near the expanded tasting room. The deck could be hot on a summer day, but the setting is peaceful.

COST: $10 for four wines.

DIRECTIONS: On Mee Lane, just east of Highway 29 about one mile north of Rutherford Crossroad.

RECOMMENDED FOR: Everyone.

Franciscan Oakville Estate

1178 Galleron Road
St. Helena, 94574
707-967-3869 or 800-529-9463
www.franciscan.com
HOURS: 10–5 daily

Franciscan has a newly refurbished tasting room and a contemporary-looking winery with a round, stone fountain out front and comfortable gardens around it. This 240-acre estate in the heart of Oakville started in 1972, but it hit its stride in the mid-1980s when—finally—they started using mostly their own grapes from their vineyards alongside Opus One, Silver Oak, Mondavi, and Groth, among others. Since then, their reputation has remained steady for quality and innovation. They were the first in Napa to make a 100 percent wild yeast Chardonnay, which they call Cuvée Savage.

Now owned by Constellation Estates, Franciscan often is considered underpriced for its quality, and they love to quote wine critic Robert Parker, who once wrote, "One might wonder why Franciscan's Napa Valley Cabernet Sauvignon sells for a fraction of Opus One when their vineyards are only separated by a road." They make Chardonnay, Merlot, Zinfandel, Cabernet Sauvignon, and their respected Bordeaux blend, Magnificat.

ATMOSPHERE: The room has soaring ceilings and skylights, big windows on three sides, and a square, polished-wood bar in the middle built around a huge wooden pillar. In the back is a wall with a large stone fireplace and shelves, making it look a bit like a library. The room manages to be modern, airy, and cozy all at once.

SERVICE: They are as friendly and professional as at any winery in the valley. Often there's a greeter to open the door and welcome you. Because of its location, this can be a busy spot, but the bar is large and generally well-staffed. Even at those times, servers manage to give tastings a bit of a personal feel and often offer an extra pour or two.

TASTING TOOLS: Good, large glasses. Spit buckets, water, and crackers handy. Very good light.

INTANGIBLES AND EXTRAS: In a busy and sometimes intimidating stretch of high-end wineries, Franciscan is reliably comfortable and good-natured. They often serve tastes from sister wineries like Mt. Veeder Winery, Ravenswood, Estancia, Veramonte, and others.

They also offer a range of tasting experiences. There is a sensory evaluation tasting daily at noon in which they help you identify a wine's components ($25), wine-and-cheese pairings daily at 1 p.m. ($25), private tastings by appointment ($30), and an outstanding blending exercise that lets visitors play winemaker and blend their own version of Magnificat daily at 11 a.m. and 2 p.m. ($25). All require reservations, but if you're there, just ask about openings.

WINE AVAILABILITY: Franciscan is widely distributed. Prices range from $17 to $40.

PICNIC PROSPECTS: None.

COST: $10 for four or more current releases. $15 and $20 for reserve tastings of four or more top-end wines. A two-for-one tasting coupon is available on the website.

DIRECTIONS: Franciscan is on the east side of Highway 29 at Galleron, which connects to the east side of the highway about a mile north of Rutherford Crossroad.

RECOMMENDED FOR: Everyone. Good place for wine novices.

Frog's Leap Winery

8815 Conn Creek Road
Rutherford, 94573
707-963-4704 or 800-959-4704
www.frogsleap.com
HOURS: 10–4 daily by appointment only; tours are generally at 10:30 a.m., 12:30 p.m., and 2:30 p.m., but it can change so call ahead

How do you not love these people? Their motto is "Time's fun when you're having flies." Their corks have "ribbit" printed on them. A warning on their bottles says "open other end." Frog's Leap is a top contender for best Napa combination of great wine and great sense of humor.

John Williams started the winery in 1982 at a site on Mill Creek in St. Helena known as the Frog Farm, and old ledgers showed the place sold frogs at the turn of the twentieth century for 33 cents a dozen. The frog theme has only grown since then.

Frog's Leap moved in 1994 to this Rutherford site that once was the Adamson Winery back in 1874. They set about renovating the original winery—they call it the Red Barn—and it's the oldest board-and-batten building in the area. They took it apart entirely, constructed an interior metal frame, then rebuilt it exactly as it was using eighty-five percent of the original wood. The Barn is now the heart of the winery that makes a pink Gamay called La Grenouille Rouganté, which translates to "The Blushing Frog," Sauvignon Blanc, Chardonnay, Zinfandel, Merlot, Syrah, Cabernet Franc, Cabernet Sauvignon, and Leapfrögmilch, a Chardonnay and Riesling blend.

ATMOSPHERE: There's an easy hospitality when you drive up and see signs that direct "visitors" to the right and "frogs" over left. Tastings and tours start at a big table in the middle of a courtyard garden (or in the barn in bad weather), and finish on an upper floor of the Red Barn looking out across the property and the flat of Rutherford. Along the way, you'll probably meet Terra, their orange cat and a star of their website.

SERVICE: They are as serious about wine as they are lighthearted about life. The tastings/tours have a good-humored, happy air, but they'll also tell you about their organic farming, solar power, and intensity when it comes to wine. Then they'll show you their frog farm.

TASTING TOOLS: Good large glasses. Spit buckets handy. Water on request. No crackers. Good light.

INTANGIBLES AND EXTRAS: This simply is a fun place to tour and taste. The feeling of playfulness is everywhere, the winery and facilities are interesting with a strong sense of history, the location is beautiful, and the wine rocks. Nice combination. Plus it's free. They also have the most entertaining winery website in Napa.

WINE AVAILABILITY: Frog's Leap is a popular, midsized winery with good distribution, but a handful of limited-release wines are best found through the winery or website. Prices range from $12 to $65.

PICNIC PROSPECTS: None.

COST: Free.

DIRECTIONS: From Highway 29, take Rutherford Crossroad (also Highway 128) east. It makes a T after one and a half miles. To the left, it becomes Conn Creek Road and stays 128. Frog's Leap is about a quarter mile east/north of the T on the left. From Silverado Trail, take Conn Creek/Highway 128 west/south, it's about one mile on the right. Look for a green mailbox on the road, and up the driveway, a big red barn with white trim and a leaping frog weather vane. There are no signs on the road. Park and go around the barn to the right to the visitor's center.

RECOMMENDED FOR: Everyone.

Grgich Hills Cellars
1829 St. Helena Highway
Rutherford, 94573
707-963-2784 or 800-532-3057
www.grgich.com
HOURS: 9:30–4:30 daily

Winemaker and co-founder Miljenko "Mike" Grgich is royalty in Napa. Besides his stints training at Beaulieu Vineyards with André Tchelistcheff and at Robert Mondavi Winery, it was a Chardonnay made by Grgich for Chateau Montelena that won as best white wine at the legendary 1976 Paris Tasting. In 1977, he partnered with Austin Hills, of the Hills Brothers Coffee family—there are no hills at Grgich Hills—to open this winery along a row of old trees in Rutherford. Over the years, Grgich's daughter, Violet, and his nephew, Ivo Jeramaz, joined the winery team.

Grgich is a native of Croatia, which explains the Croatian flag flying alongside an American flag at the winery and the Croatian coat of arms on a corner of the label. (The horse in the other corner is the Hills's family crest.) He got his first enology training at the University of Zagreb, and brought an Old World style to his winemaking. He also has a worldwide reputation. His Chardonnay has been served to two U.S. presidents, Queen Elizabeth II, King Juan Carlos of Spain, and French President François Mitterrand. But the Grgich Hills theme is that they treat all their wines like equal children. Besides the Chardonnay, they make Fumé Blanc, Merlot, Zinfandel, Cabernet Sauvignon, and Violetta, a late-harvest blend of Chardonnay and Riesling that Mike named after his daughter.

ATMOSPHERE: The winery looks unpretentious and the only real clue this is an important stop is the large parking lot. The tasting room is decidedly casual and almost rustic, with stacks of barrels on one side, wood beams, a low ceiling, and concrete floors. The big, L-shaped tasting bar is lit by bright recessed spots. It's an unfussy room and the sense is they care more about the wine than a show.

SERVICE: Many of the servers here are veterans, so, besides knowing the wine and the valley, they have a feeling of winery family about them. The bar is well staffed, and even if it's busy, there generally are enough people to make the experience feel personal.

TASTING TOOLS: OK glasses. Spit buckets, water, and crackers handy. Good light.

INTANGIBLES AND EXTRAS: Barrel tasting from 2 to 4 p.m. every Friday (the price is included in the regular $10 tasting fee). Tours ($15) at 11 a.m. and 2 p.m. on weekdays; 11 a.m. and 1:30 p.m. on weekends. Reservations are needed.

This is a comfortable place to taste, and it mixes the sense of a world-class winery with a friendly, approachable room.

WINE AVAILABILITY: Grgich Hills wines are widely distributed. Prices range from $24 to $55.

PICNIC PROSPECTS: None.

COST: $10 for six wines.

DIRECTIONS: On the west side of Highway 29 about a half mile north of Rutherford Crossroad and one mile south of Whitehall Lane.

RECOMMENDED FOR: Everyone. Comfortable spot for wine novices.

Honig Vineyard & Winery

850 Rutherford Road
Rutherford, 94573
707-963-5618 or 800-929-2217
www.honigwine.com
HOURS: 10–4 daily by appointment; they're flexible

This is another classic family winery. The Honig family bought these sixty-eight acres in the heart of Rutherford in 1968; Louis Honig kept it mostly as a farm, vineyards, and a country gathering spot for the family. He sold grapes and thought about eventually starting a winery, but died before that happened. In 1981, in his honor, his family produced the first 2,000 cases of Louis Honig Sauvignon Blanc in a tractor shed and started Honig Winery.

In 1984, grandson Michael, then twenty-two, took over managing the then-little winery, and as it's grown over the years, kept adding family members to the team. They've been an under-the-radar producer for years, but have always made wines that are well-regarded in the trade. They decided in 2005 to open a public tasting room to raise their profile.

Because Honig means honey in German, they've taken up bee-keeping as a winery hobby, which also explains the bee in the logo's H. (By the way, the hives are down by the river, far from the winery.) As for their main pursuit, Honig specializes in Sauvignon Blanc and Cabernet Sauvignon and also makes a Late Harvest Sauvignon Blanc.

ATMOSPHERE: The tasting room is just off a neat patio under trees and feels more like a sleek but comfortable dining room. It has polished, medium wood, black trim, and big windows looking out to the flat vineyards. Small, framed pictures of family and staff members add to that family feel, and tastings are done at a big, polished wood table.

SERVICE: They chose to use a table rather than bar to make the tastings personal. They go slow and let you wander out to the patio.

TASTING TOOLS: Good, big glasses. Spit buckets, water, and crackers handy.

INTANGIBLES AND EXTRAS: There's a good mix here of getting pampered a bit, yet feeling like you're meeting the family. This is an excellent, low-key winery that a lot of visitors miss, and its spot in the middle of Rutherford, off the main highways, is both beautiful and serene.

WINE AVAILABILITY: Honig wines can be found in many stores and restaurants, and at the winery or website. Prices range from $15 to $65.

PICNIC PROSPECTS: None, but they'll let you hang around the patio as long as you'd like.

COST: $10 for tasting five wines; $20 for tour and tasting.

DIRECTIONS: The long driveway is on the north side of Rutherford Crossroad about a mile east of Highway 29. There are no ornate gates. Just look for the Honig sign or flag.

RECOMMENDED FOR: Everyone.

Mumm Napa Valley
8445 Silverado Trail
Rutherford, 94573
707-967-7700 or 800-868-6272
www.mummcuveenapa.com
HOURS: 10–5 daily

Tasting at the sparkling wine houses of Napa is always special, and a Mumm motto says it exactly: purely elegant, purely festive. That's what

you're supposed to think about with sparkling wine—a little luxury, a little celebration—and that's what you get at Mumm sitting on the pretty terrace or in the open tasting room, looking across the vineyards of Rutherford and across the valley to the Mayacamas.

French Champagne house G. H. Mumm decided in 1979 to find a premium spot for an American operation, but it wasn't until 1986 that they completed this facility that looks like a ranch and barn. Mumm makes an impressive collection of sparkling wines, as well as some still wines like Chardonnay, Pinot Noir, and Pinot Gris.

ATMOSPHERE: Visitors find a table on the umbrella-covered terrace— or in the glass-walled tasting room in bad weather—and servers come by with a range of tasting options that include a single flute, a bottle to share, or a sampler flight of wines. The setting is both relaxing and plush, combining a sense of luxury with the kick-back feel of being outdoors, in among vineyards, and in a spectacularly picturesque spot.

SERVICE: Servers are polite and good-natured. They understand visitors are here to enjoy the setting along with tasting the wine, and they will let you just sit. But they have a different story to tell than at most wineries, and will explain the details of sparklings if you ask.

TASTING TOOLS: Good, small flutes. Spit buckets on request. Water and crackers at tables. Very good light.

INTANGIBLES AND EXTRAS: They have a striking art gallery that includes rotating displays and a permanent exhibit of Ansel Adams photographs that is worth taking some time to see. Mumm also offers free winery tours on the hour from

10 a.m. to 3 p.m. daily that include video presentations and a look at how sparkling wines are made. They can schedule private tours and tastings for large groups. Their high-end store has a range of art and gifts as well as the usual wine country souvenirs.

This is a place to both explore and to just sit and enjoy. Mumm, assuming everyone is driving somewhere, restricts visitors to a maximum of two full flutes of wine.

WINE AVAILABILITY: Most Mumm sparkling wines are available in stores and restaurants. The still wines are sold only through the winery or website. Prices range from $19 to $55.

PICNIC PROSPECTS: None, but you have the deck for tasting.

COST: Tasting flights are from $8.50 to $20; wines by the glass range from $5 to $15. Discount coupon on website.

DIRECTIONS: On the west side of Silverado Trail about three-quarters of a mile south of Highway 128 and a bit more than two miles north of Oakville Crossroad.

RECOMMENDED FOR: Everyone. Good spot for wine novices.

Peju Province

8466 St. Helena Highway
Rutherford, 94573
707-963-3600 or 800-446-7358
www.peju.com
HOURS: 10–6 daily

Peju is one of Napa's more distinct-looking wineries, with a bit of a wonderland touch to everything, including the flowers, fountains, and sculpture garden out front. The feature you notice first is a pointed, fifty-foot tower with a weathered, green-copper roof that has a jaunty, almost fairy-tale look to it.

Owner Tony Peju, who grew up in Aix-en-Provence, France, and his wife, Herta, started the winery in 1982 and they wanted it to have a French Provincial style to it. But they also gave it a sense of whimsy. They make some well-respected wines and their long list has a few quirky tones, too, including a Late Harvest Barrel Aged Chardonnay called Liana and a blend named Provence that mixes Merlot, Cab Franc, and Syrah with French Colombard and Sauvignon Blanc. They also offer more straight-up Sauvignon Blanc, Chardonnay, Syrah, Merlot, Cabernet Franc, Zinfandel, and Cabernet Sauvignon.

ATMOSPHERE: The tasting room, a mix of wood and stone, is inside the tower, and you feel all its height. One wall is mostly a stained-glass window with a scene of three wine muses, and the room has two tasting bars and a stairway along one wall to the top of the tower that gives a view across the valley floor. When it's busy, visitors wait to taste in groups so the servers can present and explain the wines, rather than just pour them.

SERVICE: This depends on who you get as a server/presenter, and trust us here when we say there can be a big swing. All the tastings are done as a bit of a show, and all the servers have some musical training, but the wildest show comes from Alan Arnople, who is called the Yodel Meister. His presentation includes rhyme, rap, song, and, of course, a bit of yodeling.

TASTING TOOLS: Good glasses. Spit buckets and water handy. No crackers. Good light.

INTANGIBLES AND EXTRAS: It's good fun but not entirely about the wine. This is an original, entertaining place to visit and will be memorable for less-serious tasters. It may be a little too frivolous for some earnest aficionados.

They also sell a good collection of cookbooks, sauces, vinegars, and oils.

WINE AVAILABILITY: Most wines are sold only at the winery or through the website. Prices range from $14 to $125.

PICNIC PROSPECTS: None.

COST: $7 for five wines and the floor show.

DIRECTIONS: On the east side of Highway 29 a bit less than a half mile south of Rutherford Crossroad.

RECOMMENDED FOR: Anyone who wants a fanciful, less-serious tasting.

Piña Cellars
8060 Silverado Trail
Napa, 94558
707-738-9328
www.pinanapavalley.com
HOURS: 10–4 daily; it's mostly appointment only, but if you knock and they're there, they'll be happy to let you taste

The Piña brothers—Dave, Ranndy, Larry, and John—are from a family that's been in Napa for generations and they're respected vineyard managers. In 1996, partly because they were disappointed with the wine being made from six acres they own on Howell Mountain, they started their own winery using those grapes and fruit from the thirty acres they own in Rutherford.

Their little winery on Silverado Trail with the old tractor in front—a relic of earlier days—just produces a Cabernet Sauvignon, but it's a roaring good Cabernet Sauvignon.

ATMOSPHERE: What atmosphere? The tasting room is a table on some cleared space in the working barrel room. The floor is concrete and barrels are stacked three layers high, and it feels like you're either friends invited for a tasting or that you work there. Both seem good.

SERVICE: You're likely to get served by winemakers Ted Osborne or Chuck Custodio, unless one of the brothers is roaming around. It's all extremely casual, and they'll pour whatever is open, including barrel wines from a plastic pitcher.

TASTING TOOLS: Good, large glasses and a spit bucket. No crackers or water.

INTANGIBLES AND EXTRAS: This is a place where you feel like part of the operation. It's a bit of a look inside the everyday life of a small winery. Also, Chuck's exuberant dog, Sadie, is likely to be running around, which makes it all the more friendly, but don't put your wineglass on the ground.

WINE AVAILABILITY: Piña is a small producer and most of the well-regarded wine is sold from the winery or website. Some restaurants and wine shops carry them. Prices range from $48 to $72.

PICNIC PROSPECTS: None.

COST: Free.

DIRECTIONS: On the east side of Silverado Trail just past Skellenger Lane. About one and a half miles north of Oakville Crossroad and two miles south of Highway 128.

RECOMMENDED FOR: Anyone who wants a look at a good, small winery without the trimmings.

Provenance Vineyards

1695 St. Helena Highway
Rutherford, 94573
707-968-3633
www.provenancevineyards.com
HOURS: 10–4 daily

Provenance's renowned winemaker, Tom Rinaldi, made the first vintage here in 1999 and created an instant reputation for rich, elegant Cabernets and Merlots. They also make a handful of single-vineyard reds, plus a complex Sauvignon Blanc.

The big, red, barn-looking winery was once Chateau Beaucanon, and Provenance opened a tasting room inside in 2003 with a floor made from the heads of the 900 oak barrels that produced that first 1999 Cab.

ATMOSPHERE: The outside is deceptively plain. Inside, the room is contemporary and playful. There are, for instance, bicycling jerseys for sale that say "Eat my (Rutherford) dust." The high-quality spotlights and recessed lighting give it a comfortable, modern, gallery feel. Behind the U-shaped, blond-wood-topped bar is a glass wall looking into a large barrel room.

SERVICE: Friendly and smart. You can feel an intense enthusiasm for the wines here, and if you ask, they'll go into good explanations about Rutherford soils and grapes. You can ask any wine question here—sophisticated or simple—and get a solid answer.

TASTING TOOLS: Good, large glasses. Spit buckets, water, and crackers handy. Very good light.

INTANGIBLES AND EXTRAS: It starts with the wine. Provenance has some major-league reds for tasting. And there's the challenge of reading the old cooper's marks stamped into the oak staves on the floor. (Recommendation: Put the wineglass down before bending over to read the floor.) But most of all, this is a place for wine people of all experience levels.

WINE AVAILABILITY: Although production is not huge, most can be found in shops and restaurants. Some top-end single-vineyard wines are only at the winery or website. Prices range from $19 to $75.

PICNIC PROSPECTS: None.

COST: $10 for five wines; $15 for six (three single vineyards).

DIRECTIONS: On the west side of Highway 29 about one mile north of Rutherford Crossroad.

RECOMMENDED FOR: Everyone.

Quintessa

1601 Silverado Trail
St. Helena, 94574
707-967-1601
www.quintessa.com
HOURS: Tastings and tours 10:30 a.m., 12:30 p.m. and 2:30 p.m. daily by appointment

Quintessa's sleek winery is both old school and high tech. It opened in 2002 and is built into a hillside, and works to blend with the landscape and to use eco-sensitive techniques. The gravity-flow winery is under the loading docks, so the grapes are loaded into chutes on the roof.

Owners Augustin and Valeria Huneeus are the former owners of Franciscan Estates, and they make one wine—one high-end wine—in the style of the great French châteaux: a Cabernet Sauvignon blend labeled Napa Valley Red Wine. A second label, still unnamed, is planned.

ATMOSPHERE: The winery is modern and sleek, and its front is a wide, sweeping stone wall with twenty-five-foot-tall glass doors. The small, contemporary tasting room mixes the feel of richness and of being deep inside a winery. Tasters sit at round tables made from wine barrels. The sleek wood, black metal posts, stone walls, and mix of light from overhead spots and from skylights along the edges make the room elegant but still comfortable.

SERVICE: Very polite and very knowledgeable. The detailed tour blends a sense of the land with the details of the winery. They served two wines, a current and a soon-to-be-released Quintessa, then left us to taste. Servers here seem to be aware this is an expensive tasting of an expensive wine and do not rush any part of it.

TASTING TOOLS: Good, large crystal glasses. Water, crackers, and spit buckets handy. OK light.

INTANGIBLES AND EXTRAS: Quintessa seems to understand the price of the wine, or just of the tasting, demands special treatment, and they try to deliver. The winery itself is a wonder and the view from the top of the hill behind the building is another reminder of the beauty of Napa.

WINE AVAILABILITY: Quintessa can be found in many restaurants and wine shops. Price is $110.

PICNIC PROSPECTS: None.

COST: $25 for tour and tasting of two vintages.

DIRECTIONS: On the west side of Silverado Trail, a half mile north of the intersection of Silverado and Highway 128.

RECOMMENDED FOR: People looking for the high-end experience.

Raymond Vineyard and Cellar

849 Zinfandel Lane
St. Helena, 94574
707-963-3141 or 800-525-2659
www.raymondwine.com
HOURS: 10–4 daily

The Raymonds have five generations of winemaking in Napa going back through the Beringers, one of the founding families in the valley. Roy Raymond Sr. came to Napa in 1933 as a cellar worker at Beringer, then married Martha Jane Beringer, a granddaughter of the founders, in 1936. With their sons, Roy Jr. and Walter, the Raymonds started their own winery in 1971.

The long, low visitor's center and tasting room are in what looks a bit like a modest office park, with low, stone walls and flowers, and it speaks to their straightforward, unadorned approach to winemaking. They produce a range of wines, including Sauvignon Blanc, Chardonnay, Merlot, a handful of Cabernets, and a late-harvest Chardonnay.

ATMOSPHERE: Inside, the tasting room is simple and comfortable. The medium-sized, wooden bar faces a line of windows looking across vineyards to the Mayacamas. The unpretentious feel of the building seems to spread to tasters and servers, and, even when it's crowded, there's a nice collegiality among everyone in the room.

SERVICE: They walk a line between experienced experts and low-key servers who want tasters to have fun. They're good at reading visitors, and know when to talk shop and when to explain that all Chardonnay is white.

TASTING TOOLS: Good, large glasses. Spit buckets, crackers, and water handy. Good light.

INTANGIBLES AND EXTRAS: It undersells Raymond to say they have a no-frills approach, but this is a straight-up place with good wines, and they make it easy to appreciate them.

They offer a range of tastings, depending on the day, from flights of current releases to reds to limited-production wines. Free tours at 11 a.m. daily by appointment. Private group tours and tastings available for $15 a person.

WINE AVAILABILITY: Most are available in stores and restaurants, but some reserve wines are found only at the winery or on the website. Prices range from $12.50 to $70.

PICNIC PROSPECTS: None.

COST: $7.50 or $15 for four wines, depending on the flight; a two-for-one coupon is available on the website.

DIRECTIONS: On Zinfandel Lane a bit more than a half mile east of Highway 29 and about three-quarters of a mile west of Silverado Trail.

RECOMMENDED FOR: Everyone.

Rubicon Estate

1991 St. Helena Highway
Rutherford, 94573
707-968-1100 or 800-782-4266
www.rubiconestate.com or
   www.niebaum-coppola.com
HOURS: 10–5 daily

Rubicon Estate changed its name from Niebaum-Coppola in 2006. It's one of the three or four most-visited wineries in Napa, and one of the cornerstones of the valley. It started in 1879 as Inglenook by the Finnish sea captain Gustave Niebaum. His grandnephew, John Daniel Jr., took over in 1937 and turned it into one of Napa's two post-Prohibition high-class wineries—along with

Beaulieu Vineyards. Inglenook's 1941 Cabernet Sauvignon is still cited as one of the best wines ever from Napa.

The Inglenook name was sold twice in the 1960s, and Heublein Inc. turned it into jug wine. In 1975, film director Francis Ford Coppola bought the old Niebaum Victorian home and 110 acres of the estate's vineyards and renamed it Niebaum-Coppola. He bought the historic winery and the rest of the estate in 1995. In 2006, after buying Chateau Souverain in Sonoma and renaming it Francis Coppola Estate, he changed the name here to avoid confusion and called it Rubicon after his signature wine.

The grounds are elaborate and manicured, with fountains, trees, and turn-of-the-century lampposts. The stately old winery is ivy covered and looks like a set from a Coppola movie about wineries. Rubicon produces an array of wines—some of them from Napa's premium vineyards—and the tasting room features estate wines that include Sauvignon Blanc, Chardonnay, Zinfandel, Merlot, and Cabernet Sauvignon. They also make a white blend called Blancaneaux, their flagship red named Rubicon, and Sofia Blanc de Blanc, a sparkling wine named after Francis' daughter and film director, Sofia Coppola.

ATMOSPHERE: Inside the majestic winery, the blend is part Napa wine country, part upscale Hollywood park, and that's enhanced by the valet parking and the $25 entrance (rather than "tasting") fee. The interior is ornate and refurbished, with a grand staircase leading to a second-floor museum for Coppola's movies and for Niebaum's winery. On the ground floor are a series of cellars with old wines going back to the nineteenth century.

The two large tasting rooms have high ceilings, ornamental fixtures, and a Disneyland-store feel, but with much better merchandise, ranging from crystal and ceramics to clothes and gourmet food. The big tasting bars get busy, but they're built for volume and it takes a lot to make this place feel too crowded.

SERVICE: This is an expensive tasting so servers try to give visitors a feel of personalized, unhurried attention. The servers are officially called wine guides and they know their wine and the history of the winery and the Rubicon line, and they take their time with you even when there are crowds.

TASTING TOOLS: Good, large glasses. Spit buckets and water handy. Fresh-baked bread.

INTANGIBLES AND EXTRAS: A visit here is an experience—this is the only winery in Napa with valet parking—and it's as much about the place as the wine. There is a lot to see, and do not miss the old cellars. Looking at a room with shelves of that 1941 Cab—each worth thousands of dollars at auction—is momentous in itself. It all has a pleasant sense of entertainment to it, too.

The tasting room also offers olive oil samples.

The legacy tour that looks at the history of the winery is included in the entrance fee and is offered 10:30 a.m. to 2:30 p.m. on a walk-in basis. There is also a vineyard tour ($15) daily at 11 a.m., also on a walk-in basis; a winemaking and barrel-tasting tour ($35) daily at 1 p.m., reservations required; a sensory evaluation experience ($25) daily at 10 a.m., reservations required; and a two-

hour, combination tour ($45) that finishes with a glass of their top-of-the-line Rubicon. It's offered Thursday to Sunday at 1 p.m., reservations required.

The winery also has a snug wine shop where you can buy wines by the glass and snacks, then sit on a tree-covered patio in front of the winery.

WINE AVAILABILITY: Many wines are well distributed, but some reserves are available only at the winery or through the website. Prices range from $19 to $110.

PICNIC PROSPECTS: None.

COST: $25 for entrance, legacy tour, valet parking, and tasting five wines.

DIRECTIONS: On the west side of Highway 29 just south of Rutherford Crossroad. If you're traveling north on Highway 29, don't turn left on Niebaum Lane. The winery entrance is the next left.

RECOMMENDED FOR: People looking for an upscale tasting a little on the showy side.

Rutherford Grove Winery

1673 St. Helena Highway
Rutherford, 94573
707-933-0544
www.rutherfordgrove.com
HOURS: 10–4:30 daily

One of three "Rutherford"-named wineries, this is the one on the flat-lands, and for some reason, it's often less busy than some other nearby wineries despite being right off Highway 29, and despite the comfortable, ivy-covered building surrounded by flowers, a large lawn, and a grove of eucalyptus and olive trees—not to mention the solid wines.

Rutherford Grove was started in 1993 by the Pestoni family, which has been in Napa for five generations. They make Sauvignon Blanc, Merlot, Cabernet Sauvignon, and outstanding Petite Sirah and Sangiovese.

ATMOSPHERE: The room has dark wood, vaulted ceilings with high spotlights, concrete floors, and a sense of cool peacefulness. Big, comfortable wicker chairs are set in one corner around a large fireplace, and there's often low-key jazz playing just loud enough to be relaxing.

Behind the redwood tasting bar, two-story-high glass doors open into a long barrel room. It's an easy place to take your time tasting.

SERVICE: Servers are people who've been in Napa a while, and they know their winery, their wine, and their Napa lore and gossip. There's an obligatory push or two on the wine club, but mostly they're about getting you to know their wines.

TASTING TOOLS: Small glasses. Spit buckets handy. No water or crackers. Good light.

INTANGIBLES AND EXTRAS: They rotate a range of art displays in the cases around the room, and for something a bit different, they press grape seeds for their Napa Valley Grapeseed Oil Co., which offers products like cooking oil and lavender and citrus body oils.

WINE AVAILABILITY: Some are found in restaurants and wine shops, but the only reliable bets are the winery or the website. Prices range from $14 to $40.

PICNIC PROSPECTS: Lots of tables around a big lawn and under olive and eucalyptus trees. The open, park-like setting is a good way off the highway and has been used for the Napa Valley Shakespeare Festival.

COST: $10 for five wines.

DIRECTIONS: On the west side of Highway 29, a bit more than a mile north of Rutherford Crossroad, across from Galleron Road, which intersects Highway 29 from the east.

RECOMMENDED FOR: Everyone.

Rutherford Hill Winery

200 Rutherford Hill Road
Rutherford, 94573
707-963-7194 or 800-726-5226
www.rutherfordhill.com
HOURS: 10–5 daily

The enormous, heavy wood building was constructed by Joseph Phelps in the 1960s, before he became a vintner and built his own winery. Phelps's love of dramatic, big-timber construction is clear. The massive winery is almost frightening in its scale, as if a giant, or maybe a giant's dog, lives here.

This is a popular place for visitors because of the architecture, the picnic grounds, and the cave system that runs through the mountainside for nearly a mile. Rutherford Hill, bought in 1996 by Anthony Terleto and his sons, Bill and John, has long focused on producing high-level Merlot and the Terletos have kept the tradition healthy. They make an extensive list of other wines, too, that includes, of course, a Rosé of Merlot, plus Sauvignon Blanc, Chardonnay, Sangiovese, Malbec, Syrah, Petite Verdot, and Cabernet Sauvignon.

ATMOSPHERE: The size of the tasting room is a disappointment considering the size of the building. Standing in front of the winery, you're looking up at a fifty-foot front wall and a twenty-foot-tall wood door. But inside, the room is relatively little, with two small bars and much of its floor space taken up with souvenir and wine displays. If you're expecting a fifty-foot-high ceiling, it comes up low by almost forty feet.

On a slow day, the room feels cheerful and almost intimate, with wooden bars and lots of windows behind you. On busy days, because they also sell tour tickets here, it can seem like a crowded bus station.

SERVICE: This is a noble crew. They keep up their energy and friendliness even during the busiest times. When the pace is slower, they have such a varied wine list, they're an interesting bunch.

TASTING TOOLS: OK glasses. Spit buckets handy. No water or crackers. Good light.

INTANGIBLES AND EXTRAS: Daily tours ($5) at 11:30 a.m., 1:30 p.m., and 3:30 p.m. take thirty people and fill quickly during high season and on weekends. Buy tickets in the tasting room.

Because this is an unusual facility and a relatively inexpensive visit, it can get jammed. It's a fun place to see, but not when it's busy.

WINE AVAILABILITY: Rutherford Hill wines are widely distributed, but they have a few reserves mostly available through the winery or website. Prices range from $15 to $92.

PICNIC PROSPECTS: There are picnic tables up and down the hillside under 100-year-old olive trees, and even at busy times there's usually some space. Most people go to the tables below the parking lot, which are in the trees. The tables above the parking lot and the winery, however, offer killer views of the valley.

COST: $10 for five current release wines; tour and standard tasting is $15.

DIRECTIONS: Rutherford Hill Road is on the east side of Silverado Trail, less than a quarter mile north of Highway 128. Go up the hill about a half mile, past Auberge du Soleil, to the end of the road.

RECOMMENDED FOR: Everyone—during slow times. You're taking your chances on a busy summer afternoon or weekend.

Rutherford Ranch
1680 Silverado Trail
St. Helena, 94574
707-963-3200 or 800-778-0424
www.roundhillwines.com
HOURS: 10–4:30 daily

When the winery started in 1977, owners Ernie and Virginia Van Asperen named it Roundhill after the place they honeymooned in Jamaica Hill. In 2000, they retired and sold the winery to Marco and Theo Zaninovich, who then renamed it Rutherford Ranch. The Zaninoviches are slowly removing the name Roundhill, but it will probably stay on area maps for years.

Rutherford Ranch advertises that it makes high-quality Napa wines just like its neighbors, but it won't charge over $20. Hard not to like these people. They make solid Sauvignon Blanc, Chardonnay, Merlot, Zinfandel, Cabernet Sauvignon, and, in some years, a reserve Cabernet.

ATMOSPHERE: The little tasting room is across a small, stone-filled creek from a ranch house, and is small and pleasant, with a dark-wood tasting bar under a handful of warm spots.

SERVICE: They were thrilled to see us. Our server had loads of gruff charm, poured big, and talked up the wines without getting pushy. He was a guy who liked being there, which made us like being there.

TASTING TOOLS: Good, large glasses. Spit buckets and water handy. No crackers. Good light.

INTANGIBLES AND EXTRAS: In a stretch where most of the wineries get very busy on weekends, Rutherford Ranch is often surprisingly quiet. That doesn't mean they are any less hospitable. Rutherford Ranch also sells their wines with custom labels on the bottles for places like the Monterey Bay Aquarium, Neiman Marcus, the Hotel del Coronado in San Diego, and the Royal Waikoloan in Hawaii.

WINE AVAILABILITY: All wines are available at markets and restaurants. Prices range from $8 to $16.

PICNIC PROSPECTS: None.

COST: $5 for five wines.

DIRECTIONS: On the east side of Silverado Trail just across from where Conn Creek Road/Highway 128 hits the trail from the west.

RECOMMENDED FOR: Everyone.

St. Supéry Vineyards and Winery

8440 St. Helena Highway
Rutherford, 94573
707-963-4507 or 800-942-0809
www.stsupery.com
HOURS: 10–5:30 daily May–September; 10–5 daily October–April

This is an outstanding winery to get a sense of both Napa's history and its wine. They have a demonstration vineyard out front, a strong guided tour, and one of the valley's best self-guided walks through production facilities, sensory-testing stations, and an art gallery.

In front of the winery, the large, white Victorian was built in 1882 by two of Napa's first winemakers, brothers Joseph and Louis Atkinson. It's surrounded by gardens and lawn, and fronted by a magnolia tree planted a year after the house was built and an oak a century older than that. Frenchman Edward St. Supéry took over at the turn of the twentieth century and left his name on the winery.

The property was revived in 1986 when Robert Skalli, a third-generation French winemaker, bought it. St. Supéry makes a large line of respected wines, including a well-honored Sauvignon Blanc. They also make Chardonnay (aged with and without oak), Cabernet Franc, Merlot, Syrah, Cabernet Sauvignon, Muscato, plus Élu, their red Bordeaux blend, and Virtú, a white blend of Sauvignon Blanc and Sémillon.

ATMOSPHERE: The winery building itself looks like a business complex from the outside, but inside, it's bright, modern, and energetic. A guide in the foyer will point out the walking tour up the staircase or the tasting room to the side. The large tasting room is done in tile and polished wood, and it's sleekly lit with recessed lighting and a wall of windows. The feel is breezy and contemporary.

SERVICE: There's a sense of casual professionalism, and the staff will linger and talk wine, or leave you alone if you prefer, which makes this a comfortable place for beginners. St. Supéry is another winery that gets busy on weekends and summer afternoons, and though the room is well-staffed, servers can get overwhelmed at times.

TASTING TOOLS: Good glasses. Spit buckets, water, and crackers handy. Good light.

INTANGIBLES AND EXTRAS: There is a lot to see and do here. The demonstration vineyards out front show different trellis systems and different grapes. The self-guided tour inside goes through everything from Napa Valley soils, to maps of wine regions, to the crush pad and barrel rooms. The best part is the Smell-a-Vision station that has you try to pick out aromas of wine components. St. Supéry also has an intriguing art gallery with exhibits that rotate regularly.

The guided tour ($10) also goes into the vineyards and the Atkinson house. Reservations are not needed. There is a wine shop with art and upscale knickknacks attached to the tasting room. And, the tour and tasting fee buys you a lifetime tour and tasting free pass.

WINE AVAILABILITY: St. Supéry is a major producer and distributor, though a handful of wines are sold only through the winery or website. Prices range from $18 to $70.

PICNIC PROSPECTS: None.

COST: $10 for four or five current releases; $15 for reserves; the fee buys you a lifetime tasting pass.

DIRECTIONS: On the east side of Highway 29 a half mile south of Rutherford Crossroad and one and a half miles north of Oakville Crossroad.

RECOMMENDED FOR: Everyone. Good place for wine novices.

Sawyer Cellars
8350 St. Helena Highway
Rutherford, 94573
707-963-1980 or 800-818-2252
www.sawyercellars.com
HOURS: 10–5 daily

Any winery that greets visitors with a six-foot stuffed bear standing in the doorway—wearing a waiter's apron and holding a tray with wine and glasses—is going to be an easygoing place. Sawyer, with the small, meticulously restored barn right on Highway 29, is one of those off-the-path wineries right on the highway that makes for a comfortable visit.

Charles and Joanna Sawyer, longtime lovers of Napa, finally bought their own place—what was Jaeger Vineyards—in 1994, slowly refurbished the old barn, and created a small, quality winery that makes Sauvignon Blanc, Cabernet Sauvignon, and a Bordeaux-style Meritage.

ATMOSPHERE: Besides the bear concierge, the tasting room has high windows and ceilings, and lots of light. The combination of knotted cedar walls and the polished black marble bar makes for a nice country stylishness, and a generally warm place.

SERVICE: They do on occasion get packed, but the tone is always that they're glad, and maybe a bit surprised, you dropped in. Their wine list is not long, so they don't hurry you through.

TASTING TOOLS: Good, large glasses. Spit bucket, water, and crackers handy. Very good light.

INTANGIBLES AND EXTRAS: Besides the general amiability, they sell some lighthearted souvenirs like a fairly realistic-looking fake spilled wine glass. Tours ($10 with tasting) and barrel tastings ($10) are available, both by appointment.

WINE AVAILABILITY: Their production is limited and though Sawyer wines can be found in some shops and restaurants, they're mostly available through the winery or website. Prices range from $17 to $95.

PICNIC PROSPECTS: None.

COST: $7.50 for three current releases;

a discount coupon is available on the website.

DIRECTIONS: On the east side of Highway 29 about one mile north of Oakville Crossroad and three-quarters of a mile south of Rutherford Crossroad.

RECOMMENDED FOR: Everyone.

Sequoia Grove Vineyards

8338 St. Helena Highway
Napa, 94558
707-944-2945 or 800-851-7841
www.sequoiagrove.com
HOURS: 10:30–5 daily

Sequoia Grove is one Napa's most renowned and unknown wineries. It has a big-time reputation for many of its wines, particularly its Cabernet Sauvignon and Chardonnay, and it's smack in the middle of Rutherford, yet it's almost off the beaten path for visitors.

The family-owned winery started in 1978 and is fronted by a 135-year-old farmhouse that holds the tasting room. In front of both is a small stand of redwood trees that give the winery its name. They make Gewürztraminer, Chardonnay, Syrah, Cabernet Sauvignon, and a Bordeaux blend.

ATMOSPHERE: The old farmhouse often has a winery dog or two flopped in front of the rustic-but-neat tasting room, which also is the visitor's center, store, and working barrel room. It has redwood trim, tall, barn-like ceilings and rafters, stained-glass skylights, and windows all around. It feels like the inside of one of those sequoia trees.

The small, wooden tasting bar is next to large holding tanks and it's lit by windows and some overhead spotlights and hanging lamps.

SERVICE: Their casual-but-smart style fits the winery. The servers are pretension-free, but they also appreciate that they're serving special wine.

TASTING TOOLS: Good-but-small glasses. Spit buckets handy. Water nearby from cooler. No crackers. OK light.

INTANGIBLES AND EXTRAS: The farmhouse feel is fun, the country sensibility is relaxing, and the wines are terrific. This is another winery with a soft spot for dogs. Besides their own friendly pets, they host wine tastings for partners of Guide Dogs for the Blind.

WINE AVAILABILITY: Most wines are available in stores and restaurants. Older vintages sold only through the winery or website. Prices range from $12 to $70.

PICNIC PROSPECTS: A handful of tables sit under the redwood trees. It's a pretty spot, with vineyards behind you, but it's fairly close to the highway.

COST: $10 for five wines.

DIRECTIONS: On the east side of Highway 29, one mile north of Oakville Crossroad and almost a mile south of Rutherford Crossroad.

RECOMMENDED FOR: Everyone.

Whitehall Lane Winery

1563 St. Helena Highway
St. Helena, 94574
707-963-9454 or 800-963-9454
www.whitehalllane.com
HOURS: 11–5:45 daily

Whitehall is a small winery with an excellent line of wines and a split personality for visitors. When it's quiet, it's an intimate place to taste some terrific wines at a family winery. When it's busy—and it does get busy—it's a mob scene.

Whitehall was founded in 1979 and bought by the Leonardini family of San Francisco in 1993. They put resources and skill into the winery and into sourcing grapes, and now rank among some of the premier wineries in Napa. They make Sauvignon Blanc, Chardonnay, Merlot, Cabernet Sauvignon, and a crisp dessert wine called Belmuscato.

ATMOSPHERE: The room is modern and relatively small, with subdued lighting, a green, poured-concrete bar, dark wood trim, and pale walls. Off-peak hours, it is comfortable and contemporary, and a fun place to taste. But with its spot on the highway near St. Helena, and because they stay open later than most rooms, they can get stuffed on weekend and summer afternoons.

SERVICE: They have a casual lightness to them, though these are veterans who know wine. During slower times, they will talk and joke and explain. In the busy hours, they turn into funny bartenders, but there isn't much room for wine talk.

TASTING TOOLS: OK glasses. Spit buckets and water handy. No crackers. OK light.

INTANGIBLES AND EXTRAS: It's all about timing here. Whitehall is a top producer and worth seeking out during a slower time of day.

WINE AVAILABILITY: Whitehall is well distributed, but some wines are tough to find outside the winery or website. Prices range from $15 to $90.

PICNIC PROSPECTS: None.

COST: $10 for five wines. $20 for reserve cabs.

DIRECTIONS: On the west side of Highway 29 just north of Whitehall Lane, about one and a half miles north of Rutherford Crossroad. Don't turn down Whitehall Lane—there's no access from there.

RECOMMENDED FOR: Everyone in off hours or slow times of the year. Maybe not during rush hours.

William Harrison Vineyards & Winery

1443 Silverado Trail
St. Helena, 94574
707-963-8310
www.whwines.com
HOURS: 11–5 Thursday–Monday

The big, Old West–looking winery was actually built rather recently, in 1985. It has limestone and rough-hewn wood, and looks like Ben Cartwright's house or a stagecoach station.

If the building is relatively young considering the look, winemaking in this family has some serious history. They go back to the thirteenth century in Italy, and started in California in 1902 with Antonio Perelli-Minetti's winery in Sonoma County. Antonio's grandson, William Harrison, started a mobile wine-bottling service in the early 1980s that's still a major service in the valley. Then in 1992, he began making wine in this Rutherford spot, sharing facilities with his uncle, Mario Perelli-Minetti, who's been in the wine industry for more than half a century.

This family mix is sometimes confusing, and the spot still gets called the Mario Perelli-Minetti Winery. Either way, they make some strong wines, including Chardonnay, Cabernet Franc, Cabernet Sauvignon, and a Bordeaux blend called Rutherford Red.

ATMOSPHERE: The long, thin room has the feel of a Western saloon, with heavy wood, pale walls, high ceilings, and big, square windows looking back at a low rise of vines. There are spotlights over the bar. The deck outside has tables with umbrellas and attracts crowds because no one wants to leave. The winery building sits against a row of trees, and the feel on the deck is of Napa a century ago. Except for the cars.

SERVICE: This is a fun, lively place and they have a very long, winding story to tell if you want to hear it. Their tone is casual and efficient. They can get busy, particularly later on summer and weekend afternoons, and the narrow room doesn't help. Servers try to move people off the bar if they're done, suggesting they find a spot on the deck, which is not a bad transition.

TASTING TOOLS: Good, big glasses. Spit bucket can be hard to get to in a crowd. Water handy. No crackers. Good light.

INTANGIBLES AND EXTRAS: Pretty spot with a slightly different, Old West feel, and a lesser-known winery. Good energy and relaxing deck. If the room is slow, get them to tell you the complete family wine history.

WINE AVAILABILITY: They're a small producer and the wines can be found in some shops and restaurants, but the winery or website are the best bets. Prices range from $32 to $45.

PICNIC PROSPECTS: The deck looking at the small vineyard and the hills above it is terrific, but it does get busy.

COST: $7.50 for four wines.

DIRECTIONS: On the west side of the Silverado Trail about a quarter mile south of Zinfandel Lane and one mile north of Highway 128.

RECOMMENDED FOR: Everyone.

ZD Wines
8383 Silverado Trail
Napa, 94558
800-487-7757
www.zdwines.com
HOURS: 10–4:30 daily

ZD is one of the many often-overlooked Napa wineries with gold-plated reputations. ZD wines were served at the White House in three administrations, and it has cabinets full of international medals. Yet, it's an almost-forgotten stop in Napa.

The operation started in 1968 in the Carneros region with a $3,000 ante each from aerospace engineers Gino Zepponi and Norman de Leuze—that's the ZD, though now they say it also stands for Zero Defects. Their 1969 Pinot Noir is the first wine to have a Carneros designation on the bottle. They moved to Silverado Trail and opened the winery there in 1980. After Zepponi died in 1985, the de Leuze family took over and still runs the winery.

They specialize in Chardonnay, Pinot Noir, and Cabernet Sauvignon, and they make a special wine called Abacus, which is an evolving blend of every reserve Cabernet ZD has produced.

ATMOSPHERE: The Tuscan-style winery is on a slight rise looking over the flat Rutherford vineyards. The walk from the parking lot goes past trimmed flowers and fountains and under an arbor of grapevines. The tall room, with a thirty-five-foot-high peaked ceiling, has pale-yellow walls, high windows, rust-colored floor tiles, and lots of light wood. A curved tasting bar faces the door, and behind it, windows look into a barrel room.

The feel is very Napa Valley, classy, modern, and comfortable, and though the room is not huge, they handle crowds well.

SERVICE: Also very Napa Valley, in that they know wines and seem to really like their own. They're friendly and unfussy, but this is one of the many places you can talk as much detail as you'd like and feel comfortable.

TASTING TOOLS: Good, large glasses. Spit buckets, water, and bread handy. Excellent light from a ridge over the tasting bar.

INTANGIBLES AND EXTRAS: They offer library wine tastings ($20) on Saturday mornings and wine-and-cheese tastings ($20) Sunday mornings. Reservations are needed. ZD also has one of Napa's most unique wines in its Abacus. It's what's called a Solera-style wine that blends progressive vintages—in this case, every ZD reserve Cab since 1999—and each bottling is marked by a medal telling what edition it is.

WINE AVAILABILITY: Most can be found at markets and restaurants. Some library wines and Abacus are sold only at the winery. Prices range from $30 to $60. Abacus sells for $350.

PICNIC PROSPECTS: None.

COST: $10 for three current releases; $15 for three reserve or library wines.

DIRECTIONS: On the west side of Silverado Trail about one mile south of Highway 128 and two miles north of Oakville Crossroad.

RECOMMENDED FOR: Everyone.

ST. HELENA TASTING ROOMS

Arger-Martucci Vineyards

1455 Inglewood Avenue
St. Helena, 94574
707-963-4334
www.arger-martucci.com
HOURS: 10–4 daily

The little winery and house surrounded by four acres of vineyards is a quiet surprise in a busy stretch of the valley. It's off the main highway and the tasting room is behind the pre-1900 wood winery building, through the garden and alongside a pool.

The winery here started as Villa Helena in 1985. Kosta Arger and Richard Martucci bought it in 2000—two years after they started their winemaking partnership—and turned it into a respected family-run operation. They make Chardonnay, Viognier, Pinot Noir, Syrah, Cabernet, and a sweet Sauvignon Blanc–Sémillon blend they call Dulcinea.

ATMOSPHERE: The tasting room is a bright, airy converted kitchen in what was once a guest house for the winery. The room has tall ceilings and windows looking out at the garden and pool. Visitors sit around the island in the middle of the room, and it all feels like being invited into someone's home to taste wine.

SERVICE: Winery manager Katarena Arger also makes visitors feel like friends visiting her home. She runs the tasting room with energy and enthusiasm for her family's wines, and in the rare times when the room gets busy, she has the ability to hustle without making tasters feel hurried.

TASTING TOOLS: Good, large glasses. Water and fresh bread handy. Spit bucket is a sink. Very good light.

INTANGIBLES AND EXTRAS: This is one of those little spots that's a twist from the mainstream wineries, because of its intimacy and, usually, its calm pace. Visitors here get a chance to know the people behind the winery, and might end up with Katarena sitting down with them for a glass of wine. They also offer a wine-and-cheese tasting ($10), reservations needed.

WINE AVAILABILITY: Many wines can be found in stores and restaurants. But they're small, so the winery or website are more reliable. Prices range from $22 to $50.

PICNIC PROSPECTS: None.

COST: $10 for five or more wines.

DIRECTIONS: Inglewood Avenue connects to Highway 29 from the west, and is the first street north of Zinfandel Lane on the west side. It's about a mile south of St. Helena and almost directly across from V. Sattui Winery.

RECOMMENDED FOR: Everyone.

Ballentine Vineyards

2820 St. Helena Highway North
St. Helena, 94574
707-963-7919
www.ballentinevineyards.com
HOURS: 10–5 daily

Ballentine is another of the many overlooked—or sped past—wineries with good wine. It's in the flats just north of St. Helena, and looks like it's part of Markham's large facility. Drivers sail by before they know what they've missed.

Van and Betty Ballentine have 100 years of family connections to Napa and had been growing grapes for decades. They decided to open their own winery in 1998, and are something of a rarity in Napa because they do not make a Cabernet Sauvignon. Their slightly offbeat list is well-respected for its quality and for its reasonable prices. It includes Chenin Blanc, Syrah, Cabernet Franc, Zinfandel, Zinfandel Port, and a Merlot–Cab Franc blend called Integrity.

ATMOSPHERE: The tasting room is small, and from the outside it looks like the sales office around the side of the winery building. It's neat and efficient, and plenty comfortable, but this is not a place to find the country romance of Napa, just some of its very good wine.

SERVICE: Because it's small and often slow here, the servers have plenty of time to talk about the wines and their uniqueness. And you can't help feeling you've made a personal connection.

TASTING TOOLS: Good glasses. Spit buckets handy. No water or crackers. Good light.

INTANGIBLES AND EXTRAS: When the winery opened in 1998, they made bumper stickers that said "Where the Hell is Ballentine?" They could still be printing them. But their wines are simply too good to be bypassed. For what it's worth, respected winemaker Bruce Devlin is married to Danielle Cyrot, the winemaker across the highway at St. Clement.

WINE AVAILABILITY: Some wines are found in stores and restaurants. But most of the 10,000 cases are sold through the winery or website. Prices range from $14 to $32.

PICNIC PROSPECTS: None.

COST: $5 for five wines, waived with purchase.

DIRECTIONS: On the east side of Highway 29, just north of Deer Park

Road and just past Markham Vineyards. Look for a small sign and a quick turn into the driveway.

RECOMMENDED FOR: Everyone, except people looking for pizzazz.

Beringer Vineyards
2000 Main Street
St. Helena, 94574
707-963-7115 or for tours 707-963-8989 ext 2222
www.beringer.com
HOURS: 10–6 daily May 30–October 23; 10–5 daily October 24–May 29

Beringer is the oldest continuously operating winery in Napa and one of the foundations of the wine industry in the valley. It was opened in 1876 by Beringer brothers Frederick and Jacob—after Jacob had worked as a winemaker for Charles Krug. The spectacular Rhine House on the property, constructed with basalt rock, redwood framing, slate tiles, and stained glass, was built in 1884 at the then-staggering cost of $28,000 to re-create the family home on the Rhine River in Germany.

Beringer is one of the most popular visiting spots in Napa for its stunning grounds, its garden and views, its variety of tours, its faithful re-creation of the historic site, and simply for its beauty. The actual winery, however, is across the highway. Visitors are seeing a historic district with the old winery, caves, and the Rhine House.

Beringer makes enough wines to make your head spin, and offers tastes of wines ranging from White Merlot and a Sparkling White Zinfandel to Cabernet Franc, Howell Mountain Merlot, and its top-of-the-line Private Reserve Cabernet Sauvignon.

ATMOSPHERE: The old stone winery

at the top of a hill is where they taste current releases and mid-range wines. It's a snug, wooden room near huge, old barrels, and you can feel the ancient winery around you and see some of the equipment they used more than a century ago.

The reserve room is in the Rhine House and it is a special place to taste. The middle of the house is a retail shop, but there are side rooms, hardwood staircases, and big stained-glass windows. The tasting bar is in a tall, narrow, wood-paneled room, and the feeling here is of a refined era and the winery's earlier days—mixed, now, with the fun of a boisterous wine bar.

SERVICE: Both tasting rooms are well staffed with servers who have seen a few visitors in their time yet keep up an appropriate level of enthusiasm. Because Beringer visitors range from wine novices to serious buyers, servers are versatile and seem to be good at reading the crowd. Both rooms can get packed on weekends and summer afternoons.

TASTING TOOLS: Good glasses. Water, spit buckets, and crackers handy in both locations. OK light in the old winery. Good light in the Rhine House.

INTANGIBLES AND EXTRAS: If Disneyland had a Wine Country USA, it would be like Beringer. Everything is manicured or polished, and not a leaf or grass blade is out of place. Even the fountains and stone terraces are done in stylish patterns. And that's one reason why Beringer is so popular. It is something to see, and, because of the care, it retains a Victorian charm. Some people might feel it's too polished to feel authentic, but there's still a lot to enjoy here, from the building and

gardens, to the old winemaking facilities, to the dark, gnarly oak tree behind the Rhine House, which dates back to 1787.

Beringer offers almost continuous tours that range from a thirty-minute historical tour, to a ninety-minute legacy tour that includes barrel tasting, to a semi-private, sit-down tasting of reserves. Tour prices range from $10 to $35, and include the tastings. Reservations are recommended for many of them and sign-ups are taken that day in what looks like an amusement park ticket booth but is the old carriage house by the parking lot. There are full stores in both tasting areas with glassware, ceramics, and wine art besides the usual knickknacks.

Note that there are no picnics allowed here, which is why you see a lot of people who planned to picnic at Beringer sitting with their car doors open, eating in the parking lot.

WINE AVAILABILITY: Beringer is one of the most widely available brands in America. Prices range from $12 to $100.

PICNIC PROSPECTS: None.

COST: Tastings in the Old Winery are $5 for three wines, with a two-for-one pass available on the website; reserve tastings in the Rhine House range from $8 to $15 for three wines, and possibly a Port or two.

DIRECTIONS: On the west side of Highway 29 at the north end of St. Helena, just south of the "Tunnel of Elms."

RECOMMENDED FOR: Everyone.

Charles Krug Winery

2800 Main Street
St. Helena, 94574
707-967-2200 or 800-682-5784
www.charleskrug.com
HOURS: 10:30–5 daily

Napa's wine history starts here. It is the oldest surviving winery in the valley, started by German immigrant Krug in 1861, and, maybe more importantly to some, Krug opened the first public tasting room in 1882. (Charles Krug was not, however, the first commercial winery in Napa. That belonged to John Patchett, who built a tiny stone building on the north side of Napa town in 1858.)

Charles Krug Winery has another huge role in Napa's history, because it was bought in 1943 by Cesare and Rosa Mondavi, and soon run by their sons Robert and Peter. The brothers turned it into one of Napa's major wineries and helped pioneer a range of winemaking and wine-sales innovations.

When the sons split up, and Robert opened his own winery in 1966, Peter took over management and later, his sons, Peter Jr. and Mark, joined in. They make a long list of wines, including Sauvignon Blanc, Chardonnay, Pinot Noir, Zinfandel, Merlot, Cabernet Sauvignon, Port, and a Bordeaux blend they call Family Reserve Generations.

ATMOSPHERE: The tasting room is surprisingly simple, just an unfussy wooden building under trees, with low ceilings, a long, wood bar and a row of windows behind it looking across a big courtyard at the huge, old stone winery. They're planning to refurbish the old winery and move the tasting room into it, but for now, Napa's oldest wine building—which is used for barrel storage—looks ghost-like, with closed-off windows and fraying wood. It's a contrast to the lighthearted feel in the current tasting room, which seems to have a sunny energy to it.

SERVICE: They have as much history to tell as any winery in the valley, but they don't hit you with it unless you ask. Tastings here can be breezy and simple, or serious about wine. Because of their name, they get a range of visitors, from first-timers to wine aficionados, but the room doesn't get as packed as many others in the valley.

TASTING TOOLS: Good, big glasses. Spit buckets and water handy. No crackers. Good light.

INTANGIBLES AND EXTRAS: Although they don't push it, the history is palpable, especially if you wander over to the old winery (No. 563 on the National Register of Historical Landmarks). There's also the old cider press Krug used in 1861 and a wall with a timeline of the winery and the valley.

They have a small wine-goodies store and on weekends, they do chocolate-and-Port tastings with a luscious Zinfandel Port. They also do private reserve tastings for $10 per person by appointment. They suspended their popular tours until they finish renovating the old winery.

WINE AVAILABILITY: Their wines are widely distributed, though a few, like the Zin Port, are available only through the winery or website. Prices range from $16 to $80.

PICNIC PROSPECTS: Their quiet courtyard between the tasting room and old winery has picnic tables open to the public or that can be reserved by groups of between ten and fifty.

COST: $10 for five wines. $15 for reserves.

DIRECTIONS: On the east side of Highway 29 just north of St. Helena and the "Tunnel of Elms." About a quarter mile south of Deer Park Road.

RECOMMENDED FOR: Everyone.

Corison Winery

987 St. Helena Highway
St. Helena, 94574
707-963-0826
www.corison.com
HOURS: 10–5 daily; by appointment or
drop-in if someone is there

Owner Cathy Corison, a winemaker in Napa for thirty years, including a decade at Chappellet Vineyards, started her own brand, then bought this spot just south of St. Helena in 1995. But she and her husband, William Martin, finally broke ground on this little throwback winery in 1999.

She makes Syrah, Gewürztraminer, Zinfandel, and Petite Sirah, but her focus is a highly regarded, complex Cabernet Sauvignon that is a bit lower-alcohol than some of the popular big reds and has a more subtle and classic style.

ATMOSPHERE: Although the gray-and-green, New England–style winery building with white trim is just a hundred yards or so off the highway, it feels like it's out in the country and removed from this busy stretch of Napa. Out the back door, the winery opens to vineyards that run a mile straight to the mountains.

The small tasting area is just a neat little table in the front of the big winery barrel room. It's got a concrete floor and industrial overhead lights, but the combination of vineyards outside the big, open door and the tanks all around give the pleasant reminder that this is a working winery.

SERVICE: There is rarely any kind of crowd, so the service is personal and low-key. This is also a winery that makes some sophisticated wines, and they can explain all the nuances.

TASTING TOOLS: Good, big crystal glasses. Spit buckets and water handy. No crackers. OK light.

INTANGIBLES AND EXTRAS: You get the feeling of finding an undiscovered place, which is both fun and odd, considering Corison has a respected winemaker and an address on Highway 29.

WINE AVAILABILITY: Corison can be found in some shops and restaurants, but it's mostly available through the winery or website. Prices range from $20 to $90.

PICNIC PROSPECTS: None.

COST: $10 for a handful of wines, whatever they're pouring that day.

DIRECTIONS: On the west side of Highway 29 down a long driveway about a quarter mile north of Zinfandel Lane.

RECOMMENDED FOR: Anyone looking for a smaller, out-of-the-way winery experience without going out of the way.

Flora Springs Winery & Vineyards

677 St. Helena Highway South
St. Helena, 94574
707-963-5711 or 800-913-1118
www.florasprings.com
HOURS: 10–5 daily

Flora Springs started in 1977 when the John and Flora Komes family bought a vineyard and two ghost wineries in the west side of the valley. Their children, John and Julie, and their families now run the winery that is named after their mom and the water sources on their property.

They seem to have a good time

naming their wines here. Their Sauvignon Blanc is called Soliloquy, their Bordeaux blend is Trilogy, and they have an Out of Sight Cabernet, a Wild Boar Cabernet, and a Holy Smoke Cabernet. They also make Pinot Grigio, Chardonnay, Sangiovese, Merlot, and a couple Cabs just named after their districts. The Komeses also own the Toad Hall Cellars label and pour that in this tasting room.

ATMOSPHERE: The simple storefront makes the spacious, light-wood tasting room inside a bit of a surprise. There's a large, six-sided bar in the middle of the room under bright spotlights, and some jauntily sketched murals open the room even more. There isn't much of a vineyard feel here, but the warm lighting makes it an amiable room.

SERVICE: This can be a busy spot, but the bar is well-staffed and the crew is genial. They expect a lot of tourist traffic and tend to keep the conversations simple unless you ask for details. In slower periods, they have time to talk. When it's packed on weekend afternoons, they're mostly tending bar.

TASTING TOOLS: Good glasses. Spit buckets and water handy. No crackers. Good light.

INTANGIBLES AND EXTRAS: A comfortable, good-humored place, which includes some framed wine cartoons on one wall and some of the art displayed around the room. For first-timers, this is an easy place to get your tasting legs.

WINE AVAILABILITY: Many of the wines are widely available, but a few are found only through the winery or website. Toad Hall wines are available only through the winery or websites. Prices range from $12 to $100.

PICNIC PROSPECTS: The shared courtyard behind the tasting room has plenty of tables. It's a relaxing spot but it's more coffeehouse patio than winery picnic grounds, though it does look west across vineyards to the Mayacamas Mountains.

COST: $5 for four current releases; $12 for four premium wines.

DIRECTIONS: On the west side of Highway 29. The first driveway north of Inglewood Avenue. It's next door to Dean & DeLuca and shares a courtyard with 29 Joe's Coffee House behind it.

RECOMMENDED FOR: Everyone. It's a nice stop for wine novices.

Hall Wines

401 St. Helena Highway South
St. Helena, 95474
707-967-2620 or 866-667-4255
www.hallwines.com
HOURS: 10–5:30 daily

The winery and visitor's center are in a big, white refurbished 1885 winery that once housed the Napa Valley Co-op. The walkway to the red awning over the entrance passes flower gardens and two playful metal sculptures, one a woman holding a glass sitting on a barrel named "Kegger," the other a dancing woman eating grapes called "Baccus." These will be your clue there's more sculpture and art ahead.

The winery was founded in 2002 by Craig and Kathryn Hall, who own 500 acres in Napa and Sonoma and wanted a place to make premium, Bordeaux-style wines and to mix two things they treasure, wine and art. They make Sauvignon Blanc, Merlot, and Cabernet Sauvignon.

ATMOSPHERE: This is a simple, sleek tasting room. It's done mostly in rich, dark wood, there's a high, domed ceiling, and the small bar is in one corner. There's sculpture, painting, and photography all around, and the windows and glass doors look out to vineyards.

SERVICE: They're justifiably proud of their wines here, and they say they aim for an elegant experience, but this is in no way a snooty place. They know their wines and the valley, and are welcoming and unpushy, often reminding visitors they can wander around the sculpture garden or pull out a picnic lunch.

TASTING TOOLS: Good, large glasses. Spit buckets, water, and crackers handy. Very good light.

INTANGIBLES AND EXTRAS: The tasting bar is small and can get crowded, but it's an airy room and you feel the vineyards out the door. The sculptures outside in the garden and around the arbor are from the Halls' personal collection and have an energy to them. They also sell wine by the glass if you want to sit a while.

WINE AVAILABILITY: A limited amount of wine makes it to select markets, but most are only available through the winery or website. Prices range from $20 to $65.

PICNIC PROSPECTS: The tables are under trees and look out over sculpture and the vineyards that extend to the Mayacamas range.

COST: $10 for four wines.

DIRECTIONS: On the west side of Highway 29 about a third of a mile north of Zinfandel Lane.

RECOMMENDED FOR: Everyone but beginners, unless they're sculpture fans.

Heitz Wine Cellars

436 St. Helena Highway South
St. Helena, 94574
707-963-3542
www.heitzcellar.com
HOURS: 11–4:30 daily

Joe Heitz, who started this winery in 1961, is one of the founding fathers of modern Napa and still one of its most revered winemakers. He trained under André Tchelistcheff, then bought a small winery with eight acres on Highway 29 once called "The Only One Winery," because is was the sole producer of a Grignolino.

In the mid-1960s, he formed a partnership and friendship with growers Tom and Martha May, whose Martha's Vineyard on the western flats of Oakville up against the Mayacamas Mountains is still considered one of the premier Cabernet vineyards in America. Heitz's 1966 Martha's Vineyard Cabernet, released in 1970, introduced the idea of a single-vineyard wine in Napa. Over the years, the Martha's Vineyard Cabs have been ranked among the greatest California wines produced in the twentieth century and they remain one of Napa's most acclaimed wines.

Heitz Wine Cellars is now run by Joe and Alice Heitz's children—winemaker David and winery president Kathleen—and long ago expanded and moved to a winery and ranch on Taplin Road on the eastern edge of the valley. They've remodeled the original winery building into a contemporary, cottage-sized stone tasting room. They still make a Grignolino, plus a Grignolino Rosé and Zinfandel, but specialize in their renowned Chardonnay, Cabernet Sauvignon, and Port.

ATMOSPHERE: The small, modern room has towering ceilings, sleek wood trim and floors, large, arched windows looking at vineyards in two directions, and big, overstuffed chairs in front of a stone fireplace. If it weren't for the vineyards, it would feel like an elegant mountain cabin. The tasting bar is a long, low piece of polished wood and tasting feels more like standing around a table than at a wine bar. As classy as the room is, it's surprisingly low-key for one of Napa's pioneering and important wineries.

SERVICE: It's informal and yet sophisticated. They have terrific wines to pour—for free—and they do not hurry anyone through the tasting. They hand you extensive tasting notes with each wine. They also have one of the most interesting stories to tell in the valley, but only offer when you ask. The low tasting bar makes it feel casual, as if it's a wine-tasting party.

TASTING TOOLS: Good, large glasses. Spit buckets, water, and crackers handy. Good light.

INTANGIBLES AND EXTRAS: For wine people spending any time in the valley, this is a required visit, for the setting, the history, and the wine. The room is different from some of the big, splashy places, and out back there's a crushed-granite patio with benches under a heavy trellis that looks across vineyards in every direction. It's a place to sit a bit and take in the valley.

WINE AVAILABILITY: Heitz is widely distributed, though a few wines, like the Grignolino Port, are best found through the winery or website. Prices range from $15 to $105.

PICNIC PROSPECTS: None.

COST: Free.

DIRECTIONS: On the east side of Highway 29, just north of White Lane (which is, basically, the driveway for V. Sattui).

RECOMMENDED FOR: Everyone. A special stop for wine aficionados.

Joseph Phelps Vineyards
200 Taplin Road
St. Helena, 94574
707-963-2745 or 800-707-5789
www.jpvwines.com
HOURS: 9–5 Monday–Friday; 10–4
 Saturday–Sunday; by appointment only

Joseph Phelps is another of the cornerstone wineries of modern Napa. Phelps was a contractor in the late 1960s who helped build Chateau Souverain in Sonoma's Alexander Valley and Rutherford Hill Winery, just south of his current estate. He decided that rather than just build wineries, he preferred to own one, so he bought these beautiful rolling acres south of St. Helena and in 1972 founded what would become one of Napa's most respected and varied wineries.

The winery itself is a large-scale, modern building made with massive redwood beams and glass. The front has a long, two-story-high trellis constructed from 100-year-old, recycled redwood bridge timbers and it's covered with wisteria. The back opens out to some of the 600 acres of wooded hills and rolling vineyards.

Phelps has also been an innovator. Besides a wine list that includes Sauvignon Blanc, Viognier, Chardonnay, Merlot, Syrah, and a range of respected Cabernet Sauvignons, he has labels such as the Le Mistral line of Rhone-style red blends, and the Pastiche wines that are lively, affordable red and white blends. Above them all is Insignia, a landmark wine that was California's first Bordeaux blend made under a proprietary label. In 2005, *Wine Spectator* magazine named the 2002 Insignia the number-one wine in the world.

ATMOSPHERE: The small entrance hall makes it feel a bit like checking into a hotel as visitors confirm their reservations, then, in good weather, are led out to the long, tree-covered terrace. They get a glass and a pour, then find a bench or table and mostly stare at the view. The scene from here is both peaceful and breathtaking.

Vineyard rows run down a gentle hill from the terrace edge, then off toward sharp hills and soft rolls, some covered with vines, some with trees. Farther west is Highway 29, then the Mayacamas range, and to the north is St. Helena. On bad-weather days, tastings are in the glass-walled dining room just behind the deck.

SERVICE: The tiny tasting station is set up in one corner of the terrace and tasters return to get each new wine. If it's not busy, servers find you and pour. This is a slower, more luxurious way to taste and the servers try to mix the feeling of pampering visitors with offering wine information and just letting you sit.

TASTING TOOLS: Good glasses. Some spit buckets outside. Plenty inside. No water or crackers outside. Very good light.

INTANGIBLES AND EXTRAS: This is a special kind of tasting experience. Phelps makes terrific wines and that's a good reason to come, but this is almost more about the setting and tone than the wine—until they pour the Insignia. It is a rare chance for mortal Napa visitors to taste a

wine ranked as the world's best, and this is a beautiful, quintessentially Napa spot. Plan to go slow.

WINE AVAILABILITY: Most wines are widely distributed, though some library wines and special releases can be found only at the winery. Prices range from $12.50 to $140.

PICNIC PROSPECTS: None.

COST: $20.

DIRECTIONS: Taplin is a small road on the east side of Silverado Trail about a half mile north of Zinfandel Lane. Go east on Taplin about a quarter mile and turn left through the huge wooden gate. Follow the road to the top of the hill.

RECOMMENDED FOR: Anyone looking for a slower, pampered tasting with a view.

Louis M. Martini Winery
254 St. Helena Highway South
707-968-3361 or 800-321-9463
www.louismartini.com
HOURS: 10–6 daily

This grand family of winemaking started in California in 1906, when Agostino and his son, Louis M. Martini, made wine in San Francisco. Louis M. created his own company in California's Central Valley in 1922, during Prohibition, selling sacramental and medicinal wines. He anticipated the repeal of Prohibition and moved to Napa in 1933 and built one of the corner-stones of Napa Valley.

Son Louis P. Martini took over as winemaker in 1954 and was involved until his death in 1998. His son, Michael, became the wine-maker in 1977. Through it all, the Martinis also were innovators. They were the first winemakers to buy large tracts in Carneros for vine-yards, and among the pioneers of cold fermentation, mechanical harvesters, wind machines, and research into grape clones.

The Martinis sold to E & J Gallo in 2002—the families had long been friends—and Michael remains the winemaker while his sister, Carolyn, is a director. Martini offers a long list of wines, including Pinot Gris, Chardonnay, Pinot Noir, Barbera, Merlot, an assortment of Cabernets, and Zinfandels, and Cabs from the renowned Monte Ross vineyard in Sonoma County.

ATMOSPHERE: The building looks a bit austere or industrial from the highway, which fits the Martini style of general unpretentiousness. But inside, the remodeled tasting room feels like the comfortable bar at a patio restaurant. It's small but modern and upscale, with warm lighting, tall tables, a black, polished-wood tasting bar, and a wall of glass that looks out to a large, tree-covered brick courtyard.

Visitors find setups of three glasses waiting for them, which adds to the quietly classy feel of the room.

SERVICE: This, too, has a bit of restaurant flair. Tasting flights are three wines, and each pour gets a separate glass. Servers know their wines but are content to let visitors linger over each. Tasting notes are extensive and offer real information, particularly on pairing the wines with food, and, without talking down to visitors, they're written in clear, simple language.

TASTING TOOLS: Good, large glasses. Spit buckets, crackers, and water handy. Very good light.

INTANGIBLES AND EXTRAS: The room is a bit of a surprise for one of the valley's venerable wineries. It's contemporary, with an air of low-key luxury and friendliness, and is a relatively quiet place to relax over a tasting.

WINE AVAILABILITY: Martini wines are found everywhere. A few library wines are only available at the winery or website. Prices range from $14 to $75.

PICNIC PROSPECTS: Another surprise is that the spacious, quiet courtyard, with brick walls and trim, tidy grass, and lots of flowers and trees, is still undiscovered as a picnic spot. You do need to bring your own food.

COST: Flights range from $7 to $15 for three wines.

DIRECTIONS: On the east side of Highway 29, about one mile south of St. Helena.

RECOMMENDED FOR: Everyone.

Markham Vineyards
2812 North St. Helena Highway
St. Helena, 94574
707-963-5292
www.markhamvineyards.com
HOURS: 10–5 daily

The first winery on this site was built by French immigrant Jean Laurent in 1879, and it was one of Napa's top producers before the turn of the twentieth century. But over the years, the winery went through a lot of hands and was generally dormant until Bruce Markham restarted it in 1978, using the original 6,000-square-foot building.

Then in 1988, Mercian Corp. bought the winery and built a modern stone winemaking complex and a visitor's center with fountains and plazas and space for rotating art exhibits. Markham makes a range of wines, including Sauvignon Blanc, Chardonnay, Pinot Noir, Merlot,

Zinfandel, Cabernet Franc, Petite Sirah, and Cabernet Sauvignon.

ATMOSPHERE: The mix of art and wine is big here. The modern-feeling tasting room has soaring ceilings, skylights, blond wood, and art exhibited all around. The large tasting bar has warm spotlights directly over it, and it combines with the airy room and eclectic art to create an energetic, contemporary feel.

SERVICE: The tasting room staffers seem to be both wine and art people, and they'll talk about either the current collections or their current releases.

TASTING TOOLS: Small glasses. Spit buckets and water handy. No crackers. Good light.

INTANGIBLES AND EXTRAS: Markham has a strong line of wines, but it's easy to forget that and get lost in the unusual art for sale and in the Harley Bruce Gallery inside the visitor's center. This is a place to give yourself time to look around.

WINE AVAILABILITY: The mainstream wines are well distributed, but they offer some less-distributed wines best found at the winery or on the website. Prices range from $14 to $65.

PICNIC PROSPECTS: None.

COST: $5 for four current releases; $8 for four limited-release wines; $15 for combination of two reserves and two library selections.

DIRECTIONS: On the east side of Highway 29 just past Deer Park Road.

RECOMMENDED FOR: Everyone, particularly fans of contemporary art.

Merryvale Vineyards
1000 Main Street
St. Helena, 94574
707-963-7777 or 800-326-6069
www.merryvale.com
HOURS: 10–6:30 daily

The winery was once Sunny St. Helena, started in 1937 by Cesare Mondavi before he and his family also took over Charles Krug. It was renamed Merryvale when San Francisco developer Bill Harlan bought it in 1983, and it kept the name when Jack Schlatter and his family took over in 1996.

This is a popular spot and a busy winery on the edge of St. Helena, and it's a reliably fun visit. They make a large range of wines in a handful of tiers that include Sauvignon Blanc, Chardonnay, Pinot Noir, Merlot, Zinfandel, Syrah, Cabernet Sauvignon, and two specialties, the Antigua fortified dessert wine, and Profile, their highly regarded Bordeaux blend.

ATMOSPHERE: The big tasting room is inside the middle of the winery so it has no view. Instead, it has the feel of big tanks and wood all around, with a high ceiling and bright lighting. The large bar easily accommodates a couple dozen people, but because the tasting room is open until 6:30 p.m., it can get crowded on summer and weekend afternoons. Then it turns from a more sedate tasting bar to a lively happy hour feel.

SERVICE: They offer three levels of tastings, servers know their wines, and the bar is usually well staffed. As the room changes moods, servers become more like amiable bartenders than wine folks. Don't expect them to have a lot of time for detailed conversation late in the day.

TASTING TOOLS: Good, big glasses.

Spit buckets, water, and crackers handy. Very good light.

INTANGIBLES AND EXTRAS: Their Cask Room, which is available for public rental, has one of most unique feels in the valley. It's long and thin, and lined with two stories of century-old, 2,000-gallon casks. It has a heavy wood table that can seat 120 people and seems twenty-five yards long. When the room is lined with candles, the sensibility is positively medieval. All that's missing are two knights in armor standing at the door.

Merryvale offers wine component seminars every Saturday and Sunday at 10:30 a.m. ($15) except for the fourth weekend of the month, when they have a food and wine seminar ($15). Reservations suggested for both. On the second Saturday and Sunday of every month, they offer barrel tastings from 1 p.m. to 5 p.m. ($7). No reservations needed.

Alongside the tasting room is a good-sized store with prints, paintings, and unusual ceramics, as well as the more usual clothing, sauces, and knickknacks.

WINE AVAILABILITY: Merryvale wines are widely distributed. Still, a few are available only at the winery or on the website. Prices range from $15 to $90.

PICNIC PROSPECTS: None, but this is next to Tra Vigne, one of the more popular restaurants in the valley.

COST: Flights range from $5 for current releases to $20 for a three-vintage vertical tasting of Profile.

DIRECTIONS: On the east side of Highway 29 as it enters St. Helena from the south. It's just above Charter Oak Avenue.

RECOMMENDED FOR: Everyone.

Milat Vineyards

1091 St. Helena Highway South
St. Helena, 94574
707-963-0758 or 800-546-4528
www.milat.com
HOURS: 10–5:30 daily

Since 1949, the Milat family has owned twenty acres of vineyards here, and in 1986 brothers Mike and Bob, along with their wives, Carolyn and Joyce, decided to make their own wines instead of selling the grapes. All their wines are estate grown, and they make Rosé, Chenin Blanc, Chardonnay, Merlot, Zinfandel, and Cabernet Sauvignon.

ATMOSPHERE: Milat has two very different personalities. Weekdays and weekend mornings, when it's not busy, it's a simple, charming little tasting room with a big window looking back at vineyards. You can chat up a family member or the winemaker. Late in the day, especially on weekends, it's one of the last tasting rooms open on a busy stretch of highway, and the place is a party.

SERVICE: Always friendly and adept at handling crowds. Tasting room manager Cliff Little, nephew of co-owner Mike Milat, can be both experienced sommelier or friendly bartender, as the day demands.

TASTING TOOLS: Decent glasses. No water or crackers. They'll find something to use as a spit bucket. Good light.

INTANGIBLES AND EXTRAS: At any time, this is a casual, enjoyable place, and their wines are reasonable and interesting. When it's quiet, the tastings are as individual as it gets. When it's busy, it's a place that makes the crowd fun.

Milat also rents two cottages and a loft on the property. For information, call 866-270-5669.

WINE AVAILABILITY: Some are available in stores and restaurants, but they sell eighty percent at the winery or on the website. Prices range from $9 to $44.

PICNIC PROSPECTS: None.

COST: Free, or for $5 you keep the glass, waived with purchase.

DIRECTIONS: On the west side of Highway 29 about two miles south of St. Helena and about a quarter mile north of Zinfandel Lane.

RECOMMENDED FOR: Everyone.

Prager Winery and Port Works

12881 Lewelling Lane
St. Helena, 94574
707-963-7678 or 800-969-7678
www.pragerport.com
HOURS: 10–4:30 daily

In 1978, Jim and Imogene Prager crushed their first harvest of grapes, and like many small wineries around them, made Chardonnay, Zinfandel, and Cabernet. But Jim looked around Napa for a niche and found few people making Port, a wine he loves. A Port house was born.

Since then, his three sons and his daughter have joined in running the winery, which is in a big, dark-wood building built in 1865, and in working the tasting room that feels like a daylong family party. They make some unfortified wines, like Cabernet, Merlot, and Chardonnay, but specialize in a range of Ports, including an unusual White Port, a Petite Sirah Port, and their popular Tawny Port. They also make a terrific Late Harvest Riesling.

ATMOSPHERE: If a motorcycle club produced fine Ports, this would be where they'd sell it. The boisterous, energetic tasting room is around the side of the building, through a small door behind some stairs, down an aisle crowded with barrels, and inside what looks like an unfinished rumpus room. There's no tasting bar, just someone—often Jeff Prager—sitting on a stool handing you a glass and some Port.

There are a few wooden chairs and a table, but most people stand. Or read the wood walls that are covered with money from around the world, pinned up by visitors. No one seems to know why this started, but the Prager family says it's cheaper than painting.

SERVICE: Amid the sometimes roaring party atmosphere, they still manage to explain the differences in the Ports and what makes them unique. The Pragers and whomever else is working the room let you wander, then follow with the next wine on your list. This, too, feels like a running family party.

TASTING TOOLS: Good, big glasses. Sink in side room for spit bucket. No water or crackers. OK light.

INTANGIBLES AND EXTRAS: Prager is unusual for the lighthearted energy and for the Ports. It's Napa's only winery that specializes in Port and it is the exact opposite of a stuffy Port house. They also run a two-room bed-and-breakfast along with the winery, and sell cigars, Port Vinegar, and Port Chocolate Drizzle.

WINE AVAILABILITY: Almost all their wines and Ports are sold from the tasting room or on the website. Prices range from $20 to $65.

PICNIC PROSPECTS: None.

COST: $10 for four-to-six wines and Ports.

DIRECTIONS: Lewelling is on the west side of Highway 29, a few feet north of the big Victorian of Sutter Home/Trinchero Family Estates.

RECOMMENDED FOR: Everyone, unless you really, really don't like Port.

St. Clement Vineyards
2867 North St. Helena Highway
St. Helena, 94574
707-967-3033 or 800-331-8266
www.stclement.com
HOURS: 10–5 daily

The stately Victorian on a small hill was built in 1878 by San Francisco stained-glass merchant Fritz Rosenbaum and was among the first wineries in Napa Valley. The big, gray-and-white mansion no longer functions as a winemaking facility—that's behind it—though the stone cellar is used for barrel storage. The building still has the homey charm of a bed-and-breakfast, however.

After Prohibition, the winery went through a couple owners and is now owned by Sapporo. They make Sauvignon Blanc, Chardonnay, Merlot, Cabernet Sauvignon, and a Meritage.

ATMOSPHERE: Just the walk from the parking lot up to the entrance is worth the time, because it takes you along terraced vineyards and gardens. Tastings are at two small bars in a front area that once was the dining room. The windows look down the hill and out across the valley, but for such a spectacular building the tasting area is surprisingly simple.

SERVICE: Polite, knowledgeable, and unhurried. It's a place that can get a bit crowded because it's small. There's a lot of story in this building and they'll tell you more of it when they have time.

TASTING TOOLS: Good crystal glasses. Spit buckets handy. No water or crackers. Good light.

INTANGIBLES AND EXTRAS: St. Clement has a good wine portfolio, but most people come here for the grounds. The porch and stone terrace looking across the valley make this a spectacular place to picnic or just sit for a few minutes. Fun fact: Winemaker Danielle Cyrot is married to Bruce Devlin, the winemaker at Ballentine across the highway.

WINE AVAILABILITY: Most wines are available in markets and restaurants. The best bet for some reserves is at the winery or on the website. Prices range from $16 to $80.

PICNIC PROSPECTS: There are only a few wrought-iron tables on the front veranda and they are a prime spot, so it's a good idea to call ahead to make sure they're not reserved for a winery event.

COST: $10 for five wines; a coupon for a free tasting is available on their website.

DIRECTIONS: On the west side of Highway 29, just past Deer Park Road.

RECOMMENDED FOR: Everyone, particularly if you are looking for a spot to sit for a spell.

Sutter Home Winery/Trinchero Family Estates
277 St. Helena Highway South
St. Helena, 94574
707-963-3104 or 800-967-4663
www.sutterhome.com or
   www.tfewines.com
HOURS: 10–5 daily

This is the home of the most successful mistake in American winemaking. Bob Trinchero, the winemaker for Sutter Home in the 1960s and 1970s, had surplus juice from their regular Zinfandel—just the juice, no grapes or skins—and was letting it ferment to a dry white wine that, frankly, no one bought. In 1975, mostly because they weren't paying a lot of attention, the fermentation stopped and left the wine slightly sweet (and pink, also unintended, because Trinchero accidentally let the wine have some skin contact). The result was Sutter Home White Zinfandel, which became the most popular wine in the country, and which helped launch one of the powerhouse wine companies in the U.S.

Before all that, Bob's father, Mario Trinchero, moved his family from New York in 1947 when he bought the then-dormant Sutter Home winery. They could not afford the landmark Victorian next door, which they finally bought in 1986. Now, as part of Trinchero Family Estates, they produce dozens of wines from big Zinfandels and reserve Cabernets to alcohol-free wines and the still-popular White Zinfandel.

ATMOSPHERE: The large tasting room is inside what was the old winery (they have a massive complex across the highway now) and you can still see the outline of the big doors on the re-paneled front wall. The long, two-sided tasting bar is past the gift shop and wine store woven through the room, and it looks out at the gardens surrounding the Victorian.

SERVICE: It's pretty casual here because they're used to serving visitors who came to Napa for the White Zin. But they do have a huge wine list and they do know wine.

TASTING TOOLS: Good glasses. Spit buckets, crackers, and water handy. Good light.

INTANGIBLES AND EXTRAS: This room is aimed at wine novices and

visitors not looking for big, complex reds. Trinchero makes some of those wines, they just don't expect many tasters looking for them here, which makes it a very comfortable place for wine novices. Their prices also are the lowest in Napa, with nearly two dozen wines under $10.

The restored Victorian next to the tasting room is a bed-and-breakfast inn. Information is available through the winery.

WINE AVAILABILITY: Most Sutter Home and Trinchero Family wines are distributed widely. A few are available only at the winery. Prices range from $4 to $50.

PICNIC PROSPECTS: None.

COST: The lower-tier Sutter Home wines are free; tasting the Trinchero line costs $5 for a handful of wines.

DIRECTIONS: On the west side of Highway 29, about one mile south of St. Helena.

RECOMMENDED FOR: Great place for casual wine drinkers and comfortable for wine novices. More serious wine folk might be surprised at the range in the Trinchero portfolio.

V. Sattui Winery

1111 White Lane
St. Helena, 94574
707-963-7774 or 800-799-2337
www.vsattui.com
HOURS: 9–6 daily in summer; 9–5 daily in winter

Owner Daryl Sattui resurrected the family winery that came from his great-grandfather, Vittorio, who started his winery in San Francisco in 1885. Prohibition put Vittorio out of business, but in 1976 Daryl opened what he named V. Sattui Winery just outside St. Helena. They built the European-style stone winery in 1985, but it looks a century older, with two-foot-thick walls, heavy wood beams, towers, and wine caves.

V. Sattui is one of the major tourist stops because of its look and because it has two acres of picnic space, plus a deli and gourmet cheese shop. They sell 60,000 cases of wine a year, all at the winery, and make an array of wines, including Chardonnay, Sauvignon Blanc, Gewürztraminer, Johannisberg Riesling, Merlot, Zinfandel, Cabernet, and a range of slightly sweet and fortified wines.

ATMOSPHERE: The very large tasting room could be a wine warehouse, with aisles of wines and stacks of cases in a big, open space. The very large, L-shaped wooden tasting bar is built for volume and can handle dozens of tasters easily. The tasting room is the least charming part of the winery.

SERVICE: Servers are efficient and friendly, though they also push wine sales and club membership and have what sounds like a standard pitch. It's all very casual, but our server talked more about the medals the wines won and the opportunities to save by buying in bulk, than about the actual wine.

TASTING TOOLS: Good, big glasses. Spit buckets handy. No water or crackers. Good light.

INTANGIBLES AND EXTRAS: The deli and cheese shop are enormous, and one of the best reasons for coming here, along with the picnic grounds outside. The winery does not offer tours but encourages visitors to wander through on their own.

WINE AVAILABILITY: Only at the winery or through the website. Prices range from $12 to $45.

PICNIC PROSPECTS: There are two large, grassy areas for picnics, one just outside the tasting room wing along the highway that's too close to the traffic noise and clamor. The other section is far quieter. It's back under trees by the winery building and off the road. With the large deli and scores of tables, this may be Napa's most popular place for picnics, but V. Sattui is serious about not allowing outside food, wine, or even water. It's a nice spot but the feel is a bit commercial overall.

COST: Free.

DIRECTIONS: The winery is on Highway 29 at White Lane, about a half mile north of Zinfandel Lane and about one mile south of St. Helena. It is impossible to miss.

RECOMMENDED FOR: Anyone who doesn't mind a busy place or is looking for a convenient picnic spot. Not recommended for people who want a quieter experience or who want to talk about the wine.

Benessere Vineyards

1010 Big Tree Road
St. Helena, 94574
707-963-5853
www.benesserevineyards.com
HOURS: 10–5 daily

Benessere is Italian for "well being" or "prosperity" and this small winery in an idyllic spot in the upper valley is named well. It looks like a countryside cottage set against low hills and surrounded by flowers and vineyards.

The owners, John and Ellen Benish, who bought and refurbished the winery in 1994, are from Chicago and say that moving to Napa is what gives them that feeling of Benessere, which would sound trite if it isn't so easy to believe. They've chosen Italian-style wines here, and specialize in a terrific Sangiovese. They also make Rosato di Sangiovese, Pinot Grigio, Merlot, and Zinfandel.

ATMOSPHERE: The tasting room is small and simple, with a high wooden bar, a few wine decorations, and, sometimes, Tony Bennett singing in the background. But it's the scenery out the front door that makes standing in the tasting room such a special experience.

SERVICE: This is a straightforward bunch, and they have a different style of wine to talk about than the Napa norm. Sales manager Andy Gridley, who's often in the tasting room, is a longtime Napa guy who knows the valley inside and out.

TASTING TOOLS: Good, large glasses. Spit bucket, crackers, and water handy. Good light.

INTANGIBLES AND EXTRAS: There's no way to oversell the delightful setting. Outside the tasting room is a small stone patio with benches and tables, surrounded by flowers and vineyards, and it's in a piece of the valley where the mountains on both sides are less than a mile away, giving it a nice mix of being both open and cozy.

WINE AVAILABILITY: Their Sangiovese is available in stores and restaurants. Many other wines are found only at the winery or on the website. Prices range from $18 to $45.

PICNIC PROSPECTS: There are a handful of tables scattered around the property, including a couple by the ranch house that visitors are welcome to use. The best are the tables on the front patio.

COST: $10 for four or five wines.

DIRECTIONS: At the end of Big Tree Road just after it bends. Turn east on Big Tree off Highway 29 about three miles north of St. Helena (look for the fire station).

RECOMMENDED FOR: Everyone, especially if you're looking for a pretty, slightly out-of-the-way place.

Casa Nuestra Winery and Vineyards

3451 Silverado Trail North
St. Helena, 94574
707-963-5783 or 866-844-9463
www.casanuestra.com
HOURS: 10–4:30 Monday–Saturday; by appointment, mostly

Casa Nuestra is one of the hidden treats in Napa, a small, casual, slightly offbeat winery with an independent spirit and a charming, rural setting. The name means "our house" but it should be "your house" because this is a welcoming, comfortable place to visit.

Owner Gene Kirkham, a civil rights lawyer who started the winery in 1979, works to keep the access road unpaved because he thinks it matches the mood here. The tasting room is in a rickety-looking yellow farmhouse behind some large, ancient oaks and past a lawn, a shed, and a livestock pen. Although their release is small—only 1,500 cases—they make eleven different wines including a dry Rosado, Riesling, Chenin Blanc, French Colombard, Cabernet Franc, Merlot, Cabernet Sauvignon, and a handful of red blends including their Tinto, a blend with at least nine varietals in it.

ATMOSPHERE: Kirkham gives the whole winery a bit of a 1960s, counterculture spirit. The tasting room is a big, open, and eclectically scruffy place. There's a big fireplace, psychedelic rock posters, peace signs, photos of blues and folk musicians, and a wall that's a shrine to Martin Luther King Jr. and Elvis Presley (who filmed a scene from a movie out back in the 1960s). The tasting bar is wide and looks out big windows at oak trees and the fields.

SERVICE: This group of cheery, decidedly nonserious people make the tastings feel like a fun afternoon at a little country bar, except they are decidedly wine people, too. They have a lot to tell about their unusual range of wines and their even more unusual place. Or they'll just hang out and joke with you.

TASTING TOOLS: OK glasses. Spit buckets handy. No crackers. Water on request. Good light. The room sometimes smells smoky from the fireplace.

INTANGIBLES AND EXTRAS: Laid-back, friendly, and surprising, Casa Nuestra is an easily missed winery, but it's the kind of place Napa visitors will remember for the wine, the pretty country setting, and the spirit of the people here. It's also a great, off-the-path picnic spot. They've gotten so popular, they had to go to mostly appointment-only tastings.

WINE AVAILABILITY: Very hard to find outside the winery or website. They sell out often. Prices range from $15 to $55.

PICNIC PROSPECTS: There are a handful of tables in front of the farmhouse under big oaks looking at grass and the livestock pen. It cries out for a checkered tablecloth and a picnic basket. Just sitting there feels like an escape from the world.

COST: $5 for a handful of wines, depending on what's available, waived with purchase.

DIRECTIONS: On the west side of the Silverado Trail about two and a quarter miles north of Deer Park Lane or about one and a quarter miles south of Bale Lane. Look for the small sign on Silverado and a dirt road leading west.

RECOMMENDED FOR: Everyone. This is a great discovery and a treat for people looking for something a little different in Napa.

Clos Pegase
1060 Dunaweal Lane
Calistoga, 94515
707-942-4981 or 800-366-8583
www.clospegase.com
HOURS: 10:30–5 daily

Put simply, Clos Pegase is a trip. The art, the design, the shapes, and the building and grounds come at you from all sides. There's the centuries-old oak at the end of a courtyard, framed perfectly by the building. There's the giant thumb in the vineyard. There's the huge central column at the winery entrance that looks like a massive child's toy. And there are, of course, multiple versions in painting and sculpture of Bacchus. It's all with a mix of respect for the combination of art and wine, and just a sense of playfulness.

Owners Jan and Mitsuko Shrem opened the colorful winery designed by award-winning architect Michael Graves in 1987, filled it with unusual art, and set off to help visitors find, as they say, their inner Bacchus. Besides all the art, they produce a long and varied list of wines, including Vin Gris of Merlot, Sauvignon Blanc, Chardonnay, Pinot Noir, Cabernet Franc, Merlot, and Cabernet Sauvignon.

ATMOSPHERE: The tall tasting room is filled with sculpture and paintings, and the art can overshadow the wine. The room has a tile floor and a dark mahogany bar that is backed by windows and, on one side, glass doors that lead into a barrel room filled with ancient wineglasses and models of roman-style casks.

SERVICE: At the tasting bar, it's all about the wine, though they will tell you as much about the art as you'd like. Clos Pegase says they try to make wines that are balanced and symmetrical, like their art and their building. This is another winery that can get busy, but they'll let you stay unhurried.

TASTING TOOLS: OK glasses. Spit buckets handy. No crackers or water. OK light.

INTANGIBLES AND EXTRAS: There is a lot to see here, and it can be overwhelming. This is a good place to just go slowly. There are free tours at 11 a.m. and 2 p.m.—reservations not needed—and they'll sell you wine by the glass to sip and wander, or to sit with at their picnic tables outside the tasting room.

Clos Pegase is an unusual place with a generous spirit. Their goal is

to get visitors to look around. They call it a temple to art and wine, but not one on high, just an approachable setting they hope Bacchus would like.

WINE AVAILABILITY: Most wines are found in stores and restaurants, though some reserves are available only through the winery or website. Prices range from $21 to $75.

PICNIC PROSPECTS: Tables outside the tasting room sit next to long, flat vineyards, and all around there are unusual sculptures and shapes sticking up. You can bring your own lunch or buy cheese, snacks, and wine by the glass in the tasting room.

COST: $10 for five wines; $15 for four reserve Cabs.

DIRECTIONS: Dunaweal connects to Highway 29 and to Silverado Trail about one and a half miles south of Calistoga. Clos Pegase is on the north side of the lane, across from the entrance to Sterling.

RECOMMENDED FOR: Everyone, especially if you want to add some art to the wine experience.

Cuvaison

4550 Silverado Trail
Calistoga, 94515
707-942-6266 or 800-253-9463
www.cuvaison.com
HOURS: 10–5 daily April–November;
  11–4 Sunday–Thursday, 10–5
  Friday–Saturday December–March

Cuvaison has been in this pretty spot looking across the narrow valley since 1969, but the little mission-style building with a red-tile roof that's now the visitor's center was once the whole winery. In 1979, the Schmidheiny family of Switzerland bought Cuvaison, and added vineyards in Carneros and a new winery building here.

Cuvaison makes a range of well-regarded wines, including Pinot Noir, Merlot, Syrah, and Cabernet Sauvignon, but its big seller and most renowned varietal remains its Chardonnay, which has been served at affairs of state and aboard the papal jet.

ATMOSPHERE: Always a lively little tasting room with light rock or comfortable jazz playing in the background, this is a bright place with lots of sunshine coming through windows high up the wall behind the tasting bar and from the stained-glass windows in front. There's not a lot of floor space but the feel is more energetic than crowded, and though it's popular, it's rarely too packed.

The smooth, copper bar and the earth-colored tile floor make the room modern, but there's still a sense of the tall trees around the building and the vineyards out the door.

SERVICE: Servers seem to be moving to the same light, lively rhythm of the music. They clearly know their wine but aren't particularly formal about any of it. They're more energetic than stuffy, but it's the energy of a friendly bar. They offer a complimentary pour when you walk in.

TASTING TOOLS: Good, big glasses. Spit buckets and crackers handy. No water. Good light, though the copper bar makes it a trick to see wine color.

INTANGIBLES AND EXTRAS: This is a cheerful, easy place to taste some big-league wines. The store woven through the tasting room has a variety of clothes and books and some unusual wine knickknacks. The pretty little picnic area out front adds to the unhurried atmosphere.

WINE AVAILABILITY: The Chardonnay can be found everywhere. The Pinot Noir, Merlot, and Cabernet are released in more limited supply and some wines, like the Vin Gris of Pinot Noir and the Espiritu Port are available only at the winery. Prices range from $16 to $54.

PICNIC PROSPECTS: One of the best—and easiest to find—picnic areas in the valley. The round, wooden tables sit on grass under a canopy of oaks, and though it's on Silverado Trail, you barely notice the road. Instead, you look across a beautiful, narrow stretch of the valley, at vineyards and the Mayacamas Mountains about a mile away.

COST: $8 for four current release wines. $10 for two estate and two current release wines.

DIRECTIONS: On Silverado Trail about one and a half miles south of Calistoga, just south of Dunaweal Lane.

RECOMMENDED FOR: Everyone.

Duckhorn Vineyards

1000 Lodi Lane
St. Helena, 04574
707-963-7108 or 888-354-8885
www.duckhorn.com
HOURS: 10–4 daily

The big, white, Victorian-style farmhouse looks like a throwback resort house with a wraparound veranda and white railing. It's surrounded by gardens and vineyards, and the luxury-resort feel continues as visitors walk through a sitting room with a fireplace and past what feels like a big library.

The winery is owned by one of the cornerstone families in Napa, Dan and Margaret Duckhorn, who joined with ten other families and bought ten acres near St. Helena in 1976. Dan became known as Mr. Merlot for both his early focus and the quality of his wines, and later added a widely respected Sauvignon Blanc and Cabernet Sauvignon.

Over the years, Duckhorn has expanded to create sister labels—all with duck-related names on the theory that if your name is Duckhorn you either ignore it or embrace it entirely. Dan embraced it and created Decoy (a Bordeaux blend), Goldeneye and Migration Pinot Noirs based in Sonoma County, and Paraduxx, a red blend with a Zinfandel–Cabernet Sauvignon base that now has a winery of its own in Napa's Yountville district.

ATMOSPHERE: Tastings here feel like a trip to a stylish garden restaurant. (This is one of the few tasting rooms that serve you restaurant style.) You check in at a concierge stand and get seated at tables in a room surrounded by windows, the big porch, and vineyards. The white walls and blond wood make it feel airy and open, and the table service gives it a more semi-formal restaurant feel, too.

SERVICE: They pour all your wines and introduce them—and write them down if you ask—then leave you to sip. People come by regularly to answer questions and offer as much information as you need. But when it's busy, it's harder to have a long conversation than if you were standing at a tasting bar. It's a different style, less casual than in most rooms, but it also can make visitors feel a bit more pampered.

TASTING TOOLS: Good, large glasses, and a different glass for each wine. They'll put a spit bucket on your table if you ask. Small bottles of water and crackers on the tables. Good light.

INTANGIBLES AND EXTRAS: This feels classy and unhurried, but less personal than some tasting bars. If it's a busy day, you might have to wait for a table, but it is a place where you'll never be crowded when you're tasting. Free tours daily at noon. One-hour Estate tastings at 11 a.m., 1 p.m., and 3 p.m.

WINE AVAILABILITY: Most Duckhorn wines are widely available. Best bets for some limited-production wines are the winery or website. Prices range from $25 to $125.

PICNIC PROSPECTS: None.

COST: $10 for three wines, $15 for five wines, $25 for Estate tasting.

DIRECTIONS: At Lodi Lane and Silverado Trail, about one mile north of St. Helena.

RECOMMENDED FOR: Anyone who wants a slower, sit-down tasting.

Dutch Henry Winery

4310 Silverado Trail
Calistoga, 94515
707-942-5771 or 888-224-5879
www.dutchhenry.com
HOURS: 10–5 daily; ignore the "appointment only" signs, they are happy to see you

When the family winery specializing in mostly Bordeaux varietals started in 1992, owners Scott and Les Chafen needed a name. They learned that in the mid-1800s, a man named Dutch Henry prospected in these parts for silver, then later took up with gentleman stagecoach bandit Black Bart. A winery was named. That also explains the pictures of the winery owners and staff in Western gear and shoot-outs.

ATMOSPHERE: Visitors stand on a concrete floor in a ten-by-twenty-foot opening in the barrel room, tasting wines handed out by a server, often Dennis Litman, official title: Tasting Room Guy and Ace Photographer. Outside the open doorway are the steep hills on the valley's eastern flank and a flat spot that was the original Silverado Trail. The wine descriptions and prices are on a blackboard or a plain sheet of paper, and the friendly winery dogs, including a couple Airedales named Buggsy and Teddy, often roam through to step up the casual air.

SERVICE: They know their stuff, but they are not serious. Someone says the style here reminds them of a winery down the road, and Dennis says, "Are they smart-asses, too?" Someone else asked about winery tours. "Spin around," Dennis says. "How'd you like it?" It's like tasting with high school friends.

TASTING TOOLS: Good glasses. Spit buckets handy. Bread served with olive oil and vinegar. No water. Light is mostly natural from the open door.

INTANGIBLES AND EXTRAS: This is one of those very comfortable, casual places where it's about the wine and the easy atmosphere. The bocce ball court outside is open for visitors, and the view from there looks across the narrow valley at one of Napa's notable vineyards, Sterling's Three Palms Vineyard.

WINE AVAILABILITY: Wines are sold only at the winery or through the website. Prices range from $26 to $42.

PICNIC PROSPECTS: There are a couple tables across the driveway from the winery door, but the better spot is the bench along the bocce court with its vineyard view.

COST: $10 for four or five wines, depending on what they have available.

DIRECTIONS: On the east side of Silverado Trail about three miles south of Calistoga. Look for a sign on the road and the driveway that appears to lead to someone's house.

It will take you to the tall stone building shaped like a large Monopoly piece. Tasting is through the red door in the middle, across from a couple picnic tables.

RECOMMENDED FOR: Everyone not looking for luxury.

Ehlers Estate

3222 Ehlers Lane
St. Helena, 94574
707-963-5692
www.ehlersestate.com
HOURS: 10–4 daily

The winery was built in 1886 in a spectacular spot where the valley starts to narrow. All around, you see the vines reaching to rolling hills. The three-story, tan stone building surrounded by trees is another winery that looks like an old country church.

The Ehlers name was revived in 2000 after Jean and Sylviane Leducq finished uniting the parcels of the forty-two-acre estate. Then they turned it into a nonprofit trust, and all proceeds of the winery go to the Leducq Foundation, which funds international cardiovascular research. The E on the label is wrapped around a heart. They make a handful of premium wines, including Sauvignon Blanc, Zinfandel, Cabernet Franc, and Cabernet Sauvignon.

ATMOSPHERE: The bare stone walls and beams of the nineteenth-century building give the feel of a large, old, country establishment, and the room setup, with simple couches and glass-topped tables set on barrels, could be a coffeehouse or cafe. The tasting bars are sleek, new wood, and make a classy contrast to the century-old building. The light filtering through the windows and doors gives a sense of the green outside.

SERVICE: Servers are smart and

energetic and, like in so many wineries, exude their enthusiasm for wine. They change glasses for the whites and reds.

TASTING TOOLS: Good crystal glasses. Spit buckets, water, and crackers handy. Good light from windows and overhead spots.

INTANGIBLES AND EXTRAS: The room has a station for testing your ability to identify smells. They send you off to name the scents in a series of black glasses. You bring back your guesses and get graded. The point is to learn to pay attention. Hint: Pepper and leather smell a lot alike. All proceeds from the sales of clothes and wine go to the charitable foundation.

WINE AVAILABILITY: Some are available in restaurants and shops, but most are sold only at the winery or through the website. Prices range from $20 to $75.

PICNIC PROSPECTS: None.

COST: $10 for five wines.

DIRECTIONS: Turn east on Ehlers Lane, about two miles north of St. Helena, and follow to the bend.

RECOMMENDED FOR: Everyone.

Folie à Deux Winery

3070 North St. Helena Highway
St. Helena, 94574
707-963-1160 or 800-473-4454
www.folieadeux.com
HOURS: 10–5 daily

The first story they tell is that Folie à Deux is French for "shared fantasy" and that the label shows two dancers. But really, it all comes from the winery's founding in 1981 by two psychiatrists with a love of wine and not much experience. The name more accurately translates to "folly for two," or better, "two crazy people with a shared delusion." And the dancers? Psychiatrists' ink blots.

That tells you something about this winery's lightheartedness, and you get that sense driving up to the century-old farmhouse on a knoll surrounded by flowers. Trinchero Family Estate bought the winery in 2004 but kept the same spirit and Folie à Deux's popular Ménage à Trois series of red, white, and Rosé blends. They also make Chardonnay, Syrah, Sangiovese, Barbera, Cabernet Sauvignon, and a good lineup of Zinfandels.

ATMOSPHERE: The sunny tasting room has all the feel of the old farmhouse. It's surrounded by windows looking at rolling vineyards and hills, and there's a brick fireplace in the center of the room. The floor and L-shaped bar are pale woods, warm overhead spots add texture to the light, and it's just a generally cheery place.

SERVICE: This is a popular winery and an appealing place, and they can get busy here, but the sense is more loopy insanity than being overwhelmed. When it's quiet, they have plenty to talk about, including the unusual wine combos that go into the different versions of the Ménage à Trois.

TASTING TOOLS: OK glasses. Spit buckets and pretzels handy. Water from a cooler in a corner.

INTANGIBLES AND EXTRAS: There's a wooden porch with benches on two sides of the building, and it has one of the prettier picnic spots in the area, making this a good place to just sit and be mellow. The gift shop/art store mixed in with the tasting room has an eclectic, good-humored mix of goods.

Trinchero Family Estates plans to expand the tasting facilities and add a food-wine center that they swear will be in the same spirit, but it will mean no more tasting in the farm-house.

WINE AVAILABILITY: All the Ménage à Trois wines, and most of the Cabs and Zins, can be found in stores and restaurants everywhere, but many of the others are available only through the winery or website. Prices range from $12 to $42.

PICNIC PROSPECTS: The tables are under big oaks at the top of the little hill and on the edge of vineyards. This part of the valley is filled with small rolls and short, steep peaks, and you see much of that sitting here.

COST: $10 for six wines, plus whatever else may be open.

DIRECTIONS: On the east side of Highway 29 about two miles north of St. Helena. Just south of the outlet stores.

RECOMMENDED FOR: Everyone.

Frank Family Winery

1091 Larkmead Lane
Calistoga, 94515
707-942-0859 or 800-574-9463
www.frankfamilyvineyards.com
HOURS: 10–4 daily

This is one of the liveliest winery visits in Napa, and it also comes with one of the liveliest back stories. The site started in 1884 as the historic Larkmead Winery, and was a spot for a famous Prohibition raid, when revenuers sledgehammered the tanks and sent a river of wine down the road. In 1938, it became Hanns Kornell Champagne Cellars and attracted some Hollywood A-listers, including Marilyn Monroe, who used to lounge in the winery and sip sparkling wine.

In 1992, it got another shot of Hollywood. Rich Frank, a longtime top TV executive with Disney and former president of Paramount Television Group, had made friends with winemaker Koerner Rombauer. One night, Rombauer called Frank at midnight to tell him the Kornell winery was up for sale. A day later, Frank and Rombauer owned it together. Then in 2000, a warehouse fire destroyed an enormous amount of wine from Frank Family and Rombauer, and amounted to one of the recent tragedies of Napa. They have since built a new warehouse.

The tasting room is in the small, wood-frame building just past the old, stone Larkmead Winery. Most of their wines are made at the Rombauer facility just down Silverado Trail, and they produce five sparkling wines, Chardonnay, Sangiovese, Zinfandel, Cabernet Sauvignon, and Port.

ATMOSPHERE: The sales and tasting areas feel like a temporary field office, with thin wood walls, worn carpet, and, really, not a lot of charm. Not needed. The charm comes from the high-energy, comically endowed tasting room crew. And there are Marilyn Monroe pictures everywhere, including a bigger-than-life portrait and an Andy Warhol series.

Visitors start by tasting a couple sparkling wines out front, then are gathered in groups and moved to a back bar for more wines.

SERVICE: They've managed to put together a full staff with comic timing, but they also know food and wine and talk about some unique points. They taste their Chardonnay warm here, because they say you can tell more about the wine that way. It's mostly a show, rather than a conversation, but it's a pretty good one.

TASTING TOOLS: Good glasses. Spit buckets available, but hard to reach in a crowd. No water or crackers. Good light.

INTANGIBLES AND EXTRAS: One of the most consistently fun tastings in Napa. You come here for the entertainment as much as the quality wine. They will answer any questions and chat as much you'd like.

WINE AVAILABILITY: Most wines are available in stores and restaurants as well as through the winery or website. Prices range from $25 to $70.

PICNIC PROSPECTS: A line of picnic tables sits under oak trees and looks out at vineyards.

COST: Free.

DIRECTIONS: About four miles north of St. Helena on Larkmead between Highway 29 and Silverado Trail.

RECOMMENDED FOR: Everyone. A fun spot for wine novices.

Freemark Abbey

3022 North St. Helena Highway
St. Helena, 94574
707-963-9694 or 800-963-9698
www.freemarkabbey.com
HOURS: 10–5 daily

The first thing to know is, despite the name, this winery had no church connection. It's a combination of three names, Charles Freeman, Markquand Foster, and Albert "Abbey" Aheren, Southern California businessmen who restarted the winery in 1939 after it failed during Prohibition.

Its roots go back to 1886, when Josephine Marlin Tychson started Tychson Cellars, the first California winery built and operated by a woman. An 1898 stone building is still used for barrel storage, and a later Tychson Cellars street-front building is what houses Silverado Brewing Co. The winery has gone through a handful of owners and

is now owned by the Legacy Estate group and run by winemakers Ted Edwards and Tim Bell. They make limited-production Viognier, Sangiovese, Zinfandel, Cabernet Franc, and a Late Harvest Riesling, and widely distributed Riesling, Chardonnay, Merlot, and Cabernet Sauvignon.

ATMOSPHERE: The high-ceilinged tasting room is set up like a comfortable living room with a bar at one end. There's a sitting area with a large couch and chairs in front of a brick fireplace, and French doors that lead to a sunny deck. The bar in the corner is fairly small and has bright spotlights overhead. On weekends, there's often a piano player to soften the mood even more.

SERVICE: The downside to a comfortable room on the main road is it can get very crowded, and the small bar gets packed at about ten to twelve people. It's a friendly atmosphere and the staff has a long wine list to offer—they know it well, too—but this is one of the rooms that can get too busy at peak times.

TASTING TOOLS: OK glasses. Spit buckets and water handy. No crackers. Good light.

INTANGIBLES AND EXTRAS: They make this an easy, relaxing place to taste. The deck and picnic grounds are just as comfortable. But midday on summer and harvest-season weekends, be prepared to find a crowd.

WINE AVAILABILITY: Their mainstream wines can be found in stores and restaurants across the country. The limited-production wines are available only through the winery or website. Prices range from $15 to $65.

PICNIC PROSPECTS: There are a couple tables on the bright wooden deck just outside the tasting room, and more under a big oak tree on the grass between the 1898 building and the modern winery. They are both pleasant spots, but are surrounded by buildings so there are no great vineyard views.

COST: $5 for five current releases; $10 for five reserve reds.

DIRECTIONS: On the east side of Highway 29 at Lodi Lane. It's at the back of a large parking lot behind Silverado Brewing Co.

RECOMMENDED FOR: Everyone. Avoid busy times.

Rombauer Vineyards

3522 Silverado Trail
St. Helena, 94574
707-963-5170 or 800-622-2206
www.rombauervineyards.com
HOURS: 10–5 daily

When you say Chardonnay in Napa, many, many people answer Rombauer. They make 30,000 cases and sell out in seven months. Stores around the valley often announce when the new releases come in (usually early August).

The winery on top of a wooded hill was founded by Koerner Rombauer and his late wife, Joan, in 1982. Koerner's great-aunt, Irma Rombauer, wrote *The Joy of Cooking,* and they say they've tried to spread that to the joy of wine. Koerner is also a former Braniff pilot, so there are planes and pictures all over the small tasting room, as well as pictures and posters that show his devotion to the San Francisco 49ers.

Besides Napa's "It" Chardonnay, Rombauer makes a full line of well-regarded wines, including Zinfandel, Merlot, Cabernet Sauvignon, and a Zinfandel Port.

ATMOSPHERE: The tasting room and winery are surrounded by what seems to be a mountain forest, and it makes the place feel deceptively small. Below the tasting room is a large winery and 25,000 square feet of caves. There's a long porch with benches outside that look down the steep hill.

Inside, the tasting room is ringed by windows, which gives it more of the forest feel. It has a low ceiling, three small bars, yellow walls, and small, bright spots that drop cheerful light on the bars. The room is stuffed with fun mementos from Koerner's flying days and from his celebrity friends. There are pictures or signed posters with Chuck Yeager, Garth Brooks, Barbra Streisand, and former 49ers' coach Bill Walsh.

SERVICE: It's a veteran staff and most servers have been in this room a long time, so they know their wine and Napa, and they chat rather than sell. The room can get crowded but it's always well-staffed and is always a good tasting experience.

TASTING TOOLS: Good glasses. Spit buckets, water, and crackers handy. Good light.

INTANGIBLES AND EXTRAS: Rombauer has no tasting fee and they pour a lot of wine, which makes it feel informal and old-fashioned. This also is a beautiful spot, a surprisingly wooded and secluded hilltop in the middle of the valley. Take time to stroll around and maybe just sit.

WINE AVAILABILITY: Most Rombauer wines are readily available in stores and restaurants, until they sell out of the Chardonnay. Prices range from $29 to $80.

PICNIC PROSPECTS: There are a handful of tables in the trees and down the hillside. They're terrific lunch spots, but there are only a few.

COST: Free.

DIRECTIONS: On the west side of Silverado Trail about two and a half miles north of Deer Park Road or about one mile south of Bale Lane. Go up the hill to the right.

RECOMMENDED FOR: Everyone.

Sterling Vineyards

1111 Dunaweal Lane
Calistoga, 94515
707-942-3344 or 800-726-6136
www.sterlingvineyards.com
HOURS: 10:30–4:30 daily

Sterling is a place you visit for the view, the atmosphere—and the best self-guided explanation of winemaking in the valley. It's also one of the most popular wineries, particularly for first-timers to Napa who want to spend some time at a beautiful spot. The winery was built in 1973 and refurbished in recent years.

You can see Sterling from far down the valley, a huge, white, Mediterranean-looking citadel burrowed on a hill 300 feet above the valley floor. Visitors take a three-and-a-half-minute ride on a four-person aerial tram up to the winery—with valley-wide views on the way. Then you can wander through the wine-making area on the Wine 101 tour or take either steps or an elevator to the large tasting room and deck.

They make a large range of popular wines, including Sauvignon Blanc, Chardonnay, Pinot Noir, Shiraz, Merlot, and Cabernet Sauvignon, and some of the valley's most popular single-vineyard wines, like the Winery Lake Pinot Noir and the Three Palms Merlot.

ATMOSPHERE: The big, open room has light from windows and skylights and tables scattered haphazardly to give it a casual feel. There's a large, stone fireplace and views up to the top of the valley. Much better,

though, is the stone deck outside. It's long and thin, and surrounded by pine and redwood trees, giving it an almost mountain feel. Clos Pegase winery, just across the road, is tiny 300 feet below. The view looks north across Calistoga to the mountains that rim the top of Napa Valley.

The umbrellas, small tables, and dappled sunshine make this feel like a place to hang out, though it also makes the wine tasting almost incidental.

SERVICE: Visitors walk into the atrium and get handed a glass of something interesting like Sauvignon Blanc or a blush Pinot Gris, then find a table. On weekends or when it's busy, visitors get that first glass when they get off the tram and a second taste in the middle of the self-guided tour on a terrace with a dazzling view. The idea is to spread the tasting throughout the winery and make it all feel more relaxed.

A smaller, sunny Reserve Room is open to the public, and there it's rarely too busy to go slow.

TASTING TOOLS: OK glasses. Spit buckets are large paper cups. Servers will find you water. No crackers. Very good light. (Reserve room has excellent crystal glasses, all appropriate to the varietal.)

INTANGIBLES AND EXTRAS: The experience is the reason you come. The views are among the best in the valley and the feel is relaxed, slightly indulgent, and very much like a special place.

The free, self-guided tour is outstanding. It goes out to an overlook of the crush pad and through the barrel rooms, and is accompanied by signs and videos that make it maybe the most coherent, easy-to-understand account of crushing, winemaking, and barrel use in the valley. Give yourself at least thirty minutes for the tour and listen to all the videos. They also have a full gift shop of art, ceramics, sauces, crackers, sweets, clothes, and wine knickknacks.

WINE AVAILABILITY: Most Sterling wines can be found everywhere, though a few reserves and library wines are sold only at the winery. Tasting room wines range from $15 to $25. Reserves and single-vineyard wines from $28 to $70.

PICNIC PROSPECTS: None.

COST: $15 for a tram ticket, which includes the standard five-wine tasting. Reserve room is $10 per taste. A $5 off coupon is available on the website.

DIRECTIONS: Dunaweal connects to Highway 29 and to Silverado Trail about one and a half miles south of Calistoga. Sterling is on the southern side of the lane, through a long driveway of trees, across from Clos Pegase.

RECOMMENDED FOR: Everyone. A must-visit for people looking for a view.

Tudal Family Winery

1015 Big Tree Road
St. Helena, 94574
707-963-3947
www.tudalwinery.com
HOURS: Tastings and tours are by appointment. They're flexible, but prefer Monday–Friday at 11 a.m. or 1 p.m. (We went on a Saturday.)

Tudal is a classic Napa Valley experience, a special place for anyone who has some time, and a reminder that small wineries and farming families are still the soul of the valley.

Arnold Tudal, a vegetable farmer for twenty-seven years in Alameda, across the bay from San Francisco, bought these ten acres in 1974 and planted walnut trees. A neighbor, Louis P. Martini, convinced him it

was better land for Cabernet grapes.

Over the years, Tudal has become a premier producer—his wine was a favorite of Joe DiMaggio and they were served at the White House—yet has remained a friendly country winery with a playful sense of humor and a loyalty to small farmers.

They make a Bordeaux-style Cabernet and three unusual blends they call Tractor Shed Red, Flat Bed Red, and Rag Top Red.

ATMOSPHERE: The winery office is behind the dark-wood ranch house and a large vegetable garden with a two-story wind tower. An old family tractor from the label of the Tractor Shed Red sits under a tree. There's also a red 1964 Chevy Impala convertible parked by the house and an ancient-but-functioning flatbed truck from the other labels.

Vines run up to the winery buildings, and the feeling all around is of being in the middle of low-key wine country. They taste in the small office that is wallpapered with photos of family members, friends, cats, visitors, and parties. Sometimes they taste in their tricked out "tractor shed" that has barrel storage in one room and an elegant wood table with skylights and subdued lighting in another.

SERVICE: Winemaker Ron Vuylsteke often conducts tastings and tours with the air of a guy greeting old college roomies. He's playful, casual, and happy to talk about the tiny details of winemaking or to take visitors up a metal staircase to look into the tanks. Occasionally, owner Arnold Tudal comes by and the tour has the feel of an unaffected bull session.

TASTING TOOLS: Good glasses. Water from nearby sinks. Because tastings tend to wander around the winery, bushes and gravel often become handy spit buckets. No crackers. Good light.

INTANGIBLES AND EXTRAS: This is a place you go for the people and to become part of the winery for a moment. The lovely spot and the terrific wine are a bonus. Tudal offers a combination of easy hospitality and simple, casual friendliness that catches the essence of old Napa.

WINE AVAILABILITY: The Cabs and the Tractor Shed Red (a Sangiovese-Merlot-Zinfandel blend) can be found in stores and restaurants. Other reds are only at the winery or on the website. Prices range from $15 to $45.

PICNIC PROSPECTS: None.

COST: Free.

DIRECTIONS: At the end of Big Tree Road just before it bends. Turn east on Big Tree off Highway 29 about three miles north of St. Helena (look for the fire station).

RECOMMENDED FOR: Everyone who wants to spend some time at a small, affable winery.

Twomey Cellars

1183 Dunaweal Lane
Calistoga, 94515
707-948-4801 or 800-505-4850
www.twomeycellars.com
HOURS: 9–4 Monday–Saturday

The site belonged to Stonegate Winery until 2003, when Silver Oak owner Ray Duncan took it over for his just-launched new label. (Twomey is a Duncan family name.) Although Twomey and Silver Oak share owners and winemakers, they are separate operations and there's no mention of Silver Oak at Twomey.

They use Old World–style, labor-intensive winemaking techniques, including what's called soutirage

traditional—a barrel-to-barrel, gravity-flow method for racking the wine (removing leftover solids like skins and dead yeast) that they say also decants the wine in the barrels. Twomey specializes in Merlot and Pinto Noir.

ATMOSPHERE: The winery looks like a large, white, modern country house. The tasting room has clean, spare lines with dark tile floors, a curved wooden bar topped by black granite, white walls, and a peaked white ceiling. To one side of the bar, a window looks into a barrel room and other windows around the tasting room let in the green from the trees, lawn, and vineyards surrounding the winery.

It's uncluttered and contemporary feeling, but also comfortable.

SERVICE: The service is like the room: efficient and comfortable. They have just two wines so there is no hurrying tasters. They know their wines and their valley.

TASTING TOOLS: Good, large glasses. Spit buckets and fresh bread handy. No water. OK light.

INTANGIBLES AND EXTRAS: It's a simple, straightforward tasting room in a pretty spot, but it doesn't stand out.

WINE AVAILABILITY: The Merlot is available at stores and restaurants. The Pinot is only at the winery or the website. Prices range from $40 to $65.

PICNIC PROSPECTS: None.

COST: $5 for two pours.

DIRECTIONS: Dunaweal connects to Highway 29 and to Silverado Trail about one and a half miles south of Calistoga. Twomey is just a few yards east of Highway 29.

RECOMMENDED FOR: People who want to taste a couple high-end wines.

MAYACAMAS MOUNTAINS TASTING ROOMS

Barnett Vineyards

4070 Spring Mountain Road
St. Helena, 94574
707-963-7075
www.barnettvineyards.com
HOURS: 10–4 Thursday–Monday, by appointment only

Barnett is simply a spectacular place to visit. Its wines are among the area's best and the views are dazzling. It was started in 1983 by Fionna and Hal Barnett, whose steep hillside vineyards yield deep, intense flavors. But their wines are more than big fruit. They're also graceful, balanced, and layered. And they taste even better if you're sitting on the Barnett Vineyards' deck, 2,100 feet above the valley floor, looking out at mountains, vineyards, and forever. They make Chardonnay, Pinot Noir, Merlot, and two extraordinary Cabernets.

ATMOSPHERE: This little winery looks like a villa sitting on the edge of a mountain. Some tastings are inside the barrel room that has doors opening up to the mountain, and some are on the deck that's a couple dozen yards up a path and looking out into space.

SERVICE: The tastings and tours are always small, and the people running them have been at Barnett a long time. They can get as detailed as you'd like, or just let you get lost in the wine and the views. They'd prefer to talk wine, though.

TASTING TOOLS: Good, large glasses. Spit buckets and crackers handy. They'll get water if you ask. Very good light.

INTANGIBLES AND EXTRAS: This would be special if it just had the view. And their wine would be worth the trip up the mountain if you tasted it in a hole. Together, a visit is an impressive experience. But they are serious about wine here, so don't just come for the view, come with questions and a willingness to hear what they do on Spring Mountain.

WINE AVAILABILITY: Most wines can be found in shops and restaurants, but the winery or website are your best bets. Prices range from $30 to $125.

PICNIC PROSPECTS: None.

COST: $20 for five wines and a view.

DIRECTIONS: From the bottom of Spring Mountain Road at Madrona Avenue in St. Helena, go five and a quarter miles up Spring Mountain to the top of the mountain just before the county line painted across the road. On the right, there's a cluster of eighteen mailboxes and signs for wineries. (It's the same road for Smith-Madrone.) Turn right and follow the "4070" signs to Barnett Vineyards.

RECOMMENDED FOR: Everyone who wants to spend some time on top of the world.

Chateau Potelle

3875 Mt. Veeder Road
Napa, 94558
707-255-9440
www.chateaupotelle.com
HOURS: 11–5 daily

Chateau Potelle is a welcoming, amiable place in a captivating mountain setting, and when you reach the snug, cabin-like tasting room, you're likely to be greeted by the friendly winery dogs, who, for the record, are major-league beggars. The wines are major league, too.

It was started by owners Marketta and Jean-Noël Fourmeaux, who were working as French government wine tasters and visited California in 1980 on a mission to see what was happening here. They looked around Napa and sent a telegram back to France. "Looks good," it said. "We stay."

They moved their family here, and in 1988 bought the 202 acres that is Chateau Potelle. Now they produce a range of interesting wines including a dry Rosé, a Syrah-Cab-Zinfandel-Merlot blend, a Late Harvest Chardonnay, and a Late Harvest Zin they call Zinie. Their highly praised reserve line, called VGS, includes Chardonnay, Zinfandel, Syrah, and Cabernet Sauvignon.

ATMOSPHERE: The cozy tasting room has a little tile counter, wood paneling, and a wood-burning stove in the corner. It could be a great mountain breakfast spot. It's charming without being cloying and the feel tasting here is genial friendliness. In front of the room there's a huge redwood tree and some steep vineyards, and through the window below the tasting bar is a sweeping view down the mountain.

SERVICE: This is a place with a sense of humor, and Chateau Potelle posts a series of signs suggesting questions to ask tasting room manager and general clever guy Tony Bartolomucci. Tony and company serve terrific wine here and they're good at letting you know the details of that, too.

TASTING TOOLS: Small, OK glasses. Spit bucket, water, and crackers handy. Good light.

INTANGIBLES AND EXTRAS: This is a little winery worth the effort to find. They make special wines and can explain all their techniques. The views—including from a big picnic area—are stunning, and the tone is helpful and unpretentious. It's a good place to just take in the ambience, but it's for serious wine people, too.

One caution: They are serious about a sign on the road that says: "No pets allowed. Ours get jealous." Their dogs, as friendly as they are, will bark and bark at other dogs, even if they're left in the car.

WINE AVAILABILITY: Their wines are well distributed, but they aren't huge producers and they often sell out, so the winery or the website are the best bets. Prices range from $15 to $75.

PICNIC PROSPECTS: They have tables scattered around the grounds, including on the deck behind the tasting room. All are good sites. The best spot is a series of tables under trees on the hillside below the room. They look out along some steep vineyards and down to Napa Valley.

COST: $10 for five current release wines (and whatever else Tony is pouring); or $10 for three VGS wines (and whatever else Tony is pouring).

DIRECTIONS: About one mile south on Mt. Veeder Road from where it connects to Oakville Grade. Follow the access road in almost a mile.

RECOMMENDED FOR: Everyone.

The Hess Collection Winery

4411 Redwood Road
Napa, 94558
877-707-4377
www.hesscollection.com
HOURS: 10–4 daily

This winery on the side of Mt. Veeder, if a bit off the main path, is one of the must-visits in Napa. The original stone building was built in 1903 and, in 1930, became part of

Christian Brothers when it was changed into the Mont La Salle Winery. Then, in the 1970s, Donald Hess came to Napa looking to expand his Swiss mineral water company.

Hess decided Americans would never go for bottled water, but did have the foresight to take over the winery from the Christian Brothers in 1982—rented on a ninety-nine-year lease. In 1989, he opened a dramatic tasting room and art gallery—three sleek stories of open space, white wood, and glass—built around the original stone walls of the 1903 winery.

Hess has a large portfolio of wines, including Sauvignon Blanc, a Syrah Rosé, and a Late Harvest Viognier. Their reserve line, called Hess Collection, includes Chardonnay, Zinfandel, Cabernet Sauvignon, and a layered Mountain Cuvée, a Bordeaux-like blend except it also includes Syrah.

ATMOSPHERE: The simple but impressive tasting room has an oval, polished-maple bar inside the native stone walls and the peaked ceiling of the 1903 winery. Its warm lighting is a modern contrast to the century-old stone. Through a set of glass doors, the gift shop is mixed in with the barrel room.

SERVICE: Hess requires a lot of its tasting room people because it has wine holdings all over the world, and because it has an art gallery that includes some imposing names. Servers here manage to be well-versed in all of that, and still casually friendly. There are no pretensions in the tasting room or gallery.

TASTING TOOLS: Good glasses. Spit buckets, water, and crackers handy. Good light.

INTANGIBLES AND EXTRAS: The 13,000-square-foot gallery houses Hess's collection of contemporary art featuring some international names, including Frank Stella, Francis Bacon, and Franz Gertsch. The works are unusual and visceral, like the work by Argentine Leopoldo Maler that has an old Underwood typewriter with flames shooting from it. Gertsch's photo-realism—he painted over projections of photos—are among the most memorable pieces and his *Johana III,* a portrait of a doe-eyed girl with a vaguely haunted look, will stay with you.

Hess is a unique winery in Napa, for its wines, its art, its architecture, and its spirit, and it's a place you would hate to miss.

WINE AVAILABILITY: Hess wines are found in stores and restaurants across the planet, but there still are some small-release wines found only at the winery or on the website. Prices range from $12.50 to $115.

PICNIC PROSPECTS: None.

COST: $10 for four wines, plus maybe one or two more.

DIRECTIONS: From Highway 29, take the Redwood Road/Trancas Street exit in Napa and go west on Redwood. In town, Redwood is a four-lane road. Stay in the left lane because the right will veer off to become Dry Creek Road. Stay on Redwood. That includes a left turn where it intersects with Mt. Veeder Road (which feels more like going straight). Hess is about seven miles from Highway 29.

RECOMMENDED FOR: Everyone.

Mayacamas Vineyards

1155 Lokoya Road
Napa, 94558
707-224-4030
www.mayacamas.com
HOURS: Monday–Friday by appointment

The original stone winery on the edge of a dormant volcano crater was built in 1889 by San Francisco pickle merchant John Henry Fisher and went through a handful of owners and some dormant years until Bob and Elinor Travers bought the place in 1968.

Their home is next to the old winery buildings—giving the place a feel of a small Western town—and they use some of the original concrete fermentation tanks and part of an old distillery for storage. They make Sauvignon Blanc, Chardonnay, Pinot Noir, Merlot, and a highly praised Cabernet Sauvignon.

ATMOSPHERE: The winery base and buildings, so far up in the hills, feel like an outpost in the old West. The tasting room is a tiny, bright space with a small bar and wine display, but visitors can wander out front while they taste.

SERVICE: Like many of the small wineries in the hills, they do tours and tastings together and only by appointment. There's a personal, homey feel to everything.

TASTING TOOLS: Good glasses. Spit bucket and water handy. No crackers. Good light.

INTANGIBLES AND EXTRAS: This place has an interesting story. The winery went through many hands and you have to wonder how the original owners got supplies in and wine back down the mountain. But this is a long trip for a relatively short tour, so the best reason to come is for their wine.

WINE AVAILABILITY: The wines are distributed throughout the country, but, as with many smaller wineries, the winery or website are the safest bets. Prices range from $30 to $65.

PICNIC PROSPECTS: None.

COST: Free.

DIRECTIONS: Lokoya Road runs to the west from Mt. Veeder Road. It's about six miles from Mt. Veeder's southern start (off of Redwood Road near Napa town) and about three miles from where Mt. Veeder connects to the Oakville Grade in the north. Mt. Veeder is a winding rood and Lokoya is badly marked. There are no signs for Mayacamas on Lokoya, so look carefully for the address "1155" on a post, which leads to a long dirt road up to the winery. There is one sign high in a tree, but just stay on the dirt road and it ends at Mayacamas.

RECOMMENDED FOR: People looking for Mayacamas wine or who want to see a winery road definitely less traveled.

Pride Mountain Vineyards

4026 Spring Mountain Road
St. Helena, 94574
707-963-4949
www.pridewines.com
HOURS: 11–3:30 Monday and
  Wednesday–Saturday; by appointment
  only

A renowned Spring Mountain producer with eighty acres of vineyards, this winery is part Napa County, part Sonoma, and all mountaintop. The cheerfully painted, modest-sized wood winery looks at the crests of the Mayacamas Mountains in all directions.

It was called Summit Winery when it was founded in 1890—easy to see why—but it was done in by

Prohibition thirty years later. The late Jim Pride and his family restarted the winery in 1990 and Pride Mountain still runs as a family winery and makes wines that draw big scores and terrific reviews. Their list includes Viognier, Chardonnay, Cab Franc, Merlot, Cabernet Sauvignon, and a Claret Bordeaux blend.

ATMOSPHERE: They are moving the tasting room to a corner of the winery building to give it more of a view. The current room has a rustic allure that fits the mountaintop, with a wood bar sitting on two barrels, dark wood walls, and a simple tile floor. Out the door is a porch with benches and rolling vineyards that climb over a hill. It's the kind of comfortable place with dazzling views that can almost make you forget you came for the world-class wine.

SERVICE: Even straight-up tastings require reservations—they don't want people to drive all the way up there and find a mob—so the room never gets too crowded and servers have time for everyone. They also encourage you to go slowly and wander around outside, sit on a bench, and take in the mountain.

TASTING TOOLS: Good, large glasses. Spit buckets. No water or crackers. Decent light inside. Excellent light if you wander outside.

INTANGIBLES AND EXTRAS: They have a brick inlay on their concrete crush pad that shows the Napa/Sonoma county line and a cave system under the mountain that opens at one end to even more views. Down a road below the winery, the century-old stone Summit Winery building has been restored enough to host winemaker dinners, and there's a grass picnic area next to the old building.

Like many of the Spring Mountain wineries, it takes some time to get here. In return, you get a lot: great wine and mesmerizing views. This place has some of the best of both. They offer free tours (generally once a day at 10 a.m.), but their schedule changes with the seasons.

WINE AVAILABILITY: Pride Mountain wines are in demand and are hard to find outside the winery, though some high-end wine shops carry them. Pride discontinued its online store, so most wines are now available only at the winery or by calling them. Prices range from $37 to $100.

PICNIC PROSPECTS: Appointments are required to use the picnic grounds, which is generally not a problem unless there's a winery event scheduled. The tables are in among the rolling vineyards and next to the nineteenth-century, three-story stone winery.

COST: $5 for three wines, or whatever they're pouring that day.

DIRECTIONS: From the bottom of Spring Mountain Road at Madrona Avenue in St. Helena, go five and a half miles up Spring Mountain, past the top of the mountain and past the county line painted across the road. Look for the ranch driveway on the right that says "9175" and a sign on the bottom that says "Pride." (Note: The driveway is in Sonoma County, so the numbers change to the 9000s. The driveway will head back toward Napa.)

RECOMMENDED FOR: Everyone who has the time for the trip.

Robert Keenan Winery

3660 Spring Mountain Road
St. Helena, 94574
707-963-9177
www.keenanwinery.com

HOURS: 11–4 Friday–Sunday; 11–2
Monday–Tuesday; appointments preferred

The mountainside site was planted as vineyards for the Conradi Winery in the late 1800s, then abandoned. In 1974, Robert Keenan bought the building and 180 acres of the mountain. They cleared the land and redesigned the old stone winery, opening it for the 1977 vintage.

Since then, Robert Keenan wines have developed an international reputation. The winery itself, in a beautiful clearing on the mountain, has a low-key, friendly sensibility about it. They make a lively Zinfandel, a Chardonnay/Viognier blend, and a Bordeaux blend. But they specialize in highly rated Chardonnay, Merlot, and Cabernet Sauvignon.

ATMOSPHERE: This is not a quiet, restrained tasting bar. On weekends, it feels like you've walked into a rolling party and are likely to be greeted all at once by the tasting room manager, visitors standing around holding wine, and the tasting room dogs, Scrappy and Scooby. The big, high-ceilinged room is done in rough redwood and feels like the recreation loft in a mountain lodge.

As you come in, there are sets of easy chairs around the front, and a rectangular wooden table to one side seating twelve. Behind the table is a railing, with a drop to the winery floor below. You can look over at stacked barrels or wine getting pumped into tanks. The tasting bar is in one corner of the room, under small, bright hanging lights.

SERVICE: Tasting room manager Laura Marcel runs the place like a high-energy hostess at a block party, hustling around with a casual, inclusive air. Besides the instant friendship, she explains the wines and the winemaking well, and if you're there at the end of the day, she may hustle you downstairs for some barrel tasting.

TASTING TOOLS: Good, large glasses. Spit bucket and crackers handy. No water. OK light.

INTANGIBLES AND EXTRAS: The wine is very good, and by Napa standards, reasonably priced. But that's just part of the story. The open, animated, celebratory feeling in the room is a treat and it makes you happy. It's probably not the place you'll find a detailed, sober discussion of the wine.

WINE AVAILABILITY: Their big three—Chardonnay, Merlot, and Cabernet—can be found in markets and restaurants. Some reserves and blends are only at the winery or on the website. Prices range from $18 to $79.

PICNIC PROSPECTS: Tables alongside the old winery look down on rolling vineyards planted in an open spot in the trees, then out down to the Napa Valley 1,700 feet below. It's a peaceful and breathtaking spot.

COST: Free.

DIRECTIONS: From the bottom of Spring Mountain Road at Madrona Avenue in St. Helena, go about four miles up. Look for the winery sign on the right side of the road along a stone wall and turn right. That road is winding and bumpy and ends almost a mile later at the winery.

RECOMMENDED FOR: Everyone who doesn't mind a slow, winding drive up Spring Mountain.

Schweiger Vineyards and Winery

4015 Spring Mountain Road
St. Helena, 94574
707-963-4882 or 877-963-4882
www.schweigervineyards.com
HOURS: Tours and tastings by appointment only

The Schweiger family began buying land in these mountains in the 1960s but didn't plant vines until 1981. Fred and Sally Schweiger sold their grapes for about a decade, then in 1994 decided to keep some and bottle their own wine.

This is a family operation. Son, Andrew, is the winemaker, and his wife, Paula, runs the wine club. Daughter, Diana, heads marketing and public relations. They have stopped selling grapes and now use all their fruit in their estate wines. They make Sauvignon Blanc, Chardonnay, Merlot, Cabernet Sauvignon, and Port.

ATMOSPHERE: This looks like a winery constructed by a man who also builds custom homes. The family house sits on a ridge looking out on the valley. The modern stone winery has loads of small, polished details, and even the columns and lights in the barrel room, where they conduct tastings, have a finished, upscale look.

SERVICE: It's one more Spring Mountain winery where they know it took some effort to get here and they treat visitors well. The tours are not long, but this is a beautiful spot.

TASTING TOOLS: OK glasses. Spit bucket and crackers handy. No water. OK light.

INTANGIBLES AND EXTRAS: Friendly people in a pretty spot—the winery sits in a little mountain valley surrounded by a forest that has a fairytale look to it. Winery dogs often follow you on the tour and hang around for crackers during the tastings. However, in a place this beautiful, you'd like the tasting to be outside somewhere looking at the view.

WINE AVAILABILITY: The wines can be found in stores and restaurants around the country, but their production is not huge, so the winery or website are the surest routes. Prices range from $19.50 to $85.

PICNIC PROSPECTS: None.

COST: $10 for six wines.

DIRECTIONS: From the bottom of Spring Mountain Road at Madrona Avenue in St. Helena, go just short of five miles to the vista point lookout near the mountaintop and look for the winery sign, gate, and road on the right. (Caution: Street numbers may not be consecutive as you approach the driveway. If you hit the Napa/Sonoma county line on the road, you've gone too far.)

RECOMMENDED FOR: Anyone with the time to go up the mountain for a quieter tour.

Smith-Madrone Vineyards and Winery

4022 Spring Mountain Road
St. Helena, 94574
707-963-2283
www.smithmadrone.com
HOURS: Tours and tasting by appointment (they're pretty casual about it)

In 1971, Stuart Smith says, he joined a revolution rising up in the San Francisco area, a food and wine revolution. It brought him to the mountains on the western edge of Napa, where he bought 200 acres at 1,600 to 1,800 feet to start one of the first new post-Prohibition wineries in the area.

Since then, he and his brother, Charles, have been running this small, old-school winery with old-school prices. They say they picked the name because they identify with the Madrone trees on their property—the way they blend in with the forest community and never stand alone. Also, they say, because it's better than using the name of more common plants on their land, like "Smith–Poison Oak."

They make a sophisticated Chardonnay, a balanced Cabernet, and their star is one of the rare, high-quality Rieslings in Napa.

ATMOSPHERE: This is a low-key place. Tastings start inside the small, working winery building, where Stu or Charles conduct standup tours. Out the door are a concrete crush pad, winery equipment, and a dazzling view of the Napa Valley, the Vaca Mountains, and, on clear days, the Sierra Nevada in the distance. On weekends, there may be Smith family members, including kids, wandering around.

SERVICE: There's no tasting bar or, the brothers say, much of a tour. They just pour wine, let you wander around, answer questions, and talk about winemaking and life in the Mayacamas Mountains. These are two smart guys who've been in Napa since long before the wine boom and they've seen it all.

TASTING TOOLS: Good glasses. Wine and cheese served. Spit buckets are winery drains. They'll find you water if you ask. Good light.

INTANGIBLES AND EXTRAS: Aside from the breathtaking views, this is a chance to spend time with a couple guys who are among the originals of modern Napa wine and are mini-institutions among the hillside vintners. There's also a sense of family about the place, and a feeling of what Napa was like when it was just starting to grow.

WINE AVAILABILITY: All wines can be found in stores and restaurants, but this is a small winery selling for reasonable prices and the wines go fast, particularly the Riesling. So the winery or website may be the last available places. Prices range from $20 to $45.

PICNIC PROSPECTS: Tables on a grassy ridge 1,000-plus feet above the Valley.

COST: Free.

DIRECTIONS: From the bottom of Spring Mountain Road at Madrona Avenue in St. Helena, go five and a quarter miles up Spring Mountain to the top of the mountain just before the county line painted across the road. On the right, there's a cluster of eighteen mailboxes and signs for wineries, including Smith-Madrone. (It's the same road for Barnett Vineyards.) Turn right and follow the signs to Smith-Madrone. The road is slow and bumpy, and will start downhill back toward Napa. They say, when in doubt, turn right. Mostly just follow the signs.

RECOMMENDED FOR: Everyone, particularly people who want something different from a standard tasting bar or who want a personal connection to mountain winemaking.

Spring Mountain Vineyard
2805 Spring Mountain Road
St. Helena, 94574
707-967-4188 or 877-769-4637
www.springmountainvineyard.com
HOURS: 10–4 daily; tastings only with tours, by appointment only

This winery with 850 acres running from bottom to top of the Spring Mountain district has a long and entertaining history, and has combined the operations of three wineries founded in the 1800s—La Perla, Chateau Chevalier, and Miravelle. Miravelle includes a spectacular 1884 mansion that was used in the 1980s CBS series *Falcon Crest*.

The tour here is one of the most unique in Napa because of the spectacular grounds and buildings, and it feels like a walk through a California plantation. For all the scenery, Spring Mountain, under the ownership of Jacob Safra, also has become a first-class winery, making Sauvignon Blanc, Pinot Noir, Syrah, Cabernet Sauvignon, and a Bordeaux blend called Elivette.

ATMOSPHERE: The grounds are stunning and unique, and the tour takes visitors through the 1880s barn, acres of garden, and mansion, as well as the winery and massive caves. Tastings may be in a large, open dining room inside the Miravelle mansion, in the winery caves, or, most likely, as a sit-down affair in a small, sunny cottage. All the locations are set up to give a bit of the feel of grandness.

SERVICE: Forget *Falcon Crest*. They won't even mention it unless you ask. The folks here are about wine. They'll show you some unique vineyard techniques, tell you about their winery innovations, and tell you everything you'd want to know about their winemaking and wines. They won't, however, forget to show off their grounds.

TASTING TOOLS: Good, large glasses. Spit buckets, water, and crackers handy. Light depends on location. It's best in the cottage.

INTANGIBLES AND EXTRAS: They have a special tour because of the estate, and because of the way they mix in serious talk of winemaking while showing a beautiful place.

They do not say it directly, but this is a tour and tasting for people at least a bit serious about wine.

WINE AVAILABILITY: They're slowly expanding and most wines can be found in stores and restaurants. Pinot Noir and some reserves are only at the winery or on the website. Prices range from $28 to $90.

PICNIC PROSPECTS: None.

COST: $25 for tour and five wines, waived with purchase.

DIRECTIONS: From the bottom of Spring Mountain Road at Madrona Avenue in St. Helena, go up the road a bit more than one mile and look for the sign on your left.

RECOMMENDED FOR: Everyone, but come for the wine.

Terra Valentine

3787 Spring Mountain Road
St. Helena, 94574
707-967-8340
www.terravalentine.com
HOURS: Tours by appointment only at
  10:30 a.m., 12:30 p.m., and 2:30 p.m.

This is one of the more eccentric—and spectacular—wineries in Napa because of the brilliance and the quirks of its builder, Fred Aves, who was both a genuine Renaissance man and a genuinely odd guy. Aves invented, among many other things, curb feelers for cars, and moved to the mountains of Napa in 1970.

He built a 17,000-square-foot native stone winery that's part Gothic mansion, part 1960s shrine to free thinking. He named it Yverdon, after the Swiss town his mother lived in, and decorated it with his works in stone, concrete, brass, copper, wrought iron, and stained glass. The result is a huge, fascinating, slightly weird place.

Aves stopped making wine in 1985

and died in 1998. The winery was restarted and renamed in 1999 by its current owners, Angus and Margaret Wurtele, who set about turning it into a semi-normal winery. Their Wurtele Vineyard Cabernet has earned raves and they also make Pinot Noir, Cabernet Franc, and a Sangiovese/Cabernet Sauvignon blend they call Amore.

ATMOSPHERE: Where do you start? They only offer tasting with tours here and it is a treat. The tasting room itself is a sumptuous, oak-paneled sitting room—the panels were once headed for William Randolph Hearst's castle at San Simeon—with two fireplaces and a stained-glass rendition of St. Genevieve de Paris, patron saint of winemakers, staring down at the heavy oak dining table. The rest of the winery is both functional and slightly mysterious, and it all comes with views from nearly 2,000 feet up in the mountains.

SERVICE: The tours are both whimsical and intelligent. They enjoy their unusual founding and the talents of Aves, but it's also about their wine, which is strong top to bottom. Because this is a small winery, the tours max out at twelve people and are always comfortably informal. The sit-down tasting includes top-notch cheeses and chocolate that pair with the wine.

TASTING TOOLS: Good, large glasses. A separate glass for each wine. Spit buckets, water, and crackers handy. Good light.

INTANGIBLES AND EXTRAS: This is a wild place you have to see. Aves did not settle for simplicity with any detail. There are massive, arched-wood doors held on by three-foot-long wrought-iron hinges in the shape of grapevines. There's stained glass everywhere, including a jungle scene on one wall-sized window with a cat door cut into a leopard's open mouth. There are grape clusters carved into everything, and statues, columns, polished stone, and carved wood at every turn. And most of the door handles are ornate metal fish.

The best feature is a huge barrel in the office that opens up to a circular, wrought-iron staircase inside, made to look like vines, that leads down to the barrel room.

WINE AVAILABILITY: Most of the wines, though made in relatively small amounts, can be found in shops and restaurants, but the blends are sold only at the winery or on the website. Prices range from $35 to $50.

PICNIC PROSPECTS: None.

COST: $20 for tour and tasting, waived with purchase.

DIRECTIONS: From the bottom of Spring Mountain Road at Madrona Avenue in St. Helena, go a bit more than four miles up and look for the winery sign and road on the left.

RECOMMENDED FOR: Anyone looking for something different in Napa.

CALISTOGA TASTING ROOMS

August Briggs Winery

333 Silverado Trail
Calistoga, 94515
707-942-4912
www.augustbriggswines.com
HOURS: 11:30–4:30 Thursday–Sunday

August "Joe" Briggs opened one of Napa's newest small wineries in May, 2004, after producing wines under the label Briggs & Sons Winemaking Co. since 1995. This is a family operation. Owner and winemaker Joe is often behind the tasting bar, and his parents, Betty and Bob, run the room.

The white, barn-looking winery has a red roof and sits just off Silverado Trail against a low hill on one side. They make a range of wines including Chardonnay, a handful of Pinot Noirs, Pinot Meunier, Zinfandel, Cabernet Sauvignon, and Petite Sirah.

ATMOSPHERE: The clean, modern tasting room has an easy-to-approach feel about it. The building's front is a two-story glass wall, and there's a large skylight above that, giving the sense that one side of the room is wide open to the vineyards and the eastern mountains less than a mile away.

The high ceilings are white and the room is trimmed in a rich green, which matches the pale blond wood and green-marble-topped, midsized tasting bar.

SERVICE: This is a new place and you can feel their earnestness and eagerness to please. Most people working in the room have a family connection. When Joe is pouring, the conversations can range from winemaking to the harvest quality to local gossip.

TASTING TOOLS: Good glasses. Spit buckets, water, and pretzels handy. Very good light.

INTANGIBLES AND EXTRAS: As one of the valley's newest wineries, their energy is palpable. These people are happy to be in a winery. Makes for a good experience.

WINE AVAILABILITY: Some wines are found in markets and restaurants, but as with all small-production wineries, the best bet is at the winery or on the website. Prices range from $30 to $55.

PICNIC PROSPECTS: They have a few tables out front among a few vines. The views in both directions are of the mountains that are close in on this narrow end of the valley.

COST: Free.

DIRECTIONS: On the west side of Silverado Trail about one mile south of Calistoga.

RECOMMENDED FOR: Everyone.

Bennett Lane Winery

3340 Highway 128
Calistoga, 94515
707-942-6684 or 877-629-6272
www.bennettlane.com
HOURS: 10–5:30 daily

The cheerful-looking winery is down a long driveway through a Cabernet vineyard, and has a lively villa look to it, with terra-cotta walls and a curved-tile roof. This is where the Napa Valley narrows and the mountains all around are close, which gives the building and the grounds around it the feel of fitting snugly into the top of the valley.

Owners Randy and Lisa Lynch bought the winery in 2002—it had been Vigil Vineyards—and turned this unheralded spot into one of the very friendly tasting rooms in the valley. They make well-regarded Chardonnay, Cabernet Sauvignon, and Maximus, a Cab-Merlot-Syrah blend.

ATMOSPHERE: The room is small but brightly lit and full of energy. French doors look out to a patio and vineyards. You can feel the closeness of the mountains, but still the flow of the vineyards, too. The tile floor, small marble bar, and bright overhead spotlights also add a brightness to the room.

SERVICE: Tasting room manager Jim May is a lively guy, and that's another piece of the charm here. Everyone gets treated like locals, and they assume you must know your wine because you found them. Just for fun, Jim poured a milky-yellow brew that was a two-week-old Chardonnay loaded with banana and citrus.

TASTING TOOLS: Big, good glasses. Spit buckets and water handy. No crackers. Very good light.

INTANGIBLES AND EXTRAS: This is one of those places that just adds up to something enjoyable, partly because of the location so close to the top of the valley, partly because of the gardens and grass around it, partly because of the happy spirit of the tasting room. It's a place to bring a lunch and have a picnic.

WINE AVAILABILITY: Most wines are available in stores and restaurants. Prices range from $28 to $85.

PICNIC PROSPECTS: Tables are spread around the building on the grass that separates the winery from the vineyards. They all sit right next to the vines and give views of the folds of the mountains on all sides that roll down to the valley.

COST: $10 for five or more wines; coupons are available in local free wine magazines.

DIRECTIONS: Two and a half miles north of the intersection of Highway 29 and Lincoln Avenue in Calistoga. (The main highway turns into Highway 128 past Calistoga.) Bennett Lane Winery is on the east side of the road.

RECOMMENDED FOR: Everyone.

Calistoga Cellars

1170 Tubbs Lane
Calistoga, 94515
707-942-7422
www.calistogacellars.com
HOURS: 10–4:30 Thursday–Tuesday

This winery grew out of a friendship and partnership among fraternity brothers from Iowa State, and is exactly the kind of thing most visitors wish they had thought to do. They began pooling money to buy vineyards and eventually gathered thirty-eight partners and the resources to buy the winery, a ranch house, and enough vineyards to make about 9,000 cases a year.

Most of the partners kept their day jobs, rotate vacation weeks at the nearby ranch house, and, along with managing partner Roger Louer and winemaker (and partner) Barry Gnekow, give the place a happy-to-be-here feel. They make Sauvignon Blanc, Chardonnay, Zinfandel, Merlot, and Cabernet Sauvignon.

ATMOSPHERE: From the outside, the winery and tasting room look like a simple Tuscan villa. Inside, the style is modern California, with lots of polished wood, big windows, reddish tiles, and a curved, pale green, burnished-concrete tasting bar. Through a set of glass doors you can see the working winery and its large storage tanks.

SERVICE: They're low-key and unpushy, which makes this a comfortable place for beginners.

TASTING TOOLS: Good, large glasses. Spit buckets handy. Water on request. No crackers.

INTANGIBLES AND EXTRAS: It's a straightforward, easy place to taste, and generally not as packed as some wineries. They also sell Styrofoam coolers for $5 to cart your wine around on hot days, and it makes you wonder why more wineries didn't think of that.

WINE AVAILABILITY: Many wines are available in stores and restaurants, but this is not a large producer, so the winery or website are the surest things. Prices range from $14 to $30.

PICNIC PROSPECTS: None.

COST: $7 for five wines, waived with purchase.

DIRECTIONS: Tubbs Lane is about one and a half miles north of the intersection of Highway 29 and Lincoln Avenue—Calistoga's main street—on the west side of town, and of Silverado Trail and Lincoln on the east side. (Highway 29 actually becomes Lincoln Avenue at Calistoga.) From Highway 29, go straight north at the stop light at the edge of Calistoga to Tubbs. Turn right. Calistoga Cellars is about a quarter mile up on the right. From Silverado Trail, go straight north at the stop sign where Silverado and Lincoln meet. Turn left on Tubbs. Calistoga Cellars is one mile down on the left.

RECOMMENDED FOR: Anyone looking for a smaller tasting room experience.

Chateau Montelena

1429 Tubbs Lane
Calistoga, 94515
707-942-5105
www.montelena.com
HOURS: 9:30–4 daily; Estate Cabernet tastings from 9:30–1:30 daily

Chateau Montelena is another of the cornerstone wineries in Napa for its history, its status—it was a Chateau Montelena Chardonnay that won the white wine category in the legendary 1976 Paris tasting—its grounds, and its owners, the Barrett family, who are now Napa wine royalty. Plus, of course, for its wine.

The winery building is a huge stone castle built into a hillside in 1882, though you can't tell from the tasting room side. You have to wander down the hill toward Jade Lake to get a sense of it. The tasting room entrance is above the old château, through a stone gate and under a heavy timber trellis. It feels more like you're going into a big cave or maybe a place where Hobbits would drink wine.

Chateau Montelena releases just five wines each year, including that famous Chardonnay, Riesling, Zinfandel, and two Cabernets.

ATMOSPHERE: The room feels like a big, snug cave, in part because the tasting bar is backed by the century-old stone wall of the winery. The room has heavy, dark wood posts, and generally soft lighting, except from the bright and warm spots directly over the granite tasting bar.

For a winery as renowned as Chateau Montelena, the room is a bit small and can get crowded, but that, with the stone and the lighting, adds to a dug-in, sheltered feel.

SERVICE: Maybe the oddest question mark in Napa. We've heard stories about bad service and we've had almost snooty service in the past. But on recent visits—we checked a couple times—they were charming, lighthearted, and attentive. Everyone here clearly knows wine and they know Napa, but what made our recent visits special was they were disarmingly warm. Maybe they dumped the person in charge of snooty.

TASTING TOOLS: Good, large glasses. Spit bucket, crackers, and water handy. Good light over the bar, dim around the rest of the room.

INTANGIBLES AND EXTRAS: The Estate Cabernet tasting lets visitors taste one of Napa's more consistently acclaimed wines. The tours, offered at 2 p.m. daily (for $25), take a detailed look at serious winemaking and wind up in the elegant, stone-walled Estate Room that feels like it should be guarded by knights in armor.

The grounds here are spectacular and, at a minimum, you have to walk down the steps to the front of the vine-covered winery building. Jade Lake, just below the winery, is a couple acres of man-made lake with graceful, Asian-style red bridges and pagoda-like gazebos on small islands. They no longer allow picnics here, but a walk around the peaceful lake will still lower your blood pressure.

WINE AVAILABILITY: All the wines are available in wine shops, stores, and restaurants, except the Riesling, which is found only at the winery or on the website. Prices range from $18 to $125.

PICNIC PROSPECTS: None.

COST: $10 for four current release wines; $25 for Estate Cab tasting

DIRECTIONS: Tubbs Lane is about one and a half miles north of the intersection of Highway 29 and Lincoln Avenue—Calistoga's main street—on the west side of town, and of Silverado Trail and Lincoln on the east side. (Highway 29 actually becomes Lincoln Avenue at Calistoga.) From Highway 29, go straight north at the stop light at the edge of Calistoga to Tubbs. Turn

right. Chateau Montelena is one mile up on the left. From Silverado Trail, go straight north at the stop sign where Silverado and Lincoln meet. Turn left on Tubbs. Chateau Montelena is about a quarter mile down on the right.

RECOMMENDED FOR: Everyone.

Graeser Winery
255 Petrified Forest Road
Calistoga, 94515
707-942-4437
www.graeserwinery.com
HOURS: 10–5 daily

This is a beautiful, rustic spot, and they take a traditional approach to winemaking—focusing on what they call "elegant, not overblown" Bordeaux varietals. But they have an unconventionally, very relaxed attitude, which includes a wine, Alex's Ruff Red, named after Richard's sweet German shepherd, Alex.

The carefully built, intriguing farmhouse at the center of the site dates back to 1886. The Graeser family bought the property on Diamond Mountain in 1958. Winery owner and winemaker Richard Graeser had been a produce farmer in Southern California's Imperial Valley before he took over the family property in 1983. He turned the former poultry farm into a vineyard and winery, and produced his first vintage in 1985. Besides Alex's Ruff Red, they make Sémillon, Chardonnay, Cabernet Franc, Merlot, Zinfandel, Cabernet Sauvignon, and a Cab Franc–based Bordeaux blend.

ATMOSPHERE: The house and winery are up in a clearing in the mountains surrounded by trees. They look over a long, red farm building, then up a steep, wavy hill of vines. The tasting room feels like a big farmhouse room. It has an old wood floor, a wooden tasting bar, and windows that look out to a large brick patio and the hills.

SERVICE: It would be tough to be more casual than they are here. The people are open and friendly, and pretty proud of what they have. You may find Richard serving behind the bar, and are likely to find Alex sleeping in front of it. This is a small winery, so their service is personal. They're happy to let you wander around the property or plop down at the tables on the patio or among the trees.

TASTING TOOLS: Good, large glasses. Spit buckets and water handy. No crackers. OK light.

INTANGIBLES AND EXTRAS: Graeser is only a short way off the main highway, but it feels like it's miles up in the mountains. The setting is both stunning and peaceful. This is a quick trip off the beaten path and a pretty setting that's hard to leave.

WINE AVAILABILITY: They are not large producers. Their wines are found in some Northern California restaurants and stores, but mostly at the winery or on the website. Prices range from $18 to $30.

PICNIC PROSPECTS: There are a handful of tables on the grass and under trees in front of the winery, and they have a couple tables 200 yards up a steep vineyard hill that have a view of Calistoga and the valley.

COST: $5 for five or more wines, waived with purchase.

DIRECTIONS: Petrified Forest Road is the first stop sign north of the intersection of Highway 29 and Lincoln Avenue in Calistoga. (The main highway turns into Highway 128 past Calistoga.) Graeser is one and a quarter miles up Petrified Forest Road on the left.

RECOMMENDED FOR: Everyone.

Schramsberg Vineyards

1400 Schramsberg Road
Calistoga, 94515
707-942-2414 or 800-877-3623
www.schramsberg.com
HOURS: 10–4 daily; by appointment only; tastings only with tour

In so many ways, Schramsberg is the essence of the Napa dream. When it was built in 1862 by Jacob Schram, a barber from Germany, and his wife, Annie, it became one of the premier wineries during Napa's first flourish in the late 1800s, drawing prominent visitors like Ambrose Bierce and Robert Louis Stevenson, who devoted a chapter in his book, *Silverado Squatters,* to Schramsberg.

After illness, phylloxera, and Prohibition, the winery went through years of neglect until Jamie and the late Jack Davies bought it in 1965, in part as an escape from urban life. They helped start Napa's current flourish in a place with a classic, restored Victorian, a rebuilt nineteenth-century winery, hillside vineyards, gardens, and a general idyllic feel. They were the first American winery to focus primarily on premier sparkling wines, and their wines have been served by every presidential administration since Richard Nixon crossed the Great Wall and used Schramsberg to toast Chinese Premier Chou En-lai in 1972.

ATMOSPHERE: Tours and tastings start outside by the frog pond, with the gardens all around, looking up at the 1880s house and its wide, graceful veranda. They finish with a tasting inside a simple, classy, old-wood room.

What makes this one of the more unusual tours in Napa is that it goes deep into a two-mile network of caves. It's not just the caves, it's because these are old caves, often bolstered with century-old stone and coated in places with hanging lichen. And it's because, instead of barrels, they're lined with 2.7 million bottles—walls and walls of bottles, sometimes fifteen feet high. The sense of the depth of the caves, and of the volume and effort of production, is overpowering.

SERVICE: They have one of Napa's best stories to tell, from Schram's rise and fall to the Davies restoring the dream. The tour gives a palpable feel for the work that goes into making sparkling wine and riddling the bottles with regular, sometimes daily, very small turns to slowly get the yeast and sediment to settle. The tasting is leisurely, done at small, six-person tables that are glass tops set on old sparkling wine racks. The pours are generous.

TASTING TOOLS: Good, large flutes. Separate flutes for each wine. Spit buckets on request. Water in a cooler in a corner. No crackers. Good light.

INTANGIBLES AND EXTRAS: You get the sense you're visiting the quintessence of Napa here, with its history, its beauty, and its wine. There's an impressive photo gallery of all the presidents toasting with Schramsberg, and there's the statue of the frog in the pond outside the tasting room that's become a mascot for Schramsberg. It's called Riddler's Night Out, and it's a tribute to master riddler Ramon Viera, who's worked at Schramsberg more than thirty years. The frog is wearing a tuxedo, holding a bottle in one, uh, hand, and in the other, a sparkling flute up in the air, checking the clarity of the wine in the moonlight.

Schramsberg is one of the rare premier American sparkling wine producers who use the term "champagne" on some of its labels, but it's small on the side, and it says "Napa Valley champagne" because, they say, they want people to know it ranks with the finest sparkling wine anywhere.

WINE AVAILABILITY: Their wines are well distributed, but their two top sparklings, the Reserve and J. Schram, are made in limited quantity and are hard to find outside the winery or website. They also make a Cabernet Sauvignon sold only at the winery. Prices range from $32 to $80.

PICNIC PROSPECTS: None.

COST: $25 for tour and tasting four wines.

DIRECTIONS: Off Peterson Road on the west side of Highway 29 about three miles south of Calistoga and a half mile north of Larkmead Lane. Turn up the hill onto Peterson and make a quick right on Schramsberg Road. Follow it up about a half mile.

RECOMMENDED FOR: Everyone. Maybe not for anyone who is claustrophobic.

Silver Rose Cellars

400 Silverado Trail
Calistoga, 94515
707-942-9581 or 800-995-9381
www.silverrose.com
HOURS: 10–5 daily; barrel tastings daily at 11 a.m.

This is one of the surprises in Napa because it's also a charming resort and hotel with some stellar vineyard views, and you would think the winery might be mostly a gimmick to help the resort. Not so.

Actually, owners J-Paul and Sally Dumont, who bought the property in 1985, are as serious about their winery as their inn and now produce a small line of award-winning wines. The tasting room, opened in 2000, is easy to blow past because it's so close to Calistoga, but this is worth the stop. They make Chardonnay, Merlot, and Cabernet Sauvignon.

ATMOSPHERE: The modern wood building just off Silverado Trails sits on a small lake and up against the foothills of the Vaca Mountains. The tall tasting room, done in airy earth colors, has beamed ceilings, blond wood posts, and a contemporary wooden bar. Two-story, floor-to-ceiling windows look out on the lake.

Behind the bar, a window looks into a barrel room, and around the room there are colorful prints and playfully styled cheese boards and ceramics for sale.

SERVICE: Occasionally they get tour buses rolling in, but most of the time this is an unhurried place. The servers have an easy, accepting manner and they do know their wines. The friendly woman serving us was proud to tell us some of the grapes came from her father's vineyard.

TASTING TOOLS: Good, large glasses. Spit buckets and crackers handy. No water. Good light.

INTANGIBLES AND EXTRAS: Silver Rose has a lot of little extras that make it a comfortable stop. It's right on Silverado Trail in a pretty setting, and they have a large parking lot and a cheerful room. They also have a deck for picnics, offer their barrel room for special events, and have the daily barrel tastings. They also have amazingly good, wine-filled chocolate balls, but heed their warning to eat them whole, or you'll wear the wine that's inside.

The inn and spa connected to it make it Napa's only full-on resort winery.

WINE AVAILABILITY: Most of their wines make it to stores and restaurants. Prices range from $36 to $44.

PICNIC PROSPECTS: The deck along their small lake has plenty of picnic tables and they'll sell you wine by the glass if you don't want a whole bottle with lunch.

COST: $10 for three or four wines; barrel tasting is $10.

DIRECTIONS: On the east side of Silverado Trail, about a half mile south of where Silverado meets Lincoln Avenue.

RECOMMENDED FOR: Everyone. Especially if you're staying in Calistoga.

Summers Winery
1171 Tubbs Lane
Calistoga, 94515
707-942-5508 or 866-623-1289
www.summerswinery.com
HOURS: 10:30–4:30 daily

Summers is the definition of a cheerful young winery. Their theme is "a glass of wine, a game of bocce," and the mood in the open winery and on the pleasant patio is "no worries." Plus, there's the geyser.

Jim and Beth Summers in 1996 bought what was then the San Pietro Winery, called the vineyards Villa Andriana after their daughter, and opened the bright tasting room in 1997. They make Chardonnay, Merlot, Zinfandel, Cabernet Sauvignon, Muscat Canelli, and one of the valley's rare Charbonos.

ATMOSPHERE: The sunny room has a blond-wood bar in the middle, a pale-tile floor, and a wall of windows that opens to the patio, a horse ranch behind it, and then the geyser. There's just a general easy, sassy feel here coming from the crowds, the music, and the servers.

SERVICE: It's a generally young and energetic group, and their enthusiasm for wine is evident, as is their sense of fun. The tasting room draws a young crowd because of that, but it's not a nightclub feel, just lively.

TASTING TOOLS: Good big glasses. Spit bucket, crackers, and water handy. Good light.

INTANGIBLES AND EXTRAS: First, the geyser. Summers is just down the road from one of the three official Old Faithful Geysers on the planet—the others are much bigger stars in New Zealand and, of course, Yellowstone Park. This one blows about every forty minutes—yes, it's an Old Faithful, but there still can be shifts in the eruptions—shooting thermal waters about sixty feet in the air. The geyser park charges admission and at Summers they say, it's cheaper here and you get wine. Or you can watch it while you picnic or play bocce ball.

You also get a friendly, laid-back place that's easy to approach if you're a wine rookie but clued-in enough if you want to talk wine.

WINE AVAILABILITY: Some of their wines are distributed around California, but the only sure things are the winery or website, particularly for the Charbono, which goes fast. Prices range from $18 to $46.

PICNIC PROSPECTS: The stone patio is surrounded by grass and flowers, and looks at a large horse ranch and the California Old Faithful. It's a pretty and open spot that feels more countryish than wine-countryish.

COST: $7 for six wines, refundable with wine purchase.

DIRECTIONS: Tubbs Lane is about one and a half miles north of the intersection of Highway 29 and Lincoln Avenue—Calistoga's main street—on the west side of town, and of Silverado Trail and Lincoln on the east side. (Highway 29 actually becomes Lincoln Avenue at Calistoga.) From Highway 29, go straight north at the stoplight at the edge of Calistoga to Tubbs. Turn

right. Summers Winery is about a quarter mile up on the left. From Silverado Trail, go straight north at the stop sign where Lincoln and Silverado meet. Turn left on Tubbs. Summers Winery is one mile down on the right.

RECOMMENDED FOR: Everyone. It's a particularly comfortable place for anyone intimidated by the bigger wineries.

Vincent Arroyo Winery

2362 Greenwood Avenue
Calistoga, 94515
707-942-6995
www.vincentarroyowinery.com
HOURS: 10–4:30 daily; appointments preferred

This is another place that embodies the feel of a family-owned winery, from the family members involved, to the big, gray-and-white barn next to the house, to J. J., the black Labrador doing tricks for guests—she climbs a stack of barrels and catches tennis balls tossed at her while she's up there.

Vincent Arroyo was a mechanical engineer in Silicon Valley until he bought twenty-three acres here in 1974. For years he did all the work—driving the tractor, running the cellar, and selling the wine—on his own. Now he gets some help and owns eighty-five acres, and all his grapes come from within a half mile of the winery. He makes a range of wine, including Chardonnay, Merlot, Syrah, Sangiovese, Zinfandel, Cabernet Sauvignon, and his signature wine, Petite Sirah.

ATMOSPHERE: This is as unfussy as it gets. Tasting is in front of the winery/barn on some days—which has the friendly feel of tasting in the driveway—or inside the big barrel room, which lets J. J. show off her climbing skills. There's a chalkboard listing the wines being tasted, and a general low-key sensibility.

SERVICE: Vincent often is hanging around the tasting room to chat, or pour, and he's a friendly, no-frills guy who likes talking about the land and the fun he has with wine.

TASTING TOOLS: Good, large glasses. Spit bucket and water handy. Bread and olive oils that they sell. OK light inside. Great light outside.

INTANGIBLES AND EXTRAS: It's at wineries like this where you can meet the vintner and get a sense of what it takes to build a winemaking life from the ground up. Vincent is also a dog lover and has named wines after his Labs. The specialty now is J. J.'s Blend. The small gift shop also sells J. J. apparel, including T-shirts that say "J. J.'s Friend." Plus, they have a new pup named Bodega, so expect a whole new line of shirts.

WINE AVAILABILITY: They sell only at the winery or through reservations made off their buying list. Prices range from $17 to $55.

PICNIC PROSPECTS: None.

COST: Free. $5 for groups of six or more.

DIRECTIONS: Greenwood Avenue is about three-quarters of a mile north of where Lincoln Avenue, the main street of Calistoga (and, now, Highway 29) meets Silverado Trail on the east side of town. That road changes its name to Highway 29/Lake County Highway. Turn left on Greenwood and go about a quarter mile and look for "2361" on the right. A dirt road leads to the winery.

RECOMMENDED FOR: Everyone.

Von Strasser Winery

1510 Diamond Mountain Road
Calistoga, 94515
707-942-0930
www.vonstrasser.com
HOURS: Tastings and tours by appointment only at 10:30 a.m., 1 p.m., and 3:30 p.m. daily

Owner and winemaker Rudy von Strasser bought the Diamond Mountain property with his wife, Rita, in 1990, and started replanting old vineyards, refurbishing an 1880s-vintage barn, and pushing Diamond Mountain as a separate American Viticultural Area. He won that fight in 2001.

In 1985, before they bought the site, Rudy was the first American invited to intern at Château Lafite-Rothschild in Bordeaux. He makes well-reviewed wines here in the Old World style, all from the Diamond Mountain district, that include Chardonnay, Cabernet Franc, Zinfandel, Cabernet Sauvignon, and two Bordeaux-style blends.

ATMOSPHERE: The small tasting room and office looks like a mountain cabin and it faces a rise with a small vineyard and the von Strassers' Tuscan-looking home on top. Family dogs and cats are likely to greet visitors. The tour goes into the old barn, now the center of the winery, and into 7,000 feet of caves where you can do some barrel tasting.

SERVICE: They know visitors expect a lot here, so they keep the groups small—no larger than eight—and try to make the experience feel personalized by reading their visitors and catering to what they'd like.

TASTING TOOLS: Very good glasses. Spit buckets and water handy. No crackers. Good light.

INTANGIBLES AND EXTRAS: This is a beautiful place and these are expensive tours of a winery that makes some very good and complex wines. It's for serious wine people.

WINE AVAILABILITY: Their wines are in demand and their production is small, which means most are available only at the winery or through the website. Prices range from $40 to $100.

PICNIC PROSPECTS: None.

COST: $30 for tasting and tour.

DIRECTIONS: Diamond Mountain runs off the west side of Highway 29 about two-thirds of a mile north of Dunaweal and one mile south of Lincoln Avenue. Follow Diamond Mountain three-quarters of a mile and look for the Von Strasser sign on the right. Bear to the right and go through the blue gate.

RECOMMENDED FOR: Serious wine folks.

Zahtila Vineyards

2250 Lake County Highway
Calistoga, 94515
707-942-9251
www.zahtilavineyards.com
HOURS: 10–5 daily

This is one of the smallest, most personal wineries you can find in the valley. Laura Zahtila bought the vineyards, facilities, and house in 1999 from the Traulsen family, and turned it into a boutique winery with a very informal air.

She was a technology sales specialist who now spends her energy learning how to run a winery, and she chose to try for premium reds. Zahtila focuses on Zinfandel and Cabernet Sauvignon that complement food, but they also make Chardonnay.

ATMOSPHERE: The small winery looks like a simple home with a charming rose garden from the road, and feels even more homey when Zoe, the yellow Labrador, greets vis-

itors. The snug, simple tasting room was recently added to the side of the building and is connected to the barrel room. It has a wooden bar made from redwood casks, a low ceiling, warm lighting, and looks out at a deck and the rose gardens out front.

SERVICE: They can't help but be intimate here because of the size of the place, and Laura Zahtila often pours in the tasting room with an infectious enthusiasm for her winery. Things also run at a slow pace here because this is not a winery that gets packed.

TASTING TOOLS: Small glasses. Spit bucket, crackers, and water handy. Good light.

INTANGIBLES AND EXTRAS: This is an off-the-path winery with a casual, personal feel. The stone patio and rose gardens are a quiet, sheltered spot for a picnic. Warning for the dainty: the rest room is an outhouse.

WINE AVAILABILITY: The production is small, though some wines make it to shops or restaurants. The winery or website are the best bets. Prices range from $18 to $48.

PICNIC PROSPECTS: The tables on the stone patio surrounded by the rose gardens make this one of the more unusual picnic spots in the valley. It has less the feel of wine country than just a cozy, pretty place.

COST: $5 for five wines.

DIRECTIONS: About a quarter mile north of where Lincoln Avenue, the main street of Calistoga (and, now, Highway 29), meets Silverado Trail on the east side of town. Go through the stop sign and look for the small sign on the east side of the road that is now Highway 29/Lake County Highway.

RECOMMENDED FOR: Anyone looking for a small, personal winery where they can meet the owner and her dog.

TASTING ROOM INDEX